Sustainable Development Goals Series

The **Sustainable Development Goals Series** is Springer Nature's inaugural cross-imprint book series that addresses and supports the United Nations' seventeen Sustainable Development Goals. The series fosters comprehensive research focused on these global targets and endeavours to address some of society's greatest grand challenges. The SDGs are inherently multidisciplinary, and they bring people working across different fields together and working towards a common goal. In this spirit, the Sustainable Development Goals series is the first at Springer Nature to publish books under both the Springer and Palgrave Macmillan imprints, bringing the strengths of our imprints together.

The Sustainable Development Goals Series is organized into eighteen subseries: one subseries based around each of the seventeen respective Sustainable Development Goals, and an eighteenth subseries, 'Connecting the Goals', which serves as a home for volumes addressing multiple goals or studying the SDGs as a whole. Each subseries is guided by an expert Subseries Advisor with years or decades of experience studying and addressing core components of their respective Goal.

The SDG Series has a remit as broad as the SDGs themselves, and contributions are welcome from scientists, academics, policymakers, and researchers working in fields related to any of the seventeen goals. If you are interested in contributing a monograph or curated volume to the series, please contact the Publishers: Zachary Romano [Springer; zachary.romano@springer.com] and Rachael Ballard [Palgrave Macmillan; rachael.ballard@palgrave.com].

Pushan Kumar Dutta · Bhupinder Singh ·
Vasileios Paliktzoglou · Lawrence Ibeh ·
Andi Luhur Prianto
Editors

Digital Education for a Sustainable Future

Technological Integration, SDGs, and Empowering Future Generations

palgrave
macmillan

Editors
Pushan Kumar Dutta
Amity University, Kolkata
Kadampukur, West Bengal, India

Vasileios Paliktzoglou
School of Creative Media
Bahrain Polytechnic
Isa Town, Bahrain

Andi Luhur Prianto
Social and Political Sciences
Universitas Muhammadiyah Makassar
Makassar, Indonesia

Bhupinder Singh
Sharda School of Law
Sharda University
Greater Noida, Uttar Pradesh, India

Lawrence Ibeh
Computer Science and Informatics
Berlin School of Business and Innovation
Berlin, Germany

ISSN 2523-3084 ISSN 2523-3092 (electronic)
Sustainable Development Goals Series
ISBN 978-3-032-15432-3 ISBN 978-3-032-15433-0 (eBook)
https://doi.org/10.1007/978-3-032-15433-0

Cover credit: Eugene Mymrin/Getty Images

This Palgrave Macmillan imprint is published by the registered company Springer Nature Switzerland AG
The registered company address is: Gewerbestrasse 11, 6330 Cham, Switzerland

Contents

Notes on Contributors

Dr. Vaishali Arora is a commerce graduate from the University of Delhi and also did her LL.B. from there. After completing her Masters (LL.M) from the School of Law and Legal Studies, GGSIP University, New Delhi, she qualified the UGC–NET Examination and followed her passion for teaching starting her career with Amity Law School, Noida. She has a Ph.D. from the Indian Law Institute, New Delhi, and her area of specialization is Media Law. Women & Criminal Law, Family Law-1 (Marriage & Divorce), and Law of Contract—II are her other areas of interest. With almost a decade of experience, she has two edited books (published by globally known publication brands) and diverse research papers to her credit. Besides participating in myriad conferences, training programs, etc., she has organized a plethora of national and international events of academic import in collaboration with eminent foreign law schools and NLUs. Furthermore, she has judged varied Moot Court Competitions and has been a reviewer for reputed journals.

Sanjay Balwani is faculty in Department of Electronics and Telecommunication Engineering, Jhulelal Institute of Technology, India. He has a vast experience in teaching and research.

Dr. Praful V. Barekar Assistant Professor in the Department of Computer Technology at YCCE, Nagpur, has an impressive academic background, including Ph.D. in Computer Science and Technology from RTMNU, and an M. Tech from RTMNU, Nagpur. He has over 17 years of teaching experience in the YCCE, Nagpur, and PIET, Nagpur. Additionally, he was employed at Alfatech Solutions Pvt. Ltd. in Nagpur as a software engineer. Digital Image Processing, Neural Network, Database Management Systems, Data Structures, and Operating System are just a few of the many courses in which he is an expert. His research contribution is in the field of Digital Image Processing, Video Processing, Deep Learning, and Machine Learning. Dr. Praful V. Barekar has numerous publications, patents, and copyrights, earning his recognition and membership in professional organizations like IAENG, ISTE, and IE.

Dr. Akshay Bhargava holds a Doctorate in Law (Ph.D.) with a specialization in Corporate Social Responsibility, and a Master's degree in Law (LL.M.) focusing on Corporate and Business Law. His primary academic and research interests encompass Corporate Law and Intellectual Property Rights (IPR). He has been the recipient of Best Research Paper Awards at over five international conferences and has presented more than forty research papers at various national and international seminars and academic forums. His scholarly contributions include several research publications in books, national journals, and international journals, including those indexed in Scopus.

Dr. Saurabh Chandra is an accomplished legal scholar and currently serves as an Associate Professor & Assistant Dean at the School of Law, Bennett University, India. With a robust academic foundation, he earned his Bachelor of Arts and Bachelor of Laws (B.A. LL.B.) from the prestigious Aligarh Muslim University (A.M.U.). He further specialized in Business Laws, completing his Master of Laws (LL.M.) at the renowned National Law School of India University (NLSIU), Bangalore. Dr. Chandra's academic journey culminated in a Doctorate in Law (Ph.D.) from the esteemed National Law University (NLU) Delhi. In addition to his impressive legal education from some of India's most prestigious institutions, Dr. Chandra also holds a Master's degree in Management with specialization in Human Resources in Management and another in Journalism and Mass Communication. With almost two decades of teaching experience, he has numerous publications to his credit. His expertise is complemented by a robust portfolio of scholarly publications. By bridging the gap between theoretical insights and real-world applications, Dr. Chandra's work serves as a valuable resource for academics, legal practitioners, and industry professionals alike.

Prof. Dr. Rakhi Singh Chouhan is Principal, Department of Law, Prestige Institute of Management and Research, Gwalior. Prior to this, she was Professor and Director, Chandigarh Law College, Mohali, and Amity University Gwalior. Dr Rakhi Singh brings a unique blend of expertise to the table, with a rich background encompassing both advocacy and teaching in the field of law.

Dr. Rakhi Singh, a distinguished figure in the legal community, has garnered numerous accolades throughout her illustrious career. She is gold medalist in LL.B. and is Doctorate in Law. She started her career with advocacy. She practiced in High Courts, Consumer Commission, and Debt Recovery Tribunal for 14 years and then joined academics.

Prarthana A. Deshkar, Assistant Professor in the Department of Computer Technology at YCCE, Nagpur, has an impressive academic background, including a Ph.D. in Computer Science and Engineering from RTMNU, and an M.Tech from RTMNU, Nagpur. She has over 14 years of teaching experience in the YCCE, Nagpur. Additionally, she was employed at Axiom System Pvt. Ltd. in Nagpur as a software engineer. Data mining, DBMS, OOP, and statistics for data science are just a few of the many courses in which she is an expert. Her research contribution is in the field of multi-dimensional data analysis.

Dr. Shirisha Deshpande has been in the teaching profession for 25 years and currently working as Assistant Professor in the Department of English, in Chaitanya Bharathi Institute of Technology. She published more than 30 research papers in National and International Journals, published 10 patents, and also presented papers at various national and international conferences. Her areas of specialization include English Language Teaching, English Literature, and Soft Skills Training. Dr. Deshpande has a vast teaching experience which includes teaching different subjects like General English, Communication Skills, Employability Skills, Business Communication, Technical Writing Skills, and Gender Sensitization.

Dr. Pushan Kumar Dutta is Associate Professor at Amity University Kolkata who has carved a distinctive niche in academia with over 12 years of academic experience. He earned his Ph.D. from Jadavpur University in 2015, followed by postdoctoral work as an Erasmus Mundus Scholar at the University of Oradea in Romania in 2016, which laid the foundation for a career drive for a position in institution of academic excellence.

At the forefront of his contributions is an impressive editorial portfolio. Dr. Dutta has meticulously curated and edited over 60 books in the past couple of years for globally recognized publishers such as Springer, Elsevier, IET, Taylor & Francis, Cambridge Scholar Publishers, Degruyter, and IGI Global.

Dr. Dorottya Edina, Ph.D., is a certified economist with a professional background spanning academia and the private sector. Her expertise in sustainable development, environmental accounting, and practical experience in company management aligns with her active involvement in various projects and events. Her primary research areas include sustainable development goals, circular economy, climate change and environmental control management, and ESG. She has participated in projects focused on environmental accounting, ESG, and climate change. Additionally, she is highly engaged in professional and educational activities, including curriculum developments and ESG e-learning course.

Prof. Dr. Masanori Fukui is currently a professor and researcher at Mie University in Japan. He has also served as an Associate Professor in the Faculty of Software and Information Science at Iwate Prefectural University, Japan. His research interests primarily focus on engineering, advanced manufacturing systems, intelligent technologies, and interdisciplinary applications of emerging technologies in education and industry. He has contributed to international academic collaborations, conferences, and research initiatives related to innovation, sustainable technologies, and applied engineering.

Prof. Fukui has actively promoted global academic exchange through joint research activities, technical sessions, and international conferences. He has been a regular participant in SRD conferences since 2021. His scholarly contributions emphasize practical problem-solving, technology integration, and the advancement of sustainable and intelligent systems. Through his academic and research engagements, he continues to support international cooperation in higher education and scientific development.

Ankit Garg is a researcher currently pursuing his Ph.D. at Sharda University. He holds a Master of Laws (LL.M.) in Business Laws, along with an MBA, equipping him with a robust interdisciplinary foundation. His academic contributions include presenting research articles at various prestigious national and international conferences, and his work has been published in reputable journals. He has been working for the Government of India as a legal associate, where he provides legal support for the negotiation, drafting, and review of agreements and related international legal instruments. Ankit has also worked as an associate at a corporate law firm, where he advised clients on commercial contracts, aircraft leasing and asset financing, mergers and acquisitions, and regulatory compliance.

Sureksha Garg is a law graduate, having an LL.M. in Business Laws from Amity University, Noida, and pursuing Ph.D. from Sharda University, Greater Noida.

Dr. Priya Gedam is Assistant Professor in the Post Graduate Teaching Department of Commerce at Gondwana University, Gadchiroli. She joined the university on 18th June 2016. She holds UG, PG, MPhil, and Ph.D. degrees from RTM Nagpur University, along with GDC&A. Her research interests include FDI, Industrial Management, and Financial Management. She has published 4 research articles and presented papers in international and national conferences.

Dr. Yogesh Gharpure is currently associated with Tirpude Institute of Management Education, Nagpur, as Assistant Professor. With over 20 years of teaching experience in the field of Finance and Accounting, Yogesh Gharpure also serves as the Dean of the Post-Graduate Program at the institute. Yogesh Gharpure's academic responsibilities include teaching core courses such as Financial Accounting, Cost and Management Accounting, and Financial Management, along with a range of specialized subjects in the Finance domain.

Dr. Hammouch Hind holds a Ph.D. in Economics and Management from the Faculty of Legal, Economic, and Social Sciences (FSJES) at Sidi Mohamed Ben Abdellah University in Fez, Morocco. She currently serves as Professor at the Institute for Training in Offshoring Professions in ICT and Audiovisual Sectors (IFMOTICA) in Fez and as Lecturer at FSJES Fez, where she teaches undergraduate and graduate-level courses. Her research interests span corporate social responsibility (CSR), (Environmental, Social, and Governance) ESG, management control systems, organizational and financial performance, as well as the integration of artificial intelligence in sustainable development.

Prof. Dr. rer. nat. Lawrence Ibeh, EMBA, is Lecturer and Researcher in the Faculty of Computer Science and Informatics at the Berlin School of Business and Innovation, Germany. He is the Founding Chair and Chief Research Strategist of the Berlin International Center for Multidisciplinary Research (BICMR). He holds a doctorate in Informatics and Spatial Data Science from Ludwig Maximilian University of Munich, Germany, and an Executive M.B.A. from Quantic School of Business and Technology, Washington, DC, USA. His work focuses on artificial intelligence, applied data science, digital education, sustainability analytics, spatial modeling, and responsible AI.

Dr. Deepti Jain Thakre currently serves as Assistant Professor at Ramdeobaba University (RBU), Nagpur, bringing with her over two decades of rich teaching experience in some of the city's most reputed institutions. She holds an M.Phil. and Ph.D. in English, with her research interests spanning literature, language, and humanistic studies. A dedicated academic and creative writer, Dr. Deepti has presented and published numerous research papers and poems in acclaimed national and international journals, reflecting both scholarly depth and artistic sensitivity. Her tenure as NAAC Coordinator at Anjuman College was marked by her exemplary leadership in quality assurance, institutional accreditation, and student-centric initiatives, significantly enhancing the academic culture of the institution.

Dr. Laeeq R. Janjua has a Ph.D. (Political Economy), from CAMS-USA, on PGD-COMPLIANCE. He is affiliated to COMPLIANCE OFFICE—TMF GROUP—POLAND, and he is also Lecturer at WSB University Poland. Dr. Laeeq Razzak Janjua is a finance professional working in compliance and academia, whose journey is characterized by dedication, expertise, and a commitment to excellence. Mr. Janjua's academic prowess is reflected in his extensive body of work, which includes the publication of a book on corporate social responsibility as co-author and over 40 academic research papers. These contributions have solidified his reputation as a thought leader and a respected authority in his field, earning him recognition and acclaim from peers and scholars alike.

Dr. Vijaykumar Kaluvala is a distinguished Associate Professor at KL University, Hyderabad. With a robust academic background and extensive research in financial markets, he has made significant contributions to the field. His notable work includes a comprehensive study on arbitrage trading in the BSE and NSE, focusing on market volatility and risk analysis from 2010 to 2014. Dr. Vijay is dedicated to advancing knowledge in finance and mentoring the next generation of financial experts.

Dr. Tarun Kumar Kaushik has completed his LL.B. and LL.M. from Meerut college, Meerut, affiliated with C.C.S. University Meerut and qualified UGC-NET in December 2013; thereafter, he completed his LL.D. in 2023 from Meerut College Meerut C.C.S. University Meerut also. He is having 12 years of teaching experience and has many research paper publications in Scopus Journal UGC care List Journal and peer-reviewed referred journal. He authored the book having title national green tribunal: its establishment and principles.

Roshni S. Khedgaonkar is Assistant Professor at Yeshwantrao Chavan College of Engineering (YCCE), Nagpur, with over 16 years of dedicated academic service since August 2008. Born on December 20, 1986, this accomplished academic earned a Ph.D. in Computer Science & Technology from RTMNU in 2024, specializing in cutting-edge areas including Artificial Intelligence, Image Processing, Pattern Recognition, Near Set Theory, and LaTeX. With an impressive research portfolio, they have successfully mentored 67 projects (15 M.Tech and 52 undergraduate projects) and secured funding of Rs. 33,000 for an AI-driven predictive maintenance project under the Meghe Group of Institution's Minor Research scheme. Their innovative contributions are evidenced by three granted patents covering human cognitive state classification, IoT-based toxic gas detection robotics, and pharmaceutical equipment automation, alongside two copyrights.

CMA (Dr.) Pushparaj Kulkarni currently works at Dr. Ambedkar Institute of Management Studies & Research, Nagpur (16 years). Prior to this, Pushparaj Kulkarni has worked with G.H. Raisoni Group (2 years), ICFAI (1 year). Pushparaj Kulkarni's major job profile is teaching the core courses, viz. Financial Accounting, Cost & Management Accounting, Financial Management, Taxation, and the specialized courses in Finance domain. Besides working as a full-time Assistant Professor, Pushparaj Kulkarni also affiliated as an adjourn faculty at various universities including YCMOU (Nashik), MODY University (Rajasthan), and Nagpur University. A regular faculty member at Nagpur Chapter of Cost Accountant, VANAMATI (a state-owned undertaking), WCL, and MCED.

Amit Kumar working in Dewan Law College Meerut, Indi41.

Sonika Kumari is Assistant Professor of English at NIET College, Greater Noida, Delhi NCR, and is in the final stage of completing her doctoral studies (Ph.D.) at Sharda University. Her research specialization lies in South Asian diaspora narratives and film adaptation studies, with broader interests in cultural memory, heritage studies, and pedagogy. Before joining NIET, she served as a Teaching Assistant at Sharda University for two years, gaining valuable academic and research experience. Her scholarly contributions include Scopus-indexed research papers, peer-reviewed book chapters, and poetry, published in reputed journals such as Ekphrasis Journal, Jadavpur Journal of Languages and Linguistics (JJLL), and English Studies in India (University of Kashmir). She recently published a book chapter in Springer Nature titled Trauma, Memoryscape, and Refugees: An Insight into Shyam Selvadurai's The Funny Boy. At the same time, additional works are forthcoming with Brill and Routledge (2025).

Dr. Bhrigu Raj Mourya is an accomplished legal academic and researcher with over fifteen years of teaching and administrative experience in higher education. He is presently serving as Associate Professor at MATS University, Raipur, Chhattisgarh. A UGC-NET qualified scholar, Dr. Mourya obtained his Ph.D. from Chaudhary Charan Singh University, Meerut, in 2023, where his research focused on 'The Role of DNA Profiling Evidence on the Criminal Justice System in India: An Analytical Study.' His academic portfolio includes more than 14 UGC-CARE listed publications, 6 Scopus-indexed research papers, and several authored and edited books covering diverse legal themes such as criminal law, forensic evidence, human rights, and artificial intelligence in law.

Dr. Khar Thoe Ng is an advocate for technology-focused transdisciplinary studies including STEM education integrating arts (e.g. music, art, language, and culture or abbreviated as STEAM education). She is currently affiliated with INTI International University as Senior Lecturer II teaching postgraduate subjects related to Educational Management with both teaching and supervision tasks for Master in Educational Management (MEM) and Ph.D. in Education (Ph.D. Ed). She is also Adjunct Assistant Prof. of UCSI with experience supervising doctoral students in music and arts education. She was Visiting Professor and Foreign Research Fellow in Tsukuba University, Japan, in 2010 [info. retrievable from URL: https://www.criced.tsukuba.ac.jp/staff.html]. She published extensively (>480) as lead writer, editor/chief editor, of which many books/modules/book chapters, also refereed/Scopus/WoS-indexed high impact publications, were cited/referred widely.

Dr. Vasileios Paliktzoglou, an academic and industry professional, holds a Ph.D. in Computer Science from the University of Eastern Finland. He is an active contributor to academia, serving as a guest and associate editor for prestigious journals like the Journal of Information Systems Education (JISE) and IAFOR Journal of Education. He has been a keynote speaker at several academic and industry events, sharing his insights on social computing, collaborative learning, and emerging technologies in higher education. Dr. Paliktzoglou also actively participates in international research projects, highlighting his commitment to advancing knowledge and innovation as the Book Series Editor for the 'Emerging Technologies in Education' at Vernon Press and 'AI and Education' at STAR Scholars Press. His expertise continues to shape the academic and research landscape at Bahrain Polytechnic.

Amar Pandey is a **Full-Time Research Scholar** and **Teaching Assistant** at the **School of Law**, **Bennett University (Times Group)**. He holds a **Master of Laws (LL.M) in Criminal and Security Law** from **Manipal University, Jaipur (2021-2022)**. He completed his **undergraduate studies (B.A., LL.B.)** at the **School of Law, Galgotias University (2015-2020)**. He is currently pursuing his Ph.D. with a focus on studies related to Criminal Rehabilitation.

Dr. Vivek Pimplapure currently works at Dr. Ambedkar Institute of Management Studies & Research, Nagpur (18 years). Prior to this, Dr. Vivek U Pimplapure has worked with G.S. College of Comm. and Eco. Nagpur (5 years). Dr. Vivek U Pimplapure's major job profile is teaching the core courses, viz. Financial, Cost & Management Accounting, Financial Management, Taxation, and the specialized courses in Financial Management domain. Besides working as a full-time Associate Professor also affiliated as an adjourn faculty at various universities including YCMOU (Nashik), Nagpur University. A regular faculty member at Nagpur Chapter of Cost Accountant, PHI (a state-owned undertaking), WCL, etc.

Dr. Andi Luhur Prianto is an associate professor, editor, and scholar with over 19 years of teaching and research experience in political science and government. Dean at the Faculty of Social and Political Science, Universitas Muhammadiyah Makassar, Indonesia. Previously served as Vice-Dean and Head at the Department of Government Studies, Faculty Social and Political Science, Universitas Muhammadiyah Makassar, Indonesia. Also serve as visiting research fellow at Department of Politics and Economics, Center for East-European Studies, Universitat Bremen, Germany, and as well as Chief Editor for the Otoritas : Jurnal Ilmu Pemerintahan (Political Science & Government Journal) in Web of Science (WoS) and Sinta-1 Indexed.

Prachi Priyanka is an academic and researcher whose scholarship lies at the intersections of literature, visual culture, and feminist aesthetics. She holds a Ph.D. that examines the convergences between poetry and painting, underscoring her sustained engagement with the dialogue between word and image. Her areas of academic interest span intertextuality and visual culture, Indian literature in English and in translation, partition narratives, eco-criticism, Victorian studies, and feminist literary theory. She has published extensively, with her research articles and chapters appearing in internationally recognized edited volumes from publishers such as Routledge and Lexington Books and in reputed Scopus-indexed journals. She is also the author of six books that reflect her diverse scholarly pursuits. Currently, she serves as Assistant Professor in the School of Humanities and Social Sciences at Sharda University, India, where she continues integrating teaching and research with an emphasis on critical inquiry and creative interdisciplinarity.

Dr. Ambuj Sharma is a seasoned academician and legal expert with over 17 years of experience in law education. Currently serving as the Principal of Kamkus College of Law, Ghaziabad. Dr. Sharma has authored a book titled *Artificial Intelligence in the Indian Legal System: Transformations, Challenges and Future Prospects* and contributed a chapter to an IGI Global volume on sustainable energy indexed in Scopus. He has published multiple research papers in reputed peer-reviewed journals on themes ranging from consumer protection and gender justice to personal laws and uniform civil code.

Dr. Ashok Kumar Sharma joined the Law Department of PG and Research, Meerut College (Affiliated to Ch. Charan Singh University), Meerut, after selecting through Uttar Pradesh Higher education Commission, Allahabad. The College was established in 1892 and started LL.B. in the year of 1893. He had some ten years of experience practicing law in High Court, Allahabad, before his appointment in the College as

Assistant Professor in the year of 2017. He has been a Visiting Faculty in Institute of Legal Studies, CCS University, IIMT University, and some other prestigious law schools.

Arunima Shastri is a legal academic whose work explores the evolving intersections of law, technology, and social justice. She holds an LL.M. in Corporate and Commercial Law from the National Law University, Odisha, and is currently in the final stages of her Ph.D. at Gujarat National Law University. Her doctoral research critically examines the interface between intellectual property rights, visual art, deepfakes, and digital expression in contemporary society. Her academic interests span intellectual property law, data privacy, blockchain regulation, and human rights, with a particular focus on the rights of marginalized communities, including LGBTQ+ rights. Her teaching and research emphasize bridging legal theory with technological realities, promoting a nuanced understanding of how emerging technologies challenge traditional legal frameworks. Through her scholarship and pedagogy, she contributes to advancing discourse on digital rights, creative expression, and equitable access to justice in the evolving global legal landscape.

Abhay Raj Singh is AI and Product Strategy Executive with 18+ years of experience leading business-aligned innovation, rapid product development, and platform transformation. Proven ability to convert cutting-edge research into scalable, AI-powered systems including Agentic AI and ShipAccel delivering measurable cost savings and global impact. Trusted by executive leadership to define and scale AI-first strategies that drive results and is Editor of multiple AI books, co-author of ThinkAI research, and patent-holder.

Anurag Singh working in Meerut College, Chaudhary Charan Singh University, India

Dr. Arun Prakash Singh is a dedicated academician and legal researcher with extensive experience in the field of law. He earned his Doctor of Laws (LL.D.) from Chaudhary Charan Singh University, Meerut, in 2019, where his thesis focused on 'Child Labour and Social Security System in India: A Critical Study.' He also holds an LL.M. with specializations in Banking Law, Insurance Law, Corporate Finance, and Intellectual Property Rights. Over the years, Dr. Singh has participated in numerous national and international seminars, workshops, and conferences, contributing papers on diverse legal and social themes such as

human rights, judicial reforms, and the impact of technology on law. His publications have appeared in reputed journals including the Journal of Report and Opinion and Ad Valorem. Dr. Singh has more than a decade of teaching and administrative experience and is presently serving as Principal at Bankey Bihari College of Law, Ujhani, Budaun.

Bhupinder Singh is working as Faculty of Political Science, North Bangkok University, Thailand. He has given talks at international universities, resource person in international conferences such as in Nanyang Technological University Singapore, Tashkent State University of Law Uzbekistan; KIMEP University Kazakhstan, All'ah meh Tabatabi University Iran, the Iranian Association of International Criminal law, Iran, and Hague Center for International Law and Investment, The Netherlands, Northumbria University Newcastle, UK, Taylor's University Malaysia, AFM Krakow University, Poland, European Institute for Research and Development, Georgia, Business and Technology University Georgia, Texas A & M University, USA.

Dr. Gurveer Singh is Assistant Professor at GSSDGS Khalsa College, Patiala, with over ten years of teaching experience. He earned his Ph.D. from Punjabi University, Patiala, for his research titled 'World Peace and Sikhism: Challenges and Response.' His academic journey reflects a deep commitment to exploring the philosophical and practical dimensions of peace, spirituality, and social harmony. Dr. Singh has published fifteen research papers in reputed journals and edited volumes, contributing significantly to discourse on religion and modern societal issues. His primary research interests include peace studies, interfaith dialogue, and contemporary concerns in religion, with a special focus on Sikhism. Through his scholarly work, he seeks to promote intercultural understanding and ethical engagement across faith traditions. Dr. Gurveer Singh continues to inspire students and researchers through his dedication to advancing knowledge in religion and peace-building.

Kavita R. Singh With over 16 years of teaching excellence, Dr. Kavita R. Singh stands as a pillar of academic leadership and innovation. From serving as HoD (2015–2018) to contributing as an LEC Chairperson, reviewer, and Associate Editor for reputed journals like IJREAS, her impact spans across education and research. She has chaired numerous sessions at international conferences, received prestigious research grants,

and holds more than 10 copyrights to her name. A true academic leader shaping minds and pushing boundaries in technology and research.

Dr. Devdatta Tare is Assistant Professor in the Department of Commerce, Gondwana University, Gadchiroli, Maharashtra, India. Dr. Devdatta S. Tare's qualifications are M.Com., M.B.A., UGC-NET, Ph.D., and is Assistant Professor, Gondwana University (June 2016—Present), and Assistant Professor, Datta Meghe Institute of Management Studies, Nagpur (March 2013—June 2016). Dr. Devdatta S. Tare's research interests include commerce, business management, finance (behavioral finance), and higher education administration. Dr. Devdatta S. Tare's select publications are 1. profitability analysis of selected companies in sugar industry based on their margin on sales and 2. effective performance appraisal—a study to establish correlation between employee satisfaction and optimizing business results. Dr. Devdatta S. Tare's notable achievement is Resource Person for SEBI Financial Literacy Programs (since 2015). Registered copyright for Hypothesis Validation using T-test through MS-Excel.

Dr. Avni Suresh Thakkar is Assistant Professor in the Department of Management Technology (M.B.A.) at RKNEC. With 13 years of teaching experience, 3 years in industry, and 5 years in research, she brings a rich blend of academic and practical expertise. She is actively involved in university service as a member of the Result Analysis Committee. She has contributed to research and academic administration while continuing her academic journey.

A. Vijayalakshmi is Assistant Professor in the Department of English at Chaitanya Bharathi Institute of Technology (CBIT), Hyderabad. She joined the institute on 14th February 2004 and has 20 years of teaching experience along with 9 years in research. She holds an M.A. in English Literature, PGDTE, and is currently pursuing her Ph.D. Her areas of specialization include ELT, ICT, and Soft Skills. She plays several key roles including Member of Board of Studies (BoS), ISO Coordinator, Course Coordinator for Gender Sensitization and Indian Constitution, In-charge of Soft Skills Labs, and Bridge Course Coordinator. She has published international journal papers.

Dr. Rajani Wadhai is a dedicated faculty member in the Department of Sociology at Gondwana University, Gadchiroli. She joined the university on 16th June 2016 after serving at Smt. SP College, Gogaon. With

over 5 years of teaching experience (3 years at PG and 2 years at UG level), she holds M.A., NET, SET, M.Phil., and Ph.D. in Sociology. Her research focuses on teacher–student relationships and issues of reservation in education. Her areas of specialization include Research Methodology, Criminology, Gender and Society, and Education and Society. She actively contributes as NSS Programme Officer, Member Secretary of Students' Grievance Redressal Cell, Cultural and Sports In-charge, and has coordinated NAAC workshops and other university events.

Aarushi Walgaonkar currently works as Assistant Professor at Ramdeobaba University and pursuing her Ph.D. as a Research Scholar at Nagpur University, Maharashtra. Aarushi Walgaonkar has cleared the National Eligibility Test (NET) and State Eligibility Test (SET), and completed the Post-Graduate Diploma in the Teaching of English (PGDTE). Aarushi Walgaonkar's doctoral research focuses on Children's Literature. Aarushi Walgaonkar is deeply passionate about research and enjoy contributing her ideas across diverse areas within literature. Research, for her, is not just a process but a meaningful way to explore, learn, and engage with evolving perspectives. Aarushi Walgaonkar aims to contribute actively to the academic community through insightful research, impactful teaching, and continuous learning. With a strong foundation in English studies and a commitment to scholarly growth, Aarushi Walgaonkar strives to make a positive impact in the field of literature and education.

Prof. Dr. Kittisak Wongmahesak is a distinguished academic specializing in political science, public management, and international political economy. He currently serves as Secretary of the Ph.D. Program in Political Science at North Bangkok University, Director of the Association of Legal & Political Studies in Thailand, and a Supervisor for the Post-Doctoral Fellowship Research Collaboration Program at Lincoln University College in Malaysia. He is also a Research Fellow at Shinawatra University in Thailand and Universiti Sultan Zainal Abidin in Malaysia, with adjunct professorships in Indonesia. His previous roles include Full Professor positions in China and Cyprus, as well as an Adjunct Researcher in Vietnam.

Rashi Yadav is a **Full-Time Research Scholar** and **Teaching Assistant** at the **School of Law, Bennett University (Times Group)**. He holds a **Master of Laws (LL.M) in Corporate Law** from **Guru Gobind Singh**

Indraprastha University, New Delhi (Main Campus) (2020-2021). He completed his **undergraduate studies (BA LLB)** at the **School of Law, Galgotias University (2015-2020).** He is currently pursuing his Ph.D. with a focus on studies related to Role of Judges in determining religious freedom.

Dr. Urmila Yadav is a well-known Sociologist who is currently working as Associate Professor in Sharda School of Law, Sharda University. She is actively engaged in teaching and research. She has more than 25 research papers published in various reputed national and international journals. She has published, authored, and edited books on various women and elderly related issues and has received many accolades in the academic area. She has received Awards by National Commission for Women (NCW) & Uttar Pradesh Police (Women & Safety Wing) for her excellent contribution in society. She has received financial assistance by Government of India 7 times in a short span since 2020 until date. She also owns one major research study on 'All Women Police Station Performance (Working Efficiency & Effectiveness) in Uttar Pradesh' sponsored by Govt. of India, National Commission for Women, New Delhi . She is a member of several societies and advisory boards. Dr. Urmila Yadav is continuously working in the area of women empowerment and social justice.

List of Figures

Chapter 20

CHAPTER 1

Mapping the Landscape of Digital Pedagogies: Analyzing Learner Experiences in the Digital Age

Shirisha Deshpande, Avni Suresh Thakkar, and Sanjay Balwani

Abstract The most expedited complex change occurred in schooling after the outburst of the pandemic as digitalization traveled the world and recast teaching methods and learner experiences around the globe. This chapter explores the changing contexts of teaching and learning

S. Deshpande (✉)
Department of English, Chaitanya Bharathi Institute of Technology Hyderabad, Hyderabad, Telangana, India
e-mail: shirisha_english@cbit.ac.in

A. S. Thakkar
School of Management, Shri Ramdeobaba University of Engineering and Management, Nagpur, India

S. Balwani
Department of Electronics and Telecommunication Engineering, Jhulelal Institute of Technology, Nagpur, India

P. K. Dutta et al. (eds.), *Digital Education for a Sustainable Future*, Sustainable Development Goals Series,
https://doi.org/10.1007/978-3-032-15433-0_1

in virtual and hybrid settings. It explores the ways in which digital tools, platforms, and methodologies are transforming educational practices by enabling more learner-centered engagement, personalization, and interactivity. With highlighting both popular notions in digital pedagogy including ones such as constructivist and connectivist frameworks this chapter critiques not only theory but also the emerging trends in gamification, adaptive learning, and AI-driven instruction. It examines what aspects of digital experiences extend beyond the cognitive and potentially toward emotional and social dimensions through qualitative and quantitative analysis of learner feedback. It also comments on the issues of digital inequity, Zoom fatigue, and the depersonalization of learning. Focus on inclusivity, accessibility, and the role of educators in digital transformation. Drawing on worldwide case studies, the chapter shows different ways to practice effective digital pedagogy within K–12, higher education, and continued education. The insight gleaned from this exploration is valuable for educators, policymakers, and instructional designers interested in improving the quality and equity of digital education. Placing student voices and lived experiences at the center of its approach, the study helps contribute to an ongoing rethinking of how education systems can be redesigned for a digital age.

Keywords Digital pedagogy · Learner experience · Educational technology · Online learning · Digital equity

1 Introduction

The education landscape has been caused by digital transformation to a seismic shift leading people to new ways of formal learning that is redefining bounds for how, when and where learning should take place [1]. With technology developing and growing quicker than ever, the term, "digital pedagogy" has arisen as both an answer to changes in education and a stimulus for new practices. Digital pedagogy is the practice of employing digital tools, platforms, and methodologies as a means of enhancing, extending, or transforming the acts of teaching and learning experiences in some way. Digital pedagogy is not the straightforward transmission of knowledge between teacher and learner found in physically proximate classrooms, but rather a multidimensional interactive framework based on flexibility, learner autonomy, personalization, and a much higher level of innovation into instructional and learning strategies [2].

The shift toward digital learning environments has been accelerated by many factors such as the increasing internet access, widespread use of laptops, mobile and smart devices, and Global disruptions. Such developments compels now to the usage of Learning Management Systems (LMS), virtual classrooms, AI-supported tutoring systems, gamified content, and augmented or virtual reality (AR/VR)-based simulations in a very rapid pace. Digital pedagogy is more than sprinkling in different technologies; it is a transition to a new paradigm for how we create, share, and address knowledge as huge implications for educators and learners both. This represents a paradigm shift from an instructional model delivery to a constructivist model with student engagement, which promotes critical thinking, creativity and digital literacy.

It is therefore necessary to analyze learner experiences in order to learn more about the effectiveness and impact of digital pedagogies. Digital tools have provided us with exciting new opportunities in engagement, inclusion and accessibility but they have also brought some complicated challenges related to digital fatigue and social isolation, screen addiction and unequal access to technology tools. Multiple factors as socio-economic status, geographic location, learning styles, emotional well-being all affect student experiences in digital environments [3]. The interaction between learners from different cultural perceptions of education, the different infrastructures available in those cultures, and the level of institutional support present in each culture drives the ultimate impact any digital education solution can have. This study seeks to map the shifting landscape of digital pedagogies by focusing on the voices and lived experiences of learners in multiple settings. Utilizing a multidisciplinary perspective based on relations of theories and philosophies from technology, education, psychology, and sociology, this chapter aims to gain insights into the more subtle aspects of twenty first century experiences during digital learning. Coupled with qualitative narratives and quantitative data it shows what works, what does not, and what needs to be re-imagined in the digital education space.

Digital pedagogies are not just a technology; they indicate a major change in the culture and thinking behind the philosophy of education [4]. No longer has a passive recipient of information, the learner become an active co-creator of knowledge, exploring digital environments, constructing meanings and developing communities of practice. Hence, to comprehend the landscape of digital pedagogy needs to analyze four different dimensions of technology: Technological, pedagogical, psychological, and ethical. This exploration provides an important context that can help shape policy, curriculum development, instructional design, and future research as education systems increasingly seek to be more resilient, adaptive, and equitable. In tracing the shape of digital pedagogy as viewed from the perspective of learner voice, the chapter adds to the evolution of education in the digital age an exercise that remains connected to innovative, but also equitable, compassionate, and human-centered [5].

2 Technological Tools and Platforms in Education

The infusion of tech tools and platforms into the education sector has facilitated a more dynamic delivery, access, and consumptive model of knowledge, allowing for a departure from classical learning methods. With the rise of digital pedagogy, teachers depend even more so on an ever-expanding list of digital tools to support instruction, collaboration and engagement. They vary from basic tools such as LMS to disruptive technologies like AI, VR, AR, and gamified learning environments. Each of these platforms fulfills different but complementary roles, transforming the nature of teaching and learning in diverse education contexts.

Digital education has dramatically altered the learning landscape, with Learning Management Systems such as Moodle, Canvas, and Google Classroom serving as foundational infrastructures and providing us with centralized environments for course delivery, assessments, content management, and communication [6]. These platforms help with administrative processes and give students access to learning materials and instant feedback in a more flexible manner. Also, Online platforms like Zoom, Microsoft teams, and Google meet facilitated synchronous online learning with virtual interaction for face-to-face interaction, discussions, and activities overcoming distance barriers. The more personalized and immersive technologies are rising. AI-enabled educational apps like Smart Sparrow or Carnegie Learning adaptive learning platforms analyze data and machine learning to make content available according to learning styles and paces of individual learners. By providing tailored feedback and

focused practice, this tailoring helps enhance understanding and memory. VR and AR give experiential learning where it gives the students to different simulations of real-life experiences, especially used in the field of medicine, engineering, and history where they can immerse themselves with the content of their subject [7].

Gamification integrates game mechanics including point scoring, badges, and leaderboards into educational content to increase motivation and engagement. Platforms like Kahoot! Classroom XP, Flying Classroom, Classcraft, and Quizizz are great examples of how learning can become animated and even entertaining! Mobile Learning apps will also help in providing anytime-anywhere education, bringing education even closer to a few remote and resource-poor areas. While these technologies offer many benefits to educators and students, they also necessitate thoughtful implementation and pedagogical alignment. If training and integration strategies to facilitate the technical integration of technology are not part of the plan, technology could end up as a distraction instead of an enabler. However, educators have to know these digital literacy skills and foster them with continuous professional development. The technological tools and platforms in education have opened up possibilities for more interactive, inclusive, and learner-centered pedagogies [8]. Using these innovations we will be able to convert the age-old educational experiences into immersive, engaging, and flexible learning journeys tailored for the new generation in the digital era.

3 Learner Engagement and Motivation in Digital Contexts

While learner engagement and motivation play a key role in academic success, keeping them high in digital contexts has its challenges and opportunities as well. In a face-to-face classroom, being physically present and interacting directly with others provides many natural cues for participation, accountability, and social learning. Yet, in digital learning environments—whether fully online or hybrid—the lack of physical co-presence calls for new approaches to engage learners and maintain their intrinsic motivation. For all of these reasons, then, digital pedagogy needs to be intentionally designed to facilitate engagement through interactivity, relevance, autonomy, and emotional connection.

Interactive content is the best ways to boost online learner engagement. Using multimedia resources such as video lectures, simulations,

infographics, quizzes, and drag-and-drop exercises moves things away from just reading and writing, and caters to different learning styles. The use of features like discussion boards, live polling, and collaborative documents encourage peer-to-peer interaction, which builds community and combats the isolation that frequently afflicts virtual learning environments. Video conferencing allows real-time engagement, while asynchronous platforms offer convenience and accommodate schedules and paces. Digital learning motivation is about the purpose, autonomy, and accomplishment of the learner. By including gamification elements such as point systems, badges, and progress tracking can create instant gratification and tangible goals to increase motivation [9]. Learners are provided with increased control and competence with personalized learning paths, thanks to adaptive technologies focused on their individual goals and abilities. In addition, relevance is extremely important any content that mirrors real-renowned situations or is clearly aligned with the interests of the learners will result in higher perceived value and engagement.

Digital contexts can also create barriers in the form of screen fatigue, distractions, and technological frustration that can sap motivation. Experiences that do not provide timely feedback, interfaces that are impersonal, and a design of instruction that does not engage the learner makes one feel alienated and demotivated. Hence, teachers have to implement more empathetic and learner-focused strategies such as continuous check-ins, formative assessments, and self-reflection and feedback sessions. But there is also social and emotional engagement. Students who feel that they are seen, heard and supported are more likely to stay with the learning process even when in virtual spaces. Personalized communication, sponsored group projects, recognition of contributions all help in establishing a sense of community and belonging in the digital classroom. Good learner engagement in digital spaces is the result of pedagogical design that is deliberate, inclusive, and adaptive, not a by-product of the technology itself. When educators can tailor motivational approaches to digital tools, connect them to track and use human-centered teaching practices, meaningful learning experiences can be designed featuring connectivity to a diverse population of learners in the digital age [10].

4 Equity, Access, and the Digital Divide: Cognitive and Emotional Aspects of Online Learning

The rapid expansions of digital pedagogies have exposed a wicked problem to be solved by higher education how to provide equity and access to all learners in a digitally mediated world. Although technology is seen as a means to democratize teaching and learning regardless of time and distance, it can easily create inequity or exacerbate existing inequity. The digital divide continues to dominate the experiences of learners, especially those in low-resourced communities; disparities in access to digital devices, connectivity, and digital literacy remain that this divides forms along socio-economic, geographic, gender, disability and age lines and shapes not only participation or otherwise in online learning but the quality of that participation.

Digital educational equity is not just about giving out devices or access to the Internet. This includes usability testing of culturally relevant content, language availability, assistive technologies and inclusive pedagogical strategies [11]. All these affect their cognitive engagement and emotional well-being; many others face structural barriers, such as lack of a quiet place and parent support to help learn, and lack of any access to financial money needed to study. Online education can provide empowerment for students from marginalized or vulnerable backgrounds, or it can turn into a source of stress, anxiety, and alienation. Many of these challenges are magnified without the in-person support networks that typically provide social, emotional, and academic support. In terms of cognition, learners in digital environments deal with powder kegs of self-regulation, time management, and attention all skills that follow an uneven age- and education-distribution table. Poorly designed and overly complicated digital interfaces can hinder understanding and strain attention, and continued exposure to digital screens can lead to cognitive fatigue and impaired performance. The learning differences, disabilities or both can be challenged in ways as well when a digital platform is not designed to be accessible.

So, emotionally, the learning online can result in isolation, detachment, and disconnectedness. Since there are no real time human interaction assignments, learners might miss support and hence be demotivated in return resulting in low retention or poor academic performance. Students

can be disengaged and off-put when the routines of the classroom, interaction with peers and in-person instructional guidance from a teacher are missing. The challenge of mental health concerns for e.g., the anxiety and the depression that has grown more obvious in some areas of digital learning, for example, during long stretches of distance learning [12].

Such disparities may be minimized by taking a more inclusive approach to the technology integration in schools, namely a combination of pedagogical inclusivity, competence, and emotional support. From building up infrastructure to train teachers, from developing accessible content to making mental health resources available, schools and educational institutions need to first work on digital equity. Further, policymakers and other educational stakeholders need to work together on developing frameworks that support the further digital transition so that no learner is being left behind. However, it is only through ultimately closing the digital divide and enhancing cognitive and emotional quality in online learning that we can hope to build a just, inclusive and resilient educational future in the digital age.

5 Educator Perspectives and Digital Competency

With the shift of education to digital and hybrid modes, the role of the educator has changed from that of a transmitter of knowledge to a facilitator, designer, and curator of meaningful online learning experiences. At the heart of this change is a digital competency among teachers the integration of technology with pedagogy while still being responsive enough to the varied needs of individual learners. Digital competency is more than just being a techno-savvy teacher, it includes foundation of pedagogical mastery, awareness of digital tools and its assessment, flexibility, and conscious attention to ethical, privacy, and access issues in a digital learning context.

The move to digital has been a potential positive, but also a huge strain on the educator. On the one hand, digital tools provide for more creativity, personalization, and efficiency in teaching. The possibilities of content delivery, assessment, and collaborative learning with these online platforms are endless. However, numerous educators have claimed that they are draining by the ever-present need to absorb technology and harness, frequently with constrained institutional sponsorship or mentoring. Digital fatigue among professors can affect their confidence, job satisfaction, and teaching effectiveness,particularly among those who

entered the profession through traditional pathways or whose teaching experiences have been largely analog. However, the last year has showed us that there is also the issue of keeping students engaged in a meaningful way during online learning environments. While in a face-to-face classroom body language, tone, and immediacy of interaction generally guide instructional decision making, digital spaces only deliver what we are intentionally set up to assess and to interact with [13]. There is a fine balance between audio and video tech setups and building bonds digitally, managing screen fatigue, and developing an inclusive learning experience with digital content is a mix of right and left-brain creativity and is essential and requires both technical acumen and emotional intelligence. Additionally, educators need to consider digital equity providing all students the opportunity to participate in the learning experience regardless of background or access factors.

Enhancing digital competency through professional development
Digital education-oriented training programs need to equip trainers not only on the technical aspects of technologies but also on the pedagogical aspect of things so that they would be able to overcome with new technologies/tools/platforms in the coming days. Professional growth is also sustained through collaborative learning communities, mentorship, and institutional recognition. The twenty first-century learning lives or dies by the capacity of the teacher. The skills and critical thinking, flexibility, and accessibility practices that they embody help ensure that tech continues to be a tool we build bridges with and not walls. With digital learning now an indelible part of global education systems, building the digital capacity and well-being of educators will be one of the keys in ensuring the equitable and innovative educational future people need [14].

6 Global Perspectives on Digital Pedagogies

The adoption of digital pedagogies has flourished in a multitude of ways throughout the world, influenced by disparate technological infrastructures, cultural norms, educational policy landscapes, and socio-economic climates. Digital pedagogy around the world has much to teach us, both in common challenges that nations face as they open their classrooms to technology, and in interesting innovations that are specific to local environments. Digital teaching and learning strategies are heterogeneous;

they are determined by a blend of accessibility, affordability, policy framework, and pedagogical traditions that collectively shape digital education practices globally.

Digital pedagogy is directly integrated in the educational systems of developed nations like Finland, Canada, South Korea, Singapore and more. These countries have thriving digital pipeline, teacher training and blended and personal learning-friendly policies [15]. For part of Finland's secret to doing this, the digital tools they use are woven into highly student-centered pedagogies that also focus on creativity, collaboration, etc. South Korea: Combining AI, Cloud Computing and Encounter Learning with E-Platform Learning Encounter South Korea's smart learning initiatives combine AI, smart practice and e-learning platforms to pave a road for actual-time learning analytics and adaptive instruction.

Even in developing and under-resourced regions, digital pedagogies are often limited by lack of infrastructure, lack of device and internet access, and lack of professional development for educators. But countries throughout Sub-Saharan Africa, some areas of South Asia and Latin America have discovered fortitude, using low-tech or mobile-based solutions to deliver instruction to children in far-flung and disadvantaged areas. The worldwide reactions to the COVID-19 crisis revealed both the inequalities and potential capacities of digital learning. Even as some parts of the world were able to move quickly to online learning, many struggled to keep learning on track, raising questions about digital equity, the desirability of inclusive design, and the toll of online learning on mental health. International organizations—such as UNESCO, UNICEF, and the World Bank—have since stepped up to promote digital education through financial aid, research and policy recommendations, and international cooperation and knowledge sharing [16].

The pedagogy that can be adopted also depends on cultural perceptions of technology in education. Some societies perceived digital learning as a tool for innovation and progress; in others, it was viewed with disbelief as it was suspected to undermine teachers and relations between students and teachers, and replace long-cherished traditions and values. This means that effective digital pedagogy will reverberate to walk a balance between the more universal access, engagement, and inclusion standards while resonating with local cultural norms and contextualized educational goals [17]. The global view on digital pedagogies highlights the need for subtle, contextualized approaches, cross-border cooperation and exchange of knowledge. Using one another's successes and failures as guidance, nations can move together toward digital education systems that are more equal, flexible, and learner-centered and that embrace the diversity and dynamism of the world's learning communities.

7 Challenges and Limitations in Digital Learning Environments

Although abundant for change, digital education is plagued with myriad challenges and limitations in learning and teaching using a digital form that decrease comfortability, effectiveness and inclusiveness [9]. Digital platforms are flexible, accessible, and innovative, but also raise a host of issues of equity, engagement, infrastructure, pedagogy and mental health. However, they also help us to understand the different challenges facing various groups of teachers, students, and parents during the crisis, which is crucial for developing more resilient and responsive digital education systems for diverse learners.

The digital divide remains one of the most significant barriers to realizing the potential benefits of digital learning,as it is closely linked to broader social and educational inequalities. Those from economically disadvantaged backgrounds, from rural areas, or from marginalized communities often have trouble with limited access to high-speed internet, to digital devices, and to supportive environments for learning at home [18]. Such infrastructural gaps adversely affect the participation of students in online and virtual education, resulting in learning gaps and reduced learning outcomes. Some platforms are poorly designed, and without any accessibility features they also increase exclusion for students with disabilities.

A third essential drawback is related to engagement and motivation of learners. While conventional class situation owes its strength to real time interactions, peer help, face-to-face bonding, actionable presence, virtual getting to know surroundings lacks the immediacy and emotional bandwidth that have a tendency to retain the spirit of frequent engagement. Problems include excessive screen exposure, consumptive content, and limited instantaneous feedback, all of which create conditions for cognitive overload, attention collapse, and disengagement. In the absence of well-designed interactivity and responsive content, DS IDEA slides toward boredom and irrelevance [19].

The other area that will encounter significant obstacles is in digital pedagogy itself, where many educators will need to adapt their teaching style to remain well aligned with their students. Many teachers do not get enough training and support to use technology as instruction. New materials Using online teaching will require new thinking, and new skills blending digital devices with pedagogical aims. Lack of professional development and support from the institution leads many educators to feel overwhelmed, unprepared and resistant to technology at times even despite proven benefits.

The absence of standardized and quality assured digital content and assessment. There is a wide variety of online resources and platforms, and it can be a challenge to find accurate, credible, and relevant content in line with the learning objectives. Addressing student learning in digital environments also raises further challenges, including issues of academic dishonesty, the limitations of automated feedback when it comes to more open-ended forms of assessment, and the lack of capacity to measure deeper learning outcomes such as critical thinking and collaboration [20]. The length of remote learning brought the issues of mental health and social distancing as the new important constraints. With less human contact, lower social interactions and no physical routines, numerous students are saying they're feeling more lonely, anxiety and stress, more now than prior to the pandemic. This emotional disconnection can have a detrimental effect on academic success and general quality of life.

Data privacy and cyber-security considerations are emerging as more and more critical. As learning analytics and digital assessments generate ever more data about students, it is critical that the information practices of educational institutions ensure that student information cannot be misused, breached or subject to unethical surveillance. At the same time, digital learning environments offer transformative potential and can profoundly change the way people learn; however, they still have important limitations. Tackling these issues demands a multi stakeholder approach where educators, policy makers, technologists, and learners themselves need to co-design inclusive, safe and pedagogy driven Digital Education systems that take a balanced approach to marrying technology with human touch [21].

8 Futures of Digital Pedagogy: Innovation and Transformation

Digital pedagogy is by no means static, and the changes in the digital landscape, learner expectations and societal needs destroy the tables that seem to have been set for us, and reshuffles it with more inclusive, adaptive and personalized education. With education systems transitioning from emergency remote teaching to intentional digital design, the conversation is now centered on how to design learning ecosystems that correlate the human and digital worlds sustainably. The digital pedagogy of the future cannot rest solely in the fact that a technology is present but rather how meaningfully it enhances learning opportunities, encourages autonomous critical thought, and contributes to the lifelong learning of individuals.

In the future clear directions toward pedagogies will be developed through Artificial Intelligence, machine learning and data analytics. Worldwide, adaptive learning systems are expected to deliver content tailored to learners' individual styles,performance levels, and preferences, while providing continuous feedback and support. Plan to be a VR/AR Trainer Virtual reality and augmented reality will create immersive learning environments in which students can explore complex concepts via simulation, leading to deeper understanding and engagement. This will convert static learning into dynamic, interactive representations that replicate real world context.

The increasing need for flexible, on-demand learning solutions will lead to more micro learning, modular learning, and just-in-time learning models. Decentralized education systems, such as blockchain-based credentialing, will allow learners to self-curate their learning journeys across platforms, subjects, and timelines. And this transition will further challenge entities as we know traditional institutional and cross institutional roles will begin to form—more open learning structures and organizations, more collaborative more multidisciplinary and cross-disciplinary.

The ethical and inclusive aspect of future digital pedagogy is equally important. While innovation advances, educators are responsible for ensuring that technology serves all learners equitably, while respecting privacy, accessibility, and cultural relevance. Closing this gap between innovation and practice will require professional development and digital fluency among educators. What the future holds for digital pedagogy is striking a balance between the pace at which technology evolves and the pace at which we can be pedagogically intentional while still integrating the innovative tools available to us to enrich empathy, inclusivity, and learner-centeredness in our curriculum.

9 Conclusion

Since digital pedagogy is a moving target, the need to design and implement human-centered learning environments becomes more urgent. While the literary agency will never ship kids out to work with their own massive amounts of debt, just like technological tools and platforms have transformed the educational landscape, the innovation will not lie in the technology, but in the meaningful and equitable inclusive learning experiences that technology supports. The era of digital learning has opened new avenues for personalization, flexibility, and interaction, but it has also posed new challenges everything from digital exhaustion and social isolation to equity of access and reduced human connection. So, moving away from this approach requires more careful and intentional planning of pedagogical frameworks that respond to the holistic needs of learners.

Aspects of empathy, accessibility, cultural relevance, and learner agency are highlighted in human-centered digital education. It is a demand for pedagogy that intertwines the latest technologies with compassion, community and collaboration in the teaching and learning process. We need educators with digital and emotional intelligent competencies to adapt with diverse learners context and institutions with equity deliberate policies and structures to promote well-being. The voice of the learner must be central in both the design and evaluation of digital education systems. Co-creation, feedback loops, and participatory content creation must be at the heart of necessary work to future-proof education through responsive learning to diverse experiences and needs. The next step will be to integrate technological progress and a humanistic values system to create a new educational future which is not only efficient and innovative, but also ethical, empowering, and profoundly connected to the daily experiences of the learners. This will enable digital pedagogy to be a truly transformative vehicle for inclusive and sustainable education.

References

1. Makda, F. (2025). Digital education: Mapping the landscape of virtual teaching in higher education–A bibliometric review. *Education and Information Technologies, 30*(2), 2547–2575.
2. Santoveña-Casal, S., & López, S. R. (2024). Mapping of digital pedagogies in higher education. *Education and Information Technologies, 29*(2), 2437–2458.
3. Pramesworo, I. S., Fathurrochman, I., Sembing, D., Bangkara, B. A., & Sudrajat, D. (2023). Relevance between blended learning and students' independent learning curriculum: An overview of digital age education, student and teacher engagement, technological resources. *Jurnal Kependidikan: Jurnal Hasil Penelitian dan Kajian Kepustakaan di Bidang Pendidikan, Pengajaran dan Pembelajaran, 9*(3), 858–869.
4. Wei, Z. (2024). Navigating digital learning landscapes: Unveiling the interplay between learning behaviors, digital literacy, and educational outcomes. *Journal of the Knowledge Economy, 15*(3), 10516–10546.
5. Bitar, N., & Davidovich, N. (2024). Transforming pedagogy: The digital revolution in higher education. *Education Sciences, 14*(8), 811.
6. Vaicondam, Y., Sikandar, H., Irum, S., Khan, N., & Qureshi, M. I. (2022). Research landscape of digital learning over the past 20 years: A bibliometric and visualisation analysis. *International Journal of Online and biomedical engineering, 18*(8), 4–22.
7. Putra, A. K., Bachri, S., Al Khalidy, D., & Syaiful Huda, I. A. I. (2023). Spatial acumen in the digital age: The transformative power of STEM-enriched mobile textbooks in geography. *International Journal of Interactive Mobile Technologies, 17*(23), 153–167.
8. Alam, A., & Mohanty, A. (2023). Educational technology: Exploring the convergence of technology and pedagogy through mobility, interactivity, AI, and learning tools. *Cogent Engineering, 10*(2), 2283282.
9. Väätäjä, J. O., & Ruokamo, H. (2021). Conceptualizing dimensions and a model for digital pedagogy. *Journal of Pacific Rim Psychology, 15*, 1834490921995395.
10. Bozkurt, A., & Zawacki-Richter, O. (2021). Trends and patterns in distance education (2014–2019): A synthesis of scholarly publications and a visualization of the intellectual landscape. *The International Review of Research in Open and Distance Learning, 22*(2), 19–45.
11. Rahimi, R. A., & Oh, G. S. (2024). Rethinking the role of educators in the 21st century: Navigating globalization, technology, and pandemics. *Journal of Marketing Analytics, 12*(2), 182–197.
12. Kiryakova, G., & Kozhuharova, D. (2024). The digital competences necessary for the successful pedagogical practice of teachers in the digital age. *Education Sciences, 14*(5), 507.

13. Hakimi, L., Eynon, R., & Murphy, V. A. (2021). The ethics of using digital trace data in education: A thematic review of the research landscape. *Review of Educational Research, 91*(5), 671–717.
14. Alias, N. F., & Razak, R. A. (2025). Revolutionizing learning in the digital age: A systematic literature review of microlearning strategies. *Interactive Learning Environments, 33*(1), 1–21.
15. Deák, C., & Kumar, B. (2024). A systematic review of STEAM education's role in nurturing digital competencies for sustainable innovations. *Education Sciences, 14*(3), 226.
16. Abuhassna, H., Awae, F., Adnan, M. A., Daud, M., & Almheiri, A. S. (2024). The information age for education via artificial intelligence and machine learning: a bibliometric and systematic literature analysis. *International Journal of Information and Education Technology, 14*(5), 700.
17. Rawal, D. M. (2024). Mapping of school teachers' digital competency in the context of digital infrastructure: A systematic review and empirical study of India. *Journal of Professional Capital and Community, 9*(3), 173–195.
18. Deping, Z., & Burhanudeen, H. B. (2023). Enlightenment for developing Chinese teachers' digital literacy: Comparing and analyzing international frameworks and Chinese framework. *Proceedings of EEIC, 3*, 110–130.
19. Feziyasti, A., & Ashel, H. (2025). Teaching science mapping research on integration of augmented reality technology and education for sustainable development: A bibliometric analysis. *Jurnal Penelitian Pendidikan IPA, 11*(7), 12–24.
20. Zhang, M., Akoto, M., & Li, M. (2023). Digital multimodal composing in post-secondary L2 settings: A review of the empirical landscape. *Computer Assisted Language Learning, 36*(4), 694–721.
21. Dooly, M., & Darvin, R. (2022). Intercultural communicative competence in the digital age: Critical digital literacy and inquiry-based pedagogy. *Language and Intercultural Communication, 22*(3), 354–366.

CHAPTER 2

Barriers and Breakthroughs: Assessing Equity, Access, and Innovation in Digital Learning Environments

Prarthana A. Deshkar, Kavita R. Singh, and Roshni S. Khedgaonkar

Abstract Digital Learning Environments use a critical lens to explore the systemic barriers that prevent fully inclusive participation in digital learning and share insights into breakthrough approaches that foster equitable learning outcomes. The study investigates the intersection of socio-economic context, geography, digital infrastructure, and institutional readiness for understanding learner experiences in different contexts. Shifting from traditional educational environments, it has broadened the channels of delivery, allowing for a level of innovation, flexibility, and personalization never seen before. This transition, however, has also revealed and in some cases, magnified inequities and access-related gaps. Barriers and Breakthroughs: Assessing Equity, Access, and Innovation in

P. A. Deshkar (✉) · K. R. Singh · R. S. Khedgaonkar
Department of Computer Technology, Yeshwantrao Chavan College of Engineering, Nagpur, Maharashtra, India
e-mail: prarthana.deshkar@gmail.com

P. K. Dutta et al. (eds.), *Digital Education for a Sustainable Future*, Sustainable Development Goals Series,
https://doi.org/10.1007/978-3-032-15433-0_2

using qualitative and quantitative evidence across a range of educational environments, the chapter assesses the potential for technological innovations to narrow the digital divide, specifically adaptive learning platforms, mobile technologies, and low-bandwidth solutions. It also explores the responsibility of teachers, policymakers, and designers to build a responsive digital ecosystem that directly addresses the cognitive, emotional, and cultural needs of learners. The chapter highlights ongoing challenges including restricted access to gadgets, gaps in digital literacy, and uneven quality of instruction as well as new advances that are changing the face of online education. This mapping of dynamics, in turn, informs a broader sense of what equity might even mean in digital learning, and speaks to systems-level recommendations for designing future education systems that are accessible, innovative, and human-centered.

Keywords Digital learning · Equity and access · Educational innovation · Digital divide · Inclusive pedagogy

1 Introduction

Education has entered a new phase through digital transformation that is more connected, more flexible, and more innovative than ever before. The digital landscape holds tremendous potential to boost education, through hiking up virtual classrooms, online laboratories, AI-based learning platforms, and immersive simulation or demos. But this change has not helped everyone. Digital education, while promising many possible things, has shone a spotlight on, and in many cases exacerbated, existing inequities. The harsh truth is that some pupils enjoy hi-tech glories of benchmarking and of digitally-empowered masters, and others make do with makeshift devices, patchy internet and by-and-large no support. The widening divide requires critical reflection on the hindrances to equitable participation in digital learning spaces, and more careful examination of the innovations that may hold promise for more inclusive futures of education.

Stamping out equity and access are not technical challenges but problems rooted in the socio-economic, geographic, cultural, and political contexts of learners padding out their lived experience. Many low-income and rural communities simply do not have the infrastructure, the electricity or the broadband that enables learners to access digital content. Systemic issues, like digital literacy gaps, language barriers and disabilities, still prevent full participation, even in resource-rich environments. Hence, the digital divide is multidimensional comprising not only access to technology but also the capacity to use it effectively, securely, and competently.

A few were quick on their feet, drawing on established digital infrastructures and flexible pedagogies; for many others, the disruption proved severe. Both educators and learners experienced sharp adjustment pains, emotional upheaval and varying quality of engagement. These challenges highlighted the need for inclusive digital practices that promote resilience and adaptability to new realities. They further emphasized that the conversation should not be about rethinking education in the same way that you would rethink a single model, but that what is needed is a system that can change and adapt to respond to the different needs of learners [1].

The revolution of digital learning has generated lot of innovations in the education. Recently, the edtech sector has innovated to a certain extent by making higher education more accessible for everyone, regardless of their demographic background, through mobile-based learning, low-bandwidth solutions, AI-powered adaptive platforms and open educational resources (OERs). When carefully used in accordance with sound pedagogical principles and ethical practices, tools such as these can provide significant capacity for teachers and students together to design and implement relevant, authentic educational experiences. And there are examples, from grassroots initiatives, community-based digital literacy schemes, and public-private partnerships, showing how localized and inclusive innovation can be as impactful as top-down policy change.

This chapter deep dive into the enduring challenges that inhibit digital learning equity while also exposing promising practices and models that provide scalable and sustainable solutions. With greater nuance on the interaction between structural discrepancies and technology evolution, the study aspires to offer the policymakers, educators, technologists, and learners, actionable insights. It uses international insights, a multitude of case studies and much of the data to identify the outlines of an equitable, inclusive and future-proof digital education system. The point is not just to criticize structural issues that exist, but rather to identify solutions to address them, to help create spaces in education where all learners can thrive, no matter the background. As such, this work is part of a larger vision of digital education as a vehicle of not just innovation, but also social change and equitable twenty-first-century empowerment.

2 Digital Divide: Inequalities Rooted in Infrastructure, Socio-economics, and Geography

Digital Divide is one of the most serious problems that hinder the transition to digital learning within the world, manifesting entrenched inequalities, such as unequal access in terms of infrastructure, socio-economics, and geography. Digital technologies can indeed democratize access to education, but the benefits overall tend to be unequally distributed and reinforce existing and badly exacerbated social and economic inequalities. So, this divide is a trifecta of who has access to digital tools, who has the skills to use these tools and who has the support to use them well.

Infrastructure continues to be the bedrock barrier to equitable digital learning. Power outage, limited broadband internet access, and antiquated digital devices are persistent challenges facing learners and educators alike in many low-income countries and rural areas. Even in technologically advanced nations, underdeveloped areas experience poor connectivity and obsolete hardware, thus limiting the quality and sustainability of digital education on a great scale. Such infrastructural constraints lead to students losing out with inconsistent access, delayed completion windows, or being entirely excluded from the online world [2].

Then they are part of a socio-economic factor that makes the gap larger. Those from poorer homes will typically not have their own devices and will not have a quiet place to work at home. The difficulties are multiplied when a device with limited availability needs to be shared among many learners or the caregiver has low digital literacy levels. The rising costs of data plans, software licenses, and maintenance have created another barrier to equitable access for economically disadvantaged groups. Thus, these students have to deal not only with the material obstacles involved, but also with the emotional and psychological weight of the situation, such as stress and disinterest, which reflects in their academic results.

The geography factor is equally important in defining the digital access and experience. Digital education for children cannot be delivered consistently in remote, conflict-affected or disaster-prone areas which do not have the infrastructure or institutional support for this. The core areas are generally better connected and more institutional capital is invested in them than the peripheral areas. This urban-rural divide clearly when national moves to remote learning exclude rural students from the digital dialogue.

A comprehensive and equity-driven approach is necessary to address the digital divide and need to build with governments, institutions, and technology provider's investment in infrastructure, subsidized access to devices and connectivity, and community-based digital literacy programs. It is only with equitable policies and inclusive innovation that the structural inequalities embedded within digital learning systems can be dismantled. It will never be able to unlock the promise of technology as an equalizer in education, and digital transformation will symbolize another cost in a long history of marginalization without steps taken to close the digital divide.

3 Equity in Education: Theoretical and Policy Frameworks

The principle behind educational equity comes from the idea that EACH learner, irrespective of background, deserves the opportunity to fulfill their potential. In the twenty-first-century which people live in today, this also means equitable access to digital tools, platforms, and pedagogies. A human rights-based approach to digital learning strengthens the claim that access to quality education (now inseparably linked to digital access) is a right and not a privilege. That framework highlights not only the right to education but also the duty of the state to make available inclusive, accessible, and non-discriminatory education to everyone in accordance with international legal instruments on human rights including the Universal Declaration of Human Rights (Article 26) and the UN Convention on the Rights of the Child (CRC) (Article 28) which make education a core human right based on all other human rights fundamental to the human dignity and development of all.

Global organizations have created frameworks to support equitable digital education at the policy level. The effective implementation of inclusive and equitable quality education and lifelong learning opportunities for all is evident in the UNESCO's "Education 2030 Framework for Action" and Sustainable Development Goal 4 (SDG 4). They urge the use of ICTs to close the educational gap between the different classes of people, especially the marginalized communities, girls, children with disabilities and students from fragile contexts. In the same vein, the OECD and World Bank have been promoting digital inclusion through infrastructure, teacher professional development, and open educational resources.

Policies vary greatly in scope, intent, and implementation nationally. Finland and South Korea have embraced holistic digital learning approaches that prioritize equity, teacher agency, and ubiquitous access [3]. At the same time, numerous low- and middle-income countries have launched national digital education strategies but are struggling with implementation as a result of funding limitations, lack of infrastructure and inequities across regions. A few countries have turned to public-private partnerships to widen access, while others depend on donor patronage and global partnerships.

The fulcrum toward equity in digital education lies at the intersection of human rights and actionable, context-responsive policy at the national and global level. Yet without being intended and without implementing of what is intended, policy success becomes dubious. Simply implementing systems of digital equity will not work without ongoing investment, multiple regional strategies, and consistent assessment. Policies need to be co-designed with educators, learners, and communities so that the solutions are culturally, contextually, and linguistically relevant and therefore more likely to be integrated into actual practice.

4 Access Beyond Connectivity: Devices, Skills, and Home Learning Environments

Although many people consider online access to be the gateway to digital access, access to online education is much more than access to online. Successful equitable digital learning is dependent on an ecosystem that includes having access to the devices, possessing digital literacy skills and a conducive home learning environment. So that even when the learners are, in a technical sense, "connected," without the scaffolding, the wheels fail and they fall off the bus into marginality Meaningful engagement with digital learning requires access to devices laptops, tablets, or smartphones.

But vast differences in the availability of devices persist, particularly among students from low-income homes, rural locations or refugee and disadvantaged communities [4]. The challenge to widespread programs is that many families share a single device among siblings, so student will have consistent access, while another will not. Devices differ in quality and functioning, for example, older or obsolete models may not work with current learning platforms or video conferencing tools.

The tangible and emotional context of learning at home is 50 percent shaping how things will go in the digital re-building of what used to be, and how it will have to be. With many young learners attending classes at home, crowded or noisy homes devoid of a proper study space with competing responsibilities especially for girls in some cultural contexts diminish the ability to focus and engage in the teaching-learning process which reflects in lower academic performance [5]. Regular studies and motivation to keep studying are also eventually affected due to emotional stress, economic instability, and domestic responsibilities. No less critical is the need to build digital skills both of learners and of their caregivers. Even a device and internet connectivity doesn't help if the users don't possess the digital literacy to access resources or to troubleshoot an issue by themselves. A number of students especially those still in primary school needed help from their parents or other adults, but the adults themselves may be ill prepared to support their children with online learning or simply lack the requisite digital skills. Digital learning access is more than just connectivity, though and whole of system solution that tackles device access, digital skills, and safe, stable, and nurturing home environments. This broader range of needs is why we must turn to strategies focused on making digital learning truly inclusive and serve all learners.

5 Barriers to Inclusive Participation in Digital Learning

Digital education is becoming a pillar of modern educational systems but inclusivity is still an unsolved issue. While access to knowledge is claimed to be democratized by the provision of digital learning environments, many barriers remain preventing large chunks of the population of learners from fully utilizing these. Such challenges are complex, arising from the intersections of technological and social inequities and the historical under-funding of educational systems serving marginalized populations. The main obstacles for inclusive participation are technological inaccessibility [6]. When there is connectivity, high data prices and poor educational hardware restrict learners from participating in live classes, downloading learning material, or participating in interactive learning scenarios. When digital platforms and content are not designed with accessibility in mind (for example, lacking screen readers, closed captions, or alternative text descriptions), this only compounds the barriers faced by learners with disabilities.

Making inclusion even more difficult is the fact that there is a language barrier which aside from it being a barrier in the first place where we cannot communicate with each other. It also miss out on the rest of the people around me and what they speak of because of cultural differences. A large share of digital educational content is created in the dominant global languages, which tend to marginalize non-native speakers and learners from indigenous and linguistic minority groups. Absence of localization may hinder understanding, but it further detracts from learners feeling like they belong and that their cultures matter in the curriculum. In the same way, the digital gender divide is still extensive particularly in many parts of the world. Girls and women are also kept from devices and their full use due to various access and societal concerns over safety, personal digital freedom and the freedom to learn. The important problem is the shortage of digital literacy and support systems. Students, notably from lower socio-economic backgrounds, often lack the experience of managing online platforms, digital-load and understanding what fake information is. These learners often struggle to keep up without proper training, or support from caregivers or teachers equipped with digital skills. For those families with children unable to distance learn, frustration, disenchantment and dropping out of school are near expectations without adult guides for a distance learning environment [7].

The educational institutes lack inclusive digital strategies too often. Most systems shifted to remote learning in a rush, leading to generic and cookie cutter solutions that do not account for diverse learner needs. Students with alternative learning preferences, with disabilities, or with home obligations are further marginalized by inflexible schedules, minimal interactivity, and assessments that cannot be made accessible. These challenges become even more pronounced during instances of long-term isolation or uncertainty, where the absence of emotional and psychological support an essential aspect of learner engagement compounds the issues at hand. So, addressing these barriers requires an equity lens that will inform universal access to digital learning through policies, inclusive technology design and localized content and the effective support systems. For this, stakeholders had to include learners, communities, and educators in the design of adaptive, culturally responsive, and accessible learning experiences [8]. The access is just part of the puzzle; truly inclusive digital education needs to enable, empower, provides a voice and meaningful participation in the teaching and learning process for all learners regardless of circumstances.

6 Educator Capacity and Institutional Readiness: Digital Competencies and Pedagogical Transformation

Access to technology is a key enabler of digital learning environments; however, even more critical are the digital skills of teachers and the organizational readiness to facilitate pedagogical change. Teachers are to be the link between technology and learners, so the proper integration of digital tools into the learning process is fundamentally important to guarantee quality and inclusive digital education. But for many teachers, poor training, low digital literacy, insufficient supportive systems along the way, and pedagogical conservatism have left them struggling with many issues in the classroom.

Digital competency for educators is more than just knowing how to use a computer, it is knowing what tools to select, how to design inclusive digital content, manage a virtual classroom, assess students online, and work to understand equity, privacy, and student engagement. Many teachers will have had little exposure to this kind of training, especially in developing regions of the world where teaching approaches will have been largely traditional. Continuous professional development remains essential as digital tools and platforms change so quickly, even with high-level early investment by institutions in the purpose-built financial flow. The schools, colleges, and universities should be strategic about how to use digital innovation to achieve pedagogical goals. This incorporates putting resources into ICT foundation, guaranteeing strong network, and giving access to easy to use stages and computerized assets [9]. The institutions should design supportive systems including digital help desks, peer mentoring and just in time training programs to support teachers. It takes strong leadership to create an environment that supports change, experimentation, and reflective practice.

This cannot expect pedagogical transformation just by moving from a white board to a digital screen. It requires new roles for educators, as facilitators, curators and collaborators while also promoting learner autonomy and digital literacy as well. Such a transition makes it necessary to move from content-heavy lectures to interactive, student-centric approaches leveraging multimedia, discussion forums and real-time feedback tools. Since there is no support and mapping of power structures and pathways in development, why have the school teachers feel like they are exhausting themselves, leading to digital fatigue and burnout, and even resistance to the necessary change. Hence, well-rounded policies need to touch on both the technical side of digital education and the human side of it. But at the same time, by reinforcing educator capacity and institutional preparedness, education systems will advance beyond immediate digital conditioning into sustainable pedagogical transformation, equitable, effective, and future-ready [10].

7 Innovations Bridging the Gap: Adaptive Technologies, Mobile Learning and AI-Driven Platforms

As the world of digital learning seeks to be increasingly equitable and effective, new technologies including adaptive learning systems, mobile-based education solutions, and AI-driven platforms are providing serious solutions to barriers to access, personalization and engagement. They are making subtle changes to the educational landscape, tackling some of the most endemic barriers to inclusive participation and enabling scalable and context-sensitive alternatives more often suited to different learner needs and capabilities across geographies and socio-economic spectra.

Data analytics and AI are behind adaptive learning technologies that personalize learning content to fit the performance, preferences, and speed of an individual learner. These platforms enable a tailored learning experience for each student by constantly evaluating their comprehension and providing immediate feedback, thus catering not only to the needs of students who are having difficulty but also to those who excel. Smart Sparrow, for example, Dreambox, or Knewton are tools that dynamically edit content to address gaps discovered by an educator but which may also be used to provide more effective interventions [11].

M-learning or mobile learning is a revolution especially in areas where conventional infrastructure is absent. Mobile devices are generally more ubiquitous than computers in many areas, so lightweight applications, SMS-based assessments, and downloadable content that can be stored offline open a whole new world of education. These include Khan Academy, Byju's, and Eneza Education, which used mobile technologies to provide access to curriculum-specific content in local languages to marginalized learners in remote areas.

These AI-powered education platforms are augmenting both teaching and learning through automated administrative tasks, smart recommendations, and even human-tutoring simulation experiences. Students can be led through lessons by chatbots and virtual assistants, and AI tools that track learning patterns will recommend resources targeted to the gaps identified. This ensures a more responsive and engaging learning environment that responds in real-time to learner behavior [12]. Yet, these advancements need to be deployed with proper focus on ethical concerns including data privacy, algorithmic bias, and inclusivity. These tools, when designed well and made available in an equitable manner, can reshape the educational landscape, leveling the playing field. Adaptive, mobile, and AI-enabled technologies provide tools that enable educators and institutions to overcome longstanding limitations to provide high-quality, personalized, contextual, and equitable learning experiences that fit learners where they are.

8 Learner Voices: Experiences, Challenges, and Aspirations

The impact of digital education can be better understood through the lived experiences of learners, as these experiences provide critical insights into the strengths and limitations of online and technology-enhanced learning environments. The students around the world have reported a human spectrum of reactions (and responses) to their digital learning pathways, irrespective of geography, socio-economic background and educational level. Digital learning offers a flexibility many students enjoyed, as well as a level of independence that many students welcomed [13]. Online provides a good opportunity for many (for instance, those who need to combine the studies with work or care for others) to interact with learning resources in their own time and at their own pace. Interactive tools, multimedia content, and tailored learning paths have increased engagement and motivation for students who may find difficulty in a traditional classroom delivery. In addition, it created a wider access to global content and virtual communities, broadening horizons, and encouraging cross-cultural interactions.

But they will also struggle with big challenges for learners, especially around accessibility and empathy. Low-income or rural areas where students do not have consistent or reliable internet, a personal device to use, or are unable to find a quiet place to study, are still preventing attendance. Without in-person interaction, it can be harder to maintain motivation and stay focused, resulting in isolating experiences [14]. The Mental Health Declines with poor screen experience, the lack of social interaction, and reduced support. The learners continue to be optimistic and have high expectations. They demand more inclusive, engaging and empowering digital experiences that align with their identities, help them achieve their goals and acknowledge their agency. Many students want more competition and communication with fellow students and teachers, a more responsive system and a learning space that prioritizes their mental well-being. Hearing, integrating, and acting upon learner voices in online design are not optional for digital education: they are existential. By meeting our learner where they are, institutions and policymakers can co-design equitable, human-centered digital learning systems that are able to support diverse learners to reach their fullest potential.

9 Mental Health and Emotional Well-Being in Digital Environments

In a blended or digital learning context, the learner's mental health and emotional well-being have been a burning issue. As education moves away from the traditional physical environment, much of the emotional and psychological facets of learning are often ignored. Although digital education comes with flexibility and independence to learn at individual pace, it also has a potential for rise in social isolation, stress, and emotional exhaustion if the online teaching is not planned to cater to social needs of students [15].

The biggest problem is the lack of human life in virtual environments. Students in traditional classrooms have the advantage of social cues, peer interaction, and informal teacher support all of which foster a sense of community and emotional security. The challenges caused by online learning especially delivered in asynchronous or impersonal format is that the loneliness, disconnection, and the feeling of lower motivation can ensue. The impact of this detachment may vary with respect to the user; however, for younger learners or those with special emotional needs, this feeling of disconnection can adversely affect them when it comes to engagement and academic achievement.

The extreme screen dependence and long hours of self-study of probably 6–8 hours lead to digital fatigue or virtual boredom and mental burnout. Many of them have difficulties with time management, burnout and stress because, due to the absence of tradition from home, there are no limitations of study and personal life [16]. If you have a learner who goes home to economic struggles, domestic responsibilities, or not much privacy in the home, the mind game is worse. Without access to mental health counseling or wellness services from schools in certain digital platforms, students are often left vulnerable in times when they require emotional assistance.

Mental health in digital education should not just be a supportive add-on, but rather an integral component of the necessary building blocks for effective learning. This means that institutions should recognize that retention, and learner's and institutions' success is correlated to emotional well-being. Creating inquiry-based, emotionally responsive digital learning environments makes so that technology provides not only the content but really nurtures the whole learner mind, body, and spirit. Tools, such as virtual wellness check-ins, online counseling services, mental health apps, mindfulness activities, and peer-support forums, can be integrated into digital education platforms. Also, teaching practices based in empathy and inclusion flexible due dates, check-in, socio-emotional learning content can create a healthier, more sustainable learning environment [17].

10 Data, Privacy, and Ethical Considerations in Digital Education

With the rise of data-driven platforms and technologies in digital education, data privacy and ethics have now come to the fore. Massive amounts of learner data—attendance, academic performance, behavior, and even personal identifiers—are being collected and analyzed, raising issues of consent, transparency, security, and accountability. Although this data can help provide a more personalized experience and better results, if managed irresponsibly, this can also create a big risk.

The most urgent of these issues is a failure to obtain informed consent, a failure of transparency. Neither students nor their families may know what data is being collected, and how, why, and by whom it is used [18]. Many educational technologies have no, or easily readable or accessible, privacy policy or protection, anywhere from selling the data to giving the data to a third party for any reason. This becomes especially problematic in instances where educational platforms are administered by third-party vendors, as business priorities may clash with the interest and welfare of students. An increase in data breaches and cyber-security threats in schools has revealed sensitive data and undermined trust in online systems. Universities, particularly in low resource environments, have inadequate data protection infrastructure, and this makes them attractive targets for cyber-attack. Moreover, bias in AI algorithms used in these tools e.g., predictive assessments, or automated grading can replicate and amplify social inequalities, putting marginalized learners, in particular, at risk.

Digital education in its ethical form needs transparency, data governance, and inclusivity. This data should be collected only after explicitly obtaining consent; it should be used only for educational utility and it should be kept in a secure place and not distributed to any third party. Students need to take ownership of their digital footprint. In designing all digital education tools, equity, privacy, and dignity should be equitably at the center of tool design. Conscious digital education systems, rooted in ethical principles, will ensure we build safe, equitable and rights-respecting spaces where good learning flourishes and where all higher education stakeholders feel secure, just and respected [19].

11 Conclusion and Future Scope

Education has undergone a digital transformation that, while providing new opportunities for innovation, accessibility, and individualized learning, has also revealed and in some cases exacerbated existing inequities. The many challenges in digital education range from infrastructural gaps, socio-economic gaps, digital literacy, to mental health issues. While at the same time adaptive technologies, mobile platforms and AI-powered tools provide strong opportunities to reinvent the way education is supplied and experienced, especially for marginalized or underserved learners. The digital education worth anything must be human-oriented and recognize not only the need for availability of tools but more importantly the emotional, cognitive and cultural needs of the learner. Realizing inclusive participation will require stakeholders, educators, policymakers, technologists, students, and communities to work together to ensure digital solutions are equitable, contextual and responsive. Any twenty-first-century educational reform will have to place institutional preparedness, teacher development, and computerized data privacy safeguards at the forefront.

The future of digital education is going to require continued investments in infrastructure, partnerships across sectors, and the evolution of flexible, student-centered models that are able to evolve with changing technological landscapes. It need to focus more on co-creating with learners, creating content grounded locally, and ethical approaches that are focused on justice, inclusive and well-being. We must continue to assess not just tech efficacy, but social impact and learner outcomes in research and policy. The road to a digitally inclusive and innovative education system is a never-ending journey. It requires foresight, sensitivity, and an unprecedented degree of collaboration to cross stubborn divides and to leverage the transformative potential of technology to ensure that all learners no matter where they are and no matter what they can do can benefit from it. The work is not just to go online, but to make education a force for equity, agency, and global learning justice.

References

1. Memon, F. N., & Memon, S. N. (2025). Digital divide and equity in education: Bridging gaps to ensure inclusive learning. In S. Siyal (Ed.), *Impact of digitalization on education and social sustainability* (pp. 107–130). IGI Global. https://doi.org/10.4018/979-8-3693-1854-6.ch004
2. Chikwe, C. F., Dagunduro, A. O., Ajuwon, O. A., & Ediae, A. A. (2024). Sociological barriers to equitable digital learning: A data-driven approach. *Comprehensive Research and Reviews in Multidisciplinary Studies, 2*(1), 027–034.
3. Dritsas, E., & Trigka, M. (2025). Methodological and technological advancements in E-learning. *Information, 16*(1), 56.
4. McCarthy, K. S., Crossley, S. A., Meyers, K., Boser, U., Allen, L. K., Chaudhri, V. K., et al. (2022). Toward more effective and equitable learning: Identifying barriers and solutions for the future of online education. *Technology, Mind, and Behavior, 3*(1), 24–38.

5. Bright, S., & Calvert, E. (2023). Educational technology: Barrier or bridge to equitable access to advanced learning opportunities? *Gifted Child Today, 46*(3), 187–200.
6. Okoye, K., Hussein, H., Arrona-Palacios, A., Quintero, H. N., Ortega, L. O. P., Sanchez, A. L., et al. (2023). Impact of digital technologies upon teaching and learning in higher education in Latin America: An outlook on the reach, barriers, and bottlenecks. *Education and Information Technologies, 28*(2), 2291–2360.
7. Gottschalk, F., & Weise, C. (2023). *Digital equity and inclusion in education: An overview of practice and policy in OECD countries* (OECD Education Working Papers No. 299). OECD Publishing. https://doi.org/10.1787/7cb15030-en
8. Mhlongo, S., Mbatha, K., Ramatsetse, B., & Dlamini, R. (2023). Challenges, opportunities, and prospects of adopting and using smart digital technologies in learning environments: An iterative review. *Heliyon, 9*(6), e16348.
9. Mohd Ashril, N. A. N., Chee, K. N., Yahaya, N., & Abdul Razak, R. (2025). Barriers, strategies and accessibility: Enhancing engagement and retention of learners with disabilities in MOOCs—A systematic literature review (SLR). *International Journal of Human–Computer Interaction, 41*(14), 8846–8857.
10. Eden, C. A., Chisom, O. N., & Adeniyi, I. S. (2024). Harnessing technology integration in education: Strategies for enhancing learning outcomes and equity. *World Journal of Advanced Engineering Technology and Sciences, 11*(2), 001–008.
11. Aguilar, S. J. (2020). Guidelines and tools for promoting digital equity. *Information and Learning Sciences, 121*(5/6), 285–299.
12. Vistorte, A. O. R., Deroncele-Acosta, A., Ayala, J. L. M., Barrasa, A., López-Granero, C., & Martí-González, M. (2024). Integrating artificial intelligence to assess emotions in learning environments: A systematic literature review. *Frontiers in Psychology, 15*, 1387089.
13. Ayeni, O. O., Al Hamad, N. M., Chisom, O. N., Osawaru, B., & Adewusi, O. E. (2024). AI in education: A review of personalized learning and educational technology. *GSC Advanced Research and Reviews, 18*(2), 261–271.
14. Sato, S. N., Condes Moreno, E., Rubio-Zarapuz, A., Dalamitros, A. A., Yañez-Sepulveda, R., Tornero-Aguilera, J. F., & Clemente-Suárez, V. J. (2023). Navigating the new normal: Adapting online and distance learning in the post-pandemic era. *Education Sciences, 14*(1), 19.
15. Sari, G. I., Winasis, S., Pratiwi, I., & Nuryanto, U. W. (2024). Strengthening digital literacy in Indonesia: Collaboration, innovation, and sustainability education. *Social Sciences & Humanities Open, 10*, 101100.

16. Alenezi, M., Wardat, S., & Akour, M. (2023). The need of integrating digital education in higher education: Challenges and opportunities. *Sustainability, 15*(6), 4782.
17. Eden, C. A., Chisom, O. N., & Adeniyi, I. S. (2024). Integrating AI in education: Opportunities, challenges, and ethical considerations. *Magna Scientia Advanced Research and Reviews, 10*(2), 006–013.
18. Page, A., Anderson, J., & Charteris, J. (2023). Including students with disabilities in innovative learning environments: A model for inclusive practices. *International Journal of Inclusive Education, 27*(14), 1696–1711.
19. Sahni, J. (2023). Is learning analytics the future of online education?: Assessing student engagement and academic performance in the online learning environment. *International Journal of Emerging Technologies in Learning (iJET), 18*(2), 33–49.

CHAPTER 3

Blended, Adaptive, and Micro-Learning Models: Comparing Efficacy in Digital Classrooms

A. Vijayalakshmi and Vijaykumar Kaluvala

Abstract Blended, adaptive, and micro learning are changing the face of education, complementing and in some cases replacing the traditional model in response to the quickly evolving landscape of technology and learning needs. The nature and implications of these flexible learning models are discussed in this study, which addresses the ways these models have developed, designed, and new ways in which they can be used to promote engagement and personalization and facilitate accessibility in different contexts of education. Blended learning involves mid-way

A. Vijayalakshmi (✉)
Department of English, Chaitanya Bharathi Institute of Technology Hyderabad, Hyderabad, Telangana, India
e-mail: vijayalakshmi_english@cbit.ac.in

V. Kaluvala
MBA Department, Koneru Lakshmaiah Education Foundation, Hyderabad, Telangana, India
e-mail: vijay.kumar.k@klh.edu.in

P. K. Dutta et al. (eds.), *Digital Education for a Sustainable Future*, Sustainable Development Goals Series,
https://doi.org/10.1007/978-3-032-15433-0_3

between the online digital one and the in-person foundation of a way of learning. Adaptive learning employs AI and data analytics to provide customized content and feedback on-demand based on how each learner performs, allowing you to progress at your pace. The emerging trend of micro learning addresses the need for short, focused learning modules to satisfy learners' evolving needs for just-in-time knowledge acquisition and skill development, especially in rapidly changing industries and informal learning settings. This chapter reviews criticisms of how these models address the shortcomings of traditional education by enhancing learner autonomy, supporting lifelong learning, and closing gaps in attention, motivation, and accessibility. It also looks at implementation issues like digital resources, teacher readiness, and modular content. Using case studies as well as, recent frameworks of pedagogy, the study offers institutions looking to implement these models ways to do so comprehensively and mini learning systems are a big step toward systems that focus more on students and flexibility and adaptability for the future.

Keywords Blended learning · Adaptive learning · Micro learning · Personalized education · Digital pedagogy

1 Introduction: Rethinking Education in the Digital Age

This century has brought significant changes in education, which has been transformed primarily due to ever-so-disruptive technology and learners holding different expectations. Conventional education models generally centered on the presence of a teacher or educational leader, heavier lead content, and standardized test/assessment sequences have faced growing criticism of their capacity to be effective and equitable [1]. That's a far cry from the learning experiences demanded by today's learners, who need a little more flexibility, a little of interactivity and personalization, and experiences that mirror the pace and interconnectivity of the world they live in. With digital technologies reaching every area of society, education systems are now forced to rethink the way knowledge is transmitted; accessed and experienced. At the heart of this transformation are the shift from traditional "one-size-fits-all" pedagogies, to being learner centered in approaches like blended learning, adaptive learning and micro learning.

This traditional classroom model has been a mainstay of modern education but it frequently does not account for the individual differences in learning needs, speeds, and styles. Applying delivery methods uniformly does not take into consideration the differences in comprehension speed, prior knowledge, motivation, and socio-economic background, among other factors. This has left many learners behind or disinterested. Blended learning has come forward as a hybrid model encompassing the best of both worlds of in-person instruction and flexibility with digital tools. It gives teachers the ability to expand learning beyond the walls of the classroom, provide a variety of ways to access content, and find places to connect and collaborate. In the same way, adaptive learning harnesses artificial intelligence and data analytics to enable teaching in a personalized way and in real-time, where learners can be paid in their own institutions at their own pace, depending on their performance and learning modes. On the other hand, micro learning is designed to better suit the modern learner who seems to prefer brief, specific learning units accessible anytime and anywhere which allows just-in-time skill acquisition and promotes long-term lifelong learning behaviors.

These models come together to reimagine pedagogy in a foundationally new way, with the learner at the center of the educational experience. These are not just technological innovations but pedagogical shifts that are compliant with behavioral and cognitive sciences such as spaced learning, feedback-induced reinforcement, and learner autonomy. They create new paradigms that are dynamic, responsive, and often personalized which contradict the age-old concepts of instruction time, classroom space, and educator role.

This chapter aims at analyzing effectiveness and significance of blended, adaptive, and a micro learning model in an education system park in digital classrooms. This study explores the design, delivery methods, learner engagement approaches, and assessments of these models and discusses how they can help meet diverse learner needs in formal and informal learning environments. These methods facilitate better personalization and motivation, as well as supporting common challenges such as attention span, digital fatigue, and accessibility.

The chapter domain covers the nexus of pedagogy, technology, policy and it reflects on how ready institutions might be to put such models in place, the response of educators to an adaptation of traditional practice to digital pedagogies, and the infrastructural and ethical challenges that need to be addressed to make this level of access equitable [2]. It also explores

student perception where students' perspectives are relevant for the issue of perceived autonomy, satisfaction, economic recovery, and how these compare with other learning contexts within which students have worked for e.g., online, blended, and distance. By applying this multi-dimensional perspective, the research aims to offer a comprehensive insight on the ways in which blended, adaptive, and micro learning can support more impactful and equitable education systems.

So, this exploration is not solely about comparing instructional models; rather, it is about rethinking the purpose and process of education in the digital age. The nature of learning is changing as the knowledge economy becomes the dominant economy with the need for skills and creativity, and education should also change from relying on content absorption to the agility of thinking, interaction and engagement in a complicated and unpredictable world. This study seeks to equip educators, policymakers, and technology designers with best practices, lessons of implementation, and future considered possibilities for programming digital learning environments that are innovative, inclusive, and future-driven. In so doing, it adds to the global conversation about what schooling can and should look like to meet the needs of twenty-first--century learners and citizens going forward [3].

2 Blended Learning: Bridging Physical and Virtual Classrooms

Among the many promises of educational innovation of the digital age, blended learning has evolved as one of the most significant solutions to this challenge, combining and integrating traditional face-to-face teaching and learning with online learning and instruction. Hybrid learning combines the benefits of both online and offline learning namely the real-time interaction, in-person engagement, and guided structure of a physical classroom, and the digital technologies that allow for flexibility, accessibility, and personalization of the learning experience. Given the need for diverse learning pathways to emerge at this time, the pragmatic transforming nature of blended learning has the potential to provide a shift from the current reductionist transmission-oriented aspect that further documents confusion in education systems removing from regressive, flat models.

The blended learning simply means that learners engage with content in face-to-face and online environments, frequently allowing students

to exercise agency and control over their learning i.e., rate, time, and place. This model recognizes that no one best approach nor format appeals to and helps all learners to engage and build their understanding and retention, and therefore uses a combination of formats. Blended learning, whether it be through flipped classrooms where students learn instructional content online and use class time for deeper discussions or rotational models where students rotate through digital stations and teacher-led activities, gives a more active, personalized experience of learning [4].

Blended learning also provides a means to support differentiated instruction which is one of the key advantages of the approach. Digital tools allow teachers to assign different content or assessments based on student learning levels, use analytics as indicators of student progress, and adjust their instruction to match. This fosters a differentiated learning atmosphere through which students requiring extra assistance are provided with stair step support, with advanced learners offered challenge through enrichment assignments. Online components also facilitate repeated access to lessons, guided interaction with multimedia resources, more self-paced learning, and a reduction in pressure on students and provision for different learning styles.

Blended learning is more effective through girl-student interaction. While digital learning tends to be thought of as isolating, by allowing more time in the classroom for collaborative work, project-based learning, and one-on-one mentorship, the hybrid nature of blended models often enhances communication. In a way teachers will be able to pay more attention to each student which will make a stronger pedagogical tie to each student and if they miss anything in the content like learning gaps they can find it more easily. However, blended learning can be effectively implemented with proper planning, infrastructure, and teacher training and development. Teachers need digital pedagogical competencies and assistance in developing standards-appropriate digital content while using technology authentically. To allow equity in access, schools, and institutions need to invest in LMS systems, reliable internet connectivity and appropriate devices. Blended learning is more than a passing trend or an additional tool kit is a full-fledged pedagogical framework that has the potential to redefine the future of education [5]. This fusion of face-to-face and online teaching helps to establish an adaptive learning ecosystem in which the focus on the students is at the center and will prepare them to have both the academic and the global skills to face various challenges.

3 Adaptive Learning: Personalization Through Artificial Intelligence

Within digital education, adaptive learning is a major innovation that utilizes AI to deliver personalized learning experiences based on data customized to the needs of individual students. While traditional one-size-fits-all instruction traditionally delivers the same content at the same pace as regardless of how well or poorly a learner is performing, adaptive learning systems as the name implies tailor and adjust the content, pace and order of learning materials based on a learner's performance, behavior, and engagement levels. Such smart personalization makes the learning experience adaptive and bespoke, allowing every learner to advance at an optimal pace while getting the right support and challenges according to their skill level.

Adaptive learning depends significantly on AI algorithms and learning analytics to enable the automated and continuous collection, monitoring, and analysis of learner data. Such data include quiz responses, time spent on individual topics, recurring error patterns, and navigation behavior within digital learning environments. Using this data, the system identifies strengths and gaps, as well as misconceptions, and then tailors the instructional pathway [6]. If a learner does not succeed on a given concept the platform may present further explanations, content at a lower reading level, or exercises at a lower skill level before advancing on to the next level. On the other hand, more advanced learners may be given tasks with higher orders to use their time wisely.

This model is very useful because even students with different abilities can still learn in the same way in the classroom. It supports students who need remediation without stigma and those ready to accelerate past the standard curriculum with enrichment. Adaptive platforms like DreamBox, Knewton, and Smart Sparrow have shown enhanced learning results by controlling the right level of challenge so that learning never becomes too high-stakes stress, and frustration, and disengagement caused by poorly aligned instruction, diminishes. Adaptive learning systems also provide insights that allow educators to monitor individual and group progress through real-time dashboards. Such analytics allow educators to intervene before a problem escalates, make better instructional decisions, and deliver higher-quality feedback. Adaptive learning does not replace teachers but rather enables them to provide better and more specific differentiated support. So, implementing adaptive learning is not

without its obstacles. Important considerations also include data privacy, algorithmic bias prevention, and pedagogical alignment [7]. Teachers will also need training to understand the data and incorporate the adaptive tools into their classroom methods. Wrapping up, adaptive learning driven by artificial intelligence has great potential to transform education from an inequitable, one-size-fits-all model to a more equitable and learner-centered model. Adapting to the individual needs and pace of every learner, it promotes greater comprehension, better engagement and improved academic performance across all learning environments.

4 Micro Learning: Learning in Small, Targeted Bursts: Suitability for Skill-Based, Corporate and Lifelong Learning

Micro learning is a revolutionary method of education delivery in the digital landscape, ideal for fast-paced, information-loaded world. Micro learning can be simply defined as a way to deliver content in short, focused nugget of information to meet a specific learning outcome in very little time generally utilizing videos, infographics, quizzes, or interactive modules, typically just a few minutes in length. It perfectly fits the requirement/demand of twenty-first-century learners who want to manage their work/life while also getting on-demand learning that is flexible. Hence, it also makes micro learning suitable for skill-based training, corporate learning, and lifelong education [8]. In terms of skill building, micro learning provides a direct route to building competencies in such fields as coding, language, communication or technical tool s. Micro learning takes a one-session, one-objective approach that reiterates the desired content to aid in embedding it more permanently, as opposed to long lectures or full courses. This kind of model is what platforms like Duolingo or LinkedIn Learning follows with their short lessons that can be done whenever wherever.

Micro learning is fast taking the place of traditional training in the corporate world. Its adoption by organizations is mostly to upgrade the skills of their workforce, onboard new employees, or deliver compliance training in a time- and cost-efficient manner. Micro modules are highly updateable, mobile, and can be embedded in daily workflows, meaning less time away from work for employees as they can learn as part of their roles. Such an approach is conducive to a just-in-time learning environment that maximizes productivity while nurturing a culture of continuous professional development.

Micro learning is a device that allows for lifelong learning as it gives more room for personal and professional development whenever an individual wants. Whether you are a young person trying to foster curiosity, a new employee preparing for a constantly evolving job market, or a professional wanting to keep up with current events, it caters to all learners [9]. The modular nature of the material means that learners can build up knowledge in an incremental way this makes it scalable and easier to stay motivated as well as less daunting. Micro learning works wonders in delivering specific content but lacks in providing instruction for deep conceptual learning and critical thinking development [10]. When contextually embedded in other more robust learning models, or used as a complementary approach, it is an outstanding pedagogical innovation. Micro learning responds to the penetration of efficiency, flexible, and relevance in education. It encourages skills-based, lifelong learning for varied audience segments, fits into digital consumption mindsets and time availability.

5 Student Perspectives: Motivation, Autonomy, and Challenges

Identifying student's point of view particularly involved in assessing the efficacy of digital learning models like blended, adaptive and micro learning. Modern learners today are looking for flexibility, independence and personalization, which is why they prefer digital education. Learning at your own pace and accessing different multimedia resources drives engagement and self-motivation for many learners even more so when going over complex content. By providing self-regulation and independent exploration, digital platforms enable students to own their learning path, which is one of the key components of intrinsic motivation and lifelong learning.

Students often prefer blended and adaptive models, as they provide structure while also offering more flexibility. Blended learning blends face-to-face interaction with digital components to facilitate social interaction while enhancing the experience of digital access On the other hand, adaptive learning systems are an appealing option because they respond to individual performance to prevent providing students with content

that is irrelevant to them or too challenging. Micro learning resonates strongly with those with short attention spans or limited time, providing the content in quick, bite-sized, focused bursts that play into our new found routines [11].

The challenge remains with self-directed learning where discipline and time management is required to avoid procrastination, and many find it difficult to learn in such an environment. The perception of disconnection from peers, absence of real-time response mechanisms and online fatigue can adversely affect engagement levels and academic output. Some participants, particularly in marginalized communities, still experience barriers to participation due to lack of access to devices, internet connectivity or quiet learning spaces. In general, though digital models provide important advantages concerning engagement and independence, feedback from students suggests attention to balanced instructional approaches, accessible technology, and robust support systems. Giving learners a voice makes certain that digital education develops in advanced technological, as well as socio-emotional and cognitive paths.

Learner Feedback and Performance Data

Digital learning models are defined by learner feedback and performance data, which are some of the most important predictors of success. By surveys, focus groups, and digital engagement analytics feedback, we can see how satisfied the student is, how useful he found it and what needs to be enhanced. Unlike typical online courses, MOOC platforms can be used to assess information about an individual learner such as quiz scores, time-on-task metrics, and course completion rates and provide the educator a way to adapt instructional content as needed. This data enables adaptive learning systems to provide real-time personalization, also giving educators early identification of struggling learners who can be effectively supported. But with any data comes the responsibility of context, because metrics sometimes simply miss the emotional or social barriers. At the same time, ethical data use and privacy implications need to be considered. The effective use of learner feedback and performance data supports ongoing continuous improvement of digital pedagogy and help to propel more equitable and responsive, learner-centered education when used responsibly [12]. This also enables students to reflect on their own progress and undertake self-directed study.

Preferences and Barriers Across Demographics

Digital learning attitudes and hurdles vary considerably by age, gender, class, geography and ability. While younger learners may gravitate toward gamified, social interactive platforms, adult learners often prefer micro learning formats that deliver information in a brief, flexible way. Students in urban areas are more likely to access high-speed Internet and more up-to-date devices, providing a more seamless digital learning experience while rural or low-affluent learners deal with poor connectivity and a lack of device access. In some societies, girls or women might not have the same access to digital tools due to gender norms. For students with disabilities, the problem goes further, as platforms that lack inclusive design features such as screen readers or captioning make it harder to access. Learners' immersion in content is also impacted by the diversity of cultures and languages. All demographic groups participate in online learning, but there are differences in their preferences and barriers to succeed in a digital environment, and understanding these will help to create safe digital learning environments that are inclusive of all consumers. Such digital divides call out for tailored interventions, localized content, and accessibility-focused design to bridge these gaps and support equitable educational outcomes for all learners [13].

6 Technology Infrastructure and Platform Considerations

Successful digital education rests on a solid technology infrastructure and the judicious choice of digital platforms. Blended learning, adaptive learning and micro learning models are highly successful in certain geographical hamlets, but the nature of the success is ever aligned with the technology ecosystem, its availability, reliability and scalability, around the Geography. Infrastructure is more than just an internet connection, it also includes access to devices, cloud-based storage, cyber-security, and management systems like an LMS. Stable infrastructure is essential too; even the best and most thorough pedagogical model could come undone in remote or poorly-resourced parts of the country where bandwidth is poor or power is intermittent.

The learning platforms must be user-friendly, adaptive, and inclusive to fit various types of learners. Blended learning is a common practice in the educational institutions where platforms like Google Classroom, Moodle,

Canvas are being used, while adaptive systems such as Knewton or Smart Sparrow need a complex data processing inside the backend. When it comes to micro learning, a mobile-first edtech solution that enables offline access and push notifications for instance, EdApp or Coursera's mobile app works especially well. They must be designed to work across various devices, have an easy to follow user interface, and also offer multi-lingual support to ensure optimum level of adoption and user engagement [14].

As learners enter sensitive personal information and performance metrics, platforms are subject to data protection regulations such as GDPR or its national equivalent to ensure user privacy. Schools must determine whether outsourcing to third-party platforms is ethical in terms of data consumption, then verify if the platform has sound cyber-cryptography and data retention standards in place. The centered in their classroom delivery should be the availability of technical support and training to enable the ease of movement of learners and educators within the platforms. With poorly designed onboarding (which is an investment in your digital experience) and lack of digital literacy needed to overcome the barrier, users either drop off or struggle. Training the next Gen: Institutions should spend on IT support teams, regular platform updates, and the user feedback loop. The careful structuring of the technological infrastructure and platform functionality will be the foundation to sustainably support digital education now and in the years to come [15]. These components underpin the pedagogical innovation, learner engagement, and equitable access.

7 Assessment and Feedback in Digital Environments

Evaluation and feedback are integral parts of any educational process and in digital environments; assessment is not only new in form but also presents new challenges and opportunities. Digital assessment also helps to overcome the functionality problems of many current assessment methods by avoiding rigid, static, schedule-driven forms of assessment, such as distance exams or take-home papers and provides more flexible assessment techniques which adapt to particular learning paths and time-frames. Through digital tools, formative assessments with quizzes, polls, reflections, and interactive activities can be delivered at the click of a button to give learners instant feedback, while instantly offering instructors with data about students' understanding and progress.

Specifically adaptive learning platforms utilize these automated assessments that dynamically find where students fall on a mastery scale and updating what they learn in real-time. They can analyze learner interactions, time taken to complete a task, and patterns of errors to determine where the learning gaps are [16]. Dashboards and analytics tools allow educators to track trends among individuals or groups and intervene proactively when needed. Such a data-driven feedback loop at the same time optimizes learning outcomes while also promoting self-directed learning, and guiding students on their strengths and areas of improvement.

Digital environments also open up opportunities for different types of multimodal and authentic assessment, such as e-portfolios, video presentations, blogs, or collaborative projects. These formats also offer more than rote learning and offer students the opportunity to express their understanding in flexible, creative, and real-world applications. This collaborative learning and critical thinking is further enabled through peer assessment tools and discussion forums. However, challenges remain and some of these current concerns are ensuring academic integrity in remote settings, how to eliminate bias in the process of automated grading and keeping access to assessment tools equitable. Online assessment formats can disadvantage students with limited digital literacy or a process of trial and error with an unstable internet connection [17].

Feedback should also be timely, constructive, and meaningful. Instant feedback is possible via digital platforms, but its effectiveness is contingent on good instructional design. Motivation and engagement are amplified by authentic and individual responses from educators be it through audio comments, video feedback, or one-on-one virtual meetings. While digital contexts certainly increase prospects for innovative, learner-led assessment, these opportunities need to be realized in a careful, equitable, and pedagogically informed manner.

8 Equity, Inclusion, and Accessibility: Bridging the Digital Divide

The equity, inclusion, and accessibility are both core to successful digital learning and among its biggest hurdles. The digital divide the gap between those with access to reliable internet, digital devices, and digital literacy and those without remains a factor that upholds educational inequities along socio-economic, geographic, and demographic lines.

With education systems moving so heavily into technology, the ability to engage in digital learning in a meaningful way is as much about infrastructure as it is social justice [18].

High-speed internet, personal devices, or even a quiet space to read can be scarce resources for many students in rural, low-income, or marginalized communities, making it difficult for them to participate fully. For example, learners with disabilities may come across content or platforms that are not accessible or also do not provide assistive technologies, such as screen readers, captioning, or keyboard navigation. Many of the learner populations living in underserviced areas are subjected to deeper marginalization through language barriers, content design without cultural sensitivity, or gender imbalances in the availability of the digital divide.

Digital learning in a way that inclusion is a conscious effort that must prioritize making these divides relevant. It includes spending at the community level subsidized devices and internet and mandating that platforms operate under universal-design principles. Availability in multiple languages, culturally relevant formats, and compatible with assistive technologies are all critical components of educational content [19]. Digital equity encompasses more than just hardware and software; it enables learners to have the skills and confidence to navigate digital spaces. To realize the full potential of educational technologies, we need digital literacy programs for students, parents, and educators. An equally critical component is inclusive teaching practices that acknowledge diversity among learners and respond to learner needs, backgrounds, and experiences. Equity in digital education requires a policymaking process that is truly inclusive where voices of the underrepresented contribute to design and assessment of the policies and strategies for the future of digital education. Connecting the final mile is more than a one-time answer; it is a multi-commitment to mitigate systemic inequities. Education systems have an opportunity to ensure that digital learning is genuinely equitable for all learners, regardless of where they start by tackling access barriers, leveraging inclusive pedagogies and employing accessible technology.

9 Policy Implications and Strategic Frameworks

The transition to digital education requires a complete review of educational policies and the design of strategic frameworks based on equity, innovation, and sustainability sense. With blended, adaptive and micro learning models on the rise, it is vital for policymakers to be inclusive and future-oriented with regulations that allow these models to flourish while ensuring the rights of learners are protected. Digital learning success goes beyond technology, it also needs governance structures which ensure access, quality, accountability, and ethics at all levels of education [20]. The most important policy takeaways are the requirement for a national and institutional digital educational plan that focuses on infrastructure development, capacity training, localization of content, and continuous financing. Public–private partnerships could be key mechanisms in scaling up infrastructure and innovation, particularly in low-resource settings. In addition, digital equity should be an embedded tenet in every strategic framework marginalized groups such as rural learners, students with disabilities, and economically disadvantaged students cannot be left behind.

Set up quality assurance systems to ensure the effectiveness and safety of digital platforms and content and its equitable use. Learner privacy must be safeguarded with data governance policies while analytics and AI tools need to be used ethically in education. Likewise, professional development policies need to prepare educators with the digital skills to deliver pedagogical approaches that harness those digital technologies. Interoperability standards should also be taken into account in strategic frameworks, so that educational platforms and tools can integrate smoothly across systems and geographies. The policy needs to support lifelong learning by way of acknowledgment of micro-credentials and flexible pathways in learning, allowing for learners to develop skills and credentials over time in a non-linear learning experience [21]. Policymakers need to make sure innovation is appropriately directed toward inclusion and ethical principles so that digital education actually contributes to advancing equity, empowerment, and sustainable development.

10 Conclusion and Future Directions

The combination of blended with adaptive and micro learning models heralds a new era in which higher education moves beyond traditional approaches to knowledge delivery and opens up new frontiers in knowledge uptake and experience. Such models present powerful opportunities for improved learner engagement, differentiated learning pathways, and responsiveness to varied educational needs. But they all need to be implemented well, supported by equitable infrastructure, pedagogy, and policy.

If technology is only a tool, it should be used to narrow the gap, not widen it; the use of technology must not increase existing inequalities in education. However, before we can unlock the full potential of these innovations, the digital divide needs to be bridged, accessibility ensured, learner data safeguarded, and teachers prepared for digital instruction.

The future of digital education builds on human-centered, data-informed, and context-sensitive ecosystems in the years ahead. This means scaling technological solutions, but also doing so with empathy, ethical considerations, and diversity, equity, and inclusion approaches in mind. Countries, states, schools, and communities will have to come together to co-create spaces for education that prioritize well-being, autonomy, and lifelong learning. Newer trends like AI tutors, immersive technologies (AR/VR) and blockchain for credentialing offer new potential in helping to deepen personalization and broaden access. However strategic policies that provide information on how to appropriately implement effective evidence-based innovations and rigorous evaluation procedures that assess real-world implementation are needed to use such innovations in an ethical, appropriate, and impactful way. Digital education is not a final destination but a long-term journey. Whether or not this future comes to be rests entirely on our collective ability to innovate with integrity, scale with equity, and learn through diverse experience. When approached with a strategic roadmap, digital learning can equip all learners to succeed in an increasingly connected and rapidly changing world.

References

1. Mulenga, R., & Shilongo, H. (2025). Hybrid and blended learning models: Innovations, challenges, and future directions in education. *Acta Pedagogia Asiana, 4*(1), 1–13.
2. Willberg, N. (2023). *Designing social micro-learning interventions for blended learning scenarios in higher education: Mixed methods case study at macromedia university of applied sciences.* (Doctoral dissertation. University of Westminster.
3. Ilic, P. (Ed.). (2024). *Optimizing education through micro-lessons: Engaging and adaptive learning strategies: Engaging and adaptive learning strategies.* IGI Global.
4. Mushtaq, D. M., & Iqbal, Z. (2024). Hybrid pedagogies: Assessing the effectiveness of blended and flipped learning in digital learning environments. *International Journal of Emerging Knowledge Studies, 3*(09), 662–669.

5. Vetrivel, S. C., & Mohanasundaram, T. (2024). Beyond the blackboard: Embracing hybrid learning spaces. In K. Omona & M. Kayi O'dama (Eds.), *Global perspectives on micro-learning and micro-credentials in higher education* (pp. 19). IGI Global. https://doi.org/10.4018/979-8-3693-0343-6.ch002
6. Carter, J. W., & Youssef-Morgan, C. (2022). Psychological capital development effectiveness of face-to-face, online, and Micro-learning interventions. *Education and Information Technologies, 27*(5), 6553–6575.
7. Fidan, M. (2023). The effects of microlearning-supported flipped classroom on pre-service teachers' learning performance, motivation and engagement. *Education and Information Technologies, 28*(10), 12687–12714.
8. Zhong, J., Li, Z., Hu, X., Wang, L., & Chen, Y. (2022). Effectiveness comparison between blended learning of histology practical in flipped physical classrooms and flipped virtual classrooms for MBBS students. *BMC Medical Education, 22*(1), 795.
9. Kohnke, L., Foung, D., Zou, D., & Jiang, M. (2024). Creating the conditions for professional digital competence through microlearning. *Educational Technology & Society, 27*(1), 183–197.
10. Al-Zahrani, A. M. (2024). Enhancing postgraduate students' learning outcomes through Flipped mobile-based microlearning. *Research in Learning Technology, 32*, 3110.
11. Chang, J. Y. F., Wang, L. H., Lin, T. C., Cheng, F. C., & Chiang, C. P. (2021). Comparison of learning effectiveness between physical classroom and online learning for dental education during the COVID-19 pandemic. *Journal of dental sciences, 16*(4), 1281–1289.
12. Shamir-Inbal, T., & Blau, I. (2022). Micro-learning in designing professional development for ICT teacher leaders: The role of self-regulation and perceived learning. *Professional Development in Education, 48*(5), 734–750.
13. Matzavela, V., & Alepis, E. (2021). M-learning in the COVID-19 era: Physical vs digital class. *Education and Information Technologies, 26*(6), 7183–7203.
14. Rincon-Flores, E. G., Castano, L., Guerrero Solis, S. L., Olmos Lopez, O., Rodríguez Hernández, C. F., Castillo Lara, L. A., & Aldape Valdés, L. P. (2024). Improving the learning-teaching process through adaptive learning strategy. *Smart Learning Environments, 11*(1), 27.
15. Monib, W. K., Qazi, A., Apong, R. A., & Mahmud, M. M. (2024). Investigating learners' perceptions of microlearning: Factors influencing learning outcomes. *IEEE Access, 99*, 3472113.
16. Gerbaudo, R., Gaspar, R., & Gonçalves Lins, R. (2021). Novel online video model for learning information technology based on micro learning and multimedia micro content. *Education and Information Technologies, 26*(5), 5637–5665.

17. Robles, H., Jimeno, M., Villalba, K., Mardini, I., Viloria-Nuñez, C., & Florian, W. (2023). Design of a micro-learning framework and mobile application using design-based research. *PeerJ Computer Science, 9*, e1223.
18. Deepa, M., Reba, P., Santhanamari, G., & Susithra, N. (2021). Enriched blended learning through virtual experience in microprocessors and micro-controllers course. *Journal of Engineering Education Transformations, 34*, 642–650.
19. Errabo, D. D., Dela Rosa, A., & Gonzales, L. J. M. (2024). Optimizing differentiated podcasts to promote students' self-regulation and engagement, self-efficacy and performance in asynchronous learning. *Journal of Research in Innovative Teaching & Learning, 17*(2), 368–390.
20. Alias, N. F., & Abdul Razak, R. (2023). Exploring the pedagogical aspects of microlearning in educational settings: A systematic literature review. *Malaysian Journal of Learning and Instruction (MJLI), 20*(2), 267–294.
21. Sathiyaseelan, B., Mathew, J., & Nair, S. (2024). Microlearning and learning performance in higher education: A post-test control group study. *Journal of Learning for Development, 11*(1), 1–14.

CHAPTER 4

Shifting Roles in Online Classrooms: Empowering Educators and Learners in Digital Contexts

Deepti Jain Thakre and Aarushi Walgaonkar

Abstract The development in the field of technology has revolutionized virtual education within the universities and has changed the manner in which teaching and learning take place in the contemporary digital scenario. This chapter explores the fact that teacher engagement is an indispensable factor in making any virtual learning material or experience more effective. Applying a qualitative method in the study on the basis of interpretive and phenomenological studies, the present study collected data of ten teachers and five teaching coordinators based on the interviews carried out. This chapter indicates that active teacher engagement and commitment is crucial in enabling constructive learning as well as encouraging critical thinking in pupils. Distance learning was found to be a flexible option through which learners could obtain education and they were not confined to specific time as it happened in classrooms or

D. Jain Thakre (✉) · A. Walgaonkar
Ramdeobaba University, Nagpur, India
e-mail: jaindr@rknec.edu

P. K. Dutta et al. (eds.), *Digital Education for a Sustainable Future*, Sustainable Development Goals Series,
https://doi.org/10.1007/978-3-032-15433-0_4

controlled by localization or other financial barriers posing restrictions in accessing such education. Flexibility and convenience of virtual learning made the approach accessible to a greater group of learners and redefined the way the learning process can be approached altogether. The given engagement benefits the quality of virtual education in general, leads to improved learning achievements, and assists graduates in the seamless transition to social and work environments.

Keywords Virtual education · Teacher involvement · Student engagement · Higher education quality · Online learning effectiveness

1 Introduction

The universities across the globe quickly switched to online learning due to the COVID-19 outbreak, taking advantage of Information and Communication Technologies (ICT) and platforms based on the internet, as the means of sustaining a constant interaction between the instructors and the pupils. This jump into a new regime changed the old education structure which promoted the modernization of teaching and triggering the perception of the students as adopting a more active role in learning themselves [1]. So, this transition comes without problems. Academic burnout, a process that is now well understood and defined, has been experienced by many university students manifesting it as physical and mental fatigue, an association with indifference concerning studies, a rise in absenteeism, and a fall in academic performance. This is the burnout that is commonly a result of increasing academic stress and the requirements of the virtual learning space. Research findings in a variety of areas have been indicating a significant rise in the burnout levels among the students after the pandemic and a considerable decrease in the overall interest in courses. Such withdrawal is dangerous to not only personal scholastic performance but overall learning goals of universities.

Teachers themselves have been dealing with burnout. The sudden requirement of adapting to new technologies and teaching methods has burdened the teaching profession immensely, which has led to conditions of exhaustion, anxiety, and lack of interest in their use. The stress to innovate and lack of experience in working with such virtual teaching platforms has at times been used to bring stress that impacts their work

productivity and satisfaction in their career. This strain is not only personalized on individual teachers; it may affect the university community as well creating a case of morale and overall quality of education [2].

To these dilemmas, scholars are implying that the twenty first century poses a necessity to redefine the educational techniques and frameworks at their core. This involves re-engineering instructional materials, place-of-work, interpersonal dynamics and assessment to fit the emerging facts of online learning. The system would end up repeating the evils of student dropouts and ineffective teaching without such changes. Hiding behind these challenges is the larger picture of the world around us that seems to change and transform too much, too fast the world that is termed to be a world that is liquid or in a state of transition all the time this liquidity referred to as the liquid modernity. In this kind of environment the people are forced to adjust rapidly to various situations before formal patterns or guideline are able to take a firm hold. Although such fluidity brings innovation, this innovation causes uncertainty and stress, because both teachers and students find it challenging to find stability in their educational roles [3].

The way in which an individual can overcome these challenges is the adaptiveness of the teacher thinking and staying engaged. Responsibility, commitment and motivation are factors that are closely related to teacher performance. When educators are engaged to such an extent, they play an important role in the quality of their institutions and in effect they can promote advancement in social, scientific, technological, and cultural spheres. Dynamic educators create positive learning spaces, encourage critical thinking, and outperform the students to support the achievement of their potential and boost the rest of the school system. With the above apparent relation between teacher engagement and learning outcomes, it will be essential to discuss the issue of teacher disengagement among the university teachers in online learning environments. A minimal teacher input may negatively influence their pedagogical ability, reduce the achievements of students, and lower the education quality of online studies as a whole. A question that comes to mind after this is: what actions can be performed, in order to make university teachers more engaged to promote their performance in virtual teaching.

This will not only enhance the learning process to the students but also sharpen the overall higher education. To realize this, there is a need to examine and develop measures that will encourage an increased sense of commitment and engagement of teachers in virtual classrooms. These

measures may involve establishing trust, augmenting communication mediums and promoting significant contacts between the learners and the teachers. These methods equalize the technology part of virtual learning with human relationships required in a healthy learning environment.

The chapter gives us a portrait of a modern university, straddling its own digital era challenges. It explores the transformations of the roles of teachers and students in virtual education and emphasizes the role of teacher engagement as a strong tool of promoting higher education online. The inherent assumption is that with a sincere involvement and motivation, the quality of teaching given by the teachers is enhanced, which further leads to achievement of students and reinforces the educational system as a whole. The study demands an all-round implementation of the virtual education that implies the understanding that it will need not only the implementation of some new tools and methods but also the changes in human attitude and relations. Through prioritizing empowerment of teachers and meaningful interactions higher education Universities are in a position to maneuverer through the complications behind digital learning and develop a sustainable concept of higher education in the future [4].

2 Theoretical Foundations

Online learning has fundamentally changed the way students study and what it means to be educated. It could be for the better or for the bad. This has changed the way schools work many times in the last few years. The way education, technology and interactions with other people change over time and this change is happening because of a change in the digital world that makes people think about how knowledge can be made, shared, and accessible in new ways. Online learning has made sharing information more interactive and collaborative than in a traditional classroom, when there were a lot of individuals and their roles were clear: teachers taught and students learnt with little room for change. This change not only goes against traditional ways of teaching, but it also opens up new ways to encourage creativity, independence, and participation. If it look at some of these new dimensions around changing roles, it can get a clearer idea of what sort of landscape digital technologies are making for teachers and students to work together to create educational experiences.

Virtual Learning and Modern Education

Virtual education also known as e-learning is a type of teaching which makes use of information and communication technologies (ICT) and the Internet in enabling learning. Virtual classrooms presented in this format are the digital spaces where the learning process takes place anchored on the interest, curiosity, and creativity of students, as well as personal interests. Learners use these online environments to dive into ideas and knowledge, following some existing rules, which simply means that education can take place without the physical presence in the established classroom setting. The most significant elements of successful online education is the communication between the teaching staff and students via different networks. This relationship, however, can only be effective in its true sense when a proper communication that is effective, deliberate and passionate is upheld. The students are also asked to participate actively, referring to the discretionary wealth of knowledge and experiences concerning the topic of study. Teachers constantly give them advice and feedback, which contributes to developing a more profound and valuable awareness of the subject, although they do not do it in personal interaction [5].

The environment inside the virtual classroom contributes quite much toward this understanding. The positive and supportive learning environment assists educators in understanding and reacting to needs, expectations, and challenges of students better. Such climate requires patience, empathy, and dependable help of instructors. The attributes help not only in academics but also in the emotional development of students that is also disregarded in online environments.

This is a method that is ongoing, planned, and interactive because its main aim is to reinforce the shared values and commitments involving all the participants in the learning process. Efficient integration of mentoring augurs well with the students because they also have a stable support system. It improves the performance capacity of teachers and institutional management abilities. All these aspects help in increasing the quality of higher education to be offered via virtual platforms in general. Engagement in online classes is also another important attribute of effective virtual learning. Interaction on the basis of discussion, teamwork, and observation allows students to acquire knowledge in a social way, acquiring essential academic and interpersonal skills. In an intelligent way technology becomes an enabling tool that enhances flexible and adaptable learning. Such flexibility enables education to be differentiated regarding the needs of different students to ensure a high commitment to academic excellence. This kind of strategy motivates the learners to think, form affirmed choices, and build critical thinking in the digital arena [6].

In acknowledging the revolutionary effect that virtual education is likely to make on the education sector, the educational ruling agents across the world ensure that a good balance of technology and human contact is explored. As much as it is imperative to enhance education by incorporating the emerging digital tools, it is time not to sacrifice developing social and emotional skills. People are still the key in learning, and they create a sense of community, belonging, cooperation which cannot be achieved with technology only. It is in this holistic perspective that virtual education can be understood because of the complexity between the relationship between human aspects, in the form of emotions, communication, and social interaction, and non-human aspects, which include digital platforms and technological tools. Learning can be offered beyond automated provision of content through technology as it is an ecological setting where human activity and organizational practices co-exist and enhance oneself. Such comprehensive strategy should be required to make sure that not only knowledge delivering is performed by virtual education functions but those functions also lead to active participation, engagement, and a feeling of shared responsibility of learners and educators.

Teacher Effectiveness in Online Learning

Virtual education strongly relies on the efficient work of teachers as they are the key contributors to a successful development of positive learning experiences of students. Making sure of an inclusive and supportive virtual classroom environment is one of the most important starting points of this. The empathetic approach of teachers to their students can help create the scene of comfort in which students feel secure and liked. This requires consideration of personal learning rates of students, the amount of their time and learning contexts that are unique to them through suitable technological applications that boost accessibility and interaction [7].

The other nations of the world have established the best practices in allying education with technology thus leading to transformation of learning due to their dedication toward such implementations. As an example, since the late 1990s Estonia has led the way in virtual education. The efforts like national digital platforms and the work on the elaboration of programmes aimed at the development of the teaching and learning process have contributed to the establishment of the culture which suggests the usage of the digital instruments in the educational process without any problems or difficulties to merge them with the existing educational traditions. Such advances have been fueled by the long-term engagement of both educators and learners leading to a very productive virtual learning environment. Likewise, the highly anticipatory educational technology strategies in Singapore do not only focus on technologically empowering students and teachers, but also encourages moral and inclusive utilization of digital tools. These initiatives provide the fairness to access technology that is aimed at leaving nobody behind and promoting the feeling of strong engagement and responsibility in all the members of the process.

The challenges related to the remote learning (the fear of the students, their feeling of isolation, their lack of self-confidence) can be avoided only with a properly organized strategy. A learning design that helps in taking an active participation where students learn through doing is necessary. This constructivist frame works to realize the critical and disciplined interdisciplinary thinking in the minds of the learners even in terms of following schedules and deadlines. The planning done is advisable in that there is no procrastination and frustration of students since they know their planned schedules of studying, assessment, and submissions of assignments. The instructional resources must be asynchronous like recorded lectures, video presentations, slide, and succinct summaries in order to accommodate various learning preferences and different schedules. In synchronous sessions where individuals meet punctually are to be provided to lure in the channel of stimulating discussions and reflections that are promoted by interactive technologies that underlie any form of communication and make it smooth [8].

Virtual interaction and conducting meetings are essential in ensuring engagement and communication, which depends on the nature of such meetings and interactions. There are interactive features that facilitate instant interactions between the instructor and the learners, and instructors can track the level of participation and conceptual absorption by students. This type of active communication shifts the students, who used to be the passive consumers of information, to involved learners who interact heavily with the material. Live chats, video comments and discussion forums can provide places where students have an opportunity to process, apply, and critically reflect upon what they are taught, increasing the richness of the learning environment.

In such a digital setup, there is a major shift in the role of the teacher. Educators are not content providers, but facilitators who help and assist learners on their learning process. They use multimedia devices, some of which include videoconferencing, streaming solutions, and podcasts to create interesting, involving, and engaging educational practices. Also, the virtual educator is supposed to provide their students with high-ethical standards by modifying its key teaching process referring to appropriate pedagogical premises and flexibly adopting the content delivery to satisfy the needs of different students. Practical uses of technology are not limited to the usage of traditional devices since mobile technology has become, in many ways, an influential tool in managing students and making them more productive in virtual classes [9].

In this environment, the evaluation and feedback systems are equally important. Motivation, personal responsibility, and engaged learning are promoted through a well-designed evaluation strategy that does not waste the time of the students but instead facilitates individual learning channels. Good assessment practices are not only a way to measure the level of academic achievements but also a way to pursue the ambition to constantly improve teaching and learning strategies. The respect, constructive, and timely delivery of feedback will assist the students to think about their progress, encourage intellectual development as well as create a culture of mutual respect and encouragement.

On the social level of learners there are more factors that impact the efficiency of virtual education rather seriously than these technical and procedural viewpoints. Effective communication and recognition of the social reality of the students will encourage the students to think critically and reflect. The ability to discuss various approaches helps the learners overcome their superficial assessments and deal with the deeper truths of their learning. Such active learning with the guidance of ethical issues and the direction toward offering practical solutions reinforces information storage and makes students more devoted to the learning process. The overall quality of education will rise, and the possibility of utilizing what they have learned in the course of study outside of the virtual classroom increases, when students are persuaded to engage in thoughtful and meaningful learning [10].

Virtual education thrives with active participation of the teachers, careful, considerate planning, interaction and meaningful communication, and evaluation which has to be objective, and inspiring. Ethical awareness and the emphasizing on the development of real understanding and critical thinking should be considered whenever the integration of technology is involved. A combination of these factors helps to develop a virtual learning community that is rich and supportive to the students allowing them to prosper academically as well as socially.

Virtual Higher Education

One of the major issues that most individuals are facing in the contemporary world is that they do not know whether the learned knowledge today would be of any use tomorrow. The disparate groups that form the society operate under the tensions and challenges as the society is forced to accommodate endless innovation. Education is one of the most critical processes in solving these issues, such as the problem of academic and work burnout, and facilitate inclusion in any facet that is consistent with the purposes of universities.

Healthy and clear expectations should be established to all the people involved in order to promote well-being. Burnout has been known to be a syndrome caused by ill management of the work related stress and sequentially accompanied by exhaustion, negative attitude toward work, and poor performance. Burnout may lead to poor performances in schools or school dropouts among the school going children, particularly when the demands of the teaching profession are excessive. In order to overcome this, higher education institutions must promote positive events that would help students who have low motivation, self-esteem, or are facing emotional problems due to unattained goals. Colleges are supposed to be a place of free discussion and depth of thought, to establish an enabling environment and stress free learning environment [11].

Examples across the world can emphasize the effectiveness of engagement in strengthening virtual education. In certain nations, they strongly demand an increase in commitment of university educators to enable them confront the future uncertainty based on personal integrity and responsibility. In others, students' involvement is stressed as one of the most important issues to maintain motivation during online classes. In the same way, the connection between engagement and virtual education forms a learning environment in which anxiety and uncertainty are caused by changing education models and innovative technologies. It is a method that favors greater academic engagement by planning and cooperating with educators and learners in a mature manner. Professional ethical standards are also very relevant to the enhancement of virtual learning. Ethics promotes good academic environment, and it develops a culture of collective responsibility within the university circles. Teachers become the mentors that help to instill the sense of accountability and respect, promote the correspondence that is both clear and considerate.

Emotions also play an important role in learning, as every intellectual activity is influenced by emotions. It is important for teachers to design virtual texts that promote both internal and external inspiration, which helps students to stay and remain responsible. Managing emotions positively is important to create a supportive environment where students feel connected and encouraged. Care to take care of yourself and others requires nurturing morality as a practice that strengthens community bonds. In addition, the responsible use of technology can motivate students and deepen their interest in learning. In virtual university education, teachers should be committed to continuous development, inspiration, morality, and responsibility. By embracing these qualities as kind leaders, teachers can inspire real learning that benefit both individuals and society in overall [12].

3 Need for Digital Technologies in Education

With the adoption and advancement of the globalization of education, it has become of greater urgency that the digital technologies should be incorporated. Though there existed an online system of classes, resources sharing, evaluation, and administration, their usage remained rather voluntary. The developed nations were quite ready to make this transition but the developing countries needed to adapt to it and overcome numerous obstacles. Digital tools were a necessity during this critical period as they were used to keep education systems operating all over the world. This international scenario has revealed the essence of being connected in education internationally with the help of technologies [13].

Digital platforms make students acquire the defined professional competence, including problem-solving, logical thinking, and comprehension of complicated processes. They also equip learners with an uncertain and fast-changing future where technology usage will be of more importance. The skills that the students of such tools will acquire will be essential in their careers. The process of including digital materials allows us to enrich the learning experience so that studying and teaching would be more interactive and effective. In addition, it enables institutions to have individual curriculums adapted to every student making the learning more flexible in direction. In the case of younger learners, technology in the classroom may increase engagement because children nowadays are used to various electronic devices. Lessons can be more pleasant with the help of instruments such as projectors, computers, and other modern devices that will help to take the attention of students.

The job of the teacher is being rethought at its core. In many ways, online teachers are now more than just lecturers standing at the front of the room and talking about the topic. They are also facilitators, curators, and even co-learners. It is the particular features of digital platforms that provide teachers the chance to create interesting, student-centered learning experiences that could help in this area. For example, teachers might avoid using the same lesson for everyone by using resources like discussion boards, virtual breakout rooms, and real-time collaboration software. They can also change their teaching methods to fit different learning styles, creating spaces where students are actively involved in their own education. This is a big change from old models where the teacher's authority was the most important thing in the classroom. Digital environments give teachers a chance to try out new ways of teaching, like the flipped classroom, where students watch a lesson on their own and then talk about it with the teacher. They can also get ideas from studies of literature on how to use digital technologies in the classroom. This method not only gets students more involved, but it also gives teachers more freedom so they may spend more time on higher-order abilities like critical thinking and problem-solving.

Active and technology-enhanced learning in the classroom (through interactive presentations, group work, collaborative projects, and online collaboration) makes learning more dynamic and engaging. Technology has also enabled more active participation of students by making them central to the learning process with teachers playing a guidance role toward their achievement. The plethora of digital materials has made information very accessible to learners who can share and cooperate with their colleagues via online tools such as blogs, podcasts, and wikis. These instruments facilitate creation of content, peer feedbacks, and mutual learning. Digital technology also supports innovative teaching methods, which includes gamification and flipped classes, which can significantly improve learning results. Educational approaches now often add many techniques, allowing each student to travel to personal learning. Ultimately, technology enriches the instructions by making it more attractive, meaningful and diverse learned needs.

4 Applications of Digital Technologies in Education

Use of digital technologies has proved to be useful in advancing education as it has made it easy to create learning resources and also provided additional means of engagement and collaboration among learners. The massive deployment of the Internet, along with the propagation of smart devices has brought the new era of education. Educators and instructional designers now have the task of utilizing these developments to reform the learning process, and bring quality education to everyone, independent of the site in which it is taught. Technology has also facilitated the process of learning outside the traditional classroom setting and as such, students are driven toward the impulse of creativity and achievement thus making them learn beyond normal means. Over the present times, several nations have effectively integrated remote learning due to their integration of different mediums including television, radio, internet portals, and mobile applications. The tools have simplified the attainment of information, improved retention, organized it very well, and made knowledge sharing possible [14].

The current world is dynamic, and a teacher cannot afford to be left behind in the use of any devices like smartphones and other tablets. They should make use of the web-based materials available to ensure that their teaching material remains up to date, interactive as well as dynamic. Technology is much more than entertainment-it is a question of how students, parents and teachers use it to enhance learning experiences. Thoughtful use of technology, in addition to supplementing instruction, also makes students more engaged and interested. The compatibility of e-learning platforms with mobile devices has also increased dramatically in the last few years and played a major role in increasing the accessibility and adoption of digital education. There are also specialized learning tools, such as animations, games, and AI-driven learning programs that also help serve the various learning needs. The use of technology has controlled innovations that have enabled flexibility in education in terms of age and subjects. The other aspect that is very crucial yet very little attention is given to is the role of data and analytics in the field of education. This knowledge can be used to enhance virtual classrooms, e-learning, and online tests, which contributes to the overall better learning results [15].

This is novel because it gives the teacher more options on how to teach. This is because course-ware platforms like Canvas and Moodle may create data that is useful for improvement and can show professors in real time what their students are doing and not comprehending. Teachers can utilize this information to make learning spaces more welcoming for children with special needs or who have had different experiences, change how they teach, and give specific feedback. Also, most online systems are asynchronous, which means that teachers can work from anywhere and at any time, which is something we never thought possible before. For instance, students may watch a video of a lecture whenever it was convenient for them, which would free up class time for projects or discussion. This transformation not only gives teachers greater freedom to be creative, but it also means that they have to be open to learning with their pupils, going on a journey of discovery together.

5 Challenges in Online Education and Technologies

Educative technology is a welcome aspect with numerous advantages as well as challenges especially in the application and usage of technology. Negative issues related to screen time, whether the time spent in front of a screen is actively managed by teachers or not, and equity of access have become salient, particularly after the COVID-19 pandemic. There is also a new task that educators will have to accomplish courses related to online learning, as well as make the students think critically and discuss the topic in various ways. Some students find useful to learn online, whereas others experience problems because of a large number of factors such as their inability to utilize support systems that they used to have access without any possibility. Students that would have had a hard time in the traditional classroom mode may find this to be quite difficult.

The poor quality of instruction is one of the well-known causes of constant learning problems. Most of the teachers do not possess enough knowledge in their subject areas and have not been given enough training to operate in the digital teaching environment. Technology can present possible solutions by offering training opportunities to educators either fully online or by means of blended techniques. Nonetheless, motivation too is important since some of the teachers might have the capability but lack the incentives to work effectively.

Remarkably, the low-tech approach of providing instruction at the level of students can be very efficient, particularly in the environments with limited resources. With costly high-tech solutions unavailable to most low-income areas, one should be careful to select the best strategies in terms of their harmony with the needs of learners. As video lessons and even mass online courses become more common, not all of them concentrate on early education and cover learning gaps completely. In addition, such formats frequently necessitate specific equipment and the internet access lacked by certain students at home. There may be a creative way of learning, such as gamification, that can also encourage students, but one should remember that learning can still be of a good quality without the use of only technology [16].

Economically deprived background students may lack access to smartphones or reliable internet, which makes it difficult for them to maintain it. Small learners, although often technique-luxuries, faced physical issues such as eye stress and back pain using prolonged screen. Teachers, many of whom are new to digital devices, make a lot of efforts to continue educated despite these obstacles. College students face special conflicts in practical or hand areas, as online format cannot easily repeat experienced learning. Concerns about academic dishonesty have come to light with the rise of online assessment. Nevertheless, with thoughtful design, assignments and examinations can cheat by focusing on problems-solution and deep understanding rather than memoirs. Technology can also help to automate regular tasks such as making teachers' charge, trekking attendance and grading participation. However, many students are effectively excluded from distance education, without adequate access to equipment, reliable internet, learning materials, and proper training. From low-income families, disabled families, or those who speak other languages other than the major language at home, are often required to be successful to succeed in rural or less-pillars.

The change in roles is just as big for pupils. In the online classroom, students are increasingly active participants in the learning process instead of just passive consumers of information. The collaborative and participatory nature of digital resources is what is making this transition happen. These resources give students more control over their own education. For example, Google Classroom and Microsoft Teams let students work together on group projects, share materials, and leave comments in conversations. These tools also make students feel connected and in charge. These tools are new because they let students help create knowledge instead of merely consuming it. A student might not want to raise questions or talk a lot in a lecture hall, but there are safer and fairer online areas for involvement, such anonymous discussion boards and chat rooms where everyone can see what you're saying.

6 Conclusion

Classes include various types of equipment and software in digital technology designed to support students, especially with specific access needs. The biggest advantage of integrating technology in education is the ability to reiterate and reduce tasks that take time. For example, many regular activities such as trekking attendance or monitoring student's performance can be automated, to save valuable time and effort. Beyond reducing administrative functions, technology teaches students to use digital tools to make better decisions and promote self-discipline skills. It also prepares learners for lifetime education by providing flexible access to information according to various teaching styles. Digital classes change traditional teaching by incorporating computers, internet and various electronic devices, allowing students to learn at their own pace and track their progress more effectively. With the help of customized digital materials and interactive tools, students gain more control over their learning experience. Further, such technologies are expected to play an even greater role in increasing education by creating a more attractive and efficient learning environment. Additionally, modern technologies have been important in handling complex data for important decisions related to environmental protection, such as climate change mitigation, biodiversity conservation and disaster preparations. These innovations focus on permanent development, aimed at reducing pollution, limiting environmental damage, and supporting long -term economic and social development, preserving natural resources.

References

1. Papadakis, S., Kiv, A., Kravtsov, H., Osadchyi, V., Marienko, M., Pinchuk, O., Shyshkina, M., Sokolyuk, O., Мінтій, I., Vakaliuk, T., Azarova, L., Kolgatina, L., Amelina, S., Volkova, N., Velychko, V., Striuk, A., & Семеріков, C. (2023). *Unlocking the power of synergy: The joint force of*

cloud technologies and augmented reality in education. https://doi.org/10.31812/123456789/7399

2. Karakose, T., Kocabas, I., Yirci, R., Papadakis, S., Ozdemir, T. Y., & Demirkol, M. (2022). The development and evolution of digital leadership: A bibliometric mapping approach-based study. *Sustainability, 14*(23), 16171. https://doi.org/10.3390/su142316171
3. Guamán-Carranza, A. R. (2024). Los entornos virtuales y su importancia en el desempeño docente. *Revista Arbitrada Interdisciplinaria Koinonía, 9*(17), 238–256. https://doi.org/10.35381/r.k.v9i17.3217
4. Bohara, P. S. (2024). Supporting teachers in implementing project-based learning in teaching secondary mathematics: An action research. *Advances in Mobile Learning Educational Research, 4*(2), 1122–1134. https://doi.org/10.25082/amler.2024.02.007
5. Vahos, L. E. G., Muñoz, L. E. M., & Londoño-Vásquez, D. A. (2019). Teacher's role in the meaningful learning achievement based on ICT. *Revista Encuentros, 17*(02), 1907. https://doi.org/10.15665/encuent.v17i02.1907
6. Baque-Castro, G. Y., & Vigueras-Moreno, J. A. (2021). El docente y su desempeño en la educación virtual. *Polo Del Conocimiento: Revista Científico-Profesional, 6*(3), 991–1005. https://doi.org/10.23857/pc.v6i3.2417
7. Akinbadewa, B. O., & Sofowora, O. A. (2020). The effectiveness of multimedia instructional learning packages in enhancing secondary school students' attitudes toward biology. *International Journal on Studies in Education, 2*(2), 119–133. https://doi.org/10.46328/ijonse.19
8. Chindia, B., & Wawire, S. N. (2024). Student attitudes towards smartphone use in a pre-service teacher tech course. *Advances in Mobile Learning Educational Research, 4*(1), 994–1006. https://doi.org/10.25082/amler.2024.01.011
9. Aguayo-Estremera, R., Cañadas, G. R., Ortega-Campos, E., Pradas-Hernández, L., Martos-Cabrera, B., Velando-Soriano, A., & De La Fuente-Solana, E. I. (2022). Levels of burnout and engagement after COVID-19 among psychology and nursing students in Spain: A cohort study. *International Journal of Environmental Research and Public Health, 20*(1), 10377. https://doi.org/10.3390/ijerph20010377
10. Gudmundsdottir, G., & Hathaway, D. (2020). "We always make it work": Teachers' agency in the time of crisis. *Journal of Technology and Teacher Education, 28*(2), 239–250. https://www.learntechlib.org/primary/p/216242
11. Kalogiannakis, M., & Papadakis, S. (2019). The use of developmentally mobile applications for preparing pre-service teachers to promote STEM

activities in preschool classrooms. In *Advances in educational technologies and instructional design book series* (pp. 82–100). https://doi.org/10.4018/978-1-7998-1486-3.ch005

12. Abubakar, U., Ogunlade, O. O., & Ibrahim, H. A. (2024). The influence of technology-integrated curriculum resources on student engagement and academic achievement in higher education. *Advances in Mobile Learning Educational Research, 4*(2), 1208–1223. https://doi.org/10.25082/amler.2024.02.014
13. Karakose, T., Polat, H., Yirci, R., Tülübaş, T., Papadakis, S., Ozdemir, T. Y., & Demirkol, M. (2023). Assessment of the relationships between prospective mathematics teachers' classroom management anxiety, academic self-efficacy beliefs, academic amotivation and attitudes toward the teaching profession using structural equation modelling. *Mathematics, 11*(2), 449. https://doi.org/10.3390/math11020449
14. Llagua-Arévalo, P., & Gamboa-Salinas, J. (2023). *El Burnout Post Pandemia COVID-19 en el Desempeño Laboral de las Instituciones de Educación Superior.*. 593 Digital Publisher CEIT, *8*(4), 443–460. https://doi.org/10.33386/593dp.2023.4.1849
15. Abubakar, U., & Yunusa, A. A. (2024). Investigating academic staff behavioral intention and readiness to utilise mobile devices for instructional delivery among tertiary institutions in Sokoto State, Nigeria. *Advances in Mobile Learning Educational Research, 4*(1), 1046–1057. https://doi.org/10.25082/amler.2024.01.015
16. Papadakis, S. (2023). MOOCs 2012-2022: An overview. *Advances in Mobile Learning Educational Research, 3*(1), 682–693. https://doi.org/10.25082/amler.2023.01.017

CHAPTER 5

Policy Frameworks and Regulation for Equitable Digital Education

Roshni S. Khedgaonkar, Praful V. Barekar, and Prarthana A. Deshkar

Abstract Education has been regarded as the most potent weapon to any developing nation as being a pillar to economic and social stability. In such a nation as India, which has such a large population, access to education is one aspect that needs to be facilitated in order to get the best out of its population. There has been a keen turn toward online and digital learning, with the major pillars in the endeavor being teachers, students and education materials quality. The role of teachers in shaping knowledge and development of students is central and therefore institutions should give teachers a chance to sharpen their abilities. The National Education Policy puts much emphasis on teacher training, as well as professional development focusing on the fact that future generations will be successful mainly because of a teacher. At the center of the reforms

R. S. Khedgaonkar (✉) · P. V. Barekar · P. A. Deshkar
Department of Computer Technology, Yeshwantrao Chavan College of Engineering, Nagpur, Maharashtra, India
e-mail: roshni.k86@gmail.com

P. K. Dutta et al. (eds.), *Digital Education for a Sustainable Future*, Sustainable Development Goals Series,
https://doi.org/10.1007/978-3-032-15433-0_5

of the education system are the teachers, and an effective, comprehensive policy needs to provide a quality education to every student. It is seen in this study that online and digital education is vital regarding the implementation of policies in the National Education Policy to consider how the use of technology could fall in line with the United Nations Sustainable Development Goals (SDGs) by 2030 as set by UNESCO.

Keywords Online education · Digital learning · Teacher development · National education policy · Sustainable development goals

1 Introduction

In India, a large democracy still resides in the countryside where majority of them depend on farming which is an occupation. A large portion of students in these areas are also involved in agricultural activities with their families making it unlikely that some of them will have regular and quality access to education. With such a challenge, the National Education Policy (NEP) has put so much emphasis on the growth of the online and digital forms of learning so that students in whatever part of the country will not be denied an education. The growing significance of digital education was made especially clear when the COVID-19 outbreak happened. Lockdowns that forced individuals to spend most time at home paralyzed conventional education that took place in the classroom. It was at this period when alternative and online education was presented as the only way to continue with the academic activities. The use of the virtual classroom, on-line lectures, e-learning platforms and electronic library were essential components as it gave the students a platform to accumulate knowledge without severe interruption. The experience has shown that although conventional techniques are useful, the education system should not be without flexible or technology-based solutions to help in thriving against an unpredictable crisis [1].

The NEP does not only support the transition of the educational system to the use of technology, but also puts forth the risk as well, i.e., over-dependence on technological devices, cyber security, and lack of equal access because of socio-economic differences. In order to confront these issues, the policy proposes responsible use of technology, training of teachers to use technology, and further building of infrastructure that could provide equal access to all students. It promotes production of quality digital content in various languages that can accommodate different cultural and linguistic composition of India. To aid this vision, the Government of India has launched multiple digital programs that are inclusive of all levels of education including primary and higher education. Learning materials are freely available in massive variety in platforms such as SWAYAM, DIKSHA, e-Pathshala and the National Digital Library of India that all students and teachers can access. The target of these initiatives is to ensure that there are both present needs of education as well as the projected future demands through the increased flexibility, inclusiveness, and interactivity of learning.

The Digital India campaign is one of the major forces that drive this change orientation to establish a digitally empowered society and a strong knowledge economy. That initiative is gradually transforming the learning environment by investing into internet connection, low cost gadgets, and digital literacy campaigns. More and more rural schools are equipped with smart-classrooms and interactive boards as well as the possibility to access online learning sources. This transformation is occurring because India is not only using technology and education to improve the quality of education but the country is also gradually putting in place the necessary policies to provide all children, irrespective of the complexity of the city or the locality in a village, quality education. The vision goes beyond empowering the students purely with academic knowledge; it also gives them the skills that will be crucial in their future personal and professional lives because digital skills will be the new normal [2].

2 Fair Digital Learning in NEP 2020

The National Education Policy (NEP) 2020 lays a lot of stress on the use of technology in education given its transformational nature to meet various needs of learners in the country. It focuses on technology and ways in which it can connect gaps in access, eliminate language barriers and make learning more inclusive to students of diverse socio-economic and cultural backgrounds. It should be stressed that proper application of technology in the teaching/learning process must not only enable the enhancement of interaction between students but also should help teachers to feel empowered through a possibility to gain constant support in terms of professional development. The methodology will help keep the teacher in the loop with the latest pedagogical standards and enable the staff to adjust to the changes necessitated by the digital economy.

Within its vision understood as Online and Digital Education, NEP 2020 presents several technological interventions, which are to change the way of learning. These consist of new types of artificial intelligence, robotics, virtual labs and simulated classrooms. To facilitate the successful implementation of such tools, the National Educational Technology Forum (NETF) has been suggested as an advisory panel to aid the central as well as state governments in deployment of technology in education. The forum mandate includes planning of direction to research, stimulating innovation work and facilitating partnership between education establishments and developers of technology hence making sure that technological advances are utilized effectively in classrooms [3].

The policy also embraces a number of initiatives that are driven by the government on digitalizing in an effort to increase access to quality education. On the one hand, the platform such as DIKSHA was built to facilitate teacher professional development by providing various training modules and resources; on the other hand, SWAYAM provides online courses to school and higher education learners. NEP 2020 also stipulates that there should be high-quality educational content available in all Indian major languages so that language should not be an obstacle in learning anymore. This also entails specialized resources to learners with disabilities (Divyang learners) thereby supporting the policy on inclusive education to all learners.

To realize the significance of international cooperation in the field of educational technology, NEP 2020 suggests the reinforcement of the research capabilities with the National Research Foundation. This organization will launch and broaden research in the emerging and disruptive technology and the strategy will be to adjust mentions of educative innovations of India with the international research. These efforts would be aimed at solving issues on a global platform and generating domestic progress that could enhance the quality and accessibility of education in the nation [4].

The policy also emphasizes on the best use of digital forums with regard to ICT based education provision. This involves the development of convenient audio and video interfaces to take online classes so that the process of learning could be interactive and engaging. NEP 2020 is based on the system that envisages constant availability of content and provides it to students at convenient opportunities via various sources, such as TV networks, both online and the others, which can be monitored. Virtual laboratories are also being promoted, whereby the students will be able to undertake experiments and learn in a realistic setting even in the event that physical infrastructure is unattainable.

The foundations of NEP 2020 are that teachers should be prepared to handle the needs of an online and digital education. It acknowledges the fact that efficient utilization of technology involves the need of the educators, to keep their skills intact, update their teaching methods and acquire new pedagogical approaches. To facilitate such transition, the policy recommends well-planned and beyond-surface teacher professional development programmes that would produce a technically skilled teacher, along with one who is able to create interesting and student-centered digitalized learning experiences. As NEP 2020 puts technology front and center of education transformation, it would produce an education system ready to face the future because it will be accessible and inclusive and meet international standards. It aims at providing students as well as teachers not only with the knowledge, but also with digital skills and flexibility to successfully live in a sophisticated world of constant changes [5].

3 Advantages of Digital Education

As a part of the National Education Policy (NEP) 2020, there is heavy consideration to increase access to online and digital education among learners in the nation. This is also one of its top priorities since it aims to make modern technology available to each student irrespective of his or her socio-economic background and location. In order to do so, the policy promotes institutional facilitation, i.e., the provision of a device (laptop or tablet) and stable internet connectivity. This will be done with the purpose of making the students able to use both synchronous (real-time) and asynchronous (flexible, self-paced) processes of learning. In this way, NEP 2020 will aim to make those learners who are somehow detached by reasons out of the ordinary system of conventional teaching move into the mainstream. This will be in line with the vision of the whole child development of all the students.

It is not that online and digital education as conceived under NEP 2020 constitutes giving lectures over the internet, but it is much more to do with coping with diverse learning needs of students. The policy acknowledges that learners are diverse in nature, have varying abilities and challenges and hence the policy lays emphasis on upskilling the teachers on how to use assistive and adaptive technology. This will make education more inclusive providing all students-regardless of the personal circumstances they are facing, with an equal chance to learn and excel in life. All learners must not be left behind or be disengaged in the learning process because they lack accessible learning opportunities and resources. Among the remarkable aspects of the NEP vision, one can note the idea of supporting blended learning, i.e., the type of education that combines online and offline instruction. This will enable students to learn anywhere and this will eliminate the barriers placed by geographical boundaries. There exists an added value with recorded lectures, online resource, and archived study material as the students have more time to go back to lessons and improve their understanding and revision [6].

The candidate of online and digital education is especially important to the students in the rural regions. In most rural areas, students have transport difficulties, poor weather, and infrastructure disparities that impede them to attend physical tuition sessions. These concerns were also demonstrated in a more significant way through the COVID-19 pandemic, when educational institutions had to close. Under these conditions, online training became the only salvation, and learning did not stop because of physical limitations. Another aspect of 2020 NEP that can help in solving the digital divide is to ensure that rural students receive equal access to gadgets, internet connection, and quality learning material and delete the difference among the rural and urban learning structures. The lack of digital learning opportunities in the rural regions was historically one of the factors leading to high dropout rates following school-level education. Most of the students could not enjoy any higher education mainly just because they could not move or commute to the urban centers. However, with the digitalization of education, the learners currently have the possibility to proceed with their studies at their home that significantly boosts the enrollment rates in higher education. Not only does this increase academic participation, but it also increases social and economic mobility.

In order to ensure that this dream becomes true, the government has proposed a number of digital efforts and campaigns aimed at making the process of accessing education simpler and wider reaching. These are national internet learning platform, interactive e-content and virtual classroom to help in engaging and interacting learning. It is hoped that this will be achieved by forming an educational ecosystem in which the technology will only serve to enable the opportunity to be achieved by all,

whether student or teacher to enable them to reach their great potential. The online and artificial intelligence in learning, which has been prioritized by NEP 2020, is a revolutionary move toward developing a more flexible, accommodating and future proof education system. This policy is expected to achieve this objective by using technological integration in the teaching/learning process to eliminate the geographical, infrastructure, and socio-economic inability to receive quality education as such that it can be offered to all learners in the country [7].

4 Digital Education and Changing Schooling

The New Realities of Schooling

The Covid-19 epidemic made a seismic change in the global education scenario. Whereas some new development came out-as comprehensive adopting digital technologies in teaching, focusing on student and teacher welfare, and recognition of teacher deficiency-many of these so-called "new realities" were not completely new. Instead, he intensified issues and inequalities that were already present within education systems before the epidemic. These included inequalities in access to equipment and internet connectivity, as well as variations in digital skills of teachers, students and their communities. Although the nature and severity of these challenges differ in countries and regions, many common topics have emerged.

1. Widening of Pre-Existing Inequalities

Although all schools had to quickly close, the sharp move to online learning underscored the massive divides in device access, internet access, and quality digital learning materials. Such gaps could be found not only between the countries but also inside and were often a reflection of already preexisting economic, racial, and social divisions. A digital divide soon became synonymous with the social divide as disadvantaged students in households with low income and in under-resourced areas suffered the most as a result of disrupted learning [8].

The intellectual effects have been enormous. There were substantial learning losses among many students with the largest being among those ones in developing countries or the low socioeconomic backgrounds. Such learning losses have increased gaps in achievement, decreased academic achievement and even caused school drop-outs.

Behind academics, the broader social and emotional ones were the increasing rates of depression, anxiety, childhood obesity, cases of violence against children, and chronic absences. Numerous governments put an immediate stress on so-called catch-up programmes, which are aimed at reducing lost learning levels among students. Interventions ran the spectrum of lengthening school schedules to enacting specialized remedial instructional initiatives. Awarding of such actions was used in South Asia with close to half of the countries doing so. Early evaluations of extra-tutoring schemes in certain areas, however, have cast doubt on their lasting power, with small improvements measured on student outcomes compared with control groups to whom such interventions were not applied.

2. Student Well-being

Along with learning concerns, the epidemic also had a deep and permanent impact on the student welfare. Even before Covid-19, the growing cases of childhood anxiety, loneliness and depression were being reported globally. Long isolation, uncertainty, and disintegration due to school shutdown made these issues significantly, with a global increase in mental health problems among young people. Many countries implemented post-circulatory support programs such as school-based consultations, welfare initiatives and mental health awareness campaigns. In South Asia, three-fourth of the countries introduced measures to address student welfare, although reaching scale and diverse. While the long -term effects of school closure on mental health are uncertain, early signs are disturbing and indicate the need for continuous intervention. Another area of increasing concern is the influence of social media on young mental health. Public discourse rapidly combines the use of social media with anxiety, depression and other psychological challenges among young people. Some health officials have issued a strong warning, which urge more research on social media effects and advocate safe, more regulated digital environment for children [9].

3. Shifts and Tensions in Educational Approaches

The epidemic intensified the use of digital learning methods in some countries like India, Italy and Australia. However, in many fields, schools

returned to pre-mahamari, traditional classrooms, as the restrictions were reduced. A remarkable trend was full-time, in-person teaching in most K-12 settings, despite initial expectations that hybrid or mixed models can become ideal. In some courts, "back-to-basics" approach emerged as a quick improvement for learning loss, which is more interactive, in favor of traditional teaching on student-centered education. Nevertheless, there were exceptions. In Canada and parts of Australia, as well as in the rural and remote areas of Ireland, online or mixed options continue, providing extended access to special subjects. For example, Gelic speaking communities in Ireland now use virtual classes to offer courses such as physics, which may not be locally available. Australia has seen a continuous increase in virtual school enrollment, which reflects increasing interest in online learning among some student groups.

4. Transformation of the Teaching Profession

Epidemics made unprecedented demands on teachers, many reporting tiredness, stress, and burnout. While such issues were present before Covid-19, the crisis extended them. Factors such as increase in charge, rapid adaptation to unfamiliar technologies, and administrative pressure accelerate stress. Many teachers felt overwhelmed, especially during the early months of remote learning. The lack of teacher was more visible in many countries, which aims to attract more people in the profession. In some cases, governments reduced the initial teacher education programs to speed up certification. While it helped fill the vacancies in the short term, it also expressed concern about reducing professional standards and reducing the quality of education. Teacher Attraction—In particular within the first five years of service—the condition of better working, competitive salary and constant professional development opportunities, continue to be a frequent challenge, highlighting the urgent needs of professional development [10].

5. Building Teacher Digital Competence

While significant invested in equipment, connectivity, digital platforms and educational materials during epidemics, there was less emphasis on equipping teachers with digital skills required to effectively use these resources. Many teachers struggled with rapid change in online teaching, which revealed a systemic requirement for ongoing training in digital education. Developing students' digital capacity is now a policy priority in many countries, and teachers are recognized as key agents in achieving this goal. However, existing professional standard for teachers digital skills is often widespread and lacks practical guidance for implementation. It has called teachers for continuous, well -structured professional teaching programs to help integrate technology in their teaching.

6. Wider Societal and Economic Pressures

The features of post-pandemic education systems are also struggling with challenges that directly and indirectly impact schooling. Floods, wild fires, and droughts have caused education to be disrupted in various areas due to climate related disasters. There is also the strain of resources due to political instability in some of the countries. The war in Ukraine is a case in point since the war has displaced many people, caused a refugee crisis, and added to the increases in the prices of food, energy, and basic materials in Europe, Middle East, and Africa. These disturbances exert extra pressure on education systems that are already weak.

7. Emerging Technologies and the Role of AI

The educational sector has reached a turning point amid increased use of advanced digital technologies especially the artificial intelligence (AI) and generative AIs applications. Although policy-making in this field is in its initial stages, there are already certain nations that are venturing to adopt AI into their classrooms with regulations on ethical application. An example is the implementation of ChatGPT AI in some education systems within a certain controlled environment that reflects the importance of innovation, but also making sure to respect the importance of critical thinking and avoiding over-dependence on automation.

In other areas, the introduction of AI in school is still in a developing, unregulated form and there are few references to it at national policy levels. In the meantime, pilot programs, including so-called smart classrooms in Sri Lanka, are providing teachers and students a chance to be exposed to AI-powered learning tools. Such experimentation is an indicator of an emerging discussion of how the world has come to grips with the prospects of emerging technologies without jeopardizing equity, quality, and safety of education [11].

The Covid −19 pandemic has transformed the education terrain, hastening certain alterations and intensifying inequities that existed prior to the pandemic. The problems like the loss of learning, mental health concerns, digital divide, teacher shortage, and the establishment of new technologies still have to be addressed. It is also a challenge as the education system adjusts to the new post-pandemic world by both trying to respond to the exigencies of recovery and at the same time anticipating the longer-term change and creating a clearer view of how teaching and learning may evolve. The events of the past years demonstrate that resilience, inclusivity, and innovation are key to the creation of the education systems that are resilient to future disruption and are able to support all learners equally.

5 Digital Education Policy

The scenario of digital education has led to significant changes in recent years, which has been shaped by rapid integration of technology in teaching and learning processes. As the school and education system are conducive to transferring realities, it is the growing requirement to assess whether the current policies reflect these changes adequately. The insight drawn by comparative reviews of many education systems reveals the clear difference of how countries approached for digital education before the Covid −19 epidemic, rapid adaptation during the crisis, and policy changes were observed after the reopening of schools.

- Before the COVID-19 Pandemic

Before the pandemic, some of the countries had already implemented specific digital education policies, whereas others were at the initial stage of development. Other countries had incorporated their digital learning plan under wider national innovation plans so that they did not only modernize their education systems but also meet the challenges of quality, equity and efficiency. In general, such policies were aimed at enhancing infrastructural conditions as developing internet connection and supply of devices, embedding digital technologies into curriculum delivery, developing online learning content, teacher training, and advancing digital competence development in students.

Such policies in several countries were not new but rather decades-old and showed long-term commitment toward digital change in education. By comparison, other countries were just moving toward formalized practices in the area of digital learning, and in some instances, they were instituting formal strategies in decades. Although some governments provided large sums of money to ensure such policies were met, including balancing the costs of purchasing new equipment, upgrades within the network and professional development, other governments, especially in developing countries were unable to prioritize digital learning within their national budgets [12].

There were also differences when it came to the way digital education was governed and accomplished. A federal or decentralized system left the infrastructure provision and rules of pedagogy at regional or provincial level and thus, even within a country the provision of, as well as the rules governing, together with approaches to pedagogy in different regions differed. Differences in the use of available resources did exist on a centralized system although there was more coherent directive on centralized systems whereas in some cases schools were not only high on their spending and implementation discretion.

Among the most evident ones in most education systems included a lack of systematic monitoring and evaluation of the effectiveness of their digital policy. Although sporadic forms of evaluation were in place, systematic processes to evaluate the effects of technology integration on learning, teaching and equity were far and in between.

- During the COVID-19 Pandemic

Education systems had to live up to the challenge with an urgency never seen before, as pandemic school closures spread all over the world between 2020 and 2022. However, countries with already established digital learning infrastructure and trainings programmes of teachers were in a better position to switch to remote learning. Nevertheless, even such systems had problems, especially with regards to offering equal access to the underprivileged students.

The governments worldwide had spent a lot of resources to broaden digital materials, develop online learning platforms, and transmit education through TV and radio. In other settings, there emerged central hub authorities providing web-based textbooks, syllabi, teaching classroom resources and additional materials in multiple languages. The broadcast medium, through television channels, public broadcasting, and private media houses was pertinent in giving lessons to students who had poor access to an internet connection [13].

In many countries, there were major plans that each student would now be given an electronic device-maybe a laptop or tablet-with high-speed internet connections. Additional subsidies were also provided to connectivity needs of low-income earning households. In addition to increasing the infrastructure, there were new regulations that were raised to help schools, teachers, and parents to cope with online and blended learning settings. These strategies covered many different issues, including how to plan the lessons of all types of learners and how to protect cyber security in online classes.

Countries were in a position to make the switch with low disruption where they had established one-to-one device programmes and a strong digital ecosystem including the presence of well equipped separate schools. Nonetheless, in low-resource settings, there was a lack of access, teacher readiness, and digital literacy. This contributed to further directing the digital gap, mostly to rural and low-income groups. Policy wise, certain nations established new practices and solely to deal with the pandemic situation, whereas others modified the already existing ones. Quite a number of these temporary solutions displaced pre-pandemic digital strategic education plans and instead turned their minds toward salvaging continuity in teaching by implementing short term solutions.

- After the COVID-19 Pandemic

With the restrictions of the pandemic being lifted and teaching in real life starting back up, many of the emergency digital efforts were reduced or tossed out. Rather than indicating that a paradigm shift in education provision had occurred permanently, post-reopening created a swift backlash to conventional face-to-face learning in most jurisdictions. Even the hybrid and blended forms of learning were only kept in situations where it could be taken to be special, sometimes being special rather than being mainstream.

One could clearly note policy development slowdown in digital education in certain countries. As investments in infrastructure remained, including the renovation of classrooms, increases in broadband, and an updating of facilities, few signs of widespread pedagogical innovation or strategy could be found. As an illustration, massive investments were made to replace conventional classrooms by more technologically advanced learning facilities, although the release of finer details in the course of implementation and proper allocation of resources in the capacity-building of teachers was not undertaken in most of the education systems. Even then there were some exceptions as countries leveraged the post-pandemic situation to institutionalize the national plans regarding digital-led change in education which involved schedules and roadmap of teacher training along with educational data analytics integration. Roadmaps were published in these instances to describe short-, medium- and long-term goals of utilizing data to make decisions, enhance learning and guarantee excellent delivery of digital education. There was also a weak policy framework in most education systems of emerging technologies, especially artificial intelligence (AI), a permanent challenge. Although the AI tools already started affecting the field of education, few countries have already provided even non-mandatory advice on the responsible introduction of AI practices and the ethical use of the tools [14].

6 Overall Observations

Changes in the digital education policy that occurred during the pre-pandemic, pandemic, and post-pandemic periods prove the development and the current unresolved issues. The crisis also led to the unprecedented investments in the sphere of technology and increased the pace of the transfer toward remote learning. But in numerous instances these benefits were never fully institutionalized within long-term policy systems. Those that had high pre-pandemic digital strategy fared better overall in the transition, though even they did not do very well on equity. Infrastructure constraints and money shortages were claims of many common core challenges especially in developing regions despite the new technological solutions like the use of TV and radio as a learning medium. Going into the future, creating, and maintaining the momentum during the pandemic is the major challenge. This involves not only further investment in infrastructures but also coherent policy implementations, training of teachers, equity-oriented projects, and pathways to the new technologies. In the absence of such broad planning, the likelihood of losing the gains of the crisis and opportunity to establish more future-ready and inclusive education systems can be missed.

7 Conclusion

The current era is a stage in which the world has become a place in which digital technology has established and predetermined virtually every product of life in the world. With education as one of the key aspects of social and economic development, this area has also experienced a radical change as a result of digitalization. Although the previous policies and educational commissions proposed the introduction of technology into learning and teaching processes, the actual driving force of the change was observed in recent few years and specifically following the COVID-19 pandemic hitting the world. The new reality inflicted by the pandemic rushed changes in the use of digital tech and online learning strategies so that it ceased being a tool supporting the process of education but a source of life on its own.

Previously, learners significantly depended on the single education center, staff, and facilities in the learning process. This gave rise to restriction regarding exposure to various topics, knowledge, and views. Nevertheless, the modern perspective of education focuses on students' cooperation, learning sharing, and interdisciplinary education. In this strategy, students will be given the opportunity to be exposed to various school of thoughts, they will also leverage the quality of educators working in other institutions and they will be in a position to have an expansive view of their field of study. This is conceptualized as an ecosystem whereby the institutions now do not operate in silos but rather collaborate and better the learning experience.

What has emerged is technology as the engine of this change. The online learning course, online classroom, educational applications, video conferencing tools, and interactive content help students to study without interruption despite the geographical or physical distance. The tools do not only guarantee uninterrupted learning in situations of emergencies, like the pandemic, but also provide a chance of self-paced learning, individual instruction, and worldwide resources. Lectures, live classes and discussion forums, digital libraries all see to it that the students are taught at their own ease and can even explore what is beyond the boundaries of the curriculum.

The digital divide has to be dealt with in a multifaceted manner. The projects by the government including national digital campaigns are vital in enhancing internet connectivity, access to affordable internet service, and the supply of devices to students in low-income areas. Of equal significance is the facilitation of digital literacy to make sure that both learners and teachers are educated on the use of technological devices. Another role that educational institutions could play is to collaborate with technology providers to develop cost effective and easy to use platforms to achieve the needs of various learners. Moreover, cooperation between the public and the private sector may allow providing more resources and infrastructure to distant settlements, which will make digital education possible to everyone.

On the one hand, as one looks into the future, the extent of the use of technology in education is only going to increase. With artificial intelligence, machine learning and data analytics innovations finding their way deeper in the educational space, tailored learning will become more advanced than ever before. Such technologies have the ability to analyze the data about the ,students' performance identifying strengths and weaknesses, suggest individual learning paths and monitor progress in a more accurate way. Such data-centered approach will contribute to making educational experiences more personalized.

To sum up, technology integration into the learning process is an essential and rather revolutionary move toward the creation of the future of education. It facilitates the interaction between institutions and fosters interdisciplinary learning, continuity in the event of an interruption, and skills a student in facing the dynamics of a changing world. Yet, to have its positive sides accessible to everyone, the active work should be provided on the reduction of the digital divide via enhanced infrastructure, affordable access, and digital literacy programs. With the use of technological progress, inclusive policies, and devout teachers, the perspective of a digitally powerful and enlightened population will be attained.

References

1. Kaufman, J., Diliberti, M., Hunter, G., Grant, D., Hamilton, L., Schwartz, H., Setodji, C., Snoke, J., & Young, C. (2020). *COVID-19 and the state of K-12 schools: Results and technical documentation from the fall 2020 American educator panels COVID-19 surveys*. RAND Corporation eBooks. https://doi.org/10.7249/rra168-5
2. Hamilton, L., Kaufman, J., & Diliberti, M. (2020). *Teaching and leading through a pandemic: Key findings from the American educator panels spring 2020 COVID-19 surveys*. RAND Corporation eBooks. https://doi.org/10.7249/rra168-2
3. Rankin, J. G. (2022). *First aid for teacher burnout*. https://doi.org/10.4324/9781003281320
4. Golden, G. (2020). *Education policy evaluation*. OECD Education Working Papers. https://doi.org/10.1787/9f127490-en
5. Papadakis, S., Kiv, A., Kravtsov, H., Osadchyi, V., Marienko, M., Pinchuk, O., Shyshkina, M., Sokolyuk, O., Минтій, I., Vakaliuk, T., Azarova, L., Kolgatina, L., Amelina, S., Volkova, N., Velychko, V., Striuk, A., & Семеріков, C. (2023). *Unlocking the power of synergy: The joint force of cloud technologies and augmented reality in education*. https://doi.org/10.31812/123456789/7399
6. Karakose, T., Kocabas, I., Yirci, R., Papadakis, S., Ozdemir, T. Y., & Demirkol, M. (2022). The development and evolution of digital leadership: A bibliometric mapping approach-based study. *Sustainability, 14*(23), 16171. https://doi.org/10.3390/su142316171
7. Guamán-Carranza, A. R. (2024). Los entornos virtuales y su importancia en el desempeño docente. *Revista Arbitrada Interdisciplinaria Koinonía, 9*(17), 238–256. https://doi.org/10.35381/r.k.v9i17.3217
8. Bohara, P. S. (2024). Supporting teachers in implementing project-based learning in teaching secondary mathematics: An action research. *Advances in Mobile Learning Educational Research, 4*(2), 1122–1134. https://doi.org/10.25082/amler.2024.02.007
9. Vahos, L. E. G., Muñoz, L. E. M., & Londoño-Vásquez, D. A. (2019). Teacher's role in the meaningful learning achievement based on ICT. *Revista Encuentros, 17*(02), 1907. https://doi.org/10.15665/encuent.v17i02.1907
10. Baque-Castro, G. Y., & Vigueras-Moreno, J. A. (2021). El docente y su desempeño en la educación virtual. *Polo Del Conocimiento: Revista Científico-Profesional, 6*(3), 991–1005. https://doi.org/10.23857/pc.v6i3.2417
11. Akinbadewa, B. O., & Sofowora, O. A. (2020). The effectiveness of multimedia instructional learning packages in enhancing secondary school

students' attitudes toward biology. *International Journal on Studies in Education, 2*(2), 119–133. https://doi.org/10.46328/ijonse.19

12. Chindia, B., & Wawire, S. N. (2024). Student attitudes towards smartphone use in a pre-service teacher tech course. *Advances in Mobile Learning Educational Research, 4*(1), 994–1006. https://doi.org/10.25082/amler.2024.01.011
13. Diliberti, M. K., Schwartz, H. L., & Grant, D. (2021). *Stress topped the reasons why public school teachers quit, even before COVID-19*. RAND Corporation eBooks. https://doi.org/10.7249/rra1121-2
14. Darling-Hammond, L., Saunders, R., Podolsky, A., Kini, T., Espinoza, D., Hyler, M., & Carver-Thomas, D. (2019). *Best practices to recruit and retain well-prepared teachers in all classrooms*. Learning Policy Institute. Accessed 10th August, 2025. https://learningpolicyinstitute.org/sites/default/files/product-files/Leandro_Best_Practices_Recruit_Retain_REPORT.pdf

CHAPTER 6

Leveraging Green Technologies in Schools: Sustainability and Carbon Footprint Reduction through Digital Tools

Abhay Raj Singh, Arunima Shastri, Saurabh Chandra, and Urmila Yadav

Abstract This study is exploring how Information Technology has become imperative in the promotion of environmentally sustainable activities, energy savings, and reduced carbon footprints in present-day organizations. With environmental responsibility having established itself

A. R. Singh
Pitney Bowes, Orange, CT, USA

A. Shastri
CHRIST University, Bangalore, India
e-mail: arunima.shastri@christuniversity.in

S. Chandra (✉)
School of Law, Bennett University, Greater Noida, India
e-mail: saurabhchandranls@gmail.com

U. Yadav
Sharda University, Greater Noida, India

P. K. Dutta et al. (eds.), *Digital Education for a Sustainable Future*, Sustainable Development Goals Series,
https://doi.org/10.1007/978-3-032-15433-0_6

as a strategic focus, IT takes on both a strategic role as efficiency booster as well as an enabling powerhouse of sustainable change. The chapter takes the form of survey research design to examine the perceptions of organizations and their implementation and adaptation of IT solutions to achieve sustainability objectives. It has a theoretical based on the creation of the structure of a questionnaire considering a deep study of the literature on the issue and knowledge of the specialists of the field. The chapter includes various organizational engagement factors such as organizational demographics, the current state of IT infrastructures, the level of awareness and implementation of green IT solutions and sustainability strategic plans into the future. The given method is necessary to make sure that the captured data can help understand the current state of IT adoption as well as the future orientation of organizational strategies. It provides a comprehensive outline to understand the factors that run green IT adoption and provide strategic routes to organizations to strengthen their environmental responsibility while maintaining competition in the digital economy.

Keywords Green IT · Sustainability · Energy efficiency · Carbon footprint reduction · Organizational strategy

1 Introduction

Over the past few years, the interflow of Information Technology and the notions of Green IT and sustainable development has become an extensively popular subject matter in almost every corner of the world. Due to the fast technological advancements and the ever-increasing need of the energy, more people become aware of the climate impact the big IT infrastructure may have. This awareness has prompted governments, corporations, and institutions to re-define conventional practices with a higher stake being laid on the strategies that incorporate the use of IT platforms to help counter the threats to the environment coupled with further pursuing the objectives of sustainability. The qualitative elements are incorporated in the study to develop a richer insight of the subject matter. The statistical results are complemented by interviews, case study, and narrative analyses, which provide more in-depth understandings of real world success and impediments that organizations face. The practical challenges brought to the fore by these qualitative perspectives include budgetary pressures, change resistance, technological shortcomings and patronage gaps in the policy implementation. Simultaneously, they also bring out best practices that can be emulated as industrial practices. These results are highly indictive of the need to integrate sustainable IT practices as part and parcel in the operational plans of organizations. They indicate to the necessity of collaboration between the industries, common purpose of policies, and technological improvements in finding efficient solutions to the urgent issues related to the environment. It is important to note that, in the research, proactive strategies are shown to fully incorporate Green IT practices, including energy-efficient data centers, virtualization and cloud computing, and acceptable e-waste management, to achieve significant improvements in sustainability performance of organizations and to realize cost efficiencies as well as resiliency in operations.

The recommendations arising from this research are based in the results of statistical model and cost-profit analysis. They provide practical, actionable guidance for organizations to design and implement impressive green IT strategies. These include investing in scalable and flexible infrastructure, promoting employee awareness and engagement, taking advantage of data analytics for stability tracking, and collaborating with government and non-government agencies to align with global environmental standards. Ultimately, this research contributes to the growing body of knowledge of how it can serve as a catalyst for sustainable development within organizational contexts [1].

Green IT is an elaborate concept that focuses on minimizing the impacts of IT activities on nature and increasing productivity of the technology-based systems. The major philosophy behind Green IT has been to reduce negative environmental impact of technology and at the same time make sure that the resources, especially consumption of energy is efficient, sustainable and cost effective today. This comes in form of introducing new technologies like virtualization, cloud-based computing, server consolidation and smart cooling technology in the data center. The implementation of such energy-saving activities will help organizations save considerable power, prolong the period of usage of the hardware and decline the levels of e-waste production.

An important part of sustainable IT plan is carbon footprints and their mitigation. Companies are getting more aggressive when it comes to investing on sophisticated tools and measures in order to quantify, evaluate and monitor their greenhouse gas emissions. These monitoring not only enable businesses to establish measurable sustainability objectives but also give them an opportunity to be in line with the global climate agreements like the Paris agreement, and work toward climate change mitigation globally. Other than energy-efficient hardware, and optimized software solutions, IT also transforms and makes it possible to manage the infrastructure smarter. Artificial intelligence (AI), machine learning (ML) and IoT-based environmental monitoring provide more responsive, adaptive and predictive energy management systems. Such technologies require real-time analysis and decision-making, thus, potentially cutting down on redundant energy consumption and insufficient operations by several magnitudes [2].

Besides that, the growing number of case studies, pilot projects, and best practice frameworks has turned into an effective source of knowledge to the practitioners, policymakers, and even researchers. With a review of such instances, it is possible to note not only a novelty in approach on using technology but also the successful partnerships between governments and business that have played significant roles in launching sustainable IT processes. Such partnerships emphasize the significance of the partnering efforts to fund research, roll out big projects and lay down the set regulatory provisions that promote accountable technological advancement.

The on-going transformation of the concept of Green IT shows that, sustainability in technology is far more than a mere corporate social responsibility initiative, but is a tactical imperative that affects the operational performance, brand image, and the eventual competitiveness front. Practicing environmentally friendly IT will enable businesses to cut down operating expenses, make themselves resilient to the risks of environmental change and emerge as market leaders in the shift to the low-carbon economy. It is within such a context that this paper attempts to give a detailed overview of latest trends, emerging practices, and emerging technologies that are influencing the field of Green IT and sustainable development. The examination of the latest trends, the analysis of their effects, and the recognition of the possible gaps make this research an attempt to provide practical conclusions which could be utilized in the future planning of using IT as the element of environmental awareness. The end goal is to lay the groundwork to establish a future in which both technological creativity and ecological management move forward in concert with one another toward the creation of a digitally advanced and ecologically sustainable global environment [3].

2 Relevance and Importance of the Chapter

Schools using green technology are a big step toward sustainability and transforms how we think about being responsible for the environment in schools. Schools are adopting technology to make their classrooms more environmentally friendly and lower their carbon impact. Schools are also helping to lower carbon footprints by using digital technology to make students more aware of the environment. Smart boards that use less energy, cloud-based discussion boards, and virtual labs are all instances of new technologies that use fewer resources than older ones. Online assignments and digital textbooks, for example, get rid of paper waste. Virtual experiments take the place of costly or impractical real-life ones. For example, you can learn about renewable energy sources without taking up too many non-renewable resources, or you can test the strength of a material at different temperatures. Another good thing is that smart building systems, such climate controls and automatic lighting, make schools use less energy. Students can use these tools, including apps that help them figure out their carbon footprint or games that teach them about sustainable solutions, to deal with current environmental problems in a fun way. They can also assist promote sustainability and social change. This transition turns schools become centers of green innovation by using technology that helps with instruction and environmental care. By making sustainability a part of teaching, learning, and running the school, green technologies encourage students and teachers to become advocates for a better future that is good for the world.

3 Background of Study

The Green Information Technology (Green IT) and sustainability segment has been experiencing significant innovations, both on the academic and applied level during the past decade, 2000 to 2009. It was in this decade that a shift has occurred where the technological innovation started to be regarded as an increasingly viable strategic means to resolve urgent environmental concerns and promote long-term sustainability of business. The industry authorities, academicians and organizations started to research on the application of information technology as an effective way not only in operational efficiency but also in facilitating environmental responsibility.

At this time research studies were emphasizing potential transformative properties of IT in regard to improving environmental performance especially in terms of energy efficiency, resource optimization, and carbon footprint reduction. Green IT, that include: server virtualization, use of energy-efficient equipment, data center consolidation, power management systems usage, became vital steps toward power reduction and greenhouse emission mitigation. Such initiatives not only served the purpose of environmental initiatives but also saved a lot of money to organizations and therefore made them strongly convincing reasons to be implemented [4].

Studies also underlined the importance of integrating IT on supply chain management as a way of enhancing sustainability in the industry. Incorporation of the IT-enabled system, comprising sophisticated tracking technology, computerized control system inventory and real-time data sharing program, bolstered the sense of transparency and enhanced the effectiveness of the supply chain considerably. The developments enabled effective management of resources, the reduction of wastage of materials, the optimization of logistics and the promotion of environmentally friendly purchasing habits. Technology assisted organizations in avoiding waste of resources by simplifying processes and making it possible to accurately forecast the real demand thus enabling them to achieve a balance between preventing the waste of resources and remaining competitive in the market.

There was an increasing use of IT in the transportation sector toward reaching an environmental goal as well. Smart transportations, traffic control systems, and the high technology of optimizing routes were increasingly used to decrease the traffic, enhance efficiency of travel and save fuel. These innovations were powerful contributors to emission reductions, energy efficiency, and sustainable urban movement. Collectively, the research and development of this decade outlines a paradigm change in its perception—only as an operational originator, which is recognized as an important component of environmental stability strategies. The adoption of Green IT, integration of technical solutions in supply chain operations, and the application of intelligent systems in transport showed a developed understanding of the role of technology in creating a more sustainable future. These progress showed that environmental responsibility and economic viability can go in hand, laying a strong foundation for future innovations in permanent technology practices [5].

4 Gaps of This Study

End-users behavior may be considered as a critical element toward success or failure of the Green Information Technology (Green IT) projects aimed at ensuring sustainable environment in organizations. Although eco-friendly IT solutions, such as energy-efficient data centers or cloud-based resource optimization, are now available following the increased technological achievement, there is a significant gap in the knowledge regarding human behavior in designing the solution adoption, sustained use, and high overall efficacy. The existence of this gap continues since being technologically ready is never enough; instead, perceptions, attitudes, and daily behavior of users, specifically, predict the extent to which such initiatives will result in any significant sustainability outcomes. In considering user behavior with regard to Green IT, there is a need to find out in depth psychological, social, and organizational determinants, which guide decision-making. Among the main ones, one could note the perceptions of people regarding the role of being spiritually environmentally concerned in IT practices, the level of information about the solutions of their type, as well as the personal or group motives leading to their further implementation or the lack thereof. Some users can be inspired by the environmental responsibility sense, whereas others can be stimulated by the organizational perspective, cost saving prospect, and/or by social acclaim. In contrast, the lack of awareness, the intention of perceived inconvenience, the insufficient training, or resistance to change barriers may contribute greatly to the slackening of the adoption of sustainable IT practices [6].

In work places whereby, the element of sustainability is incorporated in the corporate identity and apparent advocacy by the leadership structure, the employees tend to incorporate the aspect of Green IT in the day to day performance. Conversely, in the setting which does not prioritize the specified values or does not promote them successfully, even the most sophisticated technological gadgets can be left underused. It is important to appreciate such behavioral factors in the development of any intervention that not only offers the much needed technological resources, but also ensures a positive climate of behavior change. Specific strategies can incorporate being systematic in terms of training and development of technical and environmental literacy, creating awareness through creation of benefits that are concrete in terms of adoption of Green IT and behavioral nudges in terms of encouraging the behavior of adoption through subtle efforts without forcing anyone into strict stipulations. Economic aspects like points or rewards toward sustainable actions or rewarded achievements based on performance can also be used to further encourage people to participate and motivate a feeling of shared success [7].

The correlation between the conduct of the users and the adoption of Green IT practices is multidimensional and covers both rational and emotional factors. Although economic and efficiency factors tend to prevail at the initial stages of the decision-making process, sustainability programs are often maintained by the underlying moral principles of environmental protection and sound ethical conduct. This emphasizes that when it comes to behavior change, organizations must deal with the practical and the motivational areas of behavior change. This investigation by a mix of qualitative exploration and analysis of empirical evidence is expected to give an overall insight into the human variables that gives rise to Green IT adoption. Correlations and causal relationships between demographics of the users, their attitudes, and adoption rates can be determined with the aid of quantitative methods, whereas such qualitative approaches as interviews, focus groups, and case studies can provide subtle details into personal situations and organizational context.

The results of such an investigation will presumably benefit both the scholarly theory and practice. Theoretically, the research will contribute to different models of technology adoption by incorporating the consideration of behavioral features in technology in order to fill in a determining gap in literatures. In practical terms, it will provide the organizations with some actionable advice on how to implement user engagement, address resistance, and meshing eco-friendly IT practices with everyday operations. Green IT cannot be assessed on the complexity of the deployed technology being simple but on the willingness and the capacity of users to adjust their actions to sustainable goals. With technological innovation as well as prioritizing human engagement, the organization can create a co–operative framework that not only meets operating requirements, but also wide environmental targets. Such an approach ensures that investment in Green IT receives maximum returns—in terms of organizational performance and the collective effort to reduce the environmental impact of digital technologies [8].

5 Solving the Green IT Problem Implementing of the Information Technology

The importance of Green IT and sustainability initiatives to the present research paper will be addressed by the use of a survey-based paper design intended to track the perception, implementation, and preparation of organizations to adopt environmentally sustainable processes. The emphasis is on the implementation of the Information Technology (IT) to realize energy efficiency, carbon footprints, and incorporation of green processes in structures of organizations. The chapter includes several questions grouped into several sections including the present extent of IT adoption, the specific green IT measures adopted, difficulty areas of implementation and the future sustainability plans [9]. The steps assist in identifying the factors that carry the greatest and measurable influence on the adoption of sustainability. The chapter gives a clearer picture of the most efficient strategies of influencing the environmental responsibility in the organization through quantifying the relative impact of each initiative. This evidence-based approach will not only determine the areas that should be prioritized as it relates to investing in the areas but will also aid in development of specific policies and practices that would be established in order to achieve integration of Green IT in all the industries.

6 Limitation of Study

The discoveries and revelations available in this study will provide meaningful information to the study of the overall contribution of green IT practices toward driving sustainability development. Some limitations should be mentioned to put the outcomes in the perspective. Among the limitations is the fact that the sample used is relatively small and convenience based and can therefore have an impact on how far the results can be applied on a large population. Also, the adoption of qualitative research practices, including case studies or interviews, has the risk of subjectivity and influence of the researcher on the analysis of the findings [10].

Although these approaches offer deep and insightful opinions, they might be incomplete and the addition of a more solid questionnaire, e.g., massive surveys or even experiments might give a more comprehensive picture, which would be statistically significant. The study is also relatively short, and hence the fact that it cannot be used to capture the long-term effects of the use of green IT initiatives that occur in the long run. Longitudinal research would consequently be more applicable in measuring the slow changes and long-term effects. The impact of green IT on the sustainable development proves to be a challenge to quantify. Despite the attention given to major indicators like energy saving and carbon footprint reduction among others, there can always be more considerations that have not been exhaustedly addressed in this study like resource efficiencies, effect on the supply chain and worker engagement. Intimating measurement reviews to encompass a greater number of variables may improve the precision of a future studies.

Another factor to consider here is that external forces that might impact such issues are also highly possible; this could include changes in the economic situation, alteration of policy, or a sudden leap in technology. The influence of these external dynamics on organizational greet-IT implementation strategies can be studied further. Lastly, since the study was made in a given industry, the effect might not be related to some other professions. Extending the scope of investigation to include diverse industries will help develop more overall understanding of relationships between green IT practices and sustainable development. By accepting these boundaries, future research can address existing gaps, construct the foundation here, and contribute to more effective strategies to take advantage of green as the driver of environmental responsibility and permanent development.

7 Ethical Considerations

In this study, the rights, dignity, and privacy of study participants were preserved according to ethical principles that were given the top priority. Prior to participating, the person was explicitly advised on the objectives of the research, the process involved and the risks or advantages whenever there are no benefits. It was completely voluntary, and warm consent was obtained by all the participants, since they were informed that they could refuse the participation at any point without any adverse effects. When it comes to ensuring confidentiality, digesting information obtained during interviews, questionnaires, and other techniques, the most attention was paid to their utmost care and security. The identities of the participants were anonymized and none of their personally identifiable information became disclosed at a particular stage. The rules of data protection were observed and the personal data was used only within the scope of the research; it was stored in a secure place so that no third parties could obtain it [11]. An adherent and professional relationship was established with all the subjects and cared about their contribution and fair balance was maintained in the relationship that exists between the researcher and the subject. The study was professionally conducted by the necessary ethics committee, and followed the established ethical ethics. Such actions afforded the rights and welfare of the participants and boosted the credibility and reliability of the study as well as the integrity of the studio findings.

8 Energy and Environmental Impact

Information Technology (IT) and its effect on the environment is a highly-complicated and far-reaching issue especially when it comes to the amount of energy used by IT and its role in the creation of carbon emissions. Servers alone and particularly data centers are considered the emitter of millions of metric tons of CO2 equivalents annually because of their excessive power consumption. As an example, in certain areas it reaches beyond 28 million metric tons per year, underlining the magnitude of the problem [12].

Computer energy consumption is highly dependent on the age of the computer, specifications of the computer hardware, and the usage patterns. A desktop PC has an average power use of between 66 watts and 66 watts in idle mode and roughly 1.9 watts during sleep mode. Laptops that tend to be more energy-efficient use about 33 watts just sitting idle but draw only 1 watt again in sleep mode. Smaller components also contribute to the energy demand as a whole, with an average 17 inch LED LCD monitor consuming around 13 watts in operation, 0.4 watts in stand-by mode and approximately 0.3 watts in off-mode situations. In taking a three years perspective of usages of life cycle energy consumption by a standard computer, the summation amounts at roughly 4222 KWh. Nor at the operational phase does this energy all go to waste; surprisingly, only a third is utilized here; most is consumed in the manufacturing. In case of personal computers, the manufacturing stage contributes approximately 60 to 85 percent of the total energy input into the life cycle of the product whereas, in case of mobile phones, the figure varies between 50 and 60 percent.

Remanufacturing, on the other hand, which involves refurbishment and reuse of devices, uses only a fraction of such energy. In terms of personal computers, the energy use process contains only 5–30% of that required during first manufacture and in mobile phones only 5%. Such statistics provide a clear picture of the fact that by repairing, refurbishing, and reusing products, companies can dramatically decrease the environmental impact of their IT equipment.

9 Readiness for Clear and Comprehensive Green IT Policy

It is also necessary that a clear and comprehensive Green IT policy should be developed in order to direct sustainable technology behavior within an organization. Among such a policy, there should be energy-efficient acquisition of hardware, responsible disposal of e-wastes, and the control of carbon emanation. The frequent energy audit helps in pinpointing the areas that are not efficient, pinpoints the power consuming gear, and also indicates the areas that require improvement. Virtualization and cloud computing will enable the companies to use the resources more efficiently, use less hardware and spend less energy. Energy management technologies, like automatic sleep and dynamic frequency scaling power management capabilities also reduce energy consumption in idle cycles. Optimized cooling, management of airflows and energy-efficient technologies of hardware facilitate the achievement of data center efficiency. Training and creating awareness among the employees on such habits as powering off unutilized devices, setting power saving mechanisms will also contribute. An organized e-waste scheme, coupled with qualified recyclers, will result in safe disposal of out-dated machinery. The combination of renewable energy sources, e.g. solar or wind, minimizes the usage of the non-renewable power. Energy tracking and emissions monitoring systems are beneficial to informed decision-making and optimizing, which eventually can result in ongoing improvement. Lastly, the ability to connect with industry networks and engage in green IT research enhances the process of innovation and makes an organization in tandem with the most current green practices [13].

10 Research Discussion

The study concerning the use of Information Technology (IT) in the process of green IT project and sustainable development provides useful insights into the idea that the technology can be properly exploited in order to facilitate environmental responsibility, increase the energy consumption efficiencies, and minimize carbon footprints. These results highlight why IT plays an important role in helping to solve ecological issues and sustainable business behavior.

Another conclusion made in the study is that the only way to implement green IT initiatives is to establish strong cooperation among IT professionals, policymakers, industry leaders, and other concerned actors. This implies the need to act together and strategic cooperation in the pursuit of sustainability. The future research would be to explore cooperation models and structures which can effectively coordinate various sectors to make sure that green IT practices have smooth adoption. The study similarly finds the need of establishing clear methods and ideal practices that harness the potential of IT as far as environmental sustainability is concerned to the fullest extent. Although several case studies and examples provided by the industry are referred to throughout the study, further discussion of specific ones might help to identify the decisive factors that lead to their success, providing effective guidance to which organizations striving to implement green IT solutions in their business might be referred.

Future study may look into long-term financial gains of sustainable IT practices in the form of cost-benefit analyses and returns on investment. This would aid organizations in enacting informed decision that prioritize environmental efforts among other reasons in rationale the commitment of resource toward sustainability programs. Government policies and regulatory systems are other limiting factors to embracing green IT. There is a need to do more studies to assess the efficiency of various policy strategies, incentives, and relevant legislation in order to promote the use of technology in a manner that is environmentally conscientious. Cross-country comparisons of jurisdictions with different policy models can provide much information as to what kind of governmental intervention is the most efficient one [14].

Another area that is worth looking at is the understanding the perceptions and preferences of consumers with respect to green IT products and services. Surveys and market study organizations can provide public demand with the knowledge required to align their offerings, which increases adopting environmentally friendly IT solutions. Finally, given the rapid pace of technological advancement, ongoing research should focus on emerging innovations in green. This involves the discovery of renewable energy integration, smart grid technologies, internet of things

(IOT) applications that can support permanent technology practices. Beyond these developments, organizations can be compatible with future trends and make a meaningful contribution to global environmental goals.

11 Conclusion

The chapter endeavors into a detailed analysis of how the Information Technology (IT) can be used to drive the green IT agenda and sustainable development. The results demonstrate that IT has strong potentials in influencing the environment, energy efficiency, and reducing carbon emissions. The study highlights the importance of teamwork between IT experts, policy makers, market leaders, and other stakeholders that will facilitate the successful integration of IT, practices which are environmentally responsible. It provides significant input to the organizations in terms of what to do in order to be able to undertake the adoption of green IT rules in their business practices through the use of some real life case study examples and other industry examples. These methods should be embraced so that companies could reduce their energy loads, have a limited ecological footprint, and make a contribution in the effort to reduce the problem of climate change. Although these seem to be positive observations, there are some areas that the study has identified as vital areas that need to be conditioned. Extended research into individual case studies is warranted in order to identify the major factors which lead to successful implementation of green IT. Such an analysis would be beneficial in other organizations that want to incorporate similar initiatives by providing real-life learning lessons and recommendations to take. The economic benefits of utilizing green IT can teach an organization to prioritize its projects, optimize resources and inculcate sustainability in their fundamental business models. And one should also research the effectiveness of the current government policies and regulations in ensuring an environmentally sustainable IT practice. The international comparison of countries with various policy provisions would be a potential way to define the most influential governmental strategies, which would provide the evidence-based guidance in the policy formulation and the development of efficient incentives systems.

The other issue of concern is consumer perception and demand toward green product and services in IT. Market research and survey activities directed at finding out such preferences may inform businesses to properly align their offerings with consumer expectations, therefore, making them more likely to adopt environmentally friendly technologies. Since technology development shares a fast rate of its progress, it is also vital to consider chapters of new possibilities that might become the future of green IT. Such areas as the integration of renewable energies, smart grids, and Internet of Things (IoT) as applied to sustainability can be regarded as beneficial areas of future research. Comprehension of such dynamic trends will enable organizations to be on the cutting edge of practical sources that are sustainable to technology. The study will increase the awareness of the possibility of IT being an effective motor to bring about sustainable development. Implementation of the identified strategies and practices will enable organizations to utilize the power of IT in reducing energy consumption, minimizing environmental footprint, and helping to establish a greener planet. Further exploration of the outlined directions would not only promote the field of green IT, but also will enhance the notion of sustainability implementation in various industries that are currently experiencing enormous popularity.

References

1. Baygi, R. M., Introna, L. D., & Hultin, L. (2021). Everything flows: Studying continuous socio-technological transformation in a fluid and dynamic digital world. *MIS Quarterly, 45*(1), 423–452. https://doi.org/10.25300/misq/2021/15887
2. Zimmer, M. P., & Järveläinen, J. (2022). Digital–Sustainable Co-transformation: Introducing the triple bottom line of sustainability to digital transformation research. In IFIP Advances in Information and Communication Technology (pp. 100–111). https://doi.org/10.1007/978-3-031-15688-5_10
3. Ekardt, F., Günther, P., Hagemann, K., Garske, B., Heyl, K., & Weyland, R. (2023). Legally binding and ambitious biodiversity protection under the CBD, the global biodiversity framework, and human rights law. *Environmental Sciences Europe, 35*(1), 80. https://doi.org/10.1186/s12302-023-00786-5
4. Van Wynsberghe, A. (2021). Sustainable AI: AI for sustainability and the sustainability of AI. *AI and Ethics, 1*(3), 213–218. https://doi.org/10.1007/s43681-021-00043-6
5. Drechsler, K., Gregory, R., Wagner, H., & Tumbas, S. (2020). At the crossroads between digital innovation and digital transformation. *Communications of the Association for Information Systems, 47*, 521–538. https://doi.org/10.17705/1cais.04723

6. Christmann, A., Crome, C., Graf-Drasch, V., Oberländer, A. M., & Schmidt, L. (2024). The twin transformation butterfly. *Business & Information Systems Engineering, 66*(4), 489–505. https://doi.org/10.1007/s12599-023-00847-2
7. Zeiss, R., Ixmeier, A., Recker, J., & Kranz, J. (2020). Mobilising information systems scholarship for a circular economy: Review, synthesis, and directions for future research. *Information Systems Journal, 31*(1), 148–183. https://doi.org/10.1111/isj.12305
8. Baskerville, R. L., Myers, M. D., & Yoo, Y. (2020). Digital first: The Ontological reversal and new challenges for information systems research. *MIS Quarterly, 44*(2), 509–523. https://doi.org/10.25300/misq/2020/14418
9. Hilali, W. E., Manouar, A. E., Idrissi, M., & a. J. (2020). Reaching sustainability during a digital transformation: A PLS approach. *International Journal of Innovation Science, 12*(1), 52–79. https://doi.org/10.1108/ijis-08-2019-0083
10. Gurbaxani, V., & Dunkle, D. (2019). Gearing up for successful digital transformation. *MIS Quarterly Executive, 18*(3), 209–220. https://doi.org/10.17705/2msqe.00017
11. Hanelt, A., Bohnsack, R., Marz, D., & Marante, C. A. (2020). A systematic review of the literature on digital transformation: Insights and implications for strategy and organizational change. *Journal of Management Studies, 58*(5), 1159–1197. https://doi.org/10.1111/joms.12639
12. Vial, G. (2019). Understanding digital transformation: A review and a research agenda. *The Journal of Strategic Information Systems, 28*(2), 118–144. https://doi.org/10.1016/j.jsis.2019.01.003
13. Bashir, H. (2022). Leveraging technology to communicate sustainability-related product information: Evidence from the field. *Journal of Cleaner Production, 362*, 132508. https://doi.org/10.1016/j.jclepro.2022.132508
14. Wessel, L., Baiyere, A., Ologeanu-Taddei, R., Cha, J., & Jensen, T. B. (2021). Unpacking the difference between digital transformation and IT-enabled organizational transformation. *Journal of the Association for Information Systems, 22*(1), 102–129. https://doi.org/10.17705/1jais.00655

CHAPTER 7

Digital Feminism and Inclusion in STEM Education Platforms Bridging Gender Equality in Technology

Laeeq R. Janjua, Tarun Kumar Kaushik, and Anurag Singh

Abstract Rapid evolution of digital technologies has provided enormous opportunities to rectify some of the long-standing social inequality, especially as related to women, and encourage their empowerment in the new era. Technology as a transformative tool in increasing the involvement of women, be it in education, entrepreneurship, or in governance, helps close the gender gap by creating new tools and platforms to do so. The

L. R. Janjua
WSB University, Dąbrowa Górnicza, Poland
e-mail: laeeq.janjua@wsb.edu.pl

T. K. Kaushik (✉)
Sharda School of Law, Sharda University, Greater Noida, India
e-mail: tkaushik1982@gmail.com

A. Singh
Meerut College, Chaudhary Charan Singh University, Meerut, India

P. K. Dutta et al. (eds.), *Digital Education for a Sustainable Future*, Sustainable Development Goals Series,
https://doi.org/10.1007/978-3-032-15433-0_7

digital material, online learning facilities, and innovations in technology offer more women knowledge, expertise, and market possibilities, leading to their ability to directly be more useful in the economic and society building processes. But all is not well with the power of technology in advancing the empowerment of women. Digital opportunities may not be fully exploited by women due to various hindrances in many underdeveloped areas namely: the digital divide, cultural and social barriers, poor infrastructural networks and risks of cybersecurity attacks. The barriers demand specific interventions to make sure that all women reap the technological advantages, irrespective of their geographical/social-economic orientations.

Keywords Women's empowerment · Gender equality · Digital inclusion · Technology access · Digital divide

1 Introduction

Technology has turned to be an inseparable phenomenon in the modern world that has influenced virtually all aspects of human life including communication, employment, education, politics, and access to basic resources. Technological development however has expanded new horizons to women in particular since it has given females the opportunity to overcome social, cultural and economic barriers that have been highly established in the society. Technology has proven to be an effective mechanism by breaking down the societal barriers to facilitate in opening up the world to new futures in learning, entrepreneurship, and political action that women were previously unable to access. This chapter reviews how technology has helped to achieve gender equality by focusing on case studies, international projects, and policies, focusing on the same. The results prove the significance of cooperative outcomes, inclusive decision-making and targeted interventions that will guarantee fair access to digital opportunities. Although technology has unlimited potential to empower women, the cumulative developments require both time and effort, collaboration with other sectors and approaches capable of eliminating both technological and social impediments [1].

Women are able to link to like-minded communities of people, learn new skills, and get access to employment opportunities as well as engage in the process of public discourse, all of which was previously hampered by geography, social norms or lack of mobility. The establishment of women forward business, home work, and online learning systems that allow the more open approach toward self and career realization has also been made possible by digital inventions. Even though technology has the potential to transform, there is still a substantial gender imbalance as far as access, digital skills, and use patterns are concerned. This is the digital divide that is more pronounced in the developing and underdeveloped countries where the females tend to have the hurdles compounded with limited social norms, cultural prejudices, economic constrains and poor technological infrastructures. In such contexts, poor availability of devices, lack of a consistent internet connection, prime prices and low rate of digital literacy seriously limit the opportunities of women to enjoy the fruit of technology development. The problems associated with data security and online safety are compounded by the need to solve online harassment, cyberstalking, and online safety in general, which form residential impediments to women engaging in the online domain.

It is not just technology, but a socio-economic and political necessity to fill this gap. When women participate in social, cultural and economic development, whole communities and economies can greatly benefit through increased possibilities of contributing more to development. This can only be possible through the inclusive development of digital systems. Global and regional initiatives with the aim of shutting down digital gender differences have begun to address these concerns by focusing on strength, infrastructure development, capacity-making programs and the creation of a safe digital environment. This study attempts to detect the intensive impact of technology on women's empowerment, with special attention to how online resources and digital equipment can help women to remove obstacles and actively participate in many areas of life. By examining current challenges—including cost obstacles, online safety concerns and gaps in digital literacy and evaluating the effectiveness of efforts to address them, the purpose of research is to present practical strategies to promote inclusive digital development. Ultimately, the goal is to highlight how similar access to technology can be a catalyst for creating a fair, more inclusive society, where women are not only beneficiaries of technological progress, but also an active contribution to shape a digital future [2].

2 Gender Representation in Digital Spaces

The issue of gender representation in digital environments is very complicated and fluid; it emerges on the border of technologies, culture, and deeply anchored structures of social power. Digital spaces and virtual worlds are not neutral environments but tend to replicate and in many cases exacerbate current structural inequalities and gender norms and stereotypes. The representation of gender, perception of gender, and performance of gender on the internet has a huge implication toward inclusion, equity, and social justice. Although the digital realm can be productive in terms of creating new groupings of self-expression and empowerment, it is potentially dangerous in the sense that it is bound to perpetuate the power structures that prevail in the physical world. In an intersectional sense, what is very important to keep in mind is that, gender cannot be viewed as a stand-alone phenomenon. The interaction of several dimensions of identity: race, ethnicity, class, sexuality and disability, determines experiences with digital environments. Intersectional analysis is a feminist approach to understanding gender, which rejects the idea that any social category is a simple binary, and demonstrates how the structure of advantages and disadvantages within a specific identity group intersect with that of other groups. This strategy has also been specifically applicable to tracing how digital infrastructures and online communities are used to replicate, reproduce, or challenge wider societal divisions [3].

This is serious concern which arises on the basis of such analysis is the role of algorithmic bias. The way they go about search engines, social networks, content recommendation systems and facial recognition programmes is through the use of algorithms which will in turn be based on datasets, which usually carry the historical inequalities. Where these algorithms are not scrutinized or built on inclusively, they can continue discriminatory practices-deforming or omitting particular groups, especially based on gendered and ethnically related characteristics. Consequently, those already oppressed physically might be rendered yet again, even more, invisible, stereotyped, or even damaged online.

Such settings unintentionally erect a wall to individuals, which do not fit into these mainstream cultural definitions. The example is that enforcement of policies and community guidelines tend to indicate partiality. Moderation on Twitch has also caused female-presenting bodies particularly to be censored and regulated more than masculine bodies on the basis of the sexualization and look at femininity rather than masculinity.

Those tendencies are indicative of broader social trends to regulate both female bodies and female behaviors more strictly than those of men as the reflections of the patriarchal values [4].

The emergence of immersive virtual spaces, including the metaverse, also brings more ethical features associated with gender and racial representation. Although it is theoretically freeing to create an avatar and thus explore identity, it begs the question of authenticity, cultural appropriation as well as further solidification of stereotypes. An example is using avatars to signify a race or gender that is unrelated to the gender or race of the user, so in a sense it can be an act of empowerment at one level but at another it is normally in trouble, depending on what and why but also the cultural implications. The use of female user within male avatars commonly reports higher levels of identification with the avatar and greater feelings of affirmation of their female gender identities in the real world. Though they have the potential of using these spaces as the means to discovering oneself and search their identity, they can at the same time assist in replicating the status quo unless the rules programmed into these virtual worlds are modified.

Marginalization of women in digital spheres is not a one-off case but a reflection of an overall social trend of underestimating the voices and experiences of women either directly or indirectly silencing them. This discrimination may be direct through abuse, e.g., in harassment and specific attacks, or be structural violence, involving the structure and culture of a service directly preventing equal access. This kind of dynamic is more evident in the contexts in which women are vulnerable because of their intersecting vulnerability in migration, sexual harassment, among other aspects [5].

The digital platforms do not just provide space of exclusion, they are also transformative. Women and other marginal groups, especially those who are stressed by media coverage are employing more social media, blogs, podcasts, and other online media forms to relay individual stories, question the aggregate cultural narratives, and create networks of solidarity bridging geographical and cultural landscapes. Such online platforms can magnify the voices that are usually overlooked in conventional media and offer a platform to activism efforts in the grassroots and organizing, raise public awareness.

Solving the established inequality in the digital realm is a multidimensional challenge. Regulation is necessary so that platforms are made responsible when it comes to discrimination but policies are not the only solution. A very high level of digital literacy needs to be encouraged, which will enable users to be able to navigate, interrogate, and remake online environments. Also, the marginalized groups should actively engage in the creation, administration, and control of digital tools. It does not only represent imaginary inclusion but meaningful engagement in decision-making procedures, thru the subsidizing of techno-feminist undertakings, as well as due access to technological supplies. To make the online environment really accessible and inclusive, it is necessary to implement structural changes as well as cultural change. It means the re-allocation of power and voice, disruption of embedded biases in technical systems, supporting places where varied types of identity, expression are not merely tolerated but appreciated. By purposeful design-on the part of the institutions and on the part of the users themselves-digital space can stop being merely the replication of pre-existing social stratifications and can be turned into a means of equality, empowerment, and liberation in common [6].

3 Gender Bias in AI Systems

Artificial intelligence has become revolutionary in shaping the present world as it can be seen in just about every aspect of modern living, including regular online transactions to major decision-making areas of governance, medical practice, economics, and police. With its power persistently increasing, it is critical to actively question how AI systems perform, reproduce and, in some cases, even exacerbate pre-existing social disparities. Gender bias has been one of the most burning issues in this respect. Notably, AI is not isolated phenomena, but just a component of a wider digital ecosystem, which includes social media platforms, algorithmic recommendation systems, and data-driven technologies in general and which, as a whole, can compound and cement structural inequalities unless addressed in their entirety.

Unlike one may think, artificial intelligence systems do not ascribe to objective, unbiased work. They are informed by data on which they are trained and the worldviews of the teams that build them. When datasets involved in training are biased (that is, presenting a certain demographics overrepresented and the rest underrepresented), there is no way that the AI systems will not inherit the same biases. An example of this is that the natural language models will create biased associations, such as having one profession or trait associated with a particular gender than with another, which entrenches negative stereotypes. The demographic composition of the development teams is also important; there is a lesser chance of homogeneous teams being able to think of, identify, and impede bias in technology design. Addressing these issues needs deliberate efforts to include design principled techniques, increased diversity among the AI teams, datasets that have been highly trained and curated, and effective systems of identifying and rectifying biases during the AI lifecycle [7].

Gender bias can be present in all levels of AI development, including the very first one which is the collection of data, as well as during the actual usage in the world. An excellent case in point can be observed in voice-activated conversational agents whereby it may be based on having a female-sounding voice as the virtual assistant and assuming a voice with an added layer of firm and decisive tasks to its pairing as that which is male-sounding. These design decisions pose dangers of entrenching and normalizing old gender roles as it subliminally reinforces the image of women being subordinate and men as king. It has been reported that these digital assistants tend to react calmly or humorously to the abusive or sexist language thus marginalizing further and normalizing disrespectful treatment of women. Though there has been a slight move to implement some technology companies trying to accommodate some kind of non-binary or gender-neutral, it has not been enough, as the more obvious structures of bias can be revealed through system architecture and sets of data. This mainstream tendency can be challenged and disrupted by shifting toward gender-neutral designs of AI and delivering more customization to the users [8].

The gender bias exists in the digital circles of the information environment, as well, by using disinformation campaigns based on gender. They are strategic attempts to demoralize and spread smear about women, especially those in the leadership, activism, or other positions in the public. Such campaigns take advantage of stereotypes present in the society and paint women as irrational, inefficient and unreliable, and since male candidates cannot be easily discredited, women are demoralized when it comes to partaking in political and democratic decision-making. It does not only cause personal and professional harm to people but also undermines democratic values since it stifles different representation and views in the public discourse.

The phenomenon of gendered disinformation needs to be tackled using a multi-pronged strategy. It is essential to conduct more research in this area, especially in the countries of the Global South, where the issue is poorly documented and tend to vary even more extreme. There is also the need to strengthen legislative and policy framework to make sure that those committing acts can be held liable and active enforcement is necessary. Further, active development of digital literacy on all levels is an important protective factor. The focus on digital literacy must not be limited to technical capacities only but must connote having the potential to question the information found online, identify manipulative messages, recognize the social-political background of using the digital realm, and be good digital citizens. When people are provided with these skills, society is in a better situation to challenge the promotion of biased narratives and narrow the impact of gendered disinformation [9].

4 Online Gender-Based Violence

The theme of online safety has become one of the major areas of concern in the digital age, especially in relation to the occurrence of harassment and gender-based violence in the online platform. Such violent behaviors have a disproportionate impact on women and people in lesbian, gay, bisexual, transgender, queer, and other diverse sexual orientations, gender identities, and bodily characteristics (LGBTQ+) groups. Cyberbullying, the use and propagation of intimate images, and cyberstalking have been on the rise in cyberspace, and it is now a common disturbing behavior. Such varieties of internet violence are not merely incidental aberrations, but reflect and project underlying discrepancies and disparities, which permeate the society, out at large.

Those groups which are marginalized, especially women, people of LGBTQ + and racially or ethnically minoritized groups are likely to face a greater risk of being targeted. The systematic maltreatment tends to be disempowering to the victims bearing a silencing effect that discourages the victims to be involved in social debates, promote opinions where or communicate in online groups. This is a leading to a digital divide where people who are already underrepresented in the decision-making processes in society are yet again marginalized. The intersection of different identities tends to determine the experiences of online harassment. This might include, as in the case of a queer woman of color, the experience of also facing racial discrimination, gender-based hostilities, and homophobic abuse that combine and compound into a more multifaceted form of victimization than any one form of discrimination, taken alone. Literature continues to show that long-term online abuse has long-term effects that lead to digital exclusion, low levels of social participation, and serious psychological issues of anxiety, depression, and post-traumatic stress. These abuses are further exacerbated by structural and cultural forces, including deeply ingrained misogynistic culture, as well as the design of digital platforms, which focus on behaviors that lead to engagement, virality, and maximizing profits at the expenses of user safety. The vulnerability of the legal systems and absence of strong systems of enforcement leave the victims to continued abuse with little or no redress [10].

The online gaming industry can be considered one of the spheres where gender harassment is a very common phenomenon. In recent years, studies and surveys have found that many women and girls, who engage in the gaming process, have faced harassment, toxic behavior, and abusive language committed by male players. Anonymous nicknames and voice morphing by hiding their gender is common practice among female players as a means of protecting themselves against abuse. Such toxic environment not only discourages women to actively engage in communities of gamers but also supports stereotypical view that gaming is a male-dominated field. The few females in leadership roles in gaming-related careers-like developers, creative directors and executives- also add to lack of diversity in the plot lines, character models and design in the games. Gender norms especially harmful to women are imposed via objectification or picturing them as narrow stereotypical characters. Those trends are a reflection of other inequalities in society and provide a sign of the structural disadvantages women and the marginalized encounter in the world of science, technology, and entertainment.

The virtual world, be it in social networks or artificial intelligence, as well as in some forms of interactive entertainment, tends to reproduce gender prejudices among the population and even accelerate the pace of open expression of gender bias. It can be noted both through the tendency of harassment, as well as through misrepresentation and inability to take a substantial part in participation by minorities. These problems should be addressed in a systemic manner. Possible solutions involve the platform redesign where the issue of user safety is at the core of the work, the enhancement of compliance and law enforcement mechanisms, the introduction of active moderation tools, and the usage of digital literacy and responsible online behavior through education campaigns. Long-term engagement of non-governmental organizations, community, and autonomous watchdogs can be critical in keeping platforms and policymakers accountable. An inclusive, multidimensional approach (based on the principles of inclusivity, intersectionality, and equity) is vital to building digital spaces in which all users feel safe and comfortable due to gender identity, sexuality, and ethnical status [11].

5 Digital Activism and Gender Justice

The application of digital means to the context of gender justice is known as digital activism whereby online technologies in specific, social medium platforms and online networks, and other online platforms are used to promote the rights, safety and equality of the female and LGBTQ + populations. Such activism has transformed the path the social justice movements take to include viral information exchange, the organization of activist networks, and solidarity networks on a worldwide scale. With the arrival of Web 2.0 and the proliferation of mobile internet, the digital environments have become potent platforms of political speech and protest campaigns. Feminist and LGBTQ + movements are increasingly employing them as a measure against the rights of the second sex and minorities, to spread awareness among citizens, raise their voices, increase pressure on institutions to eliminate systematic disadvantages. The notable ones are the campaigns that raise awareness about gender-based violence, workplace harassment, race, gender, and state violence intersection. Besides sparking up debates in the society, such movements have even altered changes in legislation, change cultural discourses and even heightened institutional responsibility [12].

The most manifested layers of digital gender justice work entails the hashtag actions. Hashtags create a more fun and easy to engage process of activism by connecting personal experiences to wider, collective narratives. They enable people with different backgrounds to enter into the general discourse and advocacy without much imposed restrictions. Besides the usage of hashtags, another form of support that can be used to reach large audiences is online petitioning, online campaigns and mobilizations, which are usually organized by websites like Change.org. Narrative-based posting in blogs, video materials, podcasts, and any other short-form media on Instagram or TikTok are also critically needed to defy the dominant narratives, record their own experiences, and even tell the audience about things they do not learn at school. Some activists who use more confrontational tactics may use the tactic of hacktivism or virtual protest to lobby the censorship and subvert the oppressive machinery.

Along with the opportunities, there are certain challenges of digital activism. Women and LGBTQ+ activists are disproportionately targeted by online harassment in the form of trolling, threats, and doxxing. Another serious issue that was outlined is digital repression, which is relevant to situations where the government has used surveillance tools and censorship measures or regulations to suppress the voices of opposition. Feminist and queer content will also be made more hard-to-come-by algorithmic bias on social media platforms, potentially in the form of content moderation systems, broadly defined community standards, or commercial disincentive to display content that may prove politically unpopular. This fact demonstrates the importance of strategic and critical thinking on the issue of digital activism, especially in the sphere where online spaces are overtly regulated or controlled.

Gender-based violence and discrimination have drawn global attention by these technologies, linked local struggles to international ones, as well as has made possible the ability to organize on a decentralized level, or without the traditional hierarchies. They have also given youth or disadvantaged groups the strength to become leaders in advocacy. Studies have found that this kind of activism can alter the discourse in the society, change cultural thinking, and put pressure on the institutions (public and the ones that are privately owned) to respond to the gender disparities. Reactionary are the same people who use the same digital tools that allow progressive activism. Anti-feministic and anti-LGBTQ + organizations use digital technologies (social media algorithms, viral communication patterns, individualized streams of misinformation) to construct and advance false claims, trigger moral panic, and undermine gender justice movements. Gender equality policies, reproductive rights, and trans inclusion are often disinformation that is mobilized against to build backlash and strengthen discriminatory thought patterns. These methods corrupt the political discourse, divide societies and increase exposure of activists [13].

6 Digital Gender Gap: Challenges and Barriers

Digital gender gap can be defined as the difference between men and women in relation to access to digital technologies, the use of digital technologies and the benefits that the technologies bring. Despite the enormous potential it has to transform societies and open up new planes of opportunism, technology proceeds to give many women especially those pertaining to marginalized groups many challenges and roadblocks that limit their engagement in the online world. Such barriers are usually based on a web of cultural expectations, financial constraints and institutional inadequacies, which constrain the capacity of women to access the digital tools.

It is one of the most urgent problems of inaccessibility of technology especially in economically deprived regions and rural areas. Lots of women do not have access to cheap and dependable electronic background, including affordable devices, steady online accessibility, and good electricity supply. When these resources are accessible, the issue of affordability comes up as a significant barrier, and the women of low-income households can hardly afford buying smartphones, computers, or internet subscription. This economic constraint is also supplemented by the barrier of socio-cultural factors, in which traditional gender roles and social prescriptions decrease the interest of women toward technology. The digital tool usage is viewed as superfluous or even unacceptable to women in some cultures which perpetuates the outdated stereotypes. Societies and families might also oppose females venturing into the digital world, fearing it will affect the moral grounds, may be used wrongly or might be exposed to negative content.

The digital illiteracy is another addition to the issue. Many of the women are unable to understand and use digital tools because of their low literacy knowledge. Moreover, the exposure levels to digital platforms and a lack of specific training sets lead to the large skills gap as many women cannot use technology as a means of self- or work growth. Fears of internet safety and information protection are also a deterrent as females are more than those targeted by cyber bullying, cyber bullies, and blackmailing. They are further deterred by privacy concerns, fear of data being stolen and abuse of personal identity information.

Gender bias in technology design and content is another factor that contributes to it. Since the technological world is male-dominated, most of the digital tools and technologies do not support the needs of women. They often design products that fail to reflect gender-specific needs, and the information online is likely to be exclusive since it is designed to accommodate the needs of the targeted population which, in many instances, leave out rural women whose first language or cultural orientations are not catered to. Financial reliance is also an essential element that contributes to the survival of digital divide. The financial independence of many women restricts their ownership of and maintenance of any digital device because they depend on male members of the family on purchases. Women, in families that involve male domination over technological resources, have less access to examine and use the said technology. The digital gender divide is also further contributed to by policy and implementation gaps. Although the government and NGO-based programs are actively working on digital inclusion at the global level, not all of them are relevant to women since they lack gender-sensitive models. There is inadequate funding, poor outreach, and lack of sufficient policy implementation. Such initiatives also prove to fail of reaching their planned effects without regular checks and robust execution [14].

The digital gender gap must be approached with a multidimensional strategy, one that would eliminate the economic, cultural, educational, and policy challenges at the same time. Societies can take the step to bridge this divide by providing affordable access to technology, through digital literacy programs, protecting online environments, ensuring inclusive technological design and policy frameworks which are well funded and gender responsive. Then and only then it is possible to realize all the power of technology to empower women, strengthen equality, and introduce full inclusion to the world of the digital age.

7 Impact of Technology on Women Empowerment

In the modern digital age, women have gained independence, developed their skills and made their voices heard like never before due to technology. Accompanying the increasing accessibility of digital tools, the social, economic, and political environments of women are changing toward greater inclusiveness and the opening up of new spaces in which individuals may expand selves and actively participate in the society. Technology has given women a significant power to become empowered because geographical distances and conventional boundaries became irrelevant. Online learning portals, online classrooms, and digital resources have helped to improve access to education and sharpen skills significantly. Such advancements have increased the availability of quality education especially to women in less developed or distant regions. Technological environments have extended to present women with vocational training, coding classes, and language classes to provide them with skills that can be employed to encourage independence and subsequent career advancements [11].

Digital economy has also changed the entrepreneurial attitude of the women. E-commerce sites also give women a chance to run their businesses without necessarily building their stores and thus expand markets and customer base. Moreover, women have access to secure and convenient financial alternatives through digital wallets, mobile banking and microfinance programs, and the introduction of freelancing platforms and the freelance economy in general is making them more active agents in the global economy.

Women can now access medical, psychological, and reproductive health through telemedicine services, no matter where they are located because geographical distance is not relevant. Women are also empowered to track their health and spread awareness about personal health conditions and taking preventive care actions through health-oriented mobile phone applications and wearable fitness tracking devices. Women have also increased their participation in politics and the rest of society due to technology. The social media is a tool that supports advocacy, where women can also discuss politically, join social movements and lobby causes. Online civic platforms and even the possible electronic voting systems are becoming a facilitating factor among women since it has become simpler to be actively involved in the governance and decision-making process.

In cultural aspects, online communities allow women to share experiences, knowledge, and to offer the much-needed support to one another in an environment that is safe. The influence of the internet in exposing women to a whole array of opinions helps to take advantage of the exposure and argue against the traditional gender norms and demand their rights. Technology in the workplace has increased opportunities in terms of enabling remote working where women have been able to balance between work and personal commitments with better efficiency. Working with tools and digital platforms of collaboration and productivity is also an important factor that helps women to advance and succeed in their careers. Computer advances have helped improve safety and security, as well. Safety apps to women and real-time tracking tools will help women assist at the moment of crisis, and the awareness regarding digital safety will help women know how to protect themselves against online dangers. Moreover, the impact of women with lots of power goes even over generations, because more often than not they tend to influence and show younger generations how to make the best out of available technology and offer a cult of learning and self-confidence in the world of computers [9].

The technology has now become a driver of change toward solving the existing and arising issues among women. Digital tools enable women to achieve greater independence over their lives and make meaningful contributions to the society by increasing access to education, healthcare, economic independence and social involvements. Nevertheless, equal access is also a major priority. Filling the digital divide, reducing the affordability level, enhancing the presence of safety online are key points that need to be achieved in a world in which women are fully embraced and empowered through the transformational capabilities of technology.

8 Conclusion

Technology emerged as one of the most efficient empowering factors of women that provide them with possibilities to break down historically established boundaries and enhance equality in the contemporary digital era. It has transformed women lives a lot by way of increasing access to education, empowering women economically, increasing health of women and empowering women in social and political life. The women are increasingly having an opportunity to question their historic norms, un-stereotype, and contribute positively to their families, communities and economy through use of digital tools and platforms. As much as this has been improved, the digital gender divide is increasingly becoming a topical issue especially in rural and marginalized regions where there are economic constraints related to technology accessibility to women due to cultural factors.

9 Future Scope

Bridging such a gap requires specific steps including development of digital infrastructure, digital literacy, online safety, and low cost of technology. To accomplish these, governments, the private sector, and civil society must work together to generate open and comprehensive digital spaces that will enable all women to empower themselves. Although technology has a huge potential of fostering gender equality, its ultimate power is guaranteeing fair and wide access. Removing obstacles and promoting inclusive digital empowerment, societies will be able to unlock the potential in women, and this will lead to the more just, equitable, and sustainable future.

References

1. Baumgardner, D. M. (2025). Secondary pre-service general education teachers' self-efficacy and teaching students with disabilities (pp. 27–36). https://doi.org/10.5040/9781978748415.ch-002.
2. Ferreira, E., Silva, M. J., & Gomes, C. A. (2025). Gender dynamics in STEM education: Students and pre-service teachers' voices. *Social Sciences, 14*(4), 211. https://doi.org/10.3390/socsci14040211
3. Chan, R. C. H. (2022). A social cognitive perspective on gender disparities in self-efficacy, interest, and aspirations in science, technology, engineering, and mathematics (STEM): The influence of cultural and gender norms. *International Journal of STEM Education, 9*(1), 37. https://doi.org/10.1186/s40594-022-00352-0
4. Núñez, R. B. C., & Santero-Sánchez, R. (2023). Gender gap in STEM education. In Springer eBooks (pp. 139–162). https://doi.org/10.1007/978-3-031-45802-6_9.
5. Nectoux, S., Magee, L., & Soldatic, K. (2023). Sensing technologies, digital inclusion, and disability diversity. *Journal of Computer-Mediated Communication, 28*(5), 75–89. https://doi.org/10.1093/jcmc/zmad026
6. Baygi, R. M., Introna, L. D., & Hultin, L. (2021). Everything flows: Studying continuous socio-technological transformation in a fluid and dynamic digital world. *MIS Quarterly, 45*(1), 423–452. https://doi.org/10.25300/misq/2021/15887
7. Zimmer, M. P., & Järveläinen, J. (2022). Digital–Sustainable Co-transformation: Introducing the triple bottom line of sustainability to digital transformation research. In IFIP advances in information and communication technology (pp. 100–111). https://doi.org/10.1007/978-3-031-15688-5_10.
8. Ekardt, F., Günther, P., Hagemann, K., Garske, B., Heyl, K., & Weyland, R. (2023). Legally binding and ambitious biodiversity protection under the CBD, the global biodiversity framework, and human rights law. *Environmental Sciences Europe, 35*(1), 80. https://doi.org/10.1186/s12302-023-00786-5
9. Van Wynsberghe, A. (2021). Sustainable AI: AI for sustainability and the sustainability of AI. *AI and Ethics, 1*(3), 213–218. https://doi.org/10.1007/s43681-021-00043-6

10. Drechsler, K., Gregory, R., Wagner, H., & Tumbas, S. (2020). At the crossroads between digital innovation and digital transformation. *Communications of the Association for Information Systems, 47*, 521–538. https://doi.org/10.17705/1cais.04723
11. Williams, E., Vaisanen, H., & Padmadas, S. S. (2022). Women's economic empowerment in sub-Saharan Africa: Evidence from cross-national population data. *Demographic Research, 47*, 415–452. https://doi.org/10.4054/demres.2022.47.15
12. Raihan, M. M., Subroto, S., Chowdhury, N., Koch, K., Ruttan, E., & Turin, T. C. (2024). Dimensions and barriers for digital (in)equity and digital divide: A systematic integrative review. *Digital Transformation and Society, 4*(2), 111–127. https://doi.org/10.1108/dts-04-2024-0054
13. Avanesian, G., Zaw, H. T., Kelly, P., & Mizunoya, S. (2024). Dissecting the digital divide: A household fixed effects approach to estimating gender gaps in digital skills of youth in low- and middle-income economies. *Heliyon, 10*(12), e33127. https://doi.org/10.1016/j.heliyon.2024.e33127
14. Ullah, A. A., & Chattoraj, D. (2023). Unraveling gender dynamics in migration and remittances: An Empirical analysis of Asian Women's "Exposure to Migration". *Genealogy, 8*(1), 4. https://doi.org/10.3390/genealogy8010004

CHAPTER 8

Ethics, Privacy, and Global Law in AI-Powered Learning: Ensuring Trustworthy Educational Technologies

Praful V. Barekar, Roshni S. Khedgaonkar, and Kavita R. Singh

Abstract Artificial intelligence has entered the arena of education and technology, impacting learning environments with personalized instruction, predictive analytics and adaptive assessments. Such developments immediately raise profound questions of ethics, privacy, and legal liability. AI-powered learning tools collect massive student datasets of educational performance or behavior, leading to debates over issues of privacy and surveillance. In the absence of direct and valid data governance frameworks, these systems are at risk of being ethically overstepped by either having an unbalanced effect disproportionate on the more vulnerable students, or even trying to institutionalize built-in biases in how algorithms function. The responsible AI developers need to leverage

P. V. Barekar (✉) · R. S. Khedgaonkar · K. R. Singh
Department of Computer Technology, Yeshwantrao Chavan College of Engineering, Nagpur, Maharashtra, India
e-mail: praful.barekar20@gmail.com

P. K. Dutta et al. (eds.), *Digital Education for a Sustainable Future*, Sustainable Development Goals Series,
https://doi.org/10.1007/978-3-032-15433-0_8

a variety of stakeholder perspectives from educators and policy makers when creating frameworks for fairness, explainability, and inclusion in education technology. The legal frameworks should change as there are loopholes in the present data protection laws and intellectual property provisions to address this new environment of cross-border digital education platforms. Embedding privacy-by-design, ongoing monitoring, and stakeholder engagement in the AI lifecycle can help to increase trust, ethical use of educational technologies and reduce harms. This requires establishing an integrated framework of ethics, privacy, and law regarding human dignity and the right to quality education across all stakeholder groups that can align unfettered AI deployment with experiencing learning.

Keywords AI in Education · Data Privacy · Ethical Learning Technologies · Educational Law · Trustworthy AI

1 Introduction

Artificial intelligence is revolutionizing the education field with exploring personalized, customized learning experiences to individual students and educators, so that educational resources are directed in a strategic manner and aggregated into more active and engaging learning environments. The potential of AI in educational technology is vast, from intelligent tutoring systems and personalized learning pathways to automated grading and predictive analytics. As shown in the above examples, these developments hold promise for supporting access and equity and enhancing learning outcomes, but they also raise difficult ethical, privacy, and legal questions that have to be addressed if such technologies are to be made ethically defensible as well as consonant with education's core values. The ethical issues focused around fairness, transparency, accountability, and inclusivity. AI systems are practically a bunch of black boxes that decide important aspects about students as well as predict their performances [1]. This leaves students and educators without the ability to understand or challenge how the automate has arrived at a decision. This opacity could perpetuate bias, and further school inequality, especially when AI training data are biased by systemic societal prejudice. As such, instructional AI should prioritize algorithmic equity, make sure that discrimination in its design and application is minimized or countered through technical and structural changes, and continuously involve various stakeholders in its development and implementation.

AI is in learning environments is privacy, as these systems run based on rich troves of student data including academic records, behavior patterns, social-emotional indicators and even biometric information. The sensitivity of such data calls for using practices that are beyond minimal compliance in safeguarding the data. In many K-12 settings, student signatures can be problematic because the minor student does not understand what they are signing and has little or no choice over whether they will sign it; on a practical level, minors do not have an ability to consent under the "common rule". This further highlights the importance of privacy-by-design methods that minimizing data collection, anonymizing and encrypting such data, and only using it for its specific intended educational purposes. The commodification of education technology increases privacy pitfalls as third-party vendors can gather and commercialize information related to students, resulting in concerns over surveillance capitalism on an academic level. It is important to have transparency in data processing, opt-outs for users and regular auditing to keep student privacy intact and the trust alive in these AI systems [2].

AI is advancing more quickly in education than the regulatory environment can manage. The dynamic and autonomous nature of AI technologies is often ill-served by frameworks such as the General Data Protection Regulation (GDPR) in Europe, or even specific exemptions under the Family Education Rights Policy Act (FERPA) for example in the United States. Questions surrounding liability, when an AI system fails to accurately diagnose a student's ability to learn or reinforces discriminatory practice by the publisher of an algorithm remain largely open. In addition, there are changes in intellectual property laws related to content and datasets between the source of AI generated and established educational institutions. The convergence of online education across national boundaries will also lead to greater need for coordination of international legal standards. Compliance should be conceptualized not as a technical to-do list but as one element of a holistic program for moral custodianship of learning technologies [3].

So, inculcating trust in AI for education requires a multi-stakeholder, interdisciplinary approach. Policy makers must continue to develop and adapt frameworks to respect both innovation and individual rights. The organization recommends that developers and EdTech providers should follow ethical standards and respect privacy concerns, incorporating fairness, accountability, and transparency in AI-based systems at all points of the development lifecycle. Training and digital literacy programs are required to empower educators to comprehend and monitor the use of AI tools in their classrooms. Similarly, learners should also know what happens to their data and how algorithmic decisions impact their learning path. AI-powered learning technologies, on the other hand, can only live up to their promise and do not cause harm with robust ethical reflection and privacy systems that are built from ground-up as well as clear legal accountability. Ultimately, resistance to the adoption of AI in education should not be viewed as opposition to technology itself.Rather, it reflects a broader call for the ethical design, development, and deployment of AI systems, grounded in a commitment to human dignity, educational equity, and social justice. This ethical, privacy, and legal system will help create an innovative, yet deeply human future of education as the line between pedagogy and technology blurs.

2 AI-Powered Learning Technologies: Personalized Learning and Adaptive Systems

These industries an AI-learning technology is revolutionizing by delivering personalized learning experience and adaptive systems that can dynamically respond to the needs of individual learners. These AI-augmented platforms leverage their ability to sift through mountains of data on how students perform and navigate courses, create opportunity-ready learner paths to increase student engagement and outcomes. It leverages the machine learning algorithms to recommend content, difficulty, and sequence of learning activities based on prior knowledge surface by the student along with speed and cognitive preferences. An AI-powered language learning app, for example, might identify which grammatical structures the student struggles with and adapt the lessons to include more focused practice along with instant feedback and further explanations. It can speed up learning and drive students toward more autonomy by giving them the possibility to set their own pace of progress.

Imagine a new level of personalized learning as an adaptive system as shown above that offers real-time analytics and predictive modeling to dynamically adjust strategies for teaching. These systems are live tracking a students' learning engagement behavior, emotional responses, feedback mechanisms and adjusting when it's time to present the material asynchronously. This not only keeps people motivated, it also stops the user from having to wait too long in frustration before someone helps them out. For example, in the field of STEM education, an adaptive learning platform could automatically change from visual to interactive simulations whenever a student seems to drift off, or struggle with more conceptual topics. Adaptive systems are tools that also help teachers by providing real-time data on class-wide patterns of understanding mediocre performance in certain areas and a possible suggestion for change in the curriculum to address these shortcomings [4].

Natural Language Processing (NLP) and intelligent tutoring systems can provide better integration between personalized learning and adaptive systems while enhancing capabilities of recommender algorithms. NLP powered chatbots can act as conversational tutors, answering questions immediately and helping learners navigate through complex steps in solving problems. Recommender systems recommend related content that align with the learner's growing skills and objectives. Adaptive assessment tools diagnose conceptual gaps and recommend remedial modules before progressing to new topics.

AI in Assessment and Predictive Analytics

The gains come with significant caveats about data privacy, algorithmic bias, and access equity in AI-supported personalized and adaptive learning. In order for these systems to work, they need vast amounts of student data which obviously has to be treated securely to avoid abuse. Further, when the training datasets are biased, these recommendations and interventions could only serve to reinforce existing inequities. To do so requires algorithms whose design is open and who can be audited for bias on a routine basis, as well as inclusive co-design practices between educators, technologists, and diverse learner groups. AI enabled personalized learning and adaptive system has a robust potential that can change education to a more learner-based, efficient responsive experience [5]. These technologies can close learning gaps, stimulate motivation and prepare learners for the requisites of a digital, knowledge-driven world by weaving in intelligent analytics with dynamic content delivery.

3 Ethical Considerations in AI-Driven Education

While the infusion of AI in education creates a momentous opportunity for individualized learning, process efficiency and data-informed decision making, it also raises ethical implications that need to be addressed to ensure technology is leveraged in a way that serves learners rightly and responsibly. In essence, algorithmic bias is the fact that an AI system may learn to perpetuate bias in society by being trained on data that reflects past prejudices. By an educational frame, the biases of AI could discriminate hoarsely to students according to their learning trajectories and recommendations windows which lead those who are at margins groups unfairly toward disadvantages. Mitigating bias requires deliberate effort in systematically incorporating diversity into the data sources, having sound methods of bias detection, monitoring processes and evaluation of the system outputs to avoid automated discrimination.

Transparency and explainability matter in AI-driven education too as the case for AI transparency: Much of the power of AI can be attributed to its ability to take complex relationships and model them in ways that generalize to new data sets facilitating everything from language translation, image processing, even manipulating screenplays [6]. Explainability is essential for trust, granting stakeholders the ability to contest and validate outcomes. Ethical AI implementation requires the transparency of decision-making processes through documentation, with justifications written in a level appropriate for non-experts and policies that enforce human intervention in high-stakes educational decisions.

A related third issue is student independence and motivation. Adaptive systems can make learning more efficient, but they cannot remove autonomy over the path learners choose to take through their education. An excessive dependence on the advice of AI may thus curtail opportunities for independent thought, creative work, and self-guided learning. Thus, while ethical frameworks should promote informed decision-making among students, they also need to ensure an appropriate balance between the power of algorithms and independence. The pillar of ethical AI in education is privacy and data protection. These systems use vast amounts of personal data from academic records to behavioral patterns, and sometimes even biometric data, all of which could be a major security or privacy vulnerability if not handled correctly. Safeguarding students' rights requires taking a privacy-by-design approach, ensuring meaningful consent, and enforcing strong data governance [7]. The schools needs to be clear on what data are being collected, how those data are being used and the need they address.

The ethical considerations with AI in education require a diverse approach with educators, technologists, policymakers, and learners. Incorporating equity, trust, and human dignity into the entire life cycle of AI from design, development to deployment in education would allow educational stakeholders and civic society at large to leverage its transformative potential. There is also the issue of "equitable access". AI in education can deepen the digital divide if not planned and managed as part of a common approach where technology-supported educational practices are fine-tuned to serve underserved populations. It is filled with examples from both research and case studies that unequivocally make the case for deploying AI with ethics front-of-mind, and in a way that ensures accessibility, affordability, and inclusivity which aims to distribute its benefits as widely as possible across diverse socio-economic contexts [8].

4 Privacy Implications and Data Protection

Despite the rapid expansion of artificial intelligence in education, issues about data privacy and security are yet to be addressed since AI technologies require that a lot of sensitive learner data should be gathered, stored, and processed for grading purposes. Which may include academic records, behavior analytics, social-emotional indicators, online activity logs, and perhaps in some instances biometric data like facial recognition or voice patterns. The use of such data enables the personalization, flexibility, and predictive qualities of educational technology, but these same attributes come with a host of risks for privacy when the data is misused, mishandled, or insufficiently protected. A key privacy implication is informed consent: students, and often their parents or guardians given that they are children who in many circumstances cannot themselves give legal consent, might not understand the full extent and purpose of data collection, particularly when implemented within opaque AI systems. Learners can easily lose control of their personal data unless there is clear and transparent communication about the use of data.

Data security is another major issue, with all the data either with educational institutions or EdTech companies and hence a great lovely spot for any potential cyberattack. For example, breaches can result in hands of identity thieves, undue profiling or even direct commercial exploitation of student data [9]. Meanwhile, a proliferation of third-party platforms in online and hybrid learning environments makes it increasingly challenging to enforce privacy laws, often leaving cross-border data flows subject to inconsistent legal protections. With the introduction of regulations such as GDPR in the European Union, and FERPA in the United States not to mention the many national data protection laws that have followed suit in jurisdictions around the globe attempts to protect Personally Identifiable Information (PII) are taking shape across far-reaching educational ecosystems adopting cloud-based technologies; although how they are enforced and harmonized at this scale remains a significant challenge.

These AI-powered systems also give rise to consideration from a data minimization standpoint. The data privacy provision in this bill would allow us to make sure that the sites we send our students for school work do not collect more information than necessary, and so do not enable surveillance and profiling of students that could erode trust essential to support academic freedom [10]. A risk which originates from the way how systems are designed can be managed by developing-in privacy measures like encrypting information, anonymizing, or using secure sign-on. The sound data protection in AI-driven education is a multi-layered endeavor where thorough measures of technological vigilance commingle with timely governance procedures that adhere to the rule of law and are supported by engagement. This means that educators, policymakers, and developers must work together to develop transparent practices in data management and more equitable privacy protections between different populations which also presume accountability for mistakes. With a focus on ethical data stewardship, it can unlock the power of AI in education while supporting the core privacy rights of users to create an environment that is safe and trusted.

Nature and Sensitivity of Educational Data

Any information gathered during the process of teaching and learning, from academic records and test scores to attendance logs, behavioral patterns, learning preferences to even biometric identifiers such as facial recognition and voice recordings. Another reason this data is critically sensitive is because it reveals not only a learner's present capacities but who they are: their identity, socio-economic context, and trajectory [11]. Such data is typically collected and analyzed in AI-driven educational systems, often used to customize instruction, predict how well students might do on some benchmark, or evaluate engagement.

That sensitivity comes in the risk of misuse another way of saying unauthorized access or profiling could damage a student's reputation or opportunities. In addition, educational records are longitudinal, so the fall-out of a privacy breach can stretch over years into an individual's academic and professional career. Information is sensitive to even more when shared with third-party vendors, stored in cloud-based systems, or transmitted across jurisdictions where privacy laws often differ. Recognizing educational data as a protected category is necessary to legitimize institutional use of the technology so that both- student/teacher dignity, autonomy, and long-term security are preserved [12]. Data privacy and data security of such granular customer details should be protected by robust governance frameworks so none could be misused or exploited.

Consent Mechanisms and Data Minimization

Practical levels align well with privacy rights and consent mechanisms that are fundamental to the respect of students participating in AI-driven education. In the Minds Network, this is called informed consent: it means that students and their parents/guardians when appropriate should know what data are being collected, where they will be stored, who has access to them and how long it will be retained. The process needs to be clear, available, and without duress an implementation should not use overly technical terminology that could mask the nature of what is happening. But in reality, most of these consent agreements languish deep within miles-long terms of service that severely impair their efficacy. Data minimization is one of the key privacy principles. This task could be accomplished by gathering only the data required to meet explicitly defined learning goals, which would limit opportunities for abuse or unauthorized use in creating unintended consequences [13]. Some privacy laws for e.g., GDPR also require that organizations limit the purpose of data processing to what is strictly necessary as tightly related to purpose limitation and the principle of proportionality and upstream other direct or indirect purposes. Strong consent mechanisms and data minimization together not only build trust with learners and educational institutions but ensure that all data collection is ethical, compliant with the law, and in the long-term best interests of students.

Data Security and Cyber Threats

In AI-driven education, the most significant worry is the security of data; with more of student data stored, processed, and running across numerous connected digital applications [14]. The reason behind hacking into the educational institution and EdTech provider is pretty clear: Personal and academic records are goldmines for another form of cybercrime identity theft, fraud, unauthorized surveillance. Phishing, ransomware, data breaches and insider threats are a few examples of the many types of attacks that can threaten the security as confidentiality, integrity, and availability of educational data. Increased use of cloud services and reliance on third-party vendors also improves an attacker's likelihood to succeed because a single vulnerability in another system may lead to the exposure of sensitive information. Without an effective cybersecurity, information stored in user pod gets exposed to potential cyber threats and privacy breaches as it traverses a hostile environment.

Creating incident response procedures also helps to identify breaches which should then be handled with urgency, lessening their impact. Ideally, there should also be a training program aimed at everyone involved in the process of education- educators, administrators, and IT staff that will reinforce security awareness and help prevent common human error which continues to represent one of the biggest threats in malware attacks. With AI systems increasing in complexity, so too do cyber threats; schools need proactive, adaptive security solutions that can keep up with cutting-edge technology to preserve student-privacy and confidence in educational ecosystem [15].

5 Legal Frameworks Governing AI in Education

There is an evolving intersection between technology law, data protection regulations, intellectual property rights and education policy in the legal frameworks governing AI in Education. Just as AI is activated in the classroom, administrative processes, and remote learning sites to collect student data and turn them into algorithmic predictions through automated recommendations so do compliance authorities come into play. At a global level, high-level principles are set out in instruments such as the UNESCO recommendation on the Ethics of Artificial Intelligence (2021), which highlights human centric approaches, due diligence checks and respect for human rights when deploying AI technologies. The

EU, in contrast, is more protective: In 2018 the General Data Protection Regulation (GDPR) mandated affirmative consent, data access and correction for individuals whose data was being used.

In the US where there is not a single federal statute specific to AI, education data in particular is regulated under the Family Educational Rights and Privacy Act (FERPA) and the Children's Online Privacy Protection Act (COPPA), which dictate restrictions around collection, sharing, and use of data without parental or student consent. Countries such as Australia, Canada, and India treat AI in education as part of wider legislation on data protection but also include guidance from educational ministries. Within these laws, lie in attempts to reconcile innovation with control, providing a framework that can be used to assess whether the algorithms are fair or discriminating or accessible [16].

Such frameworks contain important provisions on transparency which ensure that students, parents, and educators know how AI tools work), accountability keeping institutions to account for the educational outcomes achieved by AI, and redress mechanisms (enabling those affected by automated decisions to challenge them). Besides this, IP law meets with AI in education on ownership of AI-generated learning resources, algorithmic templates and digital content Institutions also interact with EdTech vendors through service agreements, which must adhere to contract law.

The legal constructs are up against a runaway train of AI evolution. Some laws were written in a time when traditional information systems were the standard, so they do not account for many of the intricate AI concerns like how bias can be learned in adaptive learning algorithms or what it means to provide transparent ethical predictive analytics to track student performance. The way to bridge this is by advocating for ongoing legal reform that is designed with input from educators, policymakers, technologists, and civil society to keep AI-powered educational uses within the bounds of lawful ethical benefits [17]. This need harmonized forward-looking strategies to guide our path of innovation while also protecting the rights and future wellbeing of learners and public trust on the use of AI in learning.

Global Data Protection Laws (GDPR, FERPA, etc.)

Data protection laws with worldwide scope such as the General Data Protection Regulation (GDPR) in Europe, The Family Educational

Rights and Privacy Act (FERPA) in US), etc., have a major influence on the way AI can be used ethically and legally within education. GDPR principles include data minimization, lawful processing, purpose limitation, right to access rectification and erasure of personal data [18]. It also specifies a requirement for clear consent procedures and additional precautions for processing special categories of personal data, which is crucial in the context of AI-driven education solutions designed to interpret user data. FERPA, however, deals with the privacy of student educational records and grants parents (and eligible students) the right to inspect and amend these records while also restricting unauthorized disclosures.

Canadian Personal Information Protection and Electronic Documents Act (PIPEDA) or the Australian Privacy Act 1988, Information Security Laws have been implemented in India known as Digital Personal Data Protection Act (DPDPA). Compliance with this regulation is important not only because it's the law, but also an exercise in building trust for education technology that leverages AI. Compliance with these laws also helps ensure accountability and transparency and establishes a global minimum standard for the protection of student data privacy in an era when learning is increasingly digital and data-rich [19].

6 Conclusion and Future Aspects

Even if the scalable growth of AI in education has the potential to revolutionize education, successful edtech relies on a foundation of ethical, private, and globally compliant best practices. As cutting-edge AI systems examine vast volumes of personal data and increasingly complicated behavior, student rights protection becomes increasingly important. Frameworks focused on ethics, justice, accountability, and transparency must direct AI in education to prevent bias and privacy issues that would jeopardize equal learning opportunities. Important legal boundaries are drawn by privacy rules like the GDPR, FERPA, and other jurisdiction-specific legislation that call for secure data management, informed permission, and transparent governance over data usage. In addition to being a legal requirement, these regulations are essential for building trust among children, parents, teachers, and institutions. Globally harmonizing data protection standards while allowing for local contexts can also help educational technology providers operate responsibly across borders, thereby reducing legal conflicts through international privacy standards and dual capability multi-stakeholder consensus.

The deployment of explainable AI models (XAIs), compliance audits, and robust cyber-security measures that guard against the compromise or misuse of educational data are some examples of preventative measures that contribute to the confidence in AI-powered learning environments. In line with moral values and international legal norms, technological innovation allows us to provide learner-centered settings that uphold students' autonomy and dignity while simultaneously enabling data-driven personalization that can enhance academic results. To put it briefly, adaptive governance frameworks will be necessary to handle the quick advancements in AI. This is a multi-stakeholder process that calls for the participation of legislators, educators, technologists, attorneys, and everyone else. This is the synergy that artificial intelligence in education has to attain in order to truly empower learning by protecting privacy, rights, and confidence while laying the groundwork for a digital learning environment that is fair, safe, and ethical.

References

1. Khan, W. N. (2024). Ethical challenges of AI in education: Balancing innovation with data privacy. *AI EDIFY Journal, 1*(1), 1–13.
2. Amoo, T. A. (2025). Ethical consideration in implementing AI-based tutoring systems as educational technology tool in education: Balancing efficiency with privacy and equity in the teaching of students. *FINGER: Jurnal Ilmiah Teknologi Pendidikan, 4*(1), 34–41.
3. Muli, M. (2024). Legal and ethical implications of data privacy in artificial intelligence: A review of data privacy among learners in Kenyan secondary schools. *Journal of the Kenya National Commission for UNESCO, 5*(1), 1–11.
4. Rehan, H. (2023). Shaping the future of education with cloud and AI technologies: Enhancing personalized learning and securing data integrity in the evolving edtech landscape. *Australian Journal of Machine Learning Research & Applications, 3*(1), 359–395.
5. Alam, A. (2023). Developing a curriculum for ethical and responsible AI: A university course on safety, fairness, privacy, and ethics to prepare next generation of AI professionals. In *Intelligent communication technologies and virtual mobile networks* (pp. 879–894). Springer Nature Singapore.
6. Li, Z., & Zhang, W. (2025). Technology in education: Addressing legal and governance challenges in the digital era. *Education and Information Technologies, 30*(7), 8413–8443.
7. Holmes, W., Persson, J., Chounta, I. A., Wasson, B., & Dimitrova, V. (2022). *Artificial intelligence and education: A critical view through the lens*

of human rights, democracy and the rule of law. Council of Europe.
8. Uunona, G. N., & Goosen, L. (2023). Leveraging ethical standards in artificial intelligence technologies: A guideline for responsible teaching and learning applications. In *Handbook of research on instructional technologies in health education and allied disciplines* (pp. 310–330). IGI Global.
9. Ikwuanusi, U. F., Adepoju, P. A., & Odionu, C. S. (2023). Advancing ethical AI practices to solve data privacy issues in library systems. *International Journal of Multidisciplinary Research Updates, 6*(1), 033–044.
10. Slimi, Z., & Carballido, B. V. (2023). Navigating the ethical challenges of artificial intelligence in higher education: An analysis of seven global AI ethics policies. *TEM journal, 12*(2), 590–602.
11. Radanliev, P. (2025). AI ethics: Integrating transparency, fairness, and privacy in AI development. *Applied Artificial Intelligence, 39*(1), 2463722.
12. Adams, C., Pente, P., Lemermeyer, G., & Rockwell, G. (2023). Ethical principles for artificial intelligence in K-12 education. *Computers & Education: Artificial Intelligence, 4*, 100131.
13. Holmes, W., & Porayska-Pomsta, K. (2023). *The ethics of artificial intelligence in education* (pp. 621–653). Routledge.
14. Mhlanga, D. (2023). Open AI in education, the responsible and ethical use of ChatGPT towards lifelong learning. In *FinTech and artificial intelligence for sustainable development: The role of smart technologies in achieving development goals* (pp. 387–409). Springer Nature Switzerland.
15. Al-Zahrani, A. M. (2024). Unveiling the shadows: Beyond the hype of AI in education. *Heliyon, 10*(9), e30696.
16. Akgun, S., & Greenhow, C. (2022). Artificial intelligence in education: Addressing ethical challenges in K-12 settings. *AI and Ethics, 2*(3), 431–440.
17. Cannarsa, M. (2021). Ethics guidelines for trustworthy AI. In *The Cambridge handbook of lawyering in the digital age* (pp. 283–297).
18. Bayan, F. M., & Fayyad, M. (2024). The Ethics of AI: Navigating the moral dilemmas of Artificial Intelligence. *Arab Journal for Scientific Publishing (AJSP) ISSN, 2663*, 5798.
19. Ungerer, L., & Slade, S. (2022). Ethical considerations of artificial intelligence in learning analytics in distance education contexts. In *Learning analytics in open and distributed learning: Potential and challenges* (pp. 105–120). Springer Nature Singapore.

CHAPTER 9

Data-Driven Education for Policy and Practice: Translating Educational Big Data into Effective Policy and Instruction

Kavita R. Singh, Prarthana A. Deshkar, and Praful V. Barekar

Abstract The development for data-driven education refers to the use of big data analytics for policymaking and to improve instructional practices. With the aggregating, analyzing, and visualizing large quantities of educational data from student performance metrics to engagement patterns, decision-makers become more informed about what needs attention in order to improve learning outcomes and equity. Implementing these lessons in policy requires the interpretation of data into local contexts, pedagogical goals and resource availability. For instance, the use of data to find achievement gaps allows for specific interventions and resource allocation or innovation in curricula. Teachers can use data dashboards to personalize learning, and policymakers can monitor the impact of

K. R. Singh (✉) · P. A. Deshkar · P. V. Barekar
Department of Computer Technology, Yeshwantrao Chavan College of Engineering, Nagpur, Maharashtra, India
e-mail: singhkavita19@gmail.com

P. K. Dutta et al. (eds.), *Digital Education for a Sustainable Future*, Sustainable Development Goals Series,
https://doi.org/10.1007/978-3-032-15433-0_9

educational reforms over time. The process requires sophisticated data manipulation and collection capabilities as well as ethical use to ensure that one is not using analytics as a student rights violation tool or perpetuating biases. This seamless and integrated data-driven approach closes the loop between educational research and practice to enable agile, transparent, and accountable education systems that are responsive to emerging societal and knowledge-based demands.

Keywords Educational big data · Data-driven policy · Personalized learning · Educational analytics · Evidence-based decision-making

1 Introduction

The growing sector has gone through a rapid digital transformation, offering unprecedented opportunities to use big data to support policy-making and improve instructional strategies [1]. The principal characteristic of data-driven education is that it implies in the systematic way, the collection, analysis and interpretation of broad datasets that come from different sources like student performance records, LMS (Learning Management Systems), standardized test results, attendance logs and even behavioral engagement metrics that we could collect during a digital learning experience. Educational big data, when carefully refined and employed, is a powerful tool in making better decisions that are informed by evidence to provide equitable, personalized, and high-quality learning [2]. At a policy level, big data analytics can reveal where systematic disparities exist and how resources are being allocated, but also measure the long-term impact of educational reforms. For example, predictive analytics can predict drop out risks by recognizing early preventer indicators which prompt strategies for timely intervention. It talked about how machine learning algorithms can figure out the patterns of student learning that may lead to more curriculum coordinates with the needs and demands of society. Data insights allow teachers to informatively adjust class plans, personalize learning paths and track student progress in real time helping adaptive learning models [3].

Significance and Rationale of Chapter

Big data in teacher professional development: identifies areas of competency, offers programs to plug skill gaps and makes sure teaching methodologies are also supported by evidence [4]. Such translation of big data into policies and practices owes to the importance of strict frameworks for data governance, ethical concerns regarding student privacy, and compliance with legal requirements such as the General Data Protection Regulation (GDPR) in the EU and Family Educational Rights and Privacy Act (FERPA) in the US. In the absence of these safeguards, companies run promotional campaigns that mislead users bias amplification and loss of trust by some education agencies [5]. The educators and administrators need to be supported with capacity building in the area to become data literate and analytics interpretive.

This requires a collaborative effort between policymakers, educators, technologists, parents and students to ensure that the use of data for decision-making is aligned to local contexts and cultural sensitivities. Ultimately, the real impact of educational big data is not in the collection, but rather in the utilization extracting raw datasets to transform predictive findings advancing learning equity, resource efficiency, and long-term academic achievement. The time is ripe for education systems to move from reactive policy measures to proactive, predictive and personalized measures based on data analytics in policy making and classroom practices, thus nurturing a future where every single learner finds the pathway to thrive in a world rich with data [6].

2 Data-Driven Education: Role of Big Data Analytics in Education

Big Data analytics is transforming how education operates offering institutions, policymakers, and educator's unprecedented opportunity to use vast and varied datasets in order to improve teaching and learning, as well as administrative decision making. Modern day education revolves around data; it is produced from multiple sources like—Learning Management System, Student Information System, digital learning platforms, assessments, attendance records, social media interactions and even various sensor based devices present inside smart classrooms. Big Data analytics is the method of being able to collect, process and analyze enormous amounts of diverse and constantly expanding datasets in order to discover patterns, correlations and trends that can be used to guide tactical solutions [7]. In a metaphorical sense, this provides the infrastructure for moving from gut feel to data-informed decision making in a pedagogical context to ensure efficiency, equity, and effectiveness of the workings or mechanisms of education systems.

These insights, for example, enable predictive analytics to detect students at risk of falling behind academically due to early indicators like decreased school attendance, low levels of interaction with course content or poor results in formative assessments. Forrester reports that learning analytics similarly provides personalizing teaching: tailoring content, pace, and methods of assessment to an individual learner's strongest gift and weakest area. In addition to insights at the individual-level, Big Data analytics can also be used for better curriculum design, optimal resource allocation, improved teacher performance and more accurate outcomes of programs. Aggregated educational data might be used at the policy level, e.g., to inform reforms or the allocation of funds, as well as strategies for reaching more and better access, inclusivity in education. Using billions of data available day by day Big Data can be analyzed via predictive and prescriptive models along with the new technologies like AI/ML types in real time which understanding learner behaviors not just at present, but relating to future acts also suggest specific interventions [8].

The transformative nature of Big Data in education is also coupled with challenges related to privacy and security as well as ethical use of personal data. Student rights need to be protected in the form of existing law and regulation such as GDPR and FERPA where sensitive educational data is concerned. There is a call for building educator and administrative data literacy to identify actionable information. Big Data analytics done right can provide a powerful enabling force that accelerates the creation and maintenance of contextually-aware, personalized, differentiated educational models to deliver education for all in which every learner is empowered with the tools they need to succeed not with static one-dimensional solutions but proven dynamic methods that scale. In reality, Big Data analytics is more than just an innovation it signifies a paradigm change in how schools define, evaluate, and seek excellence in the digital era [9].

3 Sources and Types of Educational Big Data

Educational big data comes from different sources, structured, and unstructured, is the result of the complexity of learning environments. Example of these are the learning management systems (LMS) tracking of student engagements, task submissions, quiz grades, and attendance analytics. Online assessments gather performance data at a fine-grain level and school information systems (SIS) house demographic, enrollment, and academic history information [10]. EdTech tools like intelligent tutoring systems, gamified learning platforms and adaptive learning software offer a wealth of additional real-time behavioral and interaction data at scale. So, other than the academic performance, attention span, facial expressions, and even physical activity in some R&D cases with sensor-based IoT devices and biometric tools is being checked including remote learning and smart classroom. In addition, rich datasets about peer interaction and informal learning trends can be obtained from social media engagement as well as collaborative online platforms.

The administrative big data, which we might define as information collected in schools or from individuals about what they do as e.g., enrollment rates, attendance records, and institutional performance; Academic performance big data the material that fills students' report cards and test scores; Behavioral big data details how students behave while at school, how they interact with each other or teachers; Affective big data is another major category of educational mining schools are using to track learning features such as emotional responses [11]. These sources and kinds of data together provide tools for educators, policymakers, and researchers to identify trends in response rates so individual students receive personalized learning experiences increased institutional effectiveness and sharing important concerns about ethical usage and privacy protections.

Student Information Systems

Student information systems basically it would be a centralized location to store any and all of a student's information, including things like demographic details, enrollment history, attendance, grades, and academic progress. These systems serve as a framework for education management, supporting the conversations between teachers, students, and parents. SIS supports the inflow of data from different sources, which will help in tracking each individual learner's journey accurately over a period. Student information systems use robust analytics to help identify student performance trends and facilitate early interventions for students who may be at risk. The contemporary student information systems solutions come with integrated compliance tools to address local and global data protection laws so that personal information is secured [12]. Student information systems form the core of data-driven administrative decision-making and academic research by offering a single intelligible data source.

Learning Management Systems (LMS)

A learning management system (LMS) is a software application for the administration documentation, tracking reporting and delivery of electronic educational technology (also called e-learning) courses or training programs. LMS provides insights of learner engagement, knowledge gaps, and completion rates with integrated analytics for lesson improvements. They also provide personalized learning paths, adapting the content based on how an individual is performing. Also, LMS are capable of integration with SIS and other institutional systems thereby creating a smooth learning data ecosystem. LMS serves as a primary medium of converting formal educational big data generated in the course of learning into effective teaching strategies by nurturing interactions, accessibility, and accountability [13].

Assessment and Performance Data

This includes formative, summative, standardized and diagnostic test results as well as classroom-based observations. These datasets contain skill development, learning outcome and subject specific proficiency related to learning that can be measured. Performance data is rich with such patterns, pointing out areas of student strength and identifying points for instruction. This information helps in planning the instruction based on real data and thus enables the teachers to plan interventions and strategies for differentiated learning. Using more sophisticated analytics, assessment outcomes can be correlated with engagement metrics, attendance and socio-demographic factors to create a complete picture of what influences learning [14]. Performance data, in addition to enhancing academic support, is used to drive institutional policy and curriculum design, as well as resource allocation.

4 Tools and Technologies for Educational Data Processing: Data Collection and Processing Frameworks

Advance data processing tools and frameworks improved the way educational data is processed by collecting, storing, cleaning, and analyzing available datasets systematically. Data collection in education is a broad scope including various data sources like Student Information Systems (SIS), Learning Management Systems (LMS), Online Assessment systems, IoT devices in classrooms for monitoring children and digital collaboration. The structured data can include gradebooks, attendance records or demographic information and unstructured data might be student posts in a discussion forum, essays or automatic lecture capture. These collection tools use APIs, automated scripts, and cloud-based synchronization so that data from both structured and unstructured silos are collected in real time without human error and accuracy [15].

In terms of processing, frameworks, and technologies such as Apache Hadoop/Spark or Google BigQuery are used for storing the big scale educational datasets, as they provide distributed storage and computation in parallel. Preprocessing techniques like data cleaning, normalization and anonymization to ensure quality and compliance of the information with regulations such as GDPR and FERPA. There are data integration platforms such as Talend or Informatics that provide you the functionality to consolidate all datasets from different sources into master repositories where they can be used for analytics [16]. To store the data, cloud-based services like AWS Education Cloud, Microsoft Azure Education Hub and Google Cloud for Education are capable of scaling storage and computation infrastructure, with integrated machine learning models for predictive as well as prescriptive analytics.

Tools such as Artificial Intelligence (AI) and Natural Language Processing (NLP) serve to also enrich the analysis of quality data, i.e., scattered comments of students or behavior trends in logs by detecting patterns that are not apparent through the conventional statistical methods. Integration with both data acquisition and processing framework guarantees a smooth transition from data collection to insights. This combined approach not only supports evidence-based policy making but can also facilitate individualized learning, early risk identification of students in need, curriculum improvement and the optimization of education system performance [17]. Robust tools and scalable technologies allow institutions to make sense of massive volumes of raw educational data, thus turning that wealth into more actionable knowledge to support academic success and equity.

5 Translating Data into Educational Policy: Evidence-Based Decision-Making Models

Education Evidence-based Decision-making (EBDM) approaches in education, which take advantage of big data and systematic analysis to inform data-driven policies that increase student learning, advance equity, and maximize resource use [18]. These models use a mix of data points for example, student demographics, attendance, performance metrics, engagement, and of socio-economic backgrounds which can be integrated into insights that can help policymakers to design more accurate interventions for students. The process starts with capturing and scrubbing educational data from sources such as Student Information Systems (SIS), Learning Management Systems (LMS), assessment tools, and behavioral analytics platforms. Predictive modeling, data mining and machine learning are used on this data to make predictions, uncover patterns, reveal underlying causes of educational issues and predict future trends.

Education Evidence-based Decision-making frameworks take a cyclical process: defining the problem, using research to the extent possible to analyze trends, adopting policies that have evidence of effectiveness, and evaluating outcomes for future continuous improvement. For example, predictive analytics can be used to identify students that are at risk soon enough so schools faculty could intervene early with academic or mental health support [19]. The longitudinal data analysis can inform curricular reform that focuses on a specified group of students across time and space, guide teacher in-service training programs to adequately address curriculum standards; as well as help policymakers on specific schools (poor) resource allocation process. Alignment of data interpretation with evidence-based strategies for improvement is bolstered by internationally recognized frameworks (e.g., the Data Wise Improvement Process, Plan-Do-Study-Act), which serve as guides to all stakeholders.

Translation of data to policy needs strong analytics and regulations such as GDPR, FERPA, and regional privacy protection laws in place and the largest part is the collaboration with stakeholders across organizations. And by making it easy to be accurate, reliable, and contextual about data, policy-makers can keep out biases and misinterpretations which could otherwise just inflame the very inequalities they are trying to prevent [20]. It also brings on-the-ground reality to the rigorous exercise of policy formulation and last-mile delivery through qualitative insights from teachers, parents, and students. This evidence-based decision-making harnesses educational data to create overarching strategies that lead to systemic transformation. Implemented effectively, these models can help researchers and practitioners work together to both shape a more adaptive approach to education that is inclusive of the emerging new world order and responsive to changing societal needs, particularly in the rapidly evolving environment [21].

6 Challenges and Barriers

Academic challenges as well as inherent technological, institutional, ethical, and cultural obstacles can hinder the effective use of educational big data [22]. A key part of that is data quality and standardization, because inconsistent, incomplete data across systems can hinder the ability to effectively gain insights. Privacy and data protection considerations, particularly in relation to regulations such as GDPR and FERPA, require strict compliance mechanisms that can be costly, complex, and difficult to implement effectively. Moreover, educational institutions are suffering from shortage of analysis capability; while data can be found in the vast majority of systems, there is often a lack of genuine long-term capacity and structure to tackle them at an analytical level and develop insights [23]. Organizational resistance is common too—educators and administrators are often set in their ways and swayed by arguments that surveillance will increase, autonomy decrease, or qualitative elements be undermined if data-driven approaches take them over. The financial capacity means teams have restricted access to advanced analytics tools and cloud computing resources; low investment in professional development for high-quality data literacy skills. In the end, ethical dilemmas like algorithmic bias or misrepresentation of data can erode trust; transparency, equity, and human-centeredness in data practices are paramount.

Technical and Infrastructure Constraints

The major challenges are the imposition of technical and infrastructure constraints to attain data-driven systems for education. Many institutions are challenged by network bandwidth that is insufficient to move data in a timely manner from research site to another and outdated hardware and limited storage capacity incapable of storing multiple terabytes or petabytes of data on premises [24]. Comprehensive analytics are a challenge thanks to this lack of integration multiple-platform integrations are hard because legacy systems typically don't communicate with each other too well. Although cloud-based solutions are appealing, they need reliable internet connectivity instead of rural or underfunded areas. Second, security flaws in systems putting at risk data protection protocols are not only causing breaches but also diluting trust. The cost of solving for these constraints is huge in terms of investment in cutting edge infrastructure, scalable architecture and resilient security framework to manage reliability, performance, and compliance.

Skills and Capacity Gaps

The effective use of educational data analytics is largely constrained by skills and capacity gaps. This has created a unique problem for educators, administrators, and policy-makers: Few possess the requisite data literacy to understand complex datasets and translate them into effective strategies [25]. Without statistical analysis, machine learning or data visualization skills, data-driven business decisions can be misinformed or deferential to outsourced consultants. Faculty and staff training programs tend to be ad hoc or insufficient leading institutions to lack recurrent in-house analytical capability. There is a dearth of interdisciplinary professionals who understand both pedagogy and advanced analytics, further reinforcing the gap alongside comprehensive capacity-building programmes and continuous professional development.

Stakeholder Resistance

Educators, students, parents, or administrators may be skeptical about data-based practices are taking resistance from stakeholders. These include a fear that the learning process will be dehumanized, that education will become overly algorithmic or teachers over monitored and of course the old bugbear of academic freedom. Analysts can be seen as competitive threats to coal-face professionals, or the data capability itself may not be trusted in interpretation. In addition, cultural, and institutional norms often support traditional methods of evaluation which makes it challenging to integrate innovation into practice. Resistance to evidence-based practice can be difficult to overcome; however, the means through which this resistance was managed provide a template for effective strategies: transparent communication, participatory decision-making, and direct evidence of how educating workforces using data-driven approaches improves learning outcomes as well as institutional performance [25].

7 AI and Machine Learning in Education Analytics

AI and Machine Learning driven education analytics advances in deriving deeper insights from a variety of education datasets which are voluminous and extremely complex. With the aid of AI the systems can handle big data from sources like Learning Management Systems (LMS), Student Information Systems (SIS), assessments, and behavioral tracking tools and may look at hidden patterns often missed by human analysis as well. These techniques allow for predictive analytics which means predicting the student grades and whether a student will pass, drop-out or they are in need of personalized learning support helping schools to intervene better in advance. By adapting to individual learning styles, pace, and preferences content delivery through these technologies supports a more student-centered approach. NLP tools look at free-text responses, forums, and open-ended surveys to assess understanding, interest, and sentiment. AI can also improve automated grading systems, which will save educators time and eliminate mechanical tasks [26]. AI-driven analytics also support the evidence-base for resource allocation, curriculum adjustment or long-term planning in policy contexts.

But implementing it successfully will demand solid data governance, effectively integrated with ethical guidelines and transparent handling of biases or privacy concerns. With AI and ML technology inside, useful human knowledge from education experts and a "best next action" to execute that expert advice in real classrooms: education systems can help move the needle from reactive to proactive decision-making while boiling such insights into smarter teaching, learning, and administration resulting in more equitable, efficient, and effective outcomes [27].

8 Global Collaboration for Data-Driven Policy

When nations work together to share knowledge, the tools and datasets they need, policy-makers can develop locally relevant, research-based policies. International organizations, research institutions are increasingly coordinating to lay the collaborative groundwork for common data standards and interoperability frameworks as well as open-access repositories designed to allow data across different disciplines to be interoperable and comparable. Projects such as the UN's Sustainable Development Goals (SDG) data platforms, the OECD's education and economic databases or the World Health Organization's global health observatories are evidence that sharing your data can speed up responses to challenges and projects [28]. The technologies such as cloud computing, blockchain for data integrity, or large-scale analytics by artificial intelligence are empowering the robustness and scalability of world-wide data collaborations tremendously. These efforts to do real-time monitoring, predictive modeling and comparative benchmarking allow policymakers to create flexible strategies that respond dynamically to changing circumstances. Cross-border cooperation further supports capacity-building through the transfer of knowledge, technical training, and collaborative research programming that contributes to diminishing data inequity between developed versus developing zones. Such initiatives will need strong governance and regulatory oversight of data privacy, sovereignty, and ethical considerations to establish trust among stakeholders in these digital ecosystems led marketplace. In the end, global cooperation in data-driven policy-making builds collective intelligence and transparency, accountability and mutual responsibility among countries for a more effective and inclusive global governance [29].

9 Conclusion

Global collaboration for data-driven policy is a transformative pathway to smarter, more just and impactful governance on the planet's toughest challenges. Bringing together a variety of datasets powered by advanced analytics and multi-stakeholder engagement ensures that in writing policy, one works from strong evidence rather than political expediency or fragmented insights. This has been shown to hold great potential in driving forward common objectives such as the UN Sustainable Development Goals, preparation for international health-related crises, optimization of climate adaptation actions and inclusive economic development. The posting and exchange of data and know-how across borders also plays an important role in stimulating cooperation, which helps our countries be successful. Driving these potential benefits is, of course, fraught with hurdles chief among them unequal data architecture, lagging technical capability and divergent legal and ethical frameworks regulating the use of data. In the absence of remedial action, they could consign collaborative initiatives to the margins and thus continue to entrench irreparable divides.

10 Recommendations

This will require for the establishment of global data governance frameworks to guarantee interoperability of the systems and protection of privacy while offering the same chances to all nations and institutions. There should be emphasis on investments in digital infrastructure and capacity building to make it a priority, especially because that is part of the low- and middle-income countries to ensure their full participation in global data ecosystems. Finally, promoting open-data policies without compromising security and ethics will help to increase the broad base of knowledge that can be used for evidence-informed policy-making. Fourth, using new technologies like artificial intelligence, blockchain and advanced analytics can enhance the quality, transparency of data to make insights more actionable. Institutionalize multi-sector partnerships between governments, academia, private sector and civil society to ensure ongoing dialogue, knowledge sharing and collaborative problem-solving. So, embedding inclusive and equitable practices throughout the data lifecycle, including collecting, processing and applying of data will ensure that any policy decisions derived from global collaborations are truly representative, culturally sensitive and able to adequately address the needs of marginalized populations. Taken together, these steps would help the global community to generate better insights from evidence and infect its policy-making with innovation that is indigenous, more certain but likewise agiler not only smarter but also quicker, fairer, and future-fit. It will be essential to use this combination to navigate effectively in an era of twenty-first-century uncertainties with global governance is agile, transparent, and all-inclusive.

References

1. Khan, W. N. (2024). Ethical challenges of AI in education: Balancing innovation with data privacy. *AI EDIFY Journal, 1*(1), 1–13.
2. Amoo, T. A. (2025). Ethical consideration in implementing AI-based tutoring systems as educational technology tool in education: Balancing efficiency with privacy and equity in the teaching of students. *FINGER: Jurnal Ilmiah Teknologi Pendidikan, 4*(1), 34–41.
3. Muli, M. (2024). Legal and ethical implications of data privacy in artificial intelligence: A review of data privacy among learners in Kenyan secondary schools. *Journal of the Kenya National Commission for UNESCO, 5*(1), 2958–7999.
4. Fedele, A., Punzi, C., & Tramacere, S. (2024). The ALTAI checklist as a tool to assess ethical and legal implications for a trustworthy AI development in education. *Computer Law & Security Review, 53*, 105986.
5. Ramnani, S. (2024). Exploring ethical considerations of Artificial Intelligence in educational settings: An examination of bias, privacy, and accountability. *International Journal of Novel Research and Development (IJNRD), 9*(2), 2456–4184.
6. Li, Z., & Zhang, W. (2025). Technology in education: Addressing legal and governance challenges in the digital era. *Education and Information Technologies, 30*(7), 8413–8443.
7. Ismail, I. A., & Aloshi, J. M. R. (2025). Data privacy in AI-driven education: An in-depth exploration into the data privacy concerns and potential solutions. In *AI Applications and Strategies in Teacher Education* (pp. 223–252). IGI Global.
8. Ismail, I. A. (2025). Protecting privacy in ai-enhanced education: A comprehensive examination of data privacy concerns and solutions in AI-based learning. In *Impacts of Generative AI on the Future of Research and Education* (pp. 117–142).
9. Shukla, S. (2024). Principles governing ethical development and deployment of AI. *Journal of Artificial Intelligence Ethics, 7*(1), 45–60.
10. Kashefi, P., Kashefi, Y., & Ghafouri Mirsaraei, A. (2024). Shaping the future of AI: balancing innovation and ethics in global regulation. *Uniform Law Review, 29*(3), 524–548.
11. Kaddouri, M., Mhamdi, K., Chniete, I., Marhraoui, M., Khaldi, M., & Jmad, S. (2025). Adopting AI in education: Technical challenges and ethical constraints. In *Fostering Inclusive Education with AI and Emerging Technologies* (pp. 25–72). IGI Global.
12. Balan, A. (2024). Examining the ethical and sustainability challenges of legal education's AI revolution. *International Journal of the Legal Profession, 31*(3), 323–348.

13. Peñalvo, F. J. G., Alier, M., Pereira, J., & Casany, M. J. (2024). Safe, transparent, and ethical artificial intelligence: Keys to quality sustainable education (SDG4). *IJERI: International journal of Educational Research and Innovation, 22*, 1–21.
14. Radanliev, P. (2025). AI ethics: Integrating transparency, fairness, and privacy in AI development. *Applied Artificial Intelligence, 39*(1), 2463722.
15. Cheng, L., Han, J., & Nasirov, J. (2024). Ethical considerations related to personal data collection and reuse: Trust and transparency in language and speech technologies. *International Journal of Legal Discourse, 9*(2), 217–235.
16. Sumartono, E., Harliyanto, R., Situmeang, S. M. T., Siagian, D. S., & Septaria, E. (2024). The legal implications of data privacy laws, cybersecurity regulations, and AI ethics in a digital society. *The Journal of Academic Science, 1*(2), 103–110.
17. Peer Mohamed, M. S. (2024). *Exploring ethical dimensions of AI-enhanced language education: A literature perspective*. Technology in Language Teaching & Learning.
18. Ray, S., & Ray, D. P. (2024). Artificial intelligence in education: Navigating the nexus of innovation and ethics for future learning landscapes. *International Journal of Research-GRANTHAALAYAH, 11*(12), 163–174.
19. Prajapati, M. A. B. (2024). Artificially intelligent in education:"Redefining learning in the 21st century". *Journal of Educational Technology, v1*, 12818287. https://doi.org/10.5281/zenodo.12818287
20. Gilbert, C., & Gilbert, M. A. (2024). The convergence of artificial intelligence and privacy: Navigating innovation with ethical considerations. *International Journal of Scientific Research and Modern Technology (IJSRMT), 3*(9), 9–17.
21. Stracke, C. M., Chounta, I. A., & Homes, W. (2024). Global trends in scientific debates on trustworthy and ethical Artificial Intelligence and education. In *International Conference on Artificial Intelligence in Education* (pp. 254–262). Springer.
22. Chen, H. (2024). The ethical challenges of educational artificial intelligence and coping measures: A discussion in the context of the 2024 World Digital Education Conference. *Science Insights Education Frontiers, 20*(2), 3263–3281.
23. Al-Zahrani, A. M. (2024). Unveiling the shadows: Beyond the hype of AI in education. *Heliyon, 10*(9), e30696.
24. Shoghli, A., Darvish, M., & Sadeghian, Y. (2024). Balancing innovation and privacy: Ethical challenges in AI-driven healthcare. *Journal of Reviews in Medical Sciences, 4*(1), 1–11.

25. Mbah, G. O. (2024). Data privacy in the era of AI: Navigating regulatory landscapes for global businesses. *International Journal of Scientific Research and Analysis, 13*(2), 2396–2405.
26. Farooqi, M. T. K., Amanat, I., & Awan, S. M. (2024). Ethical considerations and challenges in the integration of artificial intelligence in education: A systematic review. *Journal of Excellence in Management Sciences, 3*(4), 35–50.
27. Singh, T. M., Reddy, C. K. K., Murthy, B. R., Nag, A., & Doss, S. (2025). AI and education: Bridging the gap to personalized, efficient, and accessible learning. In *Internet of behavior-based computational intelligence for smart education systems* (pp. 131–160). IGI Global.
28. Bulathwela, S., Pérez-Ortiz, M., Holloway, C., Cukurova, M., & Shawe-Taylor, J. (2024). Artificial intelligence alone will not democratise education: On educational inequality, techno-solutionism and inclusive tools. *Sustainability, 16*(2), 781.
29. Alqahtani, N., & Wafula, Z. (2025). Artificial intelligence integration: Pedagogical strategies and policies at leading universities. *Innovative Higher Education, 50*(2), 665–684.

CHAPTER 10

Educating Future Generations with AI for Legal Sustainability and SDG Compliance: Reimagining Global Insolvency and Bankruptcy Through Mediation

Sureksha Garg, Vaishali Arora, and Ankit Garg

Abstract Insolvency and bankruptcy process is vital part of financial freedom, economic system as well as institutional building. Typically constructed with adversarial, courtroom-laden models, they routinely perpetuate financial suffering, shrink asset worth, and ignore the human and sociological dynamics of corporate failure. Global insolvency and bankruptcy regimes can be reconfigured through a symbiotic merger of mediation, artificial intelligence (AI), and legal education to contribute to the advancement of the United Nations Sustainable Development Goals

S. Garg (✉) · V. Arora · A. Garg
Sharda School of Law, Sharda University, Greater Noida, India
e-mail: surekshagarg04@gmail.com

V. Arora
e-mail: vaishali.arora@sharda.ac.in

P. K. Dutta et al. (eds.), *Digital Education for a Sustainable Future*, Sustainable Development Goals Series,
https://doi.org/10.1007/978-3-032-15433-0_10

(SDGs): specifically, SDG 16 (Peace, Justice and Strong Institutions) and SDG 4 (Quality Education). Mediation represents a low cost, quick, less adversarial option promoting consensual restructuring and retaining the value of the enterprise. In combination with AI-powered analytics and online dispute resolution (ODR) platforms, mediation improves predictive risk assessment and decision-making in insolvency. It also needs to see changes in legal education to incorporate multidisciplinary skills down the line, in technology, ADR (Alternative Dispute Resolution), and sustainable development. The chapter explores comparative jurisdictions such as those in US, UK, EU, and India, and global sources such as the Singapore Convention on Mediation and UNICTRAL Models Law among others. It also assesses obstacles like regulatory intransigence, AI ethics and the digital divide.

Keywords Mediation in Insolvency · Artificial Intelligence in Legal Systems · Sustainable Development Goals (SDGs) · Legal Education Reform · Bankruptcy Law Innovation

1 Introduction

In a fast changing world economy is characterized by instability, technological innovation, and growing economic gap, there is now more emphasis on insolvency and bankruptcy laws as an essential part of economic stability and social justice. These institution building processes with adversarial judicial features are those which focus on addressing the financial distress of businesses and of individuals in ways that protect the interests of creditors and encourage economic restructuring. Yet despite being institutionally robust and emotionally and socially brutal for everyone involved today's global bankruptcy systems frequently get a bad rap for being slow, costly, and resource intensive. Against the backdrop of unprecedented challenges such as post-pandemic recovery, climate-related financial strain and digital transformation of markets, insolvency regimes which prioritize litigation as a means of addressing them warrant scrutiny. The immediate demand is for a more humane, proactive and future-fit legal system- one that marries tools of alternate dispute resolution (ADR) like mediation with artificial Intelligence (AI) and for it to be cast in the framework of United Nations Sustainable Development Goals (SDGs).

Mediation provides real practical solutions, alternative to regular bankruptcy actions. Through dialogue, cooperation, and interests-based negotiation, mediation minimizes conflict, creates an environment conducive to creative outcomes, while maintaining relationships as well as the value of a business. It gives troubled entities and creditors the ability to collaborate on restructuring plans in ways that avoid the waste and acrimony of litigation. In contrast to what is typical of legal orders that rigidly address the adjudication process, mediation tends to generate more durable and more emotionally satisfying responses. In particular, this is bad news for SMEs, start-up businesses and social businesses, which cannot afford the financial strain of multiple legal battles. A number of jurisdictions, including, but not limited to, Singapore and the European Union, have introduced structured mediation processes into their insolvency legislation; a forward-looking trend that should be echoed and further developed on the global stage [1].

Ethical and strategic use of artificial intelligence can greatly enhance mediation, and insolvency matters. Artificial intelligence based solutions can scan for early-warning signs of financial distress, propose restructuring options based on case databases, automated document processing and help conduct virtual mediation in online dispute resolution (ODR) platforms. For risk profiling, negotiation simulation and predicting judicial outcomes, machine learning algorithms may help stakeholders in making more informed decisions. Yet, although AI may make the process more efficient and promote access to justice, it will have to be employed with robust safe guards to maintain fair and transparent content, and protect sensitive financial and personal information.

It is critical that we teach these skills to the next generation of lawyers, judges, and policy experts as well as mediation skills and sustainability frameworks. If there is suspicion of it, do not just start developing here and there a new curriculum many of the existing legal curricula in many countries are still based on ancient traditions of common law, in which dispute resolution is more important than deal-making and doctrine is more important than practice. There is an immediate need for legal education reform, towards accelerating multidisciplinary components on ADR, fintech, legal tech, sustainability policy etc. If we train students to engage on digital insolvency mediation, we can educate a generation of lawyers who are prepared to deliver justice in the highly dynamic, complex, and borderless economic environment in which all operate [2].

This chapter takes an interdisciplinary approach in discussing the confluence of mediation, AI, and legal pedagogy within the domain of worldwide insolvency and bankruptcy. It considers how these components, when combined with the UN's SDGs (particularly SDG 16: Peace, Justice, and Strong Institutions, SDG 8: Decent Work and Economic Growth, SDG 4: Quality Education, and SDG 9: Industry, Innovation, and Infrastructure) can lead to more sustainable, inclusive and efficient legal and economic systems. It also considers the increasing importance on cross-border insolvency, envisaged by the UNCITRAL Model Law and the Singapore Convention on Mediation to the advancement of worldwide legal harmonization and cooperation. The chapter studies the best practices of different jurisdictions - including the United States Chapter 11 bankruptcy code, India's Insolvency and Bankruptcy Code (IBC), and the European Union Restructuring Directive to examine the way in which mediation along with AI is being incorporated in national insolvency frameworks [3].

But these changes don't come without challenges as legal conservatism and collective behaviours of opposition against IT, digital illiteracy, ethical issues, and conservative legal practice still obstruct reform. There are many nations without the regulatory framework or political infrastructure in place to bring about such radical change. In order for there to be any substantive slow of progress all levels of government, global institutions, tertiary institutions, and the public sphere must actively work to imbue legal reform processes with notions of sustainability, innovation and access [4]. The aim of this chapter is to further animate this transformative agenda by providing a holistic model that is consistent with the imperatives of global sustainability, encourages legal innovation, and advances a more democratic and egalitarian approach to financial distress and renewal [5].

2 Understanding the Global Landscape of Insolvency and Bankruptcy

The world over there has been significant evolution in the insolvency and bankruptcy landscape in recent decades, in light of changing economic structures, global trade dynamics, and increased acknowledgement on the need for an effective, holistic, and fair financial distress resolution framework [6]. Yet the details of insolvency regimes differ greatly from one jurisdiction to the other, determined by disparate legal traditions, institutional capabilities, and social and economic conditions.

In places such as the U.S., Chapter 11 is widely admired for its debtor-in-possession structure, under which companies can reorganize while in charge of day-to-day operations. It provides flexibility and court supervision, to encourage rehabilitation, not just liquidation. The UK, on the other hand, privileges creditor rights through tools such as administration and company voluntary arrangements (CVAs), in which insolvency practitioners frequently play a dominant role in reshaping troubled firms. The European Union (EU), mindful of the instrumental role of cross-border cooperation, has promulgated the Restructuring and Insolvency Directive (2019) in order to align the pre-insolvency processes and to promote business rescue culture among member states.

Some of the emerging economies like India has brought in a significant reform in the bankruptcy laws by enacting the Insolvency and Bankruptcy Code, 2016 (IBC) which consolidates the insolvency laws and ensures the reduction of time taken for the corporate resolution process. Although the IBC is a major stride towards crediting confidence and business resurgence, the same is not sheltered from criticisms on account of delays and litigation bottlenecks, insufficiency and fill-over of institutional capacities [7]. Insolvency laws in China are still at a nascent stage, and court-driven restructurings have picked up pace only in the past couple of years as market reforms have matured. Brazil, South Africa, and several nations in Southeast Asia are still struggling to create a workable balance between creditor rights, debtor protection, and the constraints.

The interesting development in the international insolvency landscape is the emergence of cross-border insolvency regimes, including the UNCITRAL Model Law on Cross-Border Insolvency, which has been adopted by more than 50 nations. This system enables courts and insolvency administrators in multiple countries to help resolve the failure of a corporation that operates in more than one country. However, discrepancies in application persist, particularly in the Global South, where insolvency regimes are frequently marred by uncertainty in procedure, inconsistent enforcement and inability in bringing their practice in line with international standards. The international insolvency and bankruptcy arena appears to be a tale of advancement and division [8]. With the world's economies more interconnected and crisis events more complex, there is an increasing requirement to have insolvency regimes that are harmonized, technology integrated and enable mediation to cater for financial distress dynamically, while also focusing on recovery and long-term economic viability and access to justice.

Cross-Border Insolvency: UNCITRAL Model Law and Multilateral Cooperation

Global insolvency is a growing phenomenon in a growingly stage-managed economy where multinational enterprises ply their trade across seamlessly crossing borders and, when they fail, the knock-on effects are often felt in a plethora of countries [9]. Domestic insolvency systems simply designed for national context are unable to manage the multi-nation collapse, and legal uncertainty, asset dissipation, and fragmented proceedings ensue. The United Nations Commission on International Trade Law (UNCITRAL) attempted to address these issues by way of the Model Law on Cross-Border Insolvency in 1997. This groundbreaking framework will foster judicial cooperation among courts and local insolvency professionals in cross-border insolvency proceedings leading to more streamlined and predictable results.

The four main tenets of the UNCITRAL Model Law are accessibility, recognition, assistance and supervision. It allows foreign debt-holders to take part in domestic insolvency proceedings and it allows for the recognition of foreign judgements and restructuring plans. The Model Law has been implemented in some states and serves as a basis for multilateral agreement. These harmonizations of laws achieve the protection of creditor rights, preservation of debtor values and coordination of restructurings across the world. But obstacles remain to multilateral cooperation on cross-border insolvency. Disparities in legal regimes and discretion, as well differences based on national interests and political will, can create barriers to unbroken implementation [10]. A large number of countries have not though followed the Model Law and also did not adopt or apply it, leading topsy-turvy in global arena. Improved international cooperation indispensable for any success in this regard would be greater international coordination through treaties, bankruptcy database sharing and improved training of Judges. It is within this framework that the combination of mediation services and AI quality tools can contribute to the enhancement of cross-border resolution processes, to the benefit of faster, fairer, and more sustainable solutions to be used in support of both global trade and investment stability and the achievement of the SDGs.

3 Case for Mediation in Insolvency and Bankruptcy

Mediation has become a potent, practical and a growing need in insolvency and bankruptcy cases as an alternative to traditional litigation with its usual high costs, delays, and adversarial impact. In the midst of financial tumult when emotions are running high, commercial relations are under strain and asset values are plummeting, mediation can create an environment where debtors, creditors, and other stakeholders collaborate to negotiate a solution that all find acceptable. Unlike court-driven processes, which are accused by some to be adversarial and transactional in nature, mediation is elastic, private, and orientated to interest-based resolution, which makes it particularly strong in insolvency contexts where maintaining value and ongoing relationships is critical. A key benefit of mediation in the context of an insolvency process is the maintenance of going concern status as well as asset value. Protracted litigation can deplete a company's reserves, tarnish its reputation, and undermine the trust necessary to reorganize [11]. Mediation is a way for the parties to resolve disputes early in the process, before you have a full-blown bankruptcy. Adverse or prolonged litigation can be especially harmful for Micro, Small, and Medium Enterprises (MSMEs) that do not have the financial strength to overcome a drawn-out litigation. Furthermore, mediated resolutions are moulded to commercial and economic realities of the case at hand rather than formulaic judicial orders, hence they are more creative and lasting.

Mediation can also minimize the costs of litigation and alleviate the burden of clogged court calendars on overwhelmed court systems. Indeed, in jurisdictions where the court system is underfunded or overburdened typical in many developing economies mediation introduces an alternative path to justice. It is processable at ODR platforms, enabling access to justice for parties which would otherwise be isolated geographically or economically. Crucially, mediation also serves the value of party or contractual autonomy, leaving the parties to mould to their own preferred solutions rather than being subject to the decisions of the courts.

From the point of view of legal sustainability and policy, mediation is in common with the SDG 16 (Peace, Justice and Strong Institutions) the promotion of inclusive, transparent, and robust justice systems. States such as Singapore, the UK, and certain EU participants have integrated processes for structured mediation within their insolvency laws underpinned by instruments such as the Singapore Convention on Mediation and the EU's Preventive Restructuring Directive. Even in India, under the new Insolvency and Bankruptcy Code (IBC), India is experimenting with pre-insolvency mediation. Mediation can address a number of systemic inadequacies in the traditional systems of insolvency, by promoting efficiency, inclusivity and economic viability. With the reform of international insolvency regulations, using mediation as an instrument of core economics is the best practise for a strong financial ecosystem and equitable law results [12].

Defining Mediation in the Legal Context

In the legal sense of the term, mediation is a structured and confidential process that occurs in non-public, in which an impartial third party ('the mediator') assists disputing parties in attempting to find a mutually acceptable resolution to their dispute. Mediators are not decision-makers like judges and arbitrators, they facilitate negotiation and resolution, and are role models for cooperation and problem solving. Mediation is based on party autonomy, flexibility and confidentiality and is well adapted for complex and confidential matters, such as insolvency cases.

Comparative Value over Litigation and Arbitration

Mediation provides some distinct differences from court proceedings and arbitration. It is less litigious, faster, and economical. Litigation and arbitration are binding, and frequently public; mediation protects relationships and privacy. It fosters the creative and interest-driven results it seeks and eschews strict procedural trappings. Parties are still in charge of the process and the final result, which leads to satisfaction with and compliance of the terms.

Early Action and Pre-Insolvency Solutions

Mediation has become more attractive for preventive restructuring and pre-insolvency scenarios whereby struggling companies can approach their creditors before insolvency proceedings are formally launched [13]. An ounce of prevention is worth a pound of cure in terms of protecting the value of the enterprise and preventing liquidation and preserving jobs.

Early conversation and willing deals on mediation can help guide companies to recovery and limit the wholesale systemic financial dislocation.

Mediation for Corporate Hospital Rehabilitation and MSME Protection

In corporate rescue and MSME safeguards, mediation is a critical tool as it provides customized solutions to meet the specific needs of micro-businesses. Many MSMEs do not have the capacity to withstand expensive and time-consuming bankruptcy processes. Round-table mediation creates an affordable and informal environment for re-scheduling debts, re-negotiating contracts and managing turnarounds preserving economic activity and jobs.

4 AI and Legal Technology in Insolvency Mediation

The application of Artificial Intelligence (AI) and legal technology in insolvency mediation is a game-changing development in the manner individuals and cooperations are managing financial distress and corporate collapse in the current century. Businesses are experiencing increasing complexity, globalization and disruption by technology, and the traditional legal mechanisms—which can be slow, expensive, and inflexible—are often ill equipped to deliver value in terms of time and perspicacity. By leveraging mediation frameworks, AI-driven tools may transform the practice of insolvency regime for the better including efficiency, accessibility and outcome predictability all in a manner that reduces the demand on courts and legal practitioners.

Predictive analytics is the most potential uses of AI in insolvency mediation. Using enormous data sets from the history of bankruptcies, AI is able to predict the probability of defaults and recommend structuring options and the financial solvency of distressed entities. These discoveries promote early action, enabling mediators and interested parties to be proactive without waiting for the business to fail. These early-warning mechanisms offer a lifeline to the country's MSMEs alerting them to financial distress when they would otherwise have no means of having their financial health monitored, and receiving legal advice promptly [14].

The major breakthrough pertains to the Online Dispute Resolution (ODR) platforms using Artificial intelligence to enable electronic mediation, automate exchange of documents as well as communicate in real time among quarrelling factions. They also overcome geographical and financial challenges to justice, particularly in cross-border insolvencies. AI can reduce the number of routine administrative tasks such as summarizing financial statements, preparing mediation briefs and organizing case files that mediators perform so that mediators can concentrate their time on the important work of facilitating dialogue and settlement. Even in more complicated cases, AI can provide decision-support tools that simulate the consequences of various user-entered conditions, which work to increase the transparency and reality of mediation scenarios [15]. The use of Natural Language Processing (NLP) can be helpful in reviewing legal contract books, spotting incoherences and determining substantial obligations the negotiation process is focusing on. AI-powered chatbots and legal assistants can also initially guide struggling businesses or creditors through the insolvency process, explain their rights and prepare them for mediation. But the use of AI in insolvency mediation does not come without its obstacles. Issues of data privacy, algorithmic bias, and opacity of AI decision-making need to be attentively handled. Sensitive financial and legal data need to be secured and comply with privacy laws.

5 Legal Education for Sustainable Futures: Reimagining Legal Curricula with AI and Mediation Skills

In the midst of rapid technological change, along with increasing economic insecurity and a shifting understanding of global justice, the conventional legal academy arrives at a most critical juncture. The law is incredibly complex, more and more entangled with digital systems, and more often called up to enable just, expedient, and sustainable results. In such conditions, the task of rethinking legal education is pressing and inescapable. Law schools need to go beyond old curricula still dominated by litigious and doctrinal mindsets, and prepare a new kind of lawyer, one that is multidisciplinary, digital-ready and ADR-competent especially mediation-based on a larger perspective of legal sustainability and the creation of constructive legal mindsets framed by the UN Sustainable Development Goals (SDGs).

This transformation includes the incorporation of the AI and mediation skills across legal curriculum. As artificial intelligence (AI) further unrolls its disruptive potential in the legal profession predictive analytics, smart legal research, document review, and ODR the lawyers of tomorrow need to be taught how to use such tools efficiently, and, more importantly, what the implications of their use are in terms of ethics, law, and society at large. It used to be that AI was an incidental piece of learning, but AI has now become a fundamental piece of legal literacy. Understanding of machine learning models, data insights, algorithmic accountability and legal tech ecosystems is a must in the new world of legal challenges, especially in niche sectors such as insolvency and bankruptcy, where the stakes are high and there is a pressing need for immediate action [16].

At the same time, mediation is taking hold as a transformative tool in legal systems, providing a collaborative, interest-based, and less expensive alternative to adversarial litigation. In the insolvency environment, where the players are frequently engaged in high-stakes negotiations at the intersection of debt, assets, and survival, mediation can provide solutions that are practical and save economic value for the business and for the stakeholders. It can argue that would imply that the legal training will need to impart both theoretical understanding and practical skills in meditation. This involves conflict resolution knowledge, communication tools and principles of negotiation, multicultural understanding, and the use of empathy in resolution. Simulations, clinical mediation services and the like, experiential modules can provide the students with opportunities to practice ADR in the real world while getting a better understanding of the rules of ethics and procedure as they pertain to ADR.

Just as crucial, is the alignment of legal education with the Sustainable Development Goals, enjoined in SDGs 4 and 16 on Quality Education and Peace, Justice, and Strong Institutions respectively. Law schools can no longer be considered as mere institutions of academic learning but as key players in the construction of resilient legal orders that contribute to justice, peace and sustainability. Reform of the curriculum to incorporate topics in climate justice, digital rights, financial inclusion, justice for social, etc. connecting law with economics, tech, policy and ethical studies [17]. For example, insolvency/bankruptcy instruction cannot limit itself to the four corners of the Insolvency Act, but should encompass comparative systems, international best practices such as the UNCITRAL Model Law, and the socio-economic consequences of financial failure. Understanding how AI tools can aid in identifying financial distress early and how mediation can retain stakeholder relationships can change the narrative for insolvency commencing with a preventative approach not a punitive one.

Building Digital Literacy in Law Students and Practitioners

Ultimately, the digital divide should be addressed in legal education to ensure that AI and mediation learning are accessible for all. In numerous regions, and specifically in developing countries, law schools do not have the necessary infrastructure and resources to provide practice-based or technology-oriented learning. A collaborative effort by governments, bar councils, international organizations, and academic associations should provide adequate funding for digital literacy programs, create open-access educational materials, and develop cross-border knowledge sharing platforms. Global best practices should be infused and interdisciplinary faculty from technology, business, and social sciences invited to enhance legal training and equip students for the changing landscape of global legal practice. The need for faculty development is equally critical. Professors at all levels should be trained in emerging legal technologies, ADR pedagogy, and SDG-aligned curriculum design. Institutional culture and rewards should support innovative teaching methods such as blended learning, flipped classrooms, and AI-augmented teaching to ensure that legal education is dynamic and responsive. In summary, it is no longer optional to reimagine legal education for a sustainable future it is mandatory. Integrating AI literacy and mediation skills in legal curricula will not only modernize the profession but also prepare future lawyers to deliver justice that is empowered by technology, inclusive, and globally coherent [18]. Law schools can train the next generation of leaders to be proactive in ensuring justice in an increasingly complex and interdependent world, which requires human-centred sustainable legal strategy.

6 Aligning Insolvency-Mediation-AI Nexus with SDGs

At the intersection of insolvency resolution, mediation and Artificial intelligence falls a unique opportunity to further the Sustainable Development Goals (SDGs) of United Nations, with particular emphasis on SDG 8 (Decent Work and Economic Growth) SDG 9 (Industry, Innovation and Infrastructure), SDG 16 (Peace, Justice and Strong Institutions) and SDG 4 (Quality Education). Most current insolvencies laws are creditor-friendly and rarely consider the concerns of business recovery, employment and long-term economies. But combining mediation, AI in insolvency procedures could promote a more balanced, inclusive and sustainable balance aiming to harmonize legal infrastructures with global development goals.

Mediation contributes to SDG 16 as it provides an alternative to litigious solutions, fosters accessible, fair and efficient dispute resolution. It promotes discussion among creditors, mitigates procedural costs and pressures, and can help to prevent the societal and economic damage that accompanies the failure of businesses. In insolvency situations, mediation can save jobs, stabilize supply lines and diminish the systemic risk from cascading defaults. Especially for the MSMEs that are essential for the achievement of SDG 8 and SDG 9, the mediation approach avoids financial distress from equating to liquidation by facilitating their restructuring in a cooperative manner [19]. AI helps insolvency systems work better and respond faster, in support of institutional innovation as a key part of SDG 9. AI systems can crunch financial information to forecast insolvency risk, pinpoint restructuring options, and automate back-office work in the mediation process. This allows for a decrease in resolution time, an increase in accuracy, and a broadened access particularly when Ex from Online Dispute Resolution (ODR) solutions are used. Such technological breakthroughs don't just enhance economic results, they drive legal accessibility, strengthening systems of justice according to SDG 16.

The intersection requires a new emphasis on legal education to ensure that the professions are equipped to engage with AI-based, ADR-focused insolvency regimes. Interdisciplinary training in AI, mediation, and sustainable finance engrafted into legal curricula can lead to legal professionals who are compatible with SDG 4 and are committed to skills development for lifelong learning and the digital and just future [20]. By linking the insolvency-mediation-AI triad with the SDGs, legal systems can play a role in fostering economic resilience, trust in institutions, and inclusive growth conditions necessary for a global recovery and future that are sustainable.

7 International Best Practices and Country Models

Recent years have seen progressive approaches to insolvency and bankruptcy around the world increasingly geared towards making processes more efficient, fair and to guarantee a sustainable outcome. A number of jurisdictions have led the way with regard to the use of mediation in insolvency and the use of technology to facilitate early intervention and stakeholder engagement. These international best practices and models offer important lessons on how countries may reform their insolvency systems with a view to the overall context of economic and social development in general.

Singapore is also a notable model with its innovative statutory system (notably the Singapore Convention on Mediation (2019)) providing for the enforcement of international mediated settlement agreements. The Insolvency, Restructuring and Dissolution Act (2020) of Singapore has introduced pre-packaged schemes of arrangement and mediation-based restructuring to encourage business rescue over liquidation. A generally pro-business legal environment, but one which has adopted ADR, particularly at the instigation of institutions like SIMC (Singapore International Mediation Centre), which highlights the best practice in balancing legal efficiency with commercial flexibility [21]. The European Union recently introduced a preventive restructuring directive (2019/1023), which calls for the creation by member states of 'early warning instruments' and 'mediation devices', in a bid to facilitate companies that are in financial difficulty but remain viable. This encourages the negotiation of solutions before formal insolvency occurs, thereby minimizing value loss and the over-crowding of courts. Nations such as Germany and France have carried out those orders through organized talks and court-controlled mediation processes. In the United States, some equivalent to UK and IRL insolvency law allows for filed Chapter 11 restructuring with the U.S. Bankruptcy Code and out of court settlement and mediation, notably with complex corporate insolvencies. Federal courts use mediation frequently for a more expedited resolution of differences, technology assists in case management that is transparent and quick.

India's own Insolvency and Bankruptcy Code, 2016, that has been traditionally litigation-centric, is now grappling with the concept of mediation and technology adoption. The move towards pre-packaged insolvency for MSMEs and digitization of insolvency tribunals are steps in the direction of an easier and consensual resolution ecosystem. These country models highlight the need for integrating legal innovation with ADR and technology. Institutional backing, legal certainty and stakeholder confidence are key to their success. In doing so they can develop insolvency systems that focus on recovery, sustainability, and inclusive justice—which is what the world will need in the post-pandemic age [22].

8 Challenges in Implementation and Compliance

The incorporation of mediation and artificial intelligence into insolvency regimes has transformative potential, but also comes with a number of difficult challenges in terms of practical application and compliance. These barriers encompass legal, institutional, technological, and sociocultural aspects and many times prevent the development of inclusive, efficient and effective insolvency systems [23]. Institutional resistance and legal conservatism is one of the biggest hurdles as the traditional lawyer-or court-centric litigation system is still considered ideal while non-adversarial approach like mediation is yet to earn the support of court's lawyers or other traditional legal practitioners. A number of insolvency practitioners and judges are insufficiently exposed to mediation skills or a 'tech law tool' that use AI and therefore that may be underused.

The fragmentation of regulation in various areas of the world often leads to uneven enforcement and prevents cooperation across borders. Although instruments such as the UNCITRAL Model Law on Cross-Border Insolvency and the Singapore Convention on Mediation offer international benchmarks, their implementation and effectiveness vary widely [24]. This non-uniform system complicates insolvency procedures of multinational companies and makes it difficult for national courts and mediators to work together. From a technical perspective, there are very real concerns about privacy, bias, and security. Financial and legal uses of AI must conform to data protection and honour the principles of transparency and fairness. AI tools, without appropriate controls, could entrench biased norms or produce results that conflict with law. The digital divide, especially in developing countries, is another reason that people do not have easy access to AI and Online Dispute Resolution (ODR) platforms thus maintaining inequality in access to justice.

An important challenge is the generation of capacities and knowledge. In many countries, legal education is outdated and mediators do not receive focus mediation skills training, let alone legal and AI knowledge and sustainability wisdom. There is a skills gap between these future legal professionals who are not prepared to lead or to support reform. Barriers are also due to lack of funds, political commitment, and public confidence in alternative approaches. Addressing these challenges will require a combination of regulatory reform, coordination across national borders, digital investment, and inclusive education [25]. It is only by persevering, collaborating, and innovating that we will enable country applications of mediation and AI in insolvency law to realize its potential to be sustainable, just, and institutionally robust.

9 Recommendations and Future Pathways: Developing AI Tools for Early Risk Assessment

Governments and commercial regulators, in cooperation with the fintech industry, academia and insolvency boards, should develop and oversee transparent, ethically informed AI models to aid in decision-making. These can be integrated into national insolvency systems, providing dashboards to identify struggling companies and recommend tailor-made mediation routes. At the same time, it is vital that these models be explainable and not exclusive, free of algorithmic bias and respectful of data protection norms. A key to promoting a proactive and healthy insolvency ecosystem is development and implementation of AI tools for early-risk assessment [26]. Early detection of financial distress is crucial to avoidable insolvencies and for businesses particularly Micro, Small & Medium Enterprises (MSME) to undertake suitable corrective action well in time. AI-enabled predictive analytics can trolled for mountains of financial, operational and market data and keep a close watch for red flags falling cash flow, credit defaults, swings in debt-to-equity ratios, sector vulnerabilities. These frameworks not only give businesses the power to initiate mediation or restructuring support at an early stage, but also provide a tool for regulators, creditors, and insolvency practitioners to respond with proportionate action.

AI-based risk assessment platforms could further be integrated into online dispute resolution (ODR) systems or insolvency portals to improve accessibility, particularly in developing economies. These tools could be offered in regional languages and be in the mobile versions to increase access for vulnerable populations and to further democratize early intervention tools [27]. The advancement of AI tools for early risk assessment serves as an important milestone for transforming the nature of insolvency law, from reactive litigation to proactive prevention. It is contributing to the achievement of SDG8 (economic growth), SDG9 (industry and innovation) and SDG16 (institutional justice) and establishes the groundwork for a digital enabled, sustainable legal-financial ecosystem.

10 Conclusion

The insolvency, mediation, and AI cocktail represent a major step in the march towards sustainable, efficient, and inclusive legal systems. Old-fashioned bankruptcy courts, which are time-consuming, uncooperative, and expensive, are nothing if not ill-suited to the intricacies of contemporary financial distress in an age of globalization and digitalization. If mediation were incorporated within insolvency regimes, stakeholders would be presented with a collaborative, interest-based process that would preserve business value, save jobs, and mitigate risks to the financial system. A combination of that with AI-powered tools would make earlier detection of financial distress possible, make the process more efficient and extend the reach to digital platforms.

For these changes to be truly transformative, though, legal education itself must evolve baking AI literacy, negotiating skills, and sustainability-mindedness into its very heart. Providing these competencies to the next generation of lawyers prepares new graduates to practice in a rapidly changing economic and technological framework. Mapping these innovations to the Sustainable Development Goals (SDGs), in particular SDGs 4, 8, 9 and 16, reflects a wider commitment to economic sustainability, institutional fairness and global solidarity. Although great progress has been accomplished, barriers to implementation still exist, like regulatory deficiencies, resistance at institutional level, ethical issues and digital divide. Solutions require a combination of government support, legal establishment, academia, and the private sector. At the end of the day, reconceiving insolvency and bankruptcy through mediation and AI is not just about strengthening legal and economic systems, but about building a more equitable, responsive, and forward-looking global regime. As we face intersecting crises and rapid change, this joined-up, people-centred approach is a road map to a justice and sustainability for generations to come.

References

1. Didea, I., & Ilie, D. M. (2025). At the intersection of technological innovations and geopolitical and economic turmoil. Echoes of Insolvency Law and Practice. *Perspectives of Law and Public Administration, 14*(1), 6–46.
2. Ayed, S. B., Matteucci, G., & Van Nam, T. (2021). Mediation and Insolvency, with a focus on developing countries. In *Compromiso con los Objetivos de Desarollo Sostenible (Commitment to the SDGs-sustainable development goals)*. JM Bosch Editor.
3. Villavicencio, K. B. (2024). The harmonization of insolvency mediation in the EU. A brief comparative analysis. *Review of International and European Economic Law, 3*(6), a1–a1.
4. Kamalnath, A., & Kaul, A. (2022). Adding mediation to India's corporate resolution process. *International Insolvency Review, 31*(2), 163–182.
5. Babaie, A. (2024). Cryptocurrency insolvency disputes: Challenges and the efficiency of mediation. *Arbitration: The International Journal of Arbitration, Mediation and Dispute Management, 90*(2), 157–179.
6. Sethi, S. (2024). ADR vis-a-vis resolution of insolvency disputes. *International Journal of Law Management & Humanities, 7*(6), 75–85.
7. Tseng, J. (2025). Insolvency of a party in international arbitration: Considerations on staying arbitration proceedings. *Journal of International Dispute Settlement, 16*(3), idaf027.
8. Olujobi, O. J. (2021). Combating insolvency and business recovery problems in the oil industry: Proposal for improvement in Nigeria's insolvency and bankruptcy legal framework. *Heliyon, 7*(2), e06123.
9. Priamsari, R. P. A. (2021). Exception of mediation procedure in bankruptcy cases according to Supreme Court regulation number 1 Year 2016. *Law Reform, 17*(1), 13–23.
10. Kumar, V. (2023). Reforms brought in the insolvency regime: The insolvency and bankruptcy code, 2016. *Indian Journal of Law and Legal Research, 5*(2), 1–12.
11. Doshi, H., & Jain, Y. (2021). The insolvency and bankruptcy framework and principle of business efficacy across different jurisdictions in the COVID era. *Business Law Review, 42*, 45–51.
12. Nuraini, A., Leon, F. M., & Usman, B. (2021). The role of non-financial factors in detecting bankruptcy by mediating financial performance. *Journal of Hunan University Natural Sciences, 48*(10), 489–499.
13. Sheehy, B., Chen, Y., Diaz-Granados, J., & Arias, C. (2024). Global norms, local priorities, and a $300 billion bankruptcy: A comparative study of bankruptcy laws of the United States and China. *American Bankruptcy Institute Law Review, 32*, 157–210.

14. Olabarrieta, U., Araujo, A., & San-Jose, L. (2021). Ethics of bankruptcy creditor. In *Handbook on ethics in finance* (pp. 441–459). Springer International Publishing.
15. Gluck, A. R., Chamblee Burch, E., & Zimmerman, A. S. (2023). Against bankruptcy: Public litigation values versus the endless quest for global peace in mass litigation. *Yale Law Journal Forum, 133*, 525–541.
16. Sharma, S., & Kansal, A. K. (2022). Insolvency and bankruptcy code, 2016 and resolution process: Retrospect and prospect. *Vinimaya, 11*, 23.
17. Alabady, H. S., & Ghazaleh, S. A. (2024). The power of the insolvency agent of a public commercial joint-stock company to protect the rights of corporate creditors. *Journal of Human Security, 20*(1), 28–32.
18. Foohey, P., & Odinet, C. K. (2023). Silencing litigation through bankruptcy. *Virginia Law Review, 109*(6), 1261–1330.
19. Tyagi, N. (2023). Indian perspective on arbitrability of insolvency disputes: Intersection, intervention and interpretation for synergy among both regimes. *Ramanujan International Journal of Business and Research, 8*(1), 70–79.
20. Đurić, Đ., Jovanović, V., & Škorić, S. (2024). Mediation settlement agreement under the Singapore convention as a cross-border restructuring instrument. *Pravo–teorija i praksa, 41*(3), 1–16.
21. Aneja, A. The connundrum between liquidation proceedings under IBC and section 230 of the companies act. *IJLRP-International Journal of Leading Research Publication, 2*(6), 22.
22. Mintah, C., Tachega, M. A., Wang, J., Kwofie, S., Addy, E., Aning-Agyei, G. P., & Arthur, A. (2025). The mediating mechanisms of how business environment affects sectoral productivity in West Africa. *Journal of the Knowledge Economy, 16*(6), 1–29.
23. Budiarti, S., Moeldjadi, M., & Wijayanti, R. (2023). Liquidity, activity, solvency, profitability on company value mediated by investment decision. *Indonesian Journal of Multidisciplinary Science, 2*(11), 3848–3864.
24. Hammond, P., & Opoku, M. O. (2023). Assessing the mediation role of corporate governance on the relationship between going concern and investor confidence. *International Journal of Economics, Business and Management Research, 7*(4), 14–31.
25. Sabri, M. F., Wijekoon, R., Abd Rahim, H., Burhan, N. A. S., Madon, Z., & Hamsan, H. H. (2022). Financial literacy, financial behavior, self-efficacy, and financial health among Malaysian households: The mediating role of money attitudes. *International Journal of Academic Research in Business and Social Sciences, 12*(13), 114–125.
26. Al Frijat, Y. S., Albawwat, I. E., & Elamer, A. A. (2024). Exploring the mediating role of corporate social responsibility in the connection between

board competence and corporate financial performance amidst global uncertainties. *Corporate Social Responsibility and Environmental Management, 31*(2), 1079–1095.
27. Eidenmüller, H., & Mayer, J. (2025). *Introducing the corporate restructuring machine: An open platform approach* (Working Paper No. 830). European Corporate Governance Institute-Law Working Paper.

CHAPTER 11

Sustainable Legal Education with Antitrust Law and AI Disruption: Comparative Legal Insights from the US and UK in the Context of Technological Integration

Ankit Garg, Vaishali Arora, and Sureksha Garg

Abstract The rapid developments of artificial intelligence technologies have rendered the antitrust enforcement far more complicated than ever before in both the US and UK. This article argues, through a comparative law lens, that AI disruption and antitrust laws intersect in a dynamic, multifaceted, and fact-specific manner, and that it is up to each jurisdiction to define competition law with regard to algorithmic collusion, data monopolies, and market concentration in the age of AI. The report scrutinizes the changing laws, policy discussions, and enforcement strategies

A. Garg (✉) · V. Arora · S. Garg
Sharda School of Law, Sharda University, Greater Noida, India
e-mail: ankgarg21@gmail.com

V. Arora
e-mail: vaishali.arora@sharda.ac.in

P. K. Dutta et al. (eds.), *Digital Education for a Sustainable Future*, Sustainable Development Goals Series,
https://doi.org/10.1007/978-3-032-15433-0_11

in each of the two nations. It also evaluates the potential of algorithmic mergers, pricing algorithms and platform competition for traditional merger and competition law policies. The study highlights the importance of a sustainable approach to legal education through a technological literacy, ethical reasoning, and an interdisciplinary preparation for future legal practitioners in a digitalized economy. The article contrasts comparative lessons to point out regulatory best practices, thereby adding to the global discussion of the challenge of the modern direction of antitrust law in the era of AI, fair competition, consumer welfare, and responsible innovation across jurisdictions.

Keywords Antitrust Law · Artificial Intelligence · Comparative Legal Analysis · Competition Regulation · Sustainable Legal Education

1 Introduction

The revolutionary emergence of AI technologies has done a great deal to change the current world markets in that it totally changes traditional business models, consumer behavior, and regulations. In clustered industries such as e-commerce, healthcare, finance, transportation, AI systems are now driving innovation and influencing not only technologies but also market structures and competitive relationships. At stake in this evolving digital ecosystem is the fate of antitrust law, a key institution of market control intended to facilitate fair competition and forestall monopolistic practices. Especially in the digital economy of advanced economies like the US and the UK, where tech economy is booming, with AI technologies increasingly part of corporate strategies, antitrust must adapt to new patterns of anti-competitive behavior. This article analyzes the interplay between antitrust law and AI-led disruption, compares how the US and the UK respond to these challenges, all the while highlighting the increasingly urgent need for future-proofed and sustainable legal education that must be actively engaged with these evolutions [1].

Historically, antitrust law has been centered on outlawing cartels, stopping the abuse of market power and reviewing mergers that could threaten competition. But AI has raised new questions that make this conversation slightly more complex and traditional antitrust tools somewhat out-of-date. For example, smart-programmed algorithms can automatically take part in price optimization, market forecasting, and consumer selection functions that may unintentionally or not lead to collusion or discrimination or negative screening. Most such algorithmic collusion takes place un-communicated with competitors, so it can be hard for regulators to prove intent, or assign liability with existing legal precedents. And, because AI relies on enormous data sets, that has given the edge to the companies with greatest access to consumer data not necessarily the companies with the most innovative ideas and who can then push aside or buy out their smaller, would-be competitors. These developments call for some recalibration of legal doctrines and regulatory strategies to preserve competitive market forces even as we nurture sustainable technological change.

In the US, competition law is based on the Sherman Act, Clayton Act, and the Federal Trade Commission Act, and enforced by the Department of Justice (DOJ) and Federal Trade Commission (FTC). United States antitrust is a case-oriented system with an over-reliance on the consumer welfare standard as a measure of injury. Conversely, the UK competition law is governed by the Competition Act 1998 and Enterprise Act 2002 in which the Competition and Markets Authority (CMA) is the key enforcement agency. The UK has chosen a more assertive and regulatory approach, concentrating increasingly on ex-ante controls, particularly in digital markets. Yet both are grappling with some of the same problems: how to spot algorithmic abuse, control the data-driven dominance of large companies and assess mergers of companies that rely on AI. Recent antitrust cases against tech giants like Google, Amazon, and Meta demonstrate that policymakers are increasingly aware of AI role in consolidating dominance but those cases also illustrate the shortcomings of existing legal tools when it comes to addressing rapidly emerging technology-enabled risks.

The US tends to focus more on market efficiency and consumer costs compared to the UK's greater focus on market structure, innovation, and fair competition. These different priorities shape the creation and enforcement of competition policy, and thereby, how AI-specific challenges like self-learning algorithms, data monopolies, and platform neutrality are met. In addition, regulatory philosophy in the UK has increasingly favored the precautionary principle and a more precautionary approach in general, whereby risk is prevented even at the risk of taking preventive action where there is none in the US. For all their differences, they are both looking at responses including regulatory sandboxes, algorithmic audit processes, and guidelines on ethical AI to enhance their supervision of digital markets. These efforts underscore the need for adaptive governance structures that can keep up with technological advances, yet also protect economic fairness and public confidence [2].

Central to this shift is the role of legal education that must equip future lawyers, regulators and policy makers with the tools to negotiate the nuances of an AI-enhanced competition law. Sustainable legal education, by this meaning, requires an interdisciplinary practice of teaching law, technology, ethics, and public policy [3]. This includes training students and practitioners to have more than a doctrinal knowledge of antitrust, but to be proficient in data analysis and digital market design. Law schools and professional training organizations must overhaul their pedagogy to integrate AI literacy, critical thinking of digital ethics and regulatory technology comfort. Developing such skills will lead to a new breed of legal professionals who can interpret and craft laws that respond intelligently to both the innovation imperative and the equity requirement [4].

AI disruption and antitrust in the US and UK looms as a defining challenge to legal orders of the twenty-first century. Comparative lessons from a legal point of view show that even though both countries are making important progress in updating their antitrust systems, enforcement effectiveness, conceptual clarity and institutional capacity are still to be addressed. Regulatory and best practices gaps can be closed through common regulation and best practice, and through an investment of effort into building the legal creative talent that is tech literate and ethically focused. As AI reshapes the boundaries of economic power, the law must adapt not just in its letter but also in its spirit supporting innovation while demanding accountability, and fostering efficiency while protecting fairness [5].

2 Antitrust Law: Key Principles and Focus

Antitrust seeks to maintain market integrity and preserve freedom of economic action by preventing exclusion, by promoting competition between the market orders, and by outlawing practices that directly or indirectly restrict market performance even where risks are concerned. Based in the economic and legal culture of liberal market economies, the antitrust law deal with conduct that impedes effective competition, distorts pricing mechanisms, or leads to the exploitation of market power [6]. The legal doctrines have developed over time to keep pace with shifting economic theories, international trade patterns and technological progress. At its heart, antitrust law centers on three main boats: abuse of dominance, cartels and merger control each of which has been designed to crack down anti-competitive behavior and it is very fabric forms the structural design of regulatory frameworks in the United States and United Kingdom.

The anti-dominance doctrine is designed to stop firms with high market power from excluding, exploiting, or discriminating against competitors or consumers. This consists of predatory pricing, refusal to deal, tying and bundling, and unfair access to bottlenecked facilities. Dominance is not illegal as such, its abuse is, because it precludes competitive pressure and establishes monopolistic structures. Establishing abuse in both US and UK law builds on a nuanced understanding of market definition, market power and the harm to consumers although the threshold is typically higher under US law, informed as it is by the consumer welfare standard.

The next basic element, the prohibition of cartels, is designed to eliminate and prevent contracts between actual or potential competitors that will impair competitive conditions. Cartels are regarded as the supreme class of antitrust violations and include such matters as price-fixing, effects on output, market sharing, and bid-rigging. These deals interfere with the competitive process and enable companies to inflate prices and stifle consumer options, sometimes in secret and across borders. Literally all over the world, for example in the US (Section 1, Sherman Act) and in the UK and there is a zero tolerance approach to conduct of this nature and criminal and civil penalties apply to deter involvement in such collusive practices [7].

The third principle, merger control, enables the competition authority to prevent corporate combinations from creating organizations with too much market power or reducing the degree of competition in a given market. Antitrust officials evaluate mergers on whether they risk harming consumers through stifled innovation, increased prices or fewer choices. The FTC in the US and the CMA in the UK both use prospective frameworks to assess whether the planned merger is expected to result in a significant impediment to effective competition. In a world of digital platforms and data-driven economy, merger control can no longer limit itself to a focus on price effects, but needs to develop a greater focus on other non-price parameters such as data concentration, entry barriers and innovation potential. In combination, these doctrines make up the cornerstone of antitrust law that is evolving as markets and technologies develop [8].

3 AI Disruption and Market Dynamics

Artificial intelligence has gained prominence as a fundamental enabler of transformation in contemporary economies, changing the dynamics of doing business and engaging with customers. AI, by providing services like predictive analytics and automated decision-making, algorithmic pricing, and targeted advertising has completely upset classical market conditions. Innovation is this kind of disruption that is happening through the development of new business models, the fast scaling of digital platforms, new types of market power, which challenge traditional antitrust doctrines. Different from previous type of technological revolutions, AI ushers in a new era of learning from data and self-improvement which is beyond the human's capability of action execution and optimization [9]. The competitive dynamics across many industries are now being shaped, if not dictated, by AI-driven actors, raising important regulatory and economic considerations in these industries for e.g., e-commerce, finance, communication, transportation, and media.

The market concentration will be the area of influence of AI on market dynamics. Companies with large datasets, computational pipes, and algorithmic knowledge out-run the proverbial bear, cementing their position through reinforcing cycles. Platform companies, such as Amazon and Google, for example, utilize artificial intelligence to hone recommendation engines, predict demand, or optimize customer interaction activities that bring more users, generate more data and improve algorithms in a virtuous cycle. This network shape provides high barriers to entry for newcomers, high reduction of market contestability, and tends to monopolistic or oligopolistic shapes. Classic antitrust tools, aimed at price-fixing or physical market shares, have a harder time gauging and restraining these intangible but immense forms of dominance.

AI powering algorithmic pricing and the use of behavioral targeting now help companies dynamically set prices on the fly, according to consumer engagements, competitor moves and market dynamics. Dynamic pricing yields efficiency gains and consumer surplus, but it can also facilitate tacit collusion where decentralized algorithms "cooperate" by pricing incrementally less than competitors but continue to compete [10]. This kind of "silent" coordination sometimes referred to as algorithmic collusion can be very difficult to identify and prosecute because it does not require evidence of intent or agreement. Likewise, AI-driven behavioral targeting is able to segment consumers and influence their buy decisions through black box and unethical means, undermining competition.

AI also reconfigures the supply chain efficiencies and labor market structures that would indirectly impact competition. Automation of logistics, predictive maintenance and computer-driven inventory control also slash costs for large companies, but introduce asymmetries for smaller ones who cannot afford or access similar technologies. In the job market, AI-enabled automation and gig economy platforms upend traditional employment structures, centralize power in the hands of digital intermediaries, and weaken the bargaining power of workers a concern increasingly seen through an antitrust lens. AI heightens the importance of innovation competition between firms along the lines of quality and price, but also through technological front-running. This realignment forces regulators to consider anti-competitive injury in new, nontraditional modes such as hindering innovation, or denying access to vital digital infrastructure [11]. As AI increasingly underpins economic activity, its disruptive influence requires rethinking of market competition, in which antitrust policy needs to fit with effective competitive strategies in fluid, data-driven space and prediction-based competition. Hence, the comprehension and the response to the disruption by AI is not simply a case of technological knowledge but a challenge for fairness as well as open markets.

4 US Perspective: Antitrust Challenges and Policy Shifts

While it comes to antitrust enforcement, the US has been long considered a forerunner in the shifting world after market changes spurred by the advent of Artificial Intelligence (AI). Based on statutory foundations such as the Sherman Act (1890), the Clayton Act (1914), and the Federal Trade Commission Act (1914), the shape of the traditional US antitrust law has been to protect competition and consumers by preventing collusion, monopolization, and anti-competitive mergers. But the rise of AI technologies presents more complicated challenges that these familiar legal structures can't easily interpret or act upon [12]. AI has empowered companies especially digital behemoths like Amazon, Google, and Meta to use tools like predictive analytics, algorithmic pricing, and data dominance to transform competition without breaking established legal definitions of antitrust behavior.

The big problem is demonstrating harm in markets that are increasingly controlled by artificial intelligence. In the US, the consumer welfare standard tends to require antitrust intervention to show that price has gone up or that output has gone down. But other AI-powered services are cheap or free in financial terms, paid for in data and attention. This obscures traditional price-based measures of harm and acres difficulties for the FTC and DOJ regulating AI-fueled dominance. And algorithmic collusion, in which self-learning pricing bots settle on uniform prices without any human input, still lies in a legal limbo under US antitrust law, which demands a showing of agreement or conscious parallelism to be enforceable.

There has been a change in policy in the US in recent years, especially now under the Biden administration they have become more aggressive with Big Tech and AI-enabled market power. President Biden's 2021 Executive Order on Promoting Competition in the American Economy hinted at a broader agenda on antitrust, urging agencies to consider labor market concentration, data privacy and platform neutrality [13].

The suing culture in US antitrust enforcement and associated litigation risks often hamper swift interlocutory action. Investigations and litigation are slow and costly they lag significantly behind the swift introduction of AI tools in the business world. Demands for legislative change, too, for an updating of antitrust laws meant to counter AI and data-driven dominance, are rising, even as congressional action is disarrayed. AI is recasting market power in forms not foreseen by twentieth-century statutes, and the US antitrust regime should keep pace striking the appropriate balance between innovation incentives and regulatory protections for the algorithms that govern much of economic life, ensuring competition and maintaining consumer welfare in the age of the algorithm.

5 UK Perspective: Regulatory Approaches and Reforms

The UK has taken a proactive and adaptable stance toward the enforcement of competition laws as a result of dynamic changes in the market due AI. The UK's competition regime which is based largely on the Competition Act 1998 (CA) 2and the Enterprise Act 2002 (EA), is administered by the Competition and Markets Authority (CMA). Sensing the AI- and digital economy-induced headwinds, the UK has become an ex-ante enforcer and regulator of increasing intensity particularly as applied to the dominant digital platforms which use AI to vacuum up data, set price intelligence agents loose, or identify consumers [14]. The Digital Markets, Competition and Consumers Bill, introducing a specialized regime for large digital firms identified as having 'Strategic Market Status' (SMS). Under this regime, the CMA "would have powers to impose conduct requirements, make market investigations and strengthen its ability to act earlier in markets to prevent harm occurring to competition." This addresses the challenge of spotting and addressing anti-competitive conduct in dynamic, AI-driven industries, where conventional enforcement frequently comes too late.

The CMA has been proactive in investigating mergers, particularly where acquisitions have the potential to foreclose future innovation, or aggregate AI capabilities. The authority stresses that innovation competition needs to be preserved and "killer acquisitions" that eliminate nascent competitors must be avoided. The UK is also building on technical capability, including AI and data science, to improve understanding of algorithmic behavior and digital ecosystems. In its adoption of ethical AI, algorithmic transparency and multidisciplinary approaches, the UK offers a model of forward-looking regulation. Its reforms are a growing testament to an evolving recognition that effective antitrust governance in the AI age demands not just legal precision, but technical understanding, institutional agility, and policy foresight to maintain competitive markets and shield consumers in a world increasingly shaped by automation and data [15].

6 Comparative Analysis: US vs UK Approaches to AI and Competition Law

The US and the UK, two jurisdictions with mature competition laws, are responding to the anti-competitive threats of Artificial Intelligence (AI) with different regulatory paradigms and enforcement postures. Although both are concerned about AI's emerging risks to market power, algorithmic collusion, and competitive neutrality, their practices differ considerably, especially in institutional design of regulators, policy measures and doctrinal emphasis. Antitrust enforcement in the US is also largely litigation-based and reactive, rooted in the now decades-old consumer welfare standard, which seeks to address clear harm normally, price increases or output cuts. This standard is challenging for assessing AI powered business practices, particularly in digital markets where services are often free of charge but confer enormous data based market power. And, while US authorities (FTC and DOJ) have then sought to explore further what might constitute harm—turning to concepts such as innovation stifling or exclusionary behavior they have struggled to do so within the confines of precedents and statute.

The UK takes a more "pro- active" and "regulatory" stance (for example that of the CMA on "ex-ante" interventions, and more specifically, in digital markets, where AI is a key driver); it is still also finding its right level of regulatory intervention. The UK Digital Markets, Competition, and Consumers Bill gives the CMA the authority to introduce conduct requirements on dominant digital companies, addresses anti-competitive conduct before it has occurred, and gives prominence to long-term innovation and contestability in markets. Compare this to the post-hoc enforcement of the US and its weak ability to prevent early-stage dominance. The other point of divergence is with regard to the regulatory approach to data. The UK has been more focused on data access, interoperability, and fairer data whereas in the US, we still are squabbling about what would legislation look like around data protection and competition [16]. The both stand before some common challenges, not least the opaqueness of algorithmic decision systems, cross-border digital operations, and a deficit of technical knowledge among enforcement bodies. For this reason, a comparative approach highlights the significance of regulatory convergence, cooperation in enforcement and the adaptation of techno-literacy to competition law. Only by bringing its legal framework into the AI- and digital-ready era will the US be equipped to join the UK in having a strong, fair and future-proof antitrust system.

7 Technological Integration and Challenges in Enforcement

The incorporation of AI technologies in market systems has been a game changer in business processes, with the added efficiencies, scalability and data-driven decision-making that was until then not available. But this swift technological integration is imposing prohibitive obstacles on antitrust enforcement, both conceptually and operationally. The landscape for traditional competition law, which had been based on market structure, pricing conduct, and consumer injury, has been changed by technological advances, obscured algorithms, automated conduct, and less tangible sources of market power. Targeted enforcement of antitrust laws in the age of AI will not only demand legal reform, but also technical architecture of digital business models. Among the core challenges is the opaqueness and complexity of AI algorithms. Such opacity also makes it extremely difficult for regulators to identify anti-competitive conduct, prove intent, or determine liability. Current legal tests, predicated on a showing of coordination or conscious parallelism, do not well account for those independent, but detrimental, results.

The dynamic and predictive aspect of AI is yet another problem faced by firms that use AI algorithms in such applications that enables the company to frequently change the strategy in response to the real-time data [17]. This immediacy can help entrench dominant positions, especially when coupled with ownership of massive data sets and infrastructure. Market power leads to a positive feedback between market dominance and the quality of an AI system: Firms with high-quality AI systems attract more users, gather more data, and improve their AI systems barring new entrants from entering the market. These feedback loops do add complexity to the traditional analysis of mergers and markets, often conducted upon the basis of static market definitions and historical data.

The enforcement authorities are often without the technical expertise and resources to pursue sophisticated, AI-informed conduct. The distance between legal and tech speak becomes ever greater. This leaves regulators playing catch-up with digital platforms and algorithmic strategies. There is an urgent requirement to bring together data scientists, AI experts and cross-disciplinary teams within competition enforcers to increase the capacity to investigate and design policy. Cross-border enforcement adds another layer of complexity to all of this, with AI-powered platforms being global entities and antitrust jurisdictions being domestic. Coordinating enforcement actions between countries, aligning standards of algorithmic transparency, and navigating jurisdictional battles also challenge the efficacy of regulation. What's more, insufficient regulation and policy prohibiting exaggeration can lead to a tug-of-war because of the fear the regulators will infringe on innovation, over-regulate emergent tech and the domination of big guys who in the meantime use that inaction to gain hegemony.

Some regulators are examining approaches such as regulatory sandboxes, compulsory algorithmic audits, and system-level surveillance to modernize enforcement tools for AI-driven markets. But these tools are just beginning to be adopted widely and standardized across the industry. AI era enforcement will thus need to become more forward-looking, tech-savvy, and globally coordinated. This transformation requires not only modest changes in legal doctrines, but also a re-conceptualization of regulatory models that can adapt to innovation not only preserving market integrity, but also consumer welfare [18].

8 Sustainable Legal Education: Preparing Future Legal Professionals

Given the ever-changing digital economy, market structures increasingly include AI or innovative technology that are being used, adopted, or further developed. As a result, it is about time that legal education adopts a complete make-over. A sustainable legal education surpasses traditional doctrine-based learning, training lawyers to have the interdisciplinary understanding, technological preparedness, and ethical sensibility necessary to engage with the emerging challenges of AI-driven competition law. As the antitrust litigations get more and more technical they include machine gun range, data cartel, and a roomful of titans the legal community, the judges and policymakers will have to find a way to both grasp and adapt to these new realities as they unfold in real-time.

The legal education needs to accept inter-disciplinarily. Law schools and vocational colleges should teach computer science, data analytics, machine learning, and digital economics. This doesn't just help build a basic understanding of how AI systems work, but also enables future lawyers to critically evaluate how these systems shape market behavior and regulatory outcomes. Partnerships with engineering and technology departments and direct experience with regulatory technology and legal technology solutions can impart pragmatic experiences that casebooks do not provide. Ethical reasoning, as well, has to be integrated more fully into what we mean today by sustainable legal education. Those questions of ethics tied to AI-driven systems largely revolve around privacy, discrimination, and accountability all of which directly collide with competition law, particularly from consumer harm or market manipulation standpoint. Those in the legal profession need to be able to assess the broader societal implications of AI deployment, and promote responsible innovation that is consistent with democratic values, transparency, and public trust [19].

Sustainable education in law needs to concentrate on lifelong learning and flexibility. In an age of rapid technological change, a static law degree is inadequate. Bar associations, legal groups, and continuing-education providers will need to provide regular training in AI advancements, digital marketplace regulation and new antitrust tactics. Focusing on critical thinking, flexibility, and legal ingenuity will help to ensure that legal professionals will be increasingly effective inside flexible legal systems. The importance of international awareness is similarly urgent. With the proliferation of AI technologies across borders the regulatory and pedagogical systems that shape them must also become globalized. Comparative law courses, analyses of international antitrust cases, and role-playing on cross-border policy can enable students to comprehend varying regulatory environments and engender international cooperation. Sustainable legal education is not a teaching reform it is a matter of strategic importance. It ensures that the future of lawyers is not just passive or reactive users but innovative designers of equitable, transparent, and technology-resilient legal regimes capable of absorbing the market-changing effects of AI in the global marketplace.

9 Policy Recommendations and Global Implications

The pervasive reconfigurations of the competitive process and market structure wrought by AI, it is clear that a multi-dimensional approach is needed to respond to it if regulation is to be effective, competition to be promoted, and innovation to be ethical. The first is the need for antitrust enforcers to update legal doctrines to suit a world of AI-specific concerns from algorithmic collusion to data-driven dominance to predictive market conduct which existing frameworks were not built to accommodate. This could involve crafting statutory definitions that cover non-price harms diminished innovation and the exploitation of personal data as well as expanding the consumer welfare standard to account for more diverse socio-economic effects.

The regulators need to incorporate, and enforce, mandatory algorithmic transparency, and the ability to audit. Firms that deploy AI systems with market-wide implications would, in fact, have to reveal algorithmic logic, decision criteria, and data sources subject to regulatory review under regulatory confidentiality [20]. Creating independent algorithmic audit authorities could increase accountability and identify harmful practices that fall out of the realm of classic antitrust review. AI firms work across border so it will require international regulation alignment. Actions led by the OECD, UNCTAD, or G7 could support cooperation on cross-border investigations, convergence of enforcement, and set best practices in the area of digital competition. The importance of investing in growing regulatory capacity cannot be overstated. Governments need to help antitrust agencies build technical capacity in AI, data science, and computational law to enforce its newly adopted regulations. That could mean investing in research hubs and public-private knowledge-sharing efforts.

The building sustainable legal education is necessary for sustained regulatory staying power. Law schools and reflex chains of professional institutions need to prepare future regulators and professionals with a more interdisciplinary, technology-informed education. These policy initiatives have far-reaching global implications: they can serve to level the playing field in AI-driven markets, mitigating digital monopolies, driving innovation and maintaining public confidence in regulatory bodies. Without strategic coordination and foresight, the unfettered ascent of AI could simply solidify economic disparities and blur democratic accountability in the digital era [21].

10 Conclusion and Future Scope

The intersection of AI and competition law raises both critical challenges and radical changes for regulators around the globe. As examined comparatively between the US and the UK, it is clear that conventional models of antitrust grounded on price- based consumer welfare and on reactive enforcement are today insufficient to grapple with the intricacies of AI-driven market structures. From algorithmic collusion to data monopolies, this emergent digital economy requires a reimagining of legal instruments and a modulation of regulatory paradigms and a clearer understanding of the technological infrastructures. But where the US pushes the litigation and nibbling policy frontiers, the UK is moving forward ex-ante in shaping these digital age markets.

The next frontier is the development of international collaboration, interdisciplinary legal teaching, and the establishment of technological-savvy regulatory bodies. Regulatory sandboxes, algorithmic audit tools and enforcement across jurisdictions are urgently required inventions in order to catch up with the rapidly expanding AI. The sustainable legal education should be the basis through which future lawyers are trained to interpret, influence, and enact these developing systems. As artificial intelligence reshapes labor markets and legal systems, a reasonable and flexible ethical approach to antitrust will be essential to protecting open competition, consumer rights, and democratic norms in the information age.

References

1. Kamara, M. (2025). The Competition Conundrum: A Comparative Study of EU and US Antitrust Approaches in the Digital Age. *Myles Kamara*, The Competition Conundrum: A Comparative Study of EU and US Antitrust Approaches in the Digital Age, 2.
2. Ganguli, P. (2024). *International perspectives on antitrust laws: A comparative study of India, the US, and the EU* (November 01, 2024).
3. Webb, J. (2022). Legal technology: The great disruption. *Lawyers in 21st Century Socities, 2*, 515–540.
4. Deutscher, E. (2022). Reshaping digital competition: The new platform regulations and the future of modern antitrust. *The Antitrust Bulletin, 67*(2), 302–340.
5. Hopster, J. K., & Maas, M. M. (2024). The technology triad: Disruptive AI, regulatory gaps and value change. *AI and Ethics, 4*(4), 1051–1069.
6. Abad, A. A. (2024). Artificial Intelligence and the future of international trade law and dispute settlement. *Contemporary Asia Arbitration Journal, 17*, 35–68.
7. Lescrauwaet, L., Wagner, H., Yoon, C., & Shukla, S. (2022). Adaptive legal frameworks and economic dynamics in emerging technologies: Navigating

the intersection for responsible innovation. *Law and Economics, 16*(3), 202–220.
8. Darvishi, K., Liu, L., & Lim, S. (2022). Navigating the nexus: Legal and economic implications of emerging technologies. *Law and Economics, 16*(3), 172–186.
9. Wang, S., Li, Y., & Khaskheli, M. B. (2024). Innovation helps with sustainable business, law, and digital technologies: Economic development and dispute resolution. *Sustainability, 16*(10), 3910.
10. Paweloszek, I., Kumar, N., & Solanki, U. (2022). Artificial Intelligence, digital technologies and the future of law: Literature review. *Futurity Economics & Law, 2*(2), 35–53.
11. Nweke, G. I., & Nweke, O. C. (2024). Harmonising strategy, innovation, and law: Navigating the path to ethical and sustainable progress. *Beijing Law Review, 15*, 200–218.
12. Tarek, A. (2023). *Mergers and acquisitions: Analysing antitrust implications and regulatory compliance* (SSRN 4518461).
13. Martin, J., & Narula, R. (2024). Balancing interests: AI, business & human rights, and the legal landscape in an era of disruption. *West Virginia Law Review, 127*(1), 1–38.
14. Wörsdörfer, M. (2022). Big tech and antitrust: An ordoliberal analysis. *Philosophy & Technology, 35*(3), 65.
15. Schrepel, T. (2021). Computational antitrust: An introduction and research agenda. *Stanford Computational Antitrust, 1*, 1.
16. Coglianese, C., & Lai, A. (2022). Antitrust by algorithm. *Stanford Computational Antitrust, 2*, 1–22.
17. Giraudo, M., Fosch-Villaronga, E., & Malgieri, G. (2024). Competing legal futures–"commodification bets" all the way from personal data to AI. *German Law Journal, 25*(7), 1095–1119.
18. Liwanda, I. (2023). Brexit, big tech, and competition law: The case for a new economic magna carta fit for the digital age. *De Lege Ferenda, 6*, 71–102.
19. Lobel, O. (2025). Technological readiness versus disruption: A framework for assessing distinct artificial intelligence policy strategies. *Emory Law Journal, 74*(5), 1055–1078.
20. Brownsword, R. (2022). Law, authority, and respect: Three waves of technological disruption. *Law, Innovation and Technology, 14*(1), 5–40.
21. Spulber, D. F. (2023). Antitrust and innovation competition. *Journal of Antitrust Enforcement, 11*(1), 5–50.

CHAPTER 12

Barriers in Digital Education: Overcoming Infrastructure, Cultural, and Financial Obstacles Fostering Sustainable Digital Education

Vivek Pimplapure, Pushparaj Kulkarni, and Yogesh Gharpure

Abstract Digital education has the potential to be transformative across a globe desperate for access to quality learning but this potential is largely still latent, mainly due to significant barriers preventing it from actualizing. The gaps in tech and infrastructure, unreliable Internet, poor

V. Pimplapure (✉) · P. Kulkarni
Dr. Ambedkar Institute of Management Studies & Research, Nagpur, India
e-mail: vivek_pimplapure@daimsr.edu.in

P. Kulkarni
e-mail: pushparaj_kulkarni@daimsr.edu.in

Y. Gharpure
Tirpude Institute of Management Education, Nagpur, India
e-mail: y.gharpure@tirpude.edu.in

P. K. Dutta et al. (eds.), *Digital Education for a Sustainable Future*, Sustainable Development Goals Series,
https://doi.org/10.1007/978-3-032-15433-0_12

hardware, no power supply further push rural/marginalized communities out of an equitable participation ground. The cultural barriers are equally critical: resistance to new technologies, insufficient digital literacy, and language barriers can all prevent learners and educators from adopting digital tools effectively. Financial pressures on institutional budgets and individual households may thereby limit the acquisition, maintenance, and upgrading of digital devices and software that multiply 'digital divides' in education. Addressing these issues will need multi-pronged approaches: investing in resilient, inclusive digital infrastructure; promoting community-based digital literacy programs; and adopting affordable access models that show how to target with enhanced affordability and interventions such as subsidies or public-private partnerships. The authors conclude that sustainable funding mechanisms need to be prioritized by policymakers, alongside a focus on culturally sensitive content and training to support patient engagement. Without addressing them holistically, one cannot aspire to create a resilient digital education ecosystem capable of responding to the needs as they change and evolve over time, while supporting lifelong learning. So, addressing infrastructure, cultural and financial barriers allows for sustainable digital education that is open, inclusive, and liberating

Keywords Digital education · Infrastructure barriers · Cultural obstacles · Financial challenges · Sustainable learning

1 Introduction

In the digital age, across the globe, food and shopping are delivered right to your doorstep; now what we just heard that education could be digitally delivered as well. Still there are major barriers to equitably and sustainably implementing these strategies, particularly in marginalized and underserved communities. These include a lack of infrastructure, steep learning curves, and cost constraints that collectively hinder the top-level growth of digital education. These are crucial barriers to address if wish to foster more responsive and sustainable educational ecosystems that serve all learners [1].

In rural and remote areas for example, the lack of reliable internet connectivity is still so high that infrastructure remains one of the surface-level barriers. Education disparities become pronounced when educational institutions use digital learning platforms, video lectures and interactive content in areas where broadband penetration lags behind. Also key: not enough access to devices like computers, tablets or smartphones many students must share them or rely on old-technology that will not support the high-tech educational software of today. This is further compounded by the lack of regulation with electricity provisions in some parts of the Global South, affecting consistency in digital learning propriety and digital infrastructure portability. It is also the absence of technical maintenance and support services which reduce the lifespan and efficacy of educational technology investments, inevitably rendering them as E-Waste items way too early for their time.

Cultural barriers are still one of the biggest limiting factors for digital education uptake. One of the most important impediments remains the digital literacy gap that affects students, educators and families reducing potential skills from technology usage. Older educators, as well as those serving communities with little prior digital experience, are left even further behind. The challenge is that the potential reasons for resistance in terms of mistrust, unfamiliarity or fear as i.e., less face-to-face interaction can tend to get people's stuck as wait for someone who will take up this argument. With the limitation of language and not having enough culturally relevant content will decrease the engagement of learners as these contents are still largely available in few global dominant languages [2]. There are gender disparities too with girls and women facing more socio-cultural restrictions on technology use, which in turn aggravates educational inequity.

To ensure equal access and long-term satisfaction, new solutions are needed to get around the new problems that come up while trying to provide sustainable digital education. Digital divides are often dependent on infrastructure, since things like slow internet access and old equipment can make it hard for people in rural or underdeveloped areas to get online. New programs are focusing on setting up offline learning platforms and cheap, solar-powered Wi-Fi hotspots to close this gap. People may be resistant to change because they believe in conventional ways of learning and are unsure of how useful technology is. This means that training programs need to be culturally conscious and show how digital tools may be useful while also taking into account the values of the area. These include the price of the gadgets and their subscriptions, which makes it hard for poorer populations to use them.

Importance of Sustainable Digital Education

Financial constraints limit institutions and households in the access and sustainability of digital education resources. Schools, especially in low-income areas, do not have the funds to spend on dieses and training because they are generally required for immediate operational expenditure under the law. Due to affordability issues, households are not able to afford buying the essential devices needed for connectivity and also internet subscriptions and data plans. Developing proprietary software and digital content costs the learner and the school tens of millions each year. Subsidized models and grants have been introduced through public-private partnerships and international aid programs, but these efforts are inherently limited in credentials and should be complemented by new, durable funding mechanisms to avoid short-term fixes that can significantly erode over time.

Tackling these intertwined barriers involved developing a full suite of strategies that were multi-dimensional. For instance, making universal broadband access a priority and through affordable and durable devices, or aligning toward a reliable power supply like solar energy as we are seeing currently take place in Tanzania. Developing community-based digital literacy programs will support teachers, students, and families in the use of technologies and make them feel confident while using it. The creation of digital content reflective of that region on the whole, in many native languages can ensure the relevance and inclusivity. This will require policy frameworks to incentivize affordable access using subsidies, tax incentives, and collaborative financing [3]. Local governments must take advantage of public-private partnerships to access technological innovation and capital. There is also the monitoring and evaluation that needs to happen ongoing to help inform implementation strategies but also a sort of accountability.

2 Understanding Barriers in Digital Education

Digital Education has immense potentials in increasing access to education, improving the quality of learning and establishing lifelong learning. But delivering on these opportunities require a profound grasp of the complex obstacles that stymie inclusive engagement and sustainable implementation. The latter are not just technical, but deeply socio-economic and cultural, defining how people can access digital learning tools, and how they actually learn with text or other rich sources words. Broadly speaking, the barriers to digital education boil down to a host of infrastructure-related challenges coupled with cultural and social obstacles and financial limitations feedback loops between all three that make dismantling them all the more complex.

It mainly concerns infrastructural barriers related to the access and quality of technological tools required for virtual learning. Any plans must necessarily build upon the requisite of reliable internet access, availability of a suitable electronic device (tablet or laptop) and consistent electricity supply in order to even consider digital learning. However, these essential services do not work everywhere, a fact that results in the digital divide barring many learners from fully participating particularly in rural or underserved areas. In addition, even in areas where infrastructure has been built, a lack of quality training and maintenance often means that existing resources are never used or quickly breakdown.

These deals with issues like digital literacy, technological attitudes, language diversity, and socio-cultural norms that affect the adoption of digital education. Without digital skills, students may not learn at all those conceived to unite the interests of the teacher with aspirations of the parent or guardian. The adoption stands in the way as well; resistance to change, chalky thoughts on digital quality and most importantly lack of interest and liking for all things traditional. In addition, educational digital content rarely captures or represents sufficiently local languages, contexts and cultural values which in turn make it less relevant for potential users [4]. The difficulties for women and other groups superimposed with digital gender gaps create further struggles, making it harder for marginalized populations to be part of the information society.

Arguably, the most palpable effects of financial pressure involve institutional capacity and individual access. Schools and families alike may not have the funds to invest in critical technologies or training, or even be able to afford devices or internet subscriptions. Software licenses and digital contents can also be expensive to acquire. Given that these barriers are as yet intractable without sustainable financing models and policy support, the scale-up potential of digital education initiatives is limited. Given this complex of interrelated challenges, it is essential to understand these barriers in order to design interventions that allow digital education systems not only to be more equitable and inclusive, but also more able to adapt and respond in ways that are appropriate for a wide variety of learners [5].

Impact of Barriers on Equity and Inclusion

The already present educational inequity is intensified with the limited reach of reliable internet access, affordable devices and electricity in rural, low-income, and marginalized communities. And cultural barriers, such as the absence of digital literacy levels tailored to closely relevant cultures matter most often in preventing different marginalized groups like girls, non-nationals and those disabled from accessing a digital arena [6].

The institutions as well as the families tend to be constrained financially that they cannot afford to spend on essential technology and resources which contribute in creating gaps in participation and learning outcomes. Those digital divides, created by these intersecting barriers, result in the marginalization of some of those least advantaged among us and exclude them from opportunities for education and potential economic mobility. To achieve that, it is of fundamental importance to answer these challenges and have digital education as an instrument of increased inclusion rather than limitation. It need policies and programs that are equity-promoting and ensure no one is left behind by closing access gaps, cultivating digital skills, and making sure the content itself is culturally responsive so all learners can capitalize on the transformative potential of digital education [7].

3 Infrastructure Challenges in Sustainable Digital Education

The unresolved infrastructural issues pose significant barriers to sustainable digital education, particularly in low-resource and rural contexts. Access to dependable internet service is a first principle of digital learning, and yet in many places people face inadequate broadband infrastructure, slow connections, or unreliable connectivity that limits their ability to connect reliably to online classes and educational content for interaction via various digital platforms. Urban areas frequently benefit from more robust infrastructure, while residents of rural and under-served communities face a digital divide. Not all learners have access to the digital devices as laptops, tablets and smartphones which is divided very unequally and many of them even share devices or use old versions which cannot run modern educational software. The differences restrict the way learners can engage with digital content to a great extent.

That is underwritten by problems of power supply as large areas of the planet, mostly in third world countries, experience power outages that disturb digital education and destroy devices. Failure to ensure access to sustainable energy solutions makes sustaining dependable digital educational ecosystems over a reasonable period of time very challenging. The operational maintenance and technical support are usually insufficient, many times absent, being opened this situation to fall into disuse or obsolescence of the equipment that in turn diminishes the return on investment in educational technology [8].

All of this poses significant challenges to be overcome if digital education is to be sustainable, but can only happen within a holistic strategy such as promoting affordable broadband, investment in rugged yet contextually relevant devices and renewable energy (such as Solar Power) to ensure continuous electricity. Efforts also need to be made for making sure that the digital education infrastructure remains sustainable for long, not only in terms of financial investments but also in terms of strengthening the technical support systems and maintenance services. But digital education will only be inclusive and sustainable, if it addresses these challenges collectively.

Internet Connectivity and Broadband Access

Digital education depends upon stable Internet and broadband access, which many areas come nowhere near to meeting. In rural and underserved geographies, online learning is disrupted by limited connectivity or slow connections, hindering access to education resources such as videos of lectures. Reducing this digital divide is essential to providing an equal access to education.

Device-Access and Hardware Restrictions

The availability of appropriate hardware such as old and outdated PCs, tablets or smartphones is still irregular more with many learners who might need to share one of their scarce resources or be burdened up with an insufficient portion of physical learning kit. The majority of our instructors believe that their research is in some way compromised due to hardware limitations, making it impossible for them to engage students effectively through the limited number of digital tools.

Electricity and Power Supply Problem

The biggest hindrance to digital learning, especially in economically backward regions is the inconsistent electricity and frequent power cuts. For digital infrastructure, power solutions that are not sustainable severely limit the usability and reliability of them.

Technological Maintenance and Support

This causes equipment to stop working and become obsolete due to the absence of technical maintenance and support services, which decreases the efficiency of digital education [9].

4 Cultural Obstacles: Digital Literacy and Skills Gaps

This includes the capacity to locate, organize, and use digital resources efficiently; an absolute prerequisite for students and ideally something we want our teachers as well as parents and indeed administrators able to demonstrate. Across many communities, notably in those that are rural, marginalized and economically deprived, a substantial proportion of learners and educators lack the initial digital skills to use educational technologies with confidence. This gap is one of exposure- to computers, to internet, and also due to poor training initiatives and socio-economic conditions that force people to prioritize basic needs over technology education [10].

Digital literacy deficits have implications at large as students need a variety of digital skills to utilize online platforms, find resources and complete assignments if they have not had specific lessons targeting these skills in an organized way than the contribution of ICT will probably be limited to lower levels of achieved engagement and possibly academic performance. Educators who feel like they are not good with technology can hesitate to include tech in their teaching and when they do, it is often poorly used which means that the quality of instruction decreases. In addition, a more unequal distribution of digital skills also means that many parents would not be capable to support their children in learning during home; this could further deepen existing inequalities.

The skills gap is not just in basic digital competency it is very much in advanced capabilities too: critical thinking, digital communication, cyber-security awareness, and content creation to name a few. The almost daily new and reinvented platforms, software and learning methods that educational technology is providing require teachers to upskill regularly. Education systems are not providing teachers the extensive professional development necessary to meet these changing requirements.

Existing cultural attitudes, as well as growing resistance to technology, make such challenges even more exacerbated. Traditional teaching practices can be highly cherished in some communities, combined with which there may be a general mistrust of or skepticism toward digital learning forms. In a world where digital content is so often presented in major global languages and tends to ignore local dialects and cultures, language can be a barrier to accessing the training or resources [11]. Gender disparities also continue to exist and the social restrictions posed upon girls are such that they are doubly denied access to technology thus widening the skill gap. There are many different types of interventions that can be implemented in order to address cultural barriers. Local digital literacy programs, customized to be culturally appropriate and available in the language of choice for the learner or educator can enable both. Two key strategies are to integrate digital skills into the formal curricula and offer continuous, context-relevant professional development for teachers [12]. Inclusive participation and respect toward addressing socio-cultural biases will definitely encourage a wider acceptability of digital education being used with greater efficiency. Digital literacy and digital skills, on this overview we give a broader view of learning through technology enabling it to be widespread while promoting equity in education systems would benefit from paying these gaps due attention.

5 Financial Barriers: Funding Constraints in Educational Institutions

This is not only the most persistent face micronutrient challenged but also to be worked out in a more sustainable and equitable manner to overcome the financial constraints many educational institutions face. Most schools, particularly in low- and middle-income countries, face financial constraints allocating resources to day-to-day operational expenses salaries, facility maintenance and basic teaching materials ahead of digital infrastructure investments needed to adopt new technologies and training personnel [13]. Unfortunately, a lack of money limits the department's capacity to buy essential hardware computers, tablets, servers and also software licenses needed for contemporary digital learning environments. As a result, schools are using outdated or inadequate technology and the advanced digital learning platforms required to teach and learn effectively is failing.

It could also limit the ability of those institutions to invest in the updates and upkeep that are required for robust digital infrastructure. Any hardware left without support and maintenance regularly, gets outdated as well as platforms go unlicensed and unsupported with the result of a downtime in digital networks impeding the continuity and quality of digital education. While some schools have implemented professional development for teachers to help point the way using technology in their teaching, many do not have the resources necessary for the kind of wide-reaching programs that are required. And this limitation of digital literacy in our teachers only further dilutes any potential for developed digital tools.

Infrastructure can be expensive: installing internet connectivity, purchasing devices and upgrading facilities to support ICT needs represent only the tip of the iceberg in terms of initial investments. Monthly or annual costs like software subscriptions, data plans, cybersecurity investments, and the requirement of technical support all serve to eat away at the wallet. These costs can tax limited education budgets, especially when governments have competing priorities or are constrained economically. In contrast, some schools, especially in urban areas or private sectors may be able to afford state of the art technology and special training, while poorer or rural communities can languish [14]. That digital divide risks exacerbating skill and learning gaps between the better-off and less well-off students that would further impede the achievement of the inclusive and equitable quality education envisaged in Sustainable Development Goals (SDGs).

Governments should mainstream digital literacy in their national education budgets and governments must also create a specific budget line for ICT infrastructure, maintenance and capability development. International development agencies and philanthropic organizations can facilitate this by providing grants, subsidies or low-interest loans earmarked for digital education initiatives that reach out to the most disadvantaged. If well-designed, public-private partnerships provide a model for tapping into the expertise and resources of the private sector in alignment with public education objectives. These could include everything from pay-what-you-can devices, to reduced license costs for software and even free training services pro bono by tech companies [15]. Lower cost alternatives such as open-source software, shared community technology centers and solar-powered digital labs can help reduce expenses while encouraging wider accessibility. Schools supported to choose scalable and modular digital infrastructure can accommodate phased investments that allow resources allocation, which will make it easier on the finances. Another example is capacity-building initiatives to train local technicians and educators, which reduce the cost of ongoing maintenance while increasing sustainability.

The transparent financial management system and effective monitoring mechanisms are required to ensure that funds earmarked for digital education are implemented efficiently and result in the desired outcomes. However, when educators, parents, and community leaders have a say in how the budget is created and oversee how it is spent, priority investments are more likely to align with actual needs. Networked school buildings can future-proof against this by enabling schools to invest strategically in digital learning and capitalize on innovative financing models and inclusionary governance to create resilient, high-quality digital learning environments. In turn, education systems will not only improve the quality of instruction and learning opportunities but also equip learners to engage in a rapidly digitalizing world allowing no student to be left behind for lack of money [16].

Public-Private Partnerships and Funding Models

Private Public partnerships (PPPs) & Innovative funding models: PPPs and other innovative financial mechanisms has become a necessary tool for addressing the financing challenge in digital education. PPPs are also a key intersection point for both public institutions and private sector entities, which can bring resources, technical expertise, and innovative solutions to address the large unmet need for digital infrastructure used in teaching-learning. Digital education can be expensive and these kinds of projects are not usually affordable for any government by itself. These solutions can be sourced by partnering with tech companies, ISPs and non-profit organizations for subsidizing devices, providing cheap internet plans, and capacity building [17].

Funding mechanisms in PPPs cover a spectrum from grants and donations to equity collaboration and for-profit models very different from traditional non-profits allow flexible solutions adapted to the diverse composition of situations. Some, for instance, target low-cost device and software solutions to schools without basic tech infrastructure; others invest in digital courseware or teacher training. Many times this comes in the form of collaborations focused on scale and sustainability, folding maintenance and training into the design of funded projects. Quality PPPs must be based on strong governance frameworks and consensually agreed targets to prevent narrow private interests from skewing public education objectives [18]. If managed properly, these partnerships can fill financing gaps, spur innovation and the development of comprehensive and resilient digital education systems to serve diverse groups of learners across a wide range of socio-economic backgrounds.

6 Strategies to Overcome Barriers

Broad-based and comprehensive strategies that deal with infrastructure deficits, cultural impediments, financial constraints, governance challenges which are not only interrelated but are often a glass ceiling on one another need to be contained. Delivering the promise of digital education requires better alignment across technology innovation, stakeholder engagement, sustainable financial solutions and enabling policy. This section provides lean start-up solutions for addressing these barriers in different geographies covering infrastructure build out and innovation, digital literacy through community programs, affordable access models and subsidies to bridge the last mile gap and policy interventions supported by a business framework [19].

Infrastructure Development and Innovation

The improving and extending the digital precinct are proposed as a base to better live with the digital divide and provoke sustainable digital education. Making seamless, universal and programmatically reliable internet connectivity is a significant bucket list item, esp. in rural and remote areas where access is either non-existent or difficult to come by. With combines of extant and new technologies including fiber optics, satellite internet, and wireless broadband while government and private sector can work in hand expand the network in service areas. The equally important is investment in affordable, resilient and context-appropriate digital devices. These devices need to be able to run contemporary educational software and operate under tough environmental conditions [20]. To make it sustainable, renewable energy, particularly solar should also be part of the infrastructure development in areas where available power is unreliable. Digital labs and charging stations powered by solar energy: This reduces the cost of running devices, while also making them more accessible. Lastly, the development of maintenance and technical support to a local level enables longer term functionality and reduces reliance on external resources.

Modular and scalable infrastructure models enable phased development that leverages existing resources, while also adapting to demands as they change. Cloud-Based Learning Ecosystems, as well as Offline-Capable Educational Platforms can decrease the need for bandwidth and widen access to learners with sparse connectivity. The modern technologies need to work within an eye and power as mentioned in this post: Infrastructure development coupled with technological innovation paves one of many paths toward more equitable and robust digital education systems [21].

Community-Based Digital Literacy Programs

To bridge the cultural and skills divide, there must be community-based digital literacy initiatives that reach out to learners, educators and parents. Engagement programs need to be contextually relevant, culturally sensitive, and linguistically accessible for effective engagement with diverse populations. Digital skills training hands-on workshops on basic computer use, internet navigation, cybersecurity awareness and educational software can impound the potency of community learning centers, libraries and schools that can act as hubs. Digital literacy programs need to be part of professional development for teachers including both pedagogical aspects and technical skills to use digital tools in teaching. Teaching techniques continue to be evolved to adapt to ever-changing technologies. The continuous format also provides teachers the confidence of delivering blended and remote learning. Increasing parental and caregiver involvement is vital in establishing a supportive home environment that encourages digital learning. Implementation of workshops and awareness campaigns could resolve the issue of reluctance to adopt technology and it can also encourage a positive perception for digital education [22].

New ideas like subsidized device programs, open-source software, and public-private partnerships are becoming more popular as ways to make digital education more accessible. Of course, sustainability also depends on adding green elements that can help the environment, such cloud-based infrastructure and devices that save power. These talks show that it need a more comprehensive strategy to innovation, adaptation, and funding that goes beyond just technology. Legislators and educators may work together to improve digital education that is open to everyone and helps all kids succeed in the digital age.

Affordable Access Models and Subsidies

There are financial impediments that innovative access models must tamp down, not only for learners and institutions alike but also for equity. Financial support such as subsidies, discounts, or financing of digital devices and internet services will help to reach families from low-income household at scale. Governments are able to partner with ISPs and tech firms that can provide zero-rated or subsidized educational content reducing the cost of data. Undertaking device donation programs, refurbishing of equipment distribution, bulk procurement can be facilitated by public-private partnership. Community technology centers with access to shared digital resources provide cost-effective entry points for learners who do not have their own devices [23].

Households can also purchase devices through microfinance or installment payment schemes that reduce the upfront cost of investment [24]. The use of open source software and digitized content freely available, brings down the licensing cost lower which makes online education more sustainable in the long run than any other method. Recruitment focused on software updates, maintenance and technical support also need to be part of sustainable financing mechanisms Since without it digital education infrastructure would not outlive its use by date. Disbursements which align with community expectations can be improved by making allocation of funds transparent and involving stakeholders when deciding how it is done.

Policy Interventions and Governance

Institutionalization of digital education with effective policy frameworks and governance structures is essential to break through these systemic barriers. Digital learning should have truly been a national education priority which means that governments allocated budgets for infrastructure, training and content development. Ensuring that digital education is integrated within wider development and climate resilience strategies will ensure it is aligned with Sustainable Development Goals and support the ability to secure funding. It is important that public policies aim at the competition between providers of connection service, so as to lower fees and improve services of quality [25].

Governance models influenced by multi-stakeholder collaborations involving government, educational facilities, private sector organizations, and civil society and communities boost resource generation, innovation and their ability to adapt to local conditions. Forming institutions or task forces to stay track of digital learning could heighten synchronization and polestar [26]. It is used to evaluate progress and gaps, and inform adjustments in policy-making. This feedback is critical to ensuring our policies remain focused on the needs of students and educators.

To address digital education barriers requires the collective strategy of infrastructure renewal, community engagement, affordability, and stable policy-making. This means addressing technological, social, financial and system challenges at the same time to build inclusive, resilient and sustainable digital learning environments. Such policies should not only widen access to education but also equip learners for full participation in the digital economy and knowledge society. It is for this reason that sustainable digital education anchored by equity and supported by innovation can signify a forceful impetus representing social transformation and progress [27].

7 Conclusion and Future Directions

The key to preparing sustainable learning environments for success in the twenty-first century is overcoming these stacked barriers to digital education through social inclusion and equity. There are infrastructure shortages, cultural hurdles, financial barriers and governance bottlenecks that have to be tackled intelligently through integrated and innovative methodologies. This need to scale up reliable internet connectivity, put money in it affordable and durable device and likewise introduce green energy solutions are important for digital division closing. Similarly, a culture of digital inclusion is nurtured as community-based digital literacy programs and ongoing professional development equip educators, learners, and families to interact with technology in the same way. New forms of funding, whether public-private partnerships or subsidies, have made digital tools and services more accessible to all by lighten the load on wallets. Sound policy frameworks and accountable, sustainable and internationalized governance.

The future of digital education is at scale, adaptable and learner-focused while centered on equity and sustainability. New technologies such as AI, AR and 5G provide fresh opportunities to make personalized learning a reality and address the inequalities that separate global citizens. But ongoing monitoring and research as well as regular engagement with stakeholders are vital to the identification of emergent challenges and appropriate response. International cooperation would provide an opportunity to share lessons and leverage resources and best practices across contexts. Through adopting whole system approaches and looking to the future, education systems can convert barriers into opportunities, to enable learners everywhere, regardless of background lead successful live in an increasingly digital world.

References

1. Singun, A. J. (2025). Unveiling the barriers to digital transformation in higher education institutions: A systematic literature review. *Discover Education, 4*(1), 37.
2. Madinah, B., & Prihatin, Y. (2024). Overcoming technology barriers to sustainable education in digital era. *Community Development, 81*, 81–95.
3. Abuali, T., & Ahmed, A. A. (2025). Challenges and opportunities in implementing E-learning in developing countries. *The Open European Journal of Social Science and Education (OEJSSE), 1*(1), 1–12.
4. Nwakoby, C. S., & Iloka, P. C. (2025). Regulatory challenges in implementing digital education in Anambra state for sustainable development. *Unizik Journal of Educational Laws and Leadership Studies, 1*(1), 28.
5. Animashaun, E. S., Familoni, B. T., & Onyebuchi, N. C. (2024). Implementing educational technology solutions for sustainable development in emerging markets. *International Journal of Applied Research in Social Sciences, 6*(6), 1158–1168.
6. Phulpoto, S. A. J., Oad, L., & Imran, M. (2024). Enhancing teacher

performance in E-learning: Addressing barriers and promoting sustainable education in public universities of Pakistan. *Pakistan Languages and Humanities Review, 8*(1), 418–429.

7. Memon, F. N., & Memon, S. N. (2025). Digital divide and equity in education: Bridging gaps to ensure inclusive learning. In *Impact of digitalization on education and social sustainability* (pp. 107–130). IGI Global.
8. Ghani, S., Malik, F., & Ullah, S. (2024). Identifications of barriers in implementation of digital technology in secondary schools of Punjab. *Pakistan Journal of Humanities and Social Sciences, 12*(1), 436–443.
9. Gbadebo, A. D. (2024). Digital transformation for educational development in Sub-Saharan Africa. *International Journal of Social Science and Religion (IJSSR), 5*(3), 397–418.
10. Siddiqi, M. M. (2024). Future of digital education: inclusive, immersive, equitable. *MediaSpace: DME Media Journal of Communication, 5*(01), 8–24.
11. Nosike, C. J. (2024). Digitalization in developing countries: Opportunities and challenges. *Nigerian Journal of Arts and Humanities, 4*(1), 2955–0343.
12. Chari, S. G. (2024). Bridging gaps, building futures: Tackling socio-economic disparities through education and technology. *London Journal of Research In Humanities and Social Sciences, 24*(16), 1–12.
13. Rydzewski, P. (2025). Digital inequality and sustainable development. *Problemy Ekorozwoju, 20*(1), 96–108.
14. Joseph, O. B., Onwuzulike, O. C., & Shitu, K. (2024). Digital transformation in education: Strategies for effective implementation. *World Journal of Advanced Research and Reviews, 23*(2), 2785–2799.
15. Glazkova, I., Falko, N., Khomenko, O., Khatuntseva, S., Rula, N., Shulzhenko, A., & Tatarin, V. (2025). Barriers in online education for displaced universities: Insights from faculty and students. *Problems and Perspectives in Management, 23*(2), 136.
16. Ajani, O. A. (2024). Sustainable transformation in South African rural universities: A digital perspective. *International Journal of Management, Knowledge and Learning, 13*(1), 113–127.
17. Aljaradin, M., Alzouebi, K., & Alkaabi, A. (2024). Online education and its impact on sustainable development goals. *International Journal of Sustainability Policy & Practice, 20*(2), 27–48.
18. Panda, A., & Gope, L. (2024). Breaking barriers: The digital revolution in girls education across India. *Journal of Interdisciplinary Studies in Education, 13*(S1), 147–171.
19. Omowole, B. M., Olufemi-Philips, A. Q., Ofadile, O. C., Eyo-Udo, N. L., & Ewim, S. E. (2024). Barriers and drivers of digital transformation in SMEs: A conceptual analysis. *International Journal of Frontline Research in Multidisciplinary Studies, 5*(2), 019–036.

20. AlAli, R., & Wardat, Y. (2024). Empowering education through digital transformation: Confronting educational wastage in basic education schools in Jordan. *International Journal of Innovative Research and Scientific Studies, 7*(3), 1148–1162.
21. Mhlanga, D. (2024). Digital transformation of education, the limitations and prospects of introducing the fourth industrial revolution asynchronous online learning in emerging markets. *Discover Education, 3*(1), 32.
22. Oshowole, S. A. (2024). *Barriers impacting the integration of classroom technology in primary schools in Lagos, Nigeria* (Doctoral dissertation). Saint Leo University.
23. Djatmiko, G. H., Sinaga, O., & Pawirosumarto, S. (2025). Digital transformation and social inclusion in public services: A qualitative analysis of e-government adoption for marginalized communities in sustainable governance. *Sustainability, 17*(7), 2908.
24. Djatmiko, G. H., Sinaga, O., & Pawirosumarto, S. (2025). Digital transformation and social inclusion in public services: A qualitative analysis of e-government adoption for marginalized communities in sustainable governance. *Sustainability, 17*(7), 2908.
25. Kamarudin, S. (2024). Strategic 4.0 in academia: A comprehensive review of digital transformation and future gaps agenda. *Business Development via AI and Digitalization, 1*, 31–40.
26. Nipo, D. T., Lily, J., Fabeil, N. F., & Jamil, I. A. A. (2024). Transforming rural entrepreneurship through digital innovation: A review on opportunities, barriers and challenges. *Journal of Management and Sustainability, 14*(2), 114–124.
27. Al-Hail, M., Zguir, M. F., & Koç, M. (2024). Exploring digital learning opportunities and challenges in higher education institutes: Stakeholder analysis on the use of social media for effective sustainability of learning–teaching–assessment in a university setting in Qatar. *Sustainability, 16*(15), 6413.

CHAPTER 13

Promoting Digital Literacy and Workforce Skills: Integrating Digital Literacy and Twenty-First-Century Skills into Curriculum Design

Devdatta Tare, Rajani Wadhai, and Priya Gedam

Abstract The developing of digital literacy and workforce skills are crucial when it comes to ensuring that students get the support they need to succeed in this ever-changing digital world. By embedding digital literacy and twenty-first-century skills including, critical processing, collaboration, creative thinking, and problem-solving into the curriculum design it better prepares students for such issues in a technological

D. Tare (✉) · R. Wadhai · P. Gedam
Gondwana University, Gadchiroli, India
e-mail: tare.devdatta@unigug.ac.in

R. Wadhai
e-mail: wadhairajani@unigug.ac.in

P. Gedam
e-mail: gedam.priya@unigug.ac.in

P. K. Dutta et al. (eds.), *Digital Education for a Sustainable Future*, Sustainable Development Goals Series,
https://doi.org/10.1007/978-3-032-15433-0_13

world and an ever-changing work place. Making Curriculum Design Work Successful curriculum design is about using an interdisciplinary approach where traditional subjects are combined with digital tools and practical application in reality. Limiting factors are meeting disparities in tech access, preparing teachers, and making material culturally inflective to equally bring learning across the socioeconomic landscape. Inclusive strategies should be adopted by policymakers and educators; the professional development of teachers must be promoted; and partnerships with industry facilitated, so that educational outcomes better meet workforce needs. Embedding digital literacy into curricula and combining twenty-first century skills enables education systems to fill the gaps in skills, empower learners and contribute to sustainable economic growth while promoting social development.

Keywords Digital literacy · Twenty-first-century skills · Curriculum design · Workforce readiness · Educational assimilation

1 Introduction

The demand for digital literacy and workforce skills has increased significantly in the rapidly changing world of today; a basic requirement to train learners to be successful in these increasingly complex and technology-driven environments. Integrating digital literacy and twenty-first-century skills into curriculum design is essential so that students have the technical know-how, but also develop critical thinking, creativity, collaboration, communication, and problem-solving skills. It empowers all individuals to develop the skills necessary to succeed in a rapidly advancing technological world, especially those who are ill-equipped at their current job due a lack of educational or training opportunities. Incorporating such abilities into educational curricula changes the nature of learning from memorization based to active experience that not only aids in innovation but also develops real-world preparedness.

Digital literacy is not just being able to use computers and software, but also knowing how to learn for the digital age; how to access, evaluate, and communicate information responsibly; and how interact with others operating in a digital environment legally. Modern skills, on the other hand have been regarded as criteria that combine cognitive and human competencies necessary for both personal and professional successfulness. This chapter looks at each idea within their big ideas to provide an inclusive framework that can help learners prepare themselves as agile, critical and socially responsible digital citizens. Curriculum mapping is crucial for accomplishing successful integration of these essential skills in a cross-curricular manner, as opposed to being treated as separate modules.

The next iteration of curriculum design thinking has to focus on interdisciplinary, project based learning practices that mimic real-world circumstances requiring active problem-solving and working in collaborative environments. Embedding digital storytelling projects in language classes or data analysis for Science and Mathematics courses assist students to use specific tools with relevancy thereby increasing their engagement and retention. Employing educational technologies, for example, interactive simulations, virtual labs and collaborative platforms not only enhances learning experiences but extends hands-on digital and cognitive skills development opportunities. A key factor to the integration of this is teacher capacity building. The reality is that educators require continual professional development to become proficient with new tools and teaching practices for twenty-first-century skill development. Institution-based teacher training programs should incorporate components of creativity, inquiry-based learning and diversity-inclusive teaching for varied learners alongside subject-specific technical skills.

Importance of Digital Literacy and Workforce Skills

There is also a need for assessment and evaluation methods to evolve with it, to encompass the vast range of digital literacy and workforce skills. If we are assessing the degree to which our students can analyze critically, work collaboratively or develop creatively traditional testing is usually inadequate. More realistic insights on competencies of learners come from formative assessments, portfolios, peer reviews and project presentations. Using rubrics that assess technical skills, along with a student's soft skills gives faculty an accurate snapshot of their performance and where they need to grow. The important to consider when introducing digital literacy into curricula is equity and inclusion. The digital divide means some of the most access-challenged students among our communities suffer disproportionately. Tasks and activities cannot be as they might for a population without such economic divides. Content deployed in the curriculum must take into account these gaps and address this shortfall with accessible content, multilingual resources, low-tech or offline options for learning. Assuredly, this makes for stronger relevance and engagement but even in the digitized era where variety rules above conformity, no learner is left behind when diverse backgrounds and learning styles are incorporated into culturally responsive pedagogy [1].

The enabling environment created through policy and institutional support is also critical for sustained operationalization. Governments and education authorities should make digital literacy and twenty-first-century skills one of the central priorities in the national educational strategies, ensure sufficient funding for its implementation and set up standards or even better guidelines. Industry collaboration can enrich curricula by mapping learning outcomes to the requirements of the workforce, ensuring internships and co-creating educational resources. This collaboration provides more resources and ensures that the course materials are keeping up with the current state of technology.

Best practice exemplars live and breathe in the hundreds of case studies attesting to success derived from embedding digital literacy and workforce skills into education. National level curriculum reforms around digital competencies have led to increased student engagement, employability and innovation Syria is a prime example. Project-based and tech-enhanced learning environments like Pokky Camp by Smarton are showing encouraging results in student creativity and critical thinking at schools and universities. The private sector partners bring in more resources and competencies to drive innovation and expand scalable quality of digital education. New groundbreaking technologies like Artificial Intelligence, Virtual Reality and 5G connectivity open up novel possibilities to increasingly individualize learning experiences narrowing skill gaps. However, these have led to a necessity of upskilling and research which teachers must embrace in order to engage with such innovations and translate into learning [2].

So, embedding digital and twenty-first-century skills into curriculum development is essential for the new era of learners in the digital age. Such integration helps us make graduates who can adapt, learn and stay employable throughout their work lives while also contributing to a more socially responsible workforce and society. Education systems that embrace innovative pedagogies, invest in teacher development, ensure equitable access, cultivate policy support can turn restrictions into opportunities enhancing inclusive and sustainable digital education for generations to come.

2 Relationship Between Digital Literacy and Workforce Competencies

Digital literacy and workforce competencies are closely related; foundations of the required skills for effective participation in the technology-driven labor markets today. Digital literacy involves the knowledge to utilize digital applications in a critical and responsible way: how to process information, communicate, collaborate, and solve with those tools. Those competencies are essentially the broader skills, knowledge, and behaviors necessary to be successful in a professional setting. Embedding digital literacy into workforce competencies means that people can do more than just use technology, they can use technology aligned to organization goals and changing work requirements.

Digital literacy is a requirement for almost all jobs in today's workforce—stretching beyond the traditional IT roles. Workers need to be able to move around in various digital communication platforms, make sense of data points, operate specific software and team communicate virtually. The core competencies of the workforce, e.g., critical thinking, adaptability, and collaboration are well served by these capabilities to improve productivity, innovation and decision-making. For example, a digitally literate employee will be able to quickly analyze vast data sets using digital tools, convey insights to cross-functional teams via online platforms and can help drive toward solution with immediate access to information.

The accelerating rate of technological change underscores the need for digital literacy to be lifelong including ongoing reskilling and up skilling to evolve with new tools and concepts. The key work force competency, learning agility or lifelong learning, one of the life skills needed for career growth. With the adoption of new technologies such as automation, artificial intelligence, and cloud computing in organizations, employees having an understanding of technology along with base level workforce skills are more likely to adapt to change; they also are able to get into the mode where innovation can be brought about.

However, academic preparation and labor market expectations remain disjointed without educational curricula deeply connected to the relationship between digital literacy and workforce competencies. Working these digital skills into learning outcomes alongside communication, teamwork, and problem-solving can lead to more well-rounded students and future employees. Companies will have a workforce that makes strong use of technology, which helps promote organizational agility and competitiveness. So, overall they both are complimentary to each other which are the two side of same coin in current scenario. Digital literacy and workforce competencies. And while digital literacy is teaching people how to use technology for work in the modern world, workforce competencies are teaching them to fit those skills within broader professional capabilities. All aimed to prepare learners for purposeful employment, future-readiness and long-term success in an era of rapid digitization and globalization [3].

The addition of digital literacy and twenty-first-century skills in the curriculum is enhancing education by equipping students for a labor market that is continuously developing and technologically demanding. New arguments are being made about how important it is to put digital skills to use in real life, along with skills like problem-solving, critical thinking, and working in groups. For example, education programs might include project-based learning, where students use digital tools like coding platforms and data analysis software to develop both technical and artistic skills while working on global issues like climate change or social justice.

3 Current Trends in Curriculum Design

Curriculum design has changed dramatically in recent years due to the rapid development of technology from training demands in the workforce and even educational paradigms. Current curriculums have been moving towards a focus on providing learners with new skills that encourage digital literacy and twenty-first century skills like creativity, collaboration, critical thinking, and adaptability. These are changes that reflect an understanding of the fact that schools must meet students where they are in a world that is both complex and interconnected, with rapidly evolving technologies.

The biggest trends is combining digital technology with traditional syllabus, changing the mode of teaching and learning. Educators are embedding digital tools and competencies across disciplines incorporating data analysis software into science classes, digital storytelling in language arts, or coding in mathematics, instead of treating digital literacy as a standalone subject. This enables students to learn digital skills in context, which increases relevance and engagement. Interactive content in the digital space including virtual labs, simulations and gamified learning are proliferating providing experiential and personalized learning to cater to different learning types. Traditional on campus face to face learning has declined, and increasingly common are blended models that comprise of F2F instruction coupled with online components which have been described as offering flexibility and reach.

Curriculum trends are also influenced by international initiatives. If anything, development organizations such as UNESCO, the OECD and The World Economic Forum have identified twenty-first-Century Skills & Digital Literacy in education frameworks of future. Many national curricula around the world have been overhauled to mirror these priorities with frameworks laid down for competencies such as critical thinking, creativity, digital citizenship, socio-emotional learning and more. The new competency-based curricula are being rolled out that emphasizes learning outcomes and mastery rather than rote memorization in several countries. Global assessments like PISA have added problem-solving and digital skills measures, consequently prompting many nations to update curricula so that new competencies can be taught. This drives a homogeneous educational reform that reduces variation, but local adaptation is still critically needed to support cultural and contextual specificity [4].

A related trend is with the increased focus on interdisciplinary and project-based learning. Undergraduate curricula, for example: are developed to encourage cross-disciplinary knowledge and skills, and assume real-world problems cannot be separated into different subject areas. Students investigate real-world problems and engage with content in context by way of project-based learning or collaborative assignments that support them to communicate effectively, develop teamwork skills, and apply knowledge. By those means, the distance between the theoretical and practical stands can be reduced to make sure that students are well informed of what might come their way needing prior preparation ahead of being recruited.

However, the upgrading of curriculum also encounters some challenges. This resistance to change has manifested in one form or another, with educators and institutions resisting either due to low digital literacy levels, inadequate training or simply being wedded to paper-and-ink teaching. Teacher professional development is an afterthought, which leads to patchy implementation of the new curricula [5]. Also, uneven access to technology and online infrastructure prevents the mainstream reach of digital-integrated curricula that rural or marginalized populations can afford putting their readiness to oblivion and widening the education divide. There is the additional danger of curricula becoming overstuffed as new digital skills are bolted on to outdated content, meaning students and educators would be under even greater pressure.

Assessment presents another challenge many assessment practices continue to rely on traditional testing, which might not necessarily represent the complex knowledge and skills that some curricula attempt to foster. This highlight illuminates an area of innovation and research that continues to be of major importance in the development of scalable assessments for twenty-first century competencies and digital literacy as well as procedures for evaluating their quality. Many education systems are looking to create innovative solutions such as adaptive learning platforms which adapt content and pacing to individual learners; competency-based progression models enabling learning mastery at its own pace; integrated teacher support systems where initial training is fused with ongoing mentorship and resources; and a whole lot of other innovation [6]. Whole-system policies designed to accommodate a coherent approach to curriculum, assessment, and teacher recruitment in the context of infrastructure investments are increasingly being promoted.

The trends in curriculum design are becoming to learner-focused and technology-endorsing facilitated for skill-based knowledge imparted education. Some of the key aspects of contemporary curricular designs include integrating digital literacy within subjects, aligning curriculum with global competency frameworks, and engaging students in interdisciplinary project-based learning. But modernization is only going to be successful if it can address the issue of teacher readiness, equity, assessment, and systemic coherence. These, and many other challenges, can be worked through to enable education systems to design curricula that will both disseminate knowledge and serve as a vehicle for empowering learners with the digital and workforce skills required in an ever-evolving world [7].

The other creative idea is to use adaptive learning technologies that customize lessons to help students become more digitally fluent while also helping them improve their communication and adaptability skills. Students can learn about AI and cloud computing while also improving their creativity and collaboration on gamified platforms like coding contests and virtual simulations.

Traditional vs. Digital-Integrated Curricula

An increasing number of colleges now require hands-on design experiences to accompany traditional curricula, which are heavily dependent on subject-specific knowledge delivered through lectures, textbooks and standardized assessments. The traditional curricula are characterized by memorization and instruction, teacher centered, low on technology integration or interdisciplinary approach. The format usually strict, with tidy subject lists and discrete instruction goals as they might be well-versed in conventional subjects, but often traditional curricula does not focus on digital skills or real-world insight enough to make learners prepared new workforce expectations.

Digital-integrated curricula embed digital literacy and tech use throughout all subjects, therefore changing pedagogy and learning style. These are active, learner-centered curricula, often deploying digital tools such as simulations, interactive media, and collaborative platforms to facilitate engagement and contextualize learning [8]. It is designed to foster cross-over between disciplines and address the twenty-first-century skills of critical thinking, creativity and communication. Digital curricula assessments typically include some form of project-based evaluation, along with rigorous formative feedback supporting deeper understanding. This shift prepares students for technology rich environments but requires robust infrastructure, teacher training and continuous updates to keep pace with technological advancements.

Global Initiatives and Best Practices

There have been a number of global initiatives that have helped in bringing curriculum reforms to the fore front developing frameworks focusing strongly on digital literacy and twenty-first-century skills. Competency-Based Education as promoted by UNESCO and OECD, is a key to a learning model more on critical thinking, problem-solving, digital citizenship and socio-emotional learnings. These frameworks are implemented in curricula around the world, to prepare graduates for both their future work and for international competition. International assessments such as PISA have begun testing skills that go beyond knowledge of content, which means curricula now focus on more global competencies.

Recommended practices are interdisciplinary, project-based learning, technology integration and inclusive pedagogy. The most successful reforms engage educators, industry, and government in a process that enables curricula to be contemporary and agile. The quality of curriculum modernization in countries is followed by effectiveness as per investment that has been made into continuous teacher professional development or into technology infrastructure [9].

Challenges in Curriculum Modernization

Most educators who are familiar with the traditional ways to teach tend to be resistant to change, may be due in part to anxiety about the new digital pedagogies or a lack of confidence in using them. Poor professional development and training exacerbate this problem, with teachers ill-equipped to teach new curriculums [10]. The result being a uniform curriculum will be adopted at the pace of its slowest adopter. There is poor internet infrastructure in many areas; and/or those who have access to such infrastructure, particularly in rural/marginalized communities, may not have digital devices. It risks further exacerbating educational inequities by widening the digital divide. That is not all, as in many educational systems with overloaded curricula that promise new-age or digital skills besides twenty-first-century ones keep adding rather than subtracting any old content and thrust, enabling them to retain dearth demands on students and teachers alike.

Existing assessment mechanisms are often slow to catch up with curricular changes; they primarily evaluate learning content, and not the breadth of skills that complex attributes like creativity or collaboration entail. Policy fragmentation and inadequate budgetary support are also common factors that undermine sustainable curriculum reforms. Meeting this challenge demands whole-society involvement and whole-of-system approaches [11].

4 Strategies for Integrating Digital Literacy and Twenty-First Century Skills

The successful integration of digital literacy and twenty-first-century skills into curricula demands a holistic, multi-leveled approach that influences what and how teachers teach and learners learn. One of the main approaches is that of curriculum mapping and alignment, which consists in progressively inserting digital and soft skills into existing subjects and learning outcomes. It is not a standalone course, but rather a theme that runs across the curriculum in language arts, mathematics, science, and social studies [12]. It does this by embedding digital skills contextually in what is meaningful to learn, and providing learners with the practical application for the development of skill through authentic tasks.

Assimilation is improved with interdisciplinary and project-based learning approaches that promote collaborative work, creativity, and critical thinking to solve complex problems. They simulate real-life experiences that help the learner to practise using digital tools coupled with cognitive and social skills. For example, students may be using data analysis tools while working on science projects or creating a multimedia presentation for a social studies assignment [13]. The project-based learning helps in communication and teamwork, important workforce competencies. The important strategy is, to use educational technology and digital tools in a proper manner. With the help of interactive platforms, virtual simulations, coding environments, and collaborative online spaces encourage active learning as well as personalized interaction. It allows for more student engagement and the opportunity to learn skills in a variety of ways. Adaptive learning systems: Adaptive digital learning environments deliver content based on the unique needs of each learner, advancing to mastery at his or her own pace [14].

The successful integration of these skills depends to a great extent on teacher training and capacity building. Educators need continuous professional learning on both digital competencies and education pedagogies to nurture twenty-first-century skills. Training was described as practice-driven, ongoing, and localized for teachers to feel secure in using the technology and implement learning tasks that focus around learners. Building a culture of innovation and flexibility in our schools and education systems is essential to ensure sustained uptake Promoting experimentation, educator collaboration and stakeholder participation enables curricula to modify itself in response to new technology and shifts in the workforce [15]. These types of approaches can add up to an approach that surrounds students with digital literacy and twenty-first-century skills in learning experiences are grounded by connection to real-world solutions, preparing them for challenges to come.

5 Measuring Digital Literacy and Skill Acquisition: Assessment and Evaluation Methods

Measuring digital literacy and the development of twenty-first-century skills creates distinct complications that need novel and integrated ways for evaluation beyond conventional testing [16]. The second type of digital competency which the educational theory denotes begs to emphasize on an exhaustive oeuvre of such skills right from those of a technical kind to rather more general in its scope; for instance; resourcefulness involving technology/critical acumen towards use of technology/ awareness about ethics and responsibilities of reading/write ability for digital mediums etc. The twenty-first-century skills of collaboration, creativity and problem-solving are diverse and highly situational, beyond what can be tested by traditional exams alone. The assessments must be diverse and authentic rather than just measuring traditional rote skills.

A key feature is formative, iterative forms of assessment that take place during learning. This model allows for almost instantaneous discernment regarding performance so that learners can reflect on their progress and educators can adjust instruction accordingly. For example, with a digital portfolio students can compile evidence of their skills in a range of forms over time (for example: stories or video presentations along with code challenges and collaborative outcomes). Portfolios provide abundant qualitative narrative around students' abilities and growth, focusing on the process much as the outcomes [17].

Project work, simulations, and real-world problem-solving tasks also work for assessing digital literacy as well as soft skills. These performance assessments require the integration and application of multiple competencies at the same time through real-world challenges as experienced by students. For instance, a team project that is related to website development or data analysis in big data applies technical knowledge with collaborative skills and analytical perspective. The use of peer and self-assessment methods also contribute to the development of metacognition, whereby students being to reflect on their learning processes in using digital skills. Rubrics with distinct evaluation criteria mapped to digital literacy standards are important to maintain consensual and transparent evaluation. So, employing technology-assisted assessment tools like adaptive quizzes and analytical platforms allow for individualized evaluation and deep visibility into learner habits and proficiency levels. These varied approaches to assessment together present a more complete image of the development and understanding that has taken place, which will guide educators in creating deeper learning experiences and assist parents in guiding their children to be prepared for today's digital age challenges [18].

6 Addressing Equity and Inclusion: Bridging the Digital Divide, Culturally Responsive Curriculum Design

Designing curricula that effectively incorporates twenty-first century skills and digital literacy cannot be done ethically or effectively without placing the lens of equity and inclusion over everything you do. Even today, the so-called digital divide is a major obstacle in deepening inequality in education [19]. But closing this gap will require a clear, consistent approach to guaranteeing that all learners regardless of their financial circumstances or where they live or wherever else are able to access the digital tools and reliable internet connections on which remote learning, in particular, depends. The schools and policymakers must focus on infrastructure investment in underserved areas and champion affordable access models be it community technology centers or income-based internet plans in order to level the digital learning playing field.

Culturally appropriate curriculum design is key to inclusion in addition to physical access. This educational approach acknowledges and honors the multi-cultural backgrounds, languages, and experiences of its learners by ensuring that learning is both authentic and interesting for all students. Local knowledge, traditions, and perspectives are incorporated into culturally responsive curricula for digital literacy and skills development in a way that acknowledges the identity of students and builds belonging. It also challenges embedded dominant narratives and biases within educational content while simultaneously fostering critical thought, and human empathy [20].

These curricula also facilitate differentiated instruction for diverse learning preferences and abilities, and offer content in accessible digital formats with full compatibility with assistive technology for learners with disabilities. Informed educators will be best positioned to design inclusive classrooms that recognize the strengths and joys of diversity when their training has integrated commitments to culturally responsive pedagogy.

Fixing equity and inclusion by addressing the digital divide and incorporating culturally responsible curriculums is vital to realizing the promise of digital literacy, workforce skills for every student. This whole-child approach helps close achievement gaps and better prepares students to be lifelong learners, effective communicators, competent team members and healthy citizens who can contribute to a diverse and interconnected world [21].

7 Role of Educational Policies and Frameworks

Educational policies and frameworks are key enablers in embedding digital literacy and twenty-first-century skills across curriculum design, making such initiatives systematic, scalable and accessible. Policies serve as the formal guidance and direction that determine priorities, allocate resources, and define standards across educational content, pedagogy and curriculum. In the absence of focused policy, efforts to update curricula often remain fragmented and can be piecemeal or forgotten very quickly [22]. Good policy allows national education goals to take stock of the characteristics and direction of global trends, for example, a broad recognition that digital skills are essential for workforce readiness and lifelong learning, while dovetailing this with solutions tailored to local contextual needs.

Policies that address other key factors e.g., the training of teachers, infrastructure development, or budgeting practices also impact schools. Professional development policies should prioritize technology literacy in delivering instruction. At the same time, policy directives can also require expansive investments in ICT infrastructure to close access gaps that create a digital divide in edu-tech. They establish the ethical and legal framework associated with data privacy, digital citizenship, and inclusive education ultimately promoting a safe and responsible utilization of technology. Incorporating the voices of stakeholders from across government, education, industry and communities in policymaking ensures that it is informed and meaningful to those with the capability to deliver; leading to greater relevance and stronger buy-in resulting in successful implementation.

The educational policies and frameworks establish the fundamental infrastructure for digital literacy and twenty-first-century skills to be embedded in curricula. They help drive action to be more coherent, ensure equity and a better deployment of resources all while maintaining quality standards and ethics, equipping education systems to get learners ready for the digital future and skills necessary in the workforce of tomorrow [23].

Digital ethics should be a big part of school curriculums so that children learn how to deal with incorrect information and privacy issues in a responsible way. By adding these skills to classes like history or arithmetic, education stays up to date and ready for the future. These strategies help students excel in many different fields and make important contributions to a digital society that is changing quickly by making sure they have both tech-savvy and adaptive abilities.

8 Conclusion

The combination of digital literacy and twenty-first-century skills in curriculum is important to help learners succeed in the ever-evolving tech-space. This integration that comes through connects the learning progressively in knowledge transmission as well as they develop critical competencies, including creativity, collaboration, problem-solving and digital citizenship. This is especially true in an academic curriculum, where interdisciplinary approaches are integrated along with active learning strategies and the intentional use of technology to develop technical competencies as well as soft skills relevant for workforce readiness and lifelong learning.

Implementation is complex and includes a variety of factors such as; teacher training, added equitable technology access for lower income students, new policies to support implementation, and innovative assessment shortcomings techniques. Bridging the digital divide and developing culturally relevant curricula is important when it comes to creating environments where all students can benefit from education in the digital age. A collaborative effort among educators, policymakers, industry partners, and communities enhances the relevance and longevity of curricula. However, continuous research, worldwide efforts, and technological developments pave the way for more growth and advancements. Through a holistic and learner-centered whole sector change, education systems can begin to reframe barriers as opportunities for students to explore ways in which they can make sense of and meaningfully contribute to increasingly digitally mediated societies. The incorporation of digital literacy and workforce skills into curricula is as much an educational-blind necessity as a lever for social and economic development in the twenty-first century.

9 Future Scope

The scope for the future of digital literacy and twenty-first-century skills to be fused within curriculum design is wide and ever-changing as new technologies enter the frame and society continues to develop. New frontiers of artificial intelligence, virtual, and augmented reality, and adaptive learning platforms promise to enable personalized, immersive, and inclusive forms of educational engagement. These tech tools can further personalize learning, boost engagement and deliver instant feedback, making it easier for learners to acquire new skills. Future curricula will also need to cover basic digital skills as well as ethical issues around their use such as data privacy, digital health, and responsible citizenship. A meaningful shift toward cross-cultural and interdisciplinary perspectives is necessary in order to equip students for global challenges and diverse work environments.

With continuous improvements and innovation present in the curriculum, combined with flexible policy framework will be backed by ongoing professional development for educators. In addition, build on industry and community partnerships to link education with workforce needs, making sure that curricula are aligned to the needs of the marketplace. The further work on designing such models for integration, and assessing best pedagogical approaches as well as evaluation tools will perfect our attempts in this direction. In conclusion, the future of curriculum design is in building flexible and equitable technology-enhanced learning ecosystems that empower every learner to thrive in a globally connected digital age.

References

1. Ndibalema, P. (2025). Digital literacy gaps in promoting 21st century skills among students in higher education institutions in Sub-Saharan Africa: A systematic review. *Cogent Education, 12*(1), 2452085.
2. Demirdis, B. (2025). Integrating digital literacy to enhance emotional and social skills in education. In T. Aldosemani & M. Lytras (Eds.), *Innovative educational frameworks for future skills and competencies* (pp. 1–38). IGI Global Scientific Publishing. https://doi.org/10.4018/979-8-3693-7555-6.ch001
3. Apata, S. B., & Oyenuga, M. O. (2025). Revolutionizing employability: The intersection of digital literacy, inclusive education, and Gen Z's skill set in the 21st century. In T. A. Ajani (Ed.), *Empowering pre-service teachers to*

enhance inclusive education through technology (pp. 155–182). IGI Global Scientific Publishing. https://doi.org/10.4018/979-8-3693-8759-7.ch006

4. Aslan, S., Alanoğlu, M., & Karabatak, S. (2025). Enhancing 21st-century teaching competencies: The key role of digital literacy in connecting pre-service teachers' TPACK. *Information Development*, Article 02666669251315841. https://doi.org/10.1177/02666669251315841
5. Haryaka, U., Razak, N. K., Rachman, F., Tung, K. Y., & Judijanto, L. (2025). Integrating digital literacy, critical thinking, and collaborative learning: Addressing contemporary challenges in 21st century education. *Journal of Hunan University Natural Sciences, 52*(3), 101–112.
6. Sharma, Y., Suri, A., Sijariya, R., & Jindal, L. (2025). Role of education 4.0 in innovative curriculum practices and digital literacy—A bibliometric approach. *E-Learning and Digital Media, 22*(1), 1–32.
7. Arora, S., Narang, S. K., Upreti, K., Singh, J., Sharma, S., & Kapoor, S. (2025). Addressing pedagogical challenges in digital literacy for the adoption of society 5.0. In B. M. Agboola & C. S. Thompson (Eds.), *Planning tools for policy, leadership, and management of education systems* (pp. 1–24). IGI Global Scientific Publishing. https://doi.org/10.4018/979-8-3693-2252-9.ch001
8. Simon, N. (2025). Towards technological literacy: Fostering digital citizenship and sustainable development education in next-generation teaching. In H. Rahman (Ed.), *Digital citizenship and building a responsible online presence* (pp. 241–258). IGI Global Scientific Publishing.
9. Kaptan, E., & Cakir, R. (2025). The effect of digital storytelling on digital literacy, 21st century skills and achievement. *Education and Information Technologies, 30*(8), 11047–11071.
10. Andong, H. A., Ubana, U. M., & Agogo, G. B. B. (2025). Building digital literacy through social work education for sustainable development. *Scientific Journal of Educational Management, Research and Law, 3*(1), 420–425.
11. Mahmud, A. F., Mahmud, M., Weda, S., & Munir, M. (2025). Digital literacy and learning interaction. *FOSTER: Journal of English Language Teaching, 6*(3), 192–210.
12. Manalu, A. N., & Wilujeng, I. (2025). How does the STEM-PjBL e-Book impact students creative thinking and digital literacy skills? *Journal of Innovation in Educational and Cultural Research, 6*(2), 297–303.
13. Boonwattanopas, D. (2025). Strategic communication to overcome challenges in digital literacy policy implementation in Japan Schools. *Jurnal Kajian Komunikasi, 13*(1), 37–54.
14. Al-Hattami, H. M. (2025). Understanding how digital accounting education fosters innovation: The moderating roles of technological self-efficacy and digital literacy. *The International Journal of Management Education, 23*(2), 101131.

15. Yang, F., Yao, R., Ren, Y., & Guo, L. (2025). Harmony in diversity: Digital literacy research in a multidisciplinary landscape. *Computers & Education, 230*, 105265.
16. Greene, J. A., & Crompton, H. (2025). Synthesizing definitions of digital literacy for the Web 3.0. *TechTrends, 69*(1), 21–37.
17. Kaletski-Maisel, G., & Jowallah, R. (2025). Empowering citizens: Preparing for the future of digital literacy and AI in education. In M. M. Kh. Hawamdeh (Ed.), *Digital citizenship and the future of AI engagement, ethics, and privacy*(pp. 133–150). IGI Global Scientific Publishing. https://doi.org/10.4018/979-8-3693-9015-3.ch005
18. Chen, J., He, X., Yin, H., Ning, Y., Wijaya, T. T., & Liu, J. (2025). Growing in organisations: The multifaceted effects of organisational support on teachers digital literacy. *British Educational Research Journal, 51*(6), 2810–2836.
19. Gupta, S., Sharma, M., & Shukla, P. (2025). From happiness curriculum to skill development: A critical evaluation of Delhi's NEEEV programme. *International Journal for Multidisciplinary Research (IJFMR), 7*(3), 1–12.
20. Afnan, H., & Maksum, M. N. R. (2025). Enhancing students soft skills through digital literacy integration in islamic education: A TPACK-based approach. *Al-Idarah: Jurnal Kependidikan Islam, 15*(1), 31–39.
21. Aborisade, P. A., Olubode-Sawe, F., Fola-Adebayo, T., Makinde, A. I., Gbenga-Owoyemi, B., Akeredolu-Ale, B., Adelabu, B., & Alese, B. K. (2025). Digital literacy levels: Realities and voices of African teachers in higher education institutions. *International Journal of Learning in Higher Education, 32*(1), 199–223.
22. Sele, Y., & Dewi, N. P. Y. A. (2025). Challenges and opportunities in preparing prospective teachers in the digital era: A critical study based on digital literacy profile. *Jurnal Eduscience, 12*(2), 524–552.
23. Ilhan, A., Aslaner, R., & Yaşaroğlu, C. (2025). Development of digital literacy skills of 21st century mathematics teachers and prospective teachers through technology assisted education. *Education and Information Technologies, 30*(8), 10837–10862.

CHAPTER 14

Digital Classrooms and Paperless Learning: A Pathway to Eco-Friendly Education

Prachi Priyanka and Sonika Kumari

Abstract The switch to digital classrooms in this case paperless online education indicates a paradoxical transformation under the umbrella of technology, which is going both way i.e., for pedagogical or learning and other environmental, holistic sustainability. Educational institutes can cut back paper usage by substituting conventional paper-based resources with digital tools like e-books, online assessments, and collaborative platforms which in return will assist to reduce deforestation rates and lower the carbon footprint. Responsiveness: The idea of responsiveness leads to being able to provide students with more interactive and personalized learning experiences regardless of geographic location through the in a digital classroom The platform supports environmentally-friendly measures, by ensuring all course materials are read online instead of

P. Priyanka (✉)
Sharda University, Greater Noida, India
e-mail: prachi.writes@gmail.com

S. Kumari
Inderprastha College of Engineering, Ghaziabad, India

P. K. Dutta et al. (eds.), *Digital Education for a Sustainable Future*, Sustainable Development Goals Series,
https://doi.org/10.1007/978-3-032-15433-0_14

being printed and thrown away after the completion of courses. Paperless learning also aligns with international goals of sustainable development, specifically with Quality Education (SDG 4) and Climate Action (SDG 13). This approach also solves logistical problems by reducing print expenses, enhancing use of resources and fueling the digital skills necessary in today's (and tomorrow's) workforce. It becomes an affordable and powerful use of the more modern digital empowered classrooms to greenify education collectively with tech-adoption.

Keywords Digital classrooms · Paperless learning · Eco-friendly education · Sustainable development · Digital literacy

1 Introduction

In the twenty-first century, education has taken an entirely new form moving from traditional chalk-and-board teaching methods to technologically enriched learning environments. The change from classroom to digital classrooms and paper learning to paperless have made great examples of how schools or universities are progressing toward a scalable, approachable and also sustainable education system. The change is not an incremental technological replacement but a strategic direction aligning with wider global environmental agendas, particularly the necessity of reducing paper waste and overall ecological footprint in education. It is an effective pathway to eco-friendly education as the use of digital tools has been integrated into education systems around the world in efforts to match up with modern learners and sustainability goals.

E-learning and digital classrooms are changing the way we learn by giving us new ways to lessen our influence on the environment. The primary points is that using digital resources instead of paper ones helps stop waste and deforestation. We don't need to make the books and other materials that our students use every day anymore. This saves millions of trees per year from the energy-intensive printing procedures that go into making them. The other change that is coming is the use of interactive digital tools like virtual labs and simulations. These tools let students do experiments like chemical reactions or ecosystem modeling without needing actual resources. This development also fosters new ideas.

Digital classrooms exercise the utilization of Information and communication technologies (ICT) to provide an immersive, interactive learning experience. Learning Management Systems (LMS) as platforms for teaching and learning; streaming services, or video-conferencing tools have enabled students and academics to access, share and create contents without the environmental impacts of only using printed materials which allows paper usage to significantly reduce. While on the one side, paperless learning is reducing dependency on textbooks, handouts, and even exam papers by delving into notes, facts online resources etc., which can further be enriched by adding some concrete information we do not know. Digital classrooms increase interest by using media-rich content, simulations, and adaptive learning systems [1]. These techniques address different learning modes and also encourage students to think critically, solve problems, build digital literacy all skills that are needed by workforce of today. Digital learning platforms also offer immediate feedback, data analytics, and progress monitoring, to help educators personalize instruction based on students' intersecting needs.

Background and Rationale

The environmental aspects to this transition are also no less persuasive. The education industry uses millions of tons of paper each year which fuels direct deforestation, water consumption, and greenhouse gas emissions. Less dependency on paper, then, is an easy way for schools and universities to contribute toward the mitigation of climate change as well as save resources. It is also aligned with the United Nations Sustainable Development Goals (SDGs), specifically Goal 4 (Quality Education) and Goal 13 (Climate Action), balancing educational progress with environmental accountability. But the path to a paperless learning environment as well as digital classrooms is not smooth. Challenges like digital disparity, weak connectivity, cyber security threats and the demand for skilled teachers are all substantial impediments to universal adoption. These challenges must be met by mutual cooperation of Governments, educational institutions, technology companies, and communities to provide fair and safe digital education for all.

Concept of Digital Classrooms

Digital classrooms and paperless learning are more of a futuristic way of bringing technological developments together with the ways we tend to care about the environment. The adoption of this model will improve learning outcomes, decrease environmental damage and ensure that students are properly suited to a digitally connected world. To make the journey sustainable in the long-run, it is not just about adopting new tools but an ethos that educationists value sustainability both for their teaching and their learners and take steps to ensure this reflects inclusivity and a constantly learning land-scape [2].

2 Education for Sustainable Development Perspective

Education for sustainable development is based on the principles of sustainable development and advocates environmental stewardship, social equity, and economic viability as essential components to human behavior toward promoting a healthy environment; Education for sustainable development is aiming to produce responsible decision-makers for preserving natural resources in society with rational consumption instead harmful ones. It is closely linked to the United Nations 2030 Agenda for Sustainable Development, Goal 4.7 ensure that all learners acquire knowledge and skills needed to promote sustainable development. The ESD view is underlined with the learning process still going well beyond information acquisition to enabling critical thinking; problem handling as interdependence and an ability of visualizing alternative futures. Preparing students to meet these challenges via ESD is an important approach in the digital classroom and paperless learning era, which fits well with ecological responsibility. Replacing paper-based materials with technology plays a supportive role for environmental outcomes by decreasing deforestation, waste generation, and the carbon footprint of educational operations.

The interactive nature of these e-learning modules enables interdisciplinary education, with environmental science, ethics, technology and social studies presented in unison to reflect the interconnectedness of sustainability challenges. Through real-world immersive activities such as collaborative online projects, virtual simulations and problem-solving exercises, learners can engage with and understand complex topics such as climate change, biodiversity loss, sustainable urban planning etc. Education for sustainable development advances inclusivity by advocating for fair access to education resources so as not to create digital divides which will leave some sectors of the communities behind in digital transformation benefits. It revolves around narrowing the digital divide, upgrading technology literacy and generating educational material that is culturally appropriate. It also highlights the need for lifelong learning, as people have to constantly learned and adapt to changes in sustainability and technology. Central to this is the role of teachers who demonstrate sustainable practices, teach about sustainability in their curriculum and use pedagogies that involve student's participation and reflection actions. Policy frameworks to enable in the digital environment should target capacity-building for educators, infrastructure investment, as well as offer open-access knowledge and learning materials. When working to integrate sustainability concepts into the very fabric of digital classrooms, not only does education transcend its role as knowledge distributor but it becomes a generator able to bring about social transformation [3]. This perspective recognizes that transformative educational innovation whether in the form of paperless education or whatever else is of course a means to an end: not something that somehow lives by itself in its own ideal realm apart from and unrelated to bigger aspirations for a more just, sustainable global society.

3 Digital Classrooms: Tools, Platforms, and Infrastructure

Digital Classrooms Digital classrooms are the same an evolution of traditional classroom but with advanced tools, platforms and infrastructure that makes learning more accessible, interactive and sustainable. In essence, a digital classroom uses Information and Communication Technologies (ICT) to either replace or add to face-to-face teaching and provides students with learning that is more interactive as well as content rich. Principal tools include Learning Management Systems (LMS) such as Classroom, Moodle and Canvas that serve as anchor points for learning content, assignments, tests and responses [4]. With these solutions, the two-way communication between the instructor and students is streamlined, as well as making resource sharing easier without having to actually use printed materials and paperless learning. Synchronous online sessions, virtual lectures, and collaborative group work can be done via video conferencing tools like Zoom, Microsoft Teams and Google Meet typically integrated with LMS platforms too for e.g., including breakout rooms and interactive whiteboards. Another pillar of eLearning is media content delivery, with videos, podcasts, animations and simulations in a format suitable for all learning types that help promote student participation. Google Drive, Dropbox and OneDrive are cloud-based storage solutions that not only allow file sharing even outside your organization, collaborative document editing in real time, or secure data management but also remove the constraints of physical storage space and further reduce environmental cost. Digital class infrastructure is more than just software, but also regarding the internet (its connectivity and speed managed), a bandwidth requirement, or digital devices like laptops, tablets Or interactive smartboards. Educational institutions also need to allocate resources for cybersecurity practices that will safeguard private information, keeping with privacy regulations. AI and adaptive learning systems AI is a set of tools designed to imitate human intelligence and adapt their processing in real time, which can be incorporated into educational experiences of students, as well as query algorithms that track the progress in student knowledge acquisition process for predicting next steps or providing educative insights to educators.

The AR/VR (Augmented Reality/Virtual Reality) solutions are extending experiential learning by creating life-style simulations through with real-world situation in a safe closed environment. More importantly, digital classrooms can be more inclusive for students with disabilities or language barriers by being accessible with screen readers, captioning tools and translation services. Comprehensive infrastructure planning will be needed to successfully implement these tools and platforms, teacher training programs, continuous technical support, and regular system upgrades [5]. Infrastructure approaches will need to address challenges for connectivity and affordability especially in rural or underserved areas, often supported through government subsidies, public-private partnerships or community level providers. Properly implemented, digital classroom tools will not only improve the quality and breadth of education but also help save the planet if it is possible to reduce paper usage, limit emissions from transport or energy consumption. They represent the foundation of a futuristic educational system that integrates technological advancements and environmental accountability.

Learning Management Systems (LMS) and Virtual Learning Environments

Digital classrooms host on Learning Management Systems (LMS) and Virtual Learning Environments (VLE), which are central to the delivery of courses in a structured manner supplemented with assessment and communication tools. These are the systems that can accommodate synchronous learning but also enable asynchronous experiences for learners in various time zones or working on different schedules. Tools like discussion boards, quizzes, grade books, and automated alerts make teaching easier and the learning experience more engaging. Replacing printed handouts with digitized course materials, LMS platforms are effectively reducing the consumption of paper and contributing toward the aim for providing environment-friendly education. They can be other applications also integrated plagiarism checkers, virtual labs, and analytics dashboards series that increases learning opportunities. LMS and VLE form the framework of a no-paper classroom environment, providing structure to deliver organization, accessibility and manageability in education [6].

Multimedia and Interactive Content

The use of multimedia and interactive content has revolutionized traditional passive learning methods into active, engaging forms of new age learning. As a part of academic hospital CME programs, inter-professional learning styles are served with the use of simulations, videos, and animations, podcasts or info-graphics which help to explain complex ideas in more ways than just one. Such interactive elements as quizzes, polls, drag-and-drop exercises and virtual experiments facilitate active enrolment leading to retention and understanding. Content like this is great for visual and auditory learners as well as helps with problem-solving, critical thinking. Tools like Edpuzzle, Nearpod, and kahoot facilitate real-time communication, prompting students to work together. Ecologically this is an advantage because multimedia resources do not require printed out worksheets, charts and physical models such as plastic tubing which reduce paper and material costs. There is no environmental impact from the use of digital content as it can be updated and distributed digitally at any time to make sure that students learn the latest and most relevant information. Thus, multimedia and other interactive resources are tools to reinforce the learning process and improve sustainability performance in education.

Cloud-Based Collaboration and Data Storage

Cloud based collaboration and storage solutions are key components to how paperless classroom should work, allowing collaborative sharing, co-editing and storing of educational content in real time. Students and educators can collaborate on documents, presentations, and spreadsheets from anywhere thanks to platforms like Google Drive, Dropbox, Microsoft OneDrive thereby promoting a culture of collaborative learning [7]. Used instead of print, USB or physical files, these tools are good for reducing waste and accessibility. The correct cloud storage can support massive multimedia files such as video lectures, research data, and interactive modules that will be tough to deal with in traditional on-premise systems. With this in mind, what becomes clear is that cloud-based tools not only enable efficient applications, but also make educational materials environmental because they leverage global resource management and collaboration to the adopt sustainable vision of digital classrooms.

Artificial Intelligence and Adaptive Learning Systems

With advancements in technology, particularly Artificial Intelligence (AI) and adaptive learning systems are revolutionizing digital classrooms for providing a personalized educational experience that will enhance learning outcomes. Learning styles and preferences are also taken into account by AI-based platforms which analyze student performance data to personalize lesson plans and make recommendations for resources. With utilizing adaptive systems, like DreamBox or Smart Sparrow, students work through material at their own optimal rate; the system dynamically adjusts content difficulty and pace as they progress. Most commonly, it manifests as intelligent tutoring systems or chatbots for academic support and increasingly in the form of predictive analytics to identify students at risk before they begin experiencing adverse outcomes [8]. These systems support resource sustainability by delivering more targeted content, thereby reducing unnecessary assignments, paper-based exercises, and overall resource wastage. In addition, teachers become more efficient as they can grade automatically and detect plagiarism while improve the curriculums with data-driven actions thanks to AI.

The guide states that by combining personalized learning with environmentally responsible measures, AI and adaptive technologies can help to advance academic achievement and also support paperless education as part of the broader sustainability mission.

4 Paperless Learning: Concepts and Practices for E-Books, Digital Notes, and Online Assessments

It has caused a monumental change how education is delivered, moving traditional printed materials to digital format making learning more accessible, interactive and most importantly sustainable. This transformation is in large part based on e-books, digital notes, and online assessments that will change how students get, interact with, and show learning. E-books integrate text, images, video, hyperlinks, and interactive quizzes into an all-in-one digital resource that can be read across devices. In contrast, platforms like Kindle and Apple Books and institutional repositories give students a library that can be held searched instantly, annotated in ways you couldn't without damaging pages and kept current [9]. This is more sustainable than printing and mailing physical books with the added benefit of putting money back in to students' pockets. Taking notes digitally extends the advantages of paperless learning, allowing students to develop, arrange, and entry their very own work across apps such as Microsoft OneNote, Evernote, or Notions. They provide handwriting capabilities with an active stylus, as well as voice recording, and embedded media to support various learning preferences, all while promoting collaborative note-taking. They all appreciate the ability to store, back up and search their notes digitally so they never lose important info again and have it at any time in no location.

With online evaluations, be it in the form of quizzes, assignments or even full-fledged exams make it convenient and easy for educators as well as students to gauge their own performance. Google Forms, Moodle and Blackboard are perfect examples of platforms that could provide assessments and real-time insights to students about where they need to focus. Together these deliver richer assessments ranging from core knowledge through to multimedia-enhanced and adaptive testing types for increased engagement and relevance environmentally, less material waste and resource use is induced by online assessments as opposed to printed answer sheets, physical exam venues and paper-based grading.

All of these strategies also foster a highly interactive, flexible, and sustainable context for learning as they help reduce the deforestation pressure associated with paper requirements of traditional activities and possibly reduce carbon emissions linked to conventional educational materials. They also follow international initiatives to embed ed-tech in the curriculum which fosters essential digital literacy, collaboration and lifelong learning skills. The key to paperless learning success, however, depends entirely on adequate digital infrastructure, available devices and proper support and training for both teachers and students. Through e-books, digital notes and online assessments as main components of instruction, institutions can promote contemporary teaching and learning practices while establishing itself as a role model for environmental care and progressive educational practices [10].

These technologies not only save resources, but they also give students hands-on experience with teaching sustainability. Digital platforms also make it feasible for people to work together in real time from different places, which cuts down on the carbon emissions that come from shipping instructional materials or commuting. New arguments also show how important gamified learning apps that teach people how to be more environmentally responsible are. Students can use these apps to put sustainability ideas into action, as when they create systems that use less energy. Digital classrooms also offer open-access, scalable resources like free online courses. This lowers the environmental impact and makes education more accessible to everyone.

5 Environmental Impact and Sustainability

Digital classrooms and paperless learning: adoption of digital classrooms for studies would be a giant step forward as it hardly leaves behind the environmental footprints of education; others objective detailed sustainability, this involves shit loads of initiatives simultaneously. For example, traditional academic models that rely on paper-based resources demand substantial deforestation as well as water usage and result in a large carbon footprint. By using digital materials instead of printed textbooks, sheets and exam papers save trees resources. But, along with to tackling environmental issues, embedding sustainability into education develops an eco-conscious mindset that helps graduates become environmentally responsible global citizens. By doing so, this shift has a dual effect: on reducing the ecological footprint of educational operations as well as on adapting pedagogical practices to global environmental agreements e.g., Paris Agreement, United Nations Sustainable Development Goals.

Reduction in Paper Usage and Deforestation

Because paper production is a resource-intensive process that needs large amounts of wood, water and energy, it presents challenges with respect to sustainability, considering the education sector is a significant consumer. Billions of paper sheets are used yearly just by schools and universities for books, handouts, and exams. This intense demand increases the pace of deforestation, loss in biodiversity, erosion of soil and imbalance on a global carbon scale. If universities make a change to e-books, digital notes and online assessments it could massively reduce the amount of paper universities get through. An average size school going completely paperless for a year would mean saving hundreds of trees and thousands of liters of water to give an instance. First, aside from the direct environmental benefits, reducing dependence on paper also reduces the demand for supply chains such as transport and packaging that contribute to environmental destruction. Secondly, it also furthers a circular economy attitude; resources are reused and recycled digitally instead of consumed and discarded physically [11].

Carbon Footprint and Energy Considerations

Education and environmentalism Both in the case of the use of paper destined for printing, as well as in terms of your carbon footprint. Using paper-based systems is a traditional format and represents a very energy-heavy production system from felling trees, pulping etc. to printing and tidings materials to schools. These stages emit significant amounts of CO_2 and other greenhouse gases which alter our climate. Going paperless for learning reduces these emissions as it requires no large scale printing or distribution. Remote and hybrid learning models also lessen the commuting by students and teachers, reducing further indirect emissions from vehicle use to access classrooms. But the digital infrastructure has an energy cost a server, a device, or any data center uses electricity to work [12]. Sustainability is reached by powering these systems with renewable energy sources and gaining widespread use of state-of-the-art technologies that are energy efficient. Both schools and universities can implement activities like recycling devices, providing excellent cloud storage as Stop-Start technology instead of charging non-stop, and promoting decreased usage on screens to mitigate the carbon footprint related to digital learning. This must address not only paper related emissions but the energy consumption to allow technology, education and other systems can reduce their environmental impact.

Alignment with UN Sustainable Development Goals

Digital classrooms and paperless learning are in direct alignment with several UN Sustainable Development Goals, which would also help to make their adoption a more compelling proposition for global educational policies. Most significantly, it promotes SDG 4 (Quality Education) by ensuring access to quality learning resources that is fully technology-enabled. Digital platforms make the same materials available for students who are homebound or living in less developed areas as they are to people enjoying a thriving educational environment. It helps support SDG 13 (Climate Action) as the approach reduces emissions through reducing paper production, transportation and waste hence climate change. Less strain on forests also contributes to SDG 15' (Life on Land) which calls for the protection, restoration and sustainable use of terrestrial ecosystems. Encouraging paperless solutions also feeds into SDG 12 (Responsible Consumption and Production) through the more efficient use of resources and reduced wastage. This practice creates a ripple effect where students will naturally embrace eco-aware practices during the rest of their life making the positive change not just immediate but long-lasting as well. With these ties, governments, NGOs and schools can work together to create policies that embed environmental responsibility into academic structures so that sustainability is inherently part of both curriculum and institutional practices.

With a paperless education, you can achieve an extensively reduce in the use of paper, leaving no carbon footprint and thereby compliant with UN Sustainable Development Goals instead to opt for building a buzzword, wider sense greener more responsible education. The challenge will be in ensuring that all have access to the digital infrastructure required, along with maintaining a focus on reliance on renewable energy and sustainable technology practices. With strategic planning and international collaboration, education can be a key enabler for significant environmental improvement by nurturing students who will strive to make the world more sustainable [13].

But there still needs to be fair access, and cheap gadgets and offline digital libraries can help make up for gaps in connectivity. Digital classrooms are the first step toward an education system that encourages a generation that cares about the environment and wants to make progress that lasts by teaching eco-friendly ideals and using technology to save resources.

6 Challenges and Limitations

Digital education has the capacity to be transformative, but needs a lot of leaps to recover as digital education is transformational in opportunity, but we must look at our efforts with searing honesty. With advance in time, the educationists have been facing significant resistance for technology adaptation which demands an extensive training and development to combine digital tools into pedagogy. The costs associated with infrastructure such as buying devices, software licenses, and keeping the lights on still remain non trivial especially in emerging markets. As a matter of fact, digital learning is not accessible to students in remote areas and under-resourced locations as it largely counts on power supply and the internet [14]. Unless these constraints are addressed with the right policy environment, focused investments, inclusive training, and programs to educate toward opportunities offered by technology-enabled education, the promise of unlocking this potential would not materialize ensuring that technology innovation will further exacerbate rather than mitigate educational inequities.

Digital Divide and Access Inequality

Although it appears to be a modernization of classrooms and paperless learning, we must bear in mind that not everyone has access to the internet; this will only accomplish increasing the educational gap. Rural, remote and economically disadvantaged regions have particularly limited access to high-speed internet, modern devices and reliable electricity. Students without these resources are very disadvantaged; they cannot fully engage in online learning or read important digital contents [15]. It should also take into consideration the gap in the quality of equipment, including connections, determined by social and economic conditions, which tends to stiffen disparities in learning. Marginalized communities might also suffer from language barrier, lack of digital literacy, and less access to technology making this exclusion multiply. The advantages of paperless education may be lost by a large part of society if no targeted interventions are made such as through government subsidies, public Wi-Fi initiatives, and even the gift of devices. The importance of tackling the digital divide is necessary for sustainable futures to be inclusive and just educational models that all students can benefit from developments in technology equally.

Cyber-security and Data Privacy Risks

With education heading in a digital direction, that problem only becomes more serious. Personal and academic data exists in the digital classroom and on the online learning platform, with collections of records, results from assessments, or logs of communication between students. This data is, however, subject to breaches, hacking and identity theft without adequate cybersecurity measures. Poor privacy mechanisms result in unauthorized sharing of data, and utilization or misappropriation which can put students as well as institutions at risk. There is also a rise in the number of phishing attacks, ransomware, and malware targeting educational institutes [16]. Most organizations do not have an in-house IT security team, and those who do often have only the most basic of protective measures which are no match for modern cyber challenges. To comply with data protection regulations such as GDPR or national privacy laws, you must do it continuously, that means monitoring your infrastructure in real time, training your employees and maintain always up to date security architecture. This reinforces trust in digital education systems, universities must invest in cybersecurity, ensure strong authentication and adopt privacy-by-design practices in all their digital platforms for learning [17].

Teacher Training and Technological Adaptation

Whether digital classrooms and paperless learning succeed or not, lies in the hand of educators who have to use tech properly in teaching. Most teachers, especially those who are used to traditional practices will have a hard time using these digital tools. But without proper training, these technologies can be underused or used inappropriately, reducing the effectiveness of teaching [18]. Professional development programs need to cover more than basic tech functionalities and include pedagogy, assessment design and student engagement in online environments. In addition, teachers need to keep up with technological developments that are happening very quickly and update their expertise on developing tools and platforms constantly. There is also resistance to change, as well as time and workload pressures that can limit adaptation. To help ease these transitions, a supportive ecosystem with mentorship programs and technical support teams in place can be useful to encourage innovation. In the end, it is educating teachers with the right knowledge and feeling more confident in using digital tools that may lead to both pedagogical quality and environmental sustainability [19].

Infrastructure and Maintenance Costs

While paperless education eliminates ongoing costs of individual printing and physical items, the financial cost of digital infrastructure is enormous. This means buying devices and ramping up your internet connectivity abilities, adding interactive boards to the equipment in your classrooms or even paying for software platforms. These upfront costs can be prohibitively high for most institutions especially those in impoverished areas. Also, the digital setup requires regular maintenance, to do patches and upgrades. Financial constraints may cause schools to use old-fashioned equipment, which ultimately affects L2 learner outcomes. We also need secure servers, backup systems and even renewable energy solutions to make our institutions sustainable. Financial burden can be reduced to a great extent collaboratively with technology providers which include strategic partnership, phased implementation plans, and shared digital resource models [20]. They must well budget and plan for long-term infrastructure, installation of digital classrooms and eco-friendly learning systems as these cost the journey.

7 Conclusion, Recommendations, and Future Directions

The expedition of digital tools in education would be a watershed movement toward wider and effective environment friendly knowledge sharing networks. Technology-enabled education saves paper, reduces deforestation, and is completely aligned to the global targets of sustainability in addition to providing superior quality learning experiences. While this promise can be met, its fulfillment is contingent on the resolution of long-polished issues ranging from the digital divide, cybersecurity threats, lack of infrastructure and a constant need for teacher training. The suggestions are to enact policies that foster digital inclusion for all, improve access to reasonably priced internet services and deploy renewable technologies for a greener power source in support of our expanding digital infrastructure. Public-private partnerships are necessary to ensure ICT literacy programs for teachers and learners. We should also look at stronger data privacy laws and open-sourcing the educational platforms to also make them more secure, accessible and affordable. These advancements in the future, with emerging technologies that include AI, immersive VR learning environments and adaptive learning algorithms among so much more will completely change how we approach education making it far more personalized, interactive and data driven. But congruent with the ideas of inclusivity and ethical frameworks, these innovations need to ensure they do not exacerbate existing inequalities. Strengthen public-private participation, mainstream sustainability objectives in education policies and as a change agent to promote innovation while ensuring equal access this can transform digital learning into a pivotal field for intertwining social advancement with environmental progress. Properly implemented and with a strategic approach, it has an important role to play in educating future generations to navigate the resource constraints of our increasingly connected global age.

References

1. Nain, V., & Prasher, R. (2025). AI-based sustainable e-learning strategies for an eco-friendly world: Transforming education. In S. Kulkarni, M. Valeri, & P. William (Eds.), *Driving business success through eco-friendly strategies* (pp. 1–20). IGI Global Scientific Publishing. https://doi.org/10.4018/979-8-3693-9750-3.ch001

2. Shah, K. N. (2025). Leveraging data science for personalizing learning experiences in eco-friendly educational systems. In S. Azar, S. K. Gupta, & K. B. Al Bataineh (Eds.), *Smart education and sustainable learning environments in smart cities* (pp. 301–316). IGI Global Scientific Publishing.
3. Mamadiyarov, Z. (2025). Empowering a sustainable future through digital learning and the SDGs. In E. Hans & A. Hans (Eds.), *Harnessing e-learning to create a sustainable future* (pp. 145–172). IGI Global Scientific Publishing. https://doi.org/10.4018/979-8-3373-0112-9.ch006
4. Aggarwal, D., Sharma, D., & Saxena, A. B. (2023). Exploring the role of artificial intelligence for augmentation of adaptable sustainable education. *Asian Journal of Advanced Research and Reports, 17*(11), 179–184.
5. Assalamah, T. M., & Hilza, I. F. (2025). Digital literacy and cultural narratives for social sustainability in primary education transformation. *Entita: Jurnal Pendidikan Ilmu Pengetahuan Sosial dan Ilmu-Ilmu Sosial, 7*(1), 1–24.
6. Rajeshwari, P., & Sivaranjani, K. (2025). E-learning revolution transforming education and training in the digital age. *Journal of Rajasthan Association for Studies in English, 22*, 1–15.
7. Ghai, A. S., Sharma, R. C., Jasola, S., & Zamfiroiu, A. (2025). Intelligent sustainable development in online learning: Insights from higher education and Industry 5.0. In A. Al Mutawa (Ed.), *Impacts of generative AI on the future of research and education* (pp. 417–444). IGI Global.
8. Singh, M. N. (2021). Inroad of digital technology in education: Age of digital classroom. *Higher Education for the Future, 8*(1), 20–30.
9. Shamim, M., Hussain, M. I., Gorde, S. U., Malik, R., Kumar, P. R., & Nagpal, P. (2022). Smart classes teaching using advanced techniques for quality education. *Journal of Positive School Psychology, 6*(5), 1891–1897.
10. Hamdan, M., & Anshari, M. (2024). Green education to promote green technological skills. In M. H. Bilal, S. Sepasgozar, & M. A. Hossain (Eds.), *Harnessing green and circular skills for digital transformation* (pp. 72–85). IGI Global Scientific Publishing. https://doi.org/10.4018/979-8-3693-2865-1.ch005
11. Yan, L., Li, Z., & Arshad, M. H. (2025). From responsibility to action: How CSR drives sustainability in higher education. *Acta Psychologica, 254*, 104831.
12. Novo, C., Zanchetta, C., Goldmann, E., & de Carvalho, C. V. (2024). The use of gamification and web-based apps for sustainability education. *Sustainability, 16*(8), 3197.
13. Koiwanit, J., Areerob, Y., Saepoo, S., & Filimonau, V. (2024, August). Sustainable practices and environmental impact assessment in a life long learning center. In *Proceedings of the 10th World Congress on New Technologies (NewTech'24) Barcelona, Spain* (pp. 25–27). Avestia Publishing.

14. Taracina, J. N. (2023). Acceptability and effectiveness of a proposed attendance monitoring system (ASAP) for safety of the stakeholders. *Scholarum: Journal of Education, 2*(2), 52–56.
15. Sachan, A. (2021, July). Proposed contemplations to make current modern cities normally more eco-friendly and sustainable. In *2021 International Congress of Advanced Technology and Engineering (ICOTEN)* (pp. 1–6). IEEE.
16. Malhotra, L., & Bhatia, H. K. (2021). From walls to clouds: SWOCs of online learning from voices of prospective teacher educators in India in response to Covid-19. *The Online Journal of Distance Education and e-Learning, 9*(1), 92–105.
17. Tejero, O. M. C. (2022). Residual post-pandemic ICT literacy in higher education: The case of foreign language teachers and students in Japan. *Human Review. International Humanities Review/Revista Internacional de Humanidades, 13*(1), 1–10.
18. Luthra, A. (2024). Green-blue sustainability initiatives for higher education institutions. *Nagarlok-Quarterly Journal of Urban Affairs, 56*(4), 411–429.
19. Qummar, M. H., Farooq, K., Muhammad, Z., & Yusliza, M. Y. (2023, November). Intelligent human resource management: A pathway toward environmental performance. In *The Global Conference on Entrepreneurship and the Economy in an Era of Uncertainty* (pp. 579–593). Springer Nature Singapore.
20. Angelaki, M. E., Bersimis, F., Karvounidis, T., & Douligeris, C. (2024). Towards more sustainable higher education institutions: Implementing the sustainable development goals and embedding sustainability into the information and computer technology curricula. *Education and Information Technologies, 29*(4), 5079–5113.

CHAPTER 15

Global Sacred Values with Sustainable Future: Transforming Religious Education Through Digital Platforms

Gurveer Singh, Bhupinder Singh, and Saurabh Chandra

Abstract Digital platforms ensure that sacred teachings can be kept authentic and deliver immersive adaptive learning experiences which then make one resonate more deeply with both spiritual concepts and sustainability positions. Framing it this manner stands between tradition and modernity which ensure religious education is actively a part of the Sustainable Development Goals (SDGs) in step with quality training, peaceful coexistence, and environmental stewardship.

G. Singh (✉)
Department of Religious Studies, General Shivdev Singh Diwan Gurbachan Singh Khalsa College, Patiala, India
e-mail: gurveer2020@gmail.com

B. Singh
North Bangkok University, Bangkok, Thailand

S. Chandra
School of Law, Bennett University, Greater Noida, India

P. K. Dutta et al. (eds.), *Digital Education for a Sustainable Future*, Sustainable Development Goals Series,
https://doi.org/10.1007/978-3-032-15433-0_15

This chapter explains the importance of sacred values, which are significant aspects of moral narrative and social structure that have traditionally helped guide behavior in the right direction. Beyond pragmatic justifications, they provide a normative basis for visioning and understanding where we need to go in shaping the future wish to create whether that pertains to ensuring an equitable society, sustainable world, or cultural heritage that is transmitted from one generation to another. This chapter exploring the ways in which religious education can be both reimagined and scaled across continents that has usually been delivered through face-to-face interactions. The examples prepared in this study allow religious education to have boundaries from an area to be mythical in the educational, using technological innovations in interactive e-learning, virtual community, and immersive media, toward inclusivity and adaptation to diverse learners. It highlights the role of digital transformation in religious education to train ethically and socially responsible global citizens fostering a sustainable and harmonious future.

Keywords Sacred values · Religious education · Sustainable future · Digital platforms · Moral transformation

1 Introduction

The role of the sacred, which is enshrined in the moral and spiritual fabric of societies around the world, has been established throughout history to distinguish our actions as human beings from animals, suggesting that something inherently meaningful lies beyond our base instincts. Rooted in religious doctrines, spiritual lineages, and moral codes, these values transcend the ever changing whims of popular culture by providing universal truths that answers to the age-old questions of what it means to be human are based upon. Sacred values that bind us to protecting the planet, caring for all life on Earth, and safeguarding our common resources can serve as a unified call to action, binding us across cultures and generations in one shared purpose, a sustainable future for all on our miraculous blue oasis. These are composed of values such as compassion, equity, sustainability, and solidarity deriving from humanity, stewardship of earth, respect for life, justice, and peace which have clear parallel in United Nations

Sustainable Development Goals (SDGs). Integrating these enduring principles into social practices can cultivate the moral strength that sustains coherency and sustainable development, preventing material progress from undermining human welfare or ecological equilibrium [1].

The broader idea of how converting this key site of religious education through digital means is not a question primarily of pedagogical innovation; in many senses, it indicates a new model for the role faith communities can play in shaping global sustainability. In a world that is increasingly grappling with the myriad ways in which technological development, economic globalization, and environmental crises are undermining core social values, including value-for-money and resourcefulness, sacred values seem to offer something of a reprieve. If these values are incorporated within the digital learning ecosystems, they can use that to develop ethically inclined global citizens who have an ability to reconcile what they believe in spiritually with how they live sustainably. As such, the current vicissitudes can evolve combining tradition and technology to unify around beliefs that break religiously inspired barriers while respecting cultural differences.

Digitally transform religious education that is rooted in the holy values, or else our spiritual inheritance will remain idle as an aging legacy, leading us nowhere in shaping a viable future for mankind. Using the vast communication, access, and flexibility benefits of digital platforms, faith traditions can address wider populations on an intergenerational dialogue platform to mobilize ethical change locally and globally. This overlap of sacred values, sustainability imperatives, and digital innovation can provide a blueprint to re-conceptualizing religious education into a formative influence for humanity that supports it in finding its group integrity toward cohesively ensuring an ecologically balanced society [2].

Background and Significance of Sacred Values in Digital Education

Religious education has historically been a key channel to pass down the sacred values from one generation to all its subsequent generations. In earlier times, these instructions would be passed from one generation to a new through human interaction in religious places or within the family home and community like on storytelling form or in written form. Ultimately, while these traditional and time-honored methods have proven to maintain the authenticity and cultural continuity of the art form, they are often very regional in level of influence and scope both for engagement at scale, accessibly, or even adaptability in an ever-evolving world where global challenges require quick; all-inclusive; and innovative solutions [3]. The enhanced technologies and emphasis of the digital revolution, the advent of the internet, mobile technologies, and interactive media have presented an extraordinary series of opportunities with which to increase the reach and effectiveness in religious education. Breaking down boundaries of geography, culture, and language, digital platforms help in spreading the sacred teachings which eventually brings different communities closer to each other. This shift is not just a convenience; it is essential for these sacred values to be both alive and unchanging in their role of influencing the modern conduct of humanity [4].

There is even greater potential for the digitization of these tools to align with eco-theological principles, making them a clear frontier in terms of the integration of faith and ecology. Interactive and immersive learning experiences on digital platforms, such as virtual reality pilgrimages, AI-driven personalized study guides, or gamified moral instruction, can themselves be considered sacred teachings that breathe life into the past wisdom of a tradition making it more accessible to younger generations. The build bridges across the planet to connect communities with one another so that they can learn from one another in environmental stewardship, conflict resolution, and social justice best practices which were formed around spiritual understanding [5]. The sacred digitization enables visioning ground-up curricula able to embed sustainable development principles at the heart of religious education from an early age, by training ethical consciousness paired with environmental and social responsibility. In these way, sacred values are conserved while being collectively harnessed for emergency global problems like climate change, inequality, and cultural erosion [6].

Interlinking Sacred Values with Sustainability Goals

They intersect with the United Nations Sustainable Development Goals (SDGs) that express commonly embraced human rights including protection of the environment, social justice, and peace. This belief in care for creation, along with ethical use of resources and responsibility to future generations are core principles of sustainability reinforced throughout religious teachings across traditions [7]. The second reason to frame sustainability within sacred moral contexts is that faith communities are also able to inspire greater commitment to climate action, poverty reduction, and community well-being. Such a moral grounding reorientates our understanding of sustainability from technical and policy into spiritual imperatives, leading to a more comprehensive approach that serves both the material needs of all people, while contributing significantly to global long-term planetary well-being [8].

Rationale for Digital Transformation in Religious Education

As the world becomes interconnected, there is a need for religious education to be more available, applicable, and valuable in contemporary society pushing digital transformation. Interactive media, virtual classrooms, and multilingual resources are only the many forms of digital platforms that get over geographical, linguistic, and also social borders. They also offer tools for bringing in modern pressing social topics like climate change, inequality, and ethical technology use—into religious teaching. They are modernized to keep them current and relevant as inspirations to create World Ethics, and this gives learners an ability to use spiritual basis of ethical ideas in practical solutions as answers now in sustainability [9].

2 Sacred Values in a Global Context: Universal Ethical Principles and Human Dignity

Sacred values articulate themselves through different religious traditions and cultural worlds, but they are finally an expression of the same fundamental emotional logic that transcends geographic, linguistic, and even doctrinal frontiers. Ultimately, it represents timeless values compassion, justice, honesty, respect for life and the Earth, and a recognition of the dignity due every human being that have traditionally been fundamental to guiding individual and communal moral compasses everywhere [10]. This includes core religious values that are enshrined in the sacred texts, oral traditions, rituals, and communal practices of all major world religions: Christianity, Islam, Hinduism, Buddhism, and Judaism; as well as Sikhism and various Indigenous spiritualities. The ideas that are buried within these values really does allow for a sort of common ground that has a shared intentionality toward thinking about how best to encourage human well-being, peaceful coexistence, and the continuance of all existence. This commonality may sound underwhelming but it is deep and, for example, can be invaluable as a platform to encourage dialogue between religions, partnership between stakeholders, or determination by the whole of the international community.

In a fast-paced, high-tech, global era of environmental destruction and social strife and widening economic gulfs, the re-inscription of sacred ideals is both an issue of religious survival and one that depends upon it for the nurturing of human dignity. Complicated values and messy arguments fall away: All human beings have value, regardless of color, creed, genitalia, or status [11]. This assertion is in line with international human rights frameworks and core to the Sustainable Development Goals (SDGs), which aim to promote equality, justice, and inclusive development. This includes the sacred principle of stewardship (central to many world religions) that informs global calls on climate action and responsible consumption, as well as the value of compassion driving humanitarian aid, poverty alleviation, and peace building. Rooting sustainability in sacred values lifts global challenges up from mere policy initiatives to ethical mandates.

The sacred values in a global context call for interconnectedness to be acknowledged of humans with other humans and as well with non-human nature. From this high view everything becomes unified from the clever to exploitive, and instead of exploitation we are now advocating cooperation, care, and reciprocity. It moves us away from short-term profits to long-term sustainability, leading to social structures and patterns of behavior that recognize life's fragility. Crucial to this is the accommodation of various values that constitute a common moral language through which diverse cultures and faith communities can join in a common effort without having to relinquish their distinct understanding of these teachings.

Ultimately, sacred values serve as an ethical compass of human dignity that resonates across even the most diverse societies to help form a moral direction toward social justice, security, and survival. Incorporating these values in education, governance, and community development especially through modern avenues like digital technologies can pave way for a more compassionate and respectful global ethic [12]. This ethic can help transcend ideological divides, model the virtues of collaborative problem-solving, and maintain the moral motivation required to confront immediate crises in a sustainable way. With renewing the connection between our sacred values and positive social norms, these types of abhorrent events would not just be counter to human dignity allow they might even cease to exist in future generations [13].

3 Sustainable Future and Sacred Values

It also has a strong moral base in sacred values that are common to all the religions of the world when we consider that a sustainable future means one where economic growth, social equity, and environmental health can really be reconciled without each undermining the other. These values of compassion, stewardship, justice, moderation, and respect for life provide a moral compass for responding to the dual challenges of climate change and biodiversity loss on one hand and poverty with social inequality on the other. In the wisdom of many sacred teachings, Earth as God's Holy Trust, or gift to humanity as a sacred trust, is highlighted [14]. This spiritual view of sustainability helps move the concept from a loci of technical policy to that of ethical responsibility, prompting higher levels of individual and collective engagement with care for earth ecology and its creatures as well as social justice.

Sacred values also inspire a holistic view of the world, where human and planetary health is mutually inclusive. They encourage action that addresses the concerns of those furthest behind, promotes access to resources in an equitable way, and fosters a culture of peace as a necessary condition for sustainable development. The moderation in wanting and nature worship as advanced by many religious traditions might be the same commitment to low consumption and wildlife conservancy required for a successful transition to implementing the UN Sustainable Development Goals (SDGs). If those spiritual principles are embedded on different levels, such as education, politics, and worldwide presence of digital practices, societies will be full of environment-friendly and ethical citizens. In sum, incorporating sacred values into the work of sustainability guarantees progress will continue to be linked with compassion, equity, and long-range planetary stewardship as a means for deepening humanity in order that it strides toward an inclusive, prosperous future where social and ecological integrity are both honored respectfully [15].

Sacred Teachings and Environmental Stewardship

Regardless of the Creator in whom one believes, creation stories provide sacred instructions concerning the protection of their natural gift to future generations, buried soils and ancient aquifers included. The stewardship concept or khalifah follows the Islamic belief in environmentalism the idea that humans should be caretakers of the Earth. Hinduism and Buddhism stress interconnectedness with all nature and promote a reverence for all life oxymoronic to ahimsa, non-violence. For indigenous spiritualities, the Earth is a living being and should be treated in kind. These viewpoints take environmental responsibility from regulatory compliance to an ethical and spiritual obligation which drives sustainable behavior rooted in cherishing life.

These teachings promote restraint, containment, and a sense of non-waste much more in alignment with modern ecological ideals. Faiths must embed these sacred values in public awareness and policies on the environment through use of digital platforms to leverage their huge networks for action on climate change, conservation, and restoration [16]. This link between conscience and savings does more than just reinforce green advocacy; it establishes a paradigm of positive earth stewardship. In this way, the sacred words make environmental stewardship not an action of choice but a powerful duty on moral and spiritual grounds.

Social Justice, Equity, and Inclusion Using Faith Principles

Faith traditions over the centuries have taught the values of social justice, equity, and inclusion, acknowledging that every human being has inherent dignity and worth. Sacred texts and teachings often exhort compassion for the marginalized, fairness in commerce, and an end to persecution. Christianity preaches love for all, regardless of social status; zakat (charitable giving) facilitates economic justice in Islam; the principle of seva (selfless service) promotes equality and a sense of community in Sikhism; while compassion (karuna) leads Buddhists to consider everyone, including women and poor people. The principles are inspired by the Sustainable Development Goals (especially SDGs 1, 5, and 10). Those teachings, when woven into religious education, ignite social movements that decry injustices within the systems and underpin individual rights to go with opportunities for everyone. Through digital platforms, this impact is increased through a global connection of faith-based initiatives and the additional work that comes along with those campaigns and resources [17]. This in turn allows integration for communities to leverage eradication of inequality through what it referred as synergy between moral persuasion and practical action. In other words, sacred values centered around justice and inclusion develop a moral foundation that drives individuals and societies to tear down walls, shield those who live in the margins, and set up just systems where all cultures are honored and every person can flourish.

Sacred Values as Catalysts for Peace-Building and Harmony

Christianity tells its followers to "love your enemies," Islam stresses the importance of such (peace-making or reconciliation) and Buddhism teaches non-violence these are but a few examples that show how religious teachings inspire conflict resolution that is underpinned by empathy and an ethos of morality. The traditional wisdom of the First Nations tribes generally emphasizes mutual aid and living in balance with people and nature. It does this by promoting these messages that are fundamentally opposed to divisiveness and acts of hostility, enabling a little more dialogue and cooperation. Vigilant in their dedicated insistence that peace is not just the cessation of violence, but the dynamic nurturing of empathy and respect, sacred values motivate change processes that mend relations and redeem societies. These messages can be broadcast by digital platforms and allow for the development of their virtual counterpart, opening opportunities for interfaith dialogues, conflict mediation training, and collaboration in humanitarian projects. Those relations of mutual empathy across global divides challenge stereotypes created by latent, colonial ways of thinking and cultivate networks of solidarity. In the end, they serve as the driver that lifts peacemaking yet higher above mere political agreements to genuine harmonization rooted in shared values and respect [18].

4 Religious Education in the Digital Era: Preserving Authenticity in Digital Religious Content

The digital revolution has changed religious education forever, enabling new possibilities for teaching sacred texts of great but threatened value. Religious education is no longer limited to physical spaces, such as temples, churches, mosques, synagogues, or any other community center because of the rise in e-learning platforms, mobile application solutions that provide religious theory and practices and even virtual reality experiences. Overwhelmingly positive reactions thus far have created opportunities for enhancement and improvement [19]. The power of reach and immediacy that digital media confer is equally seen to potentially challenge factual validity, contextual integrity, and originality in representation of religious references. Misunderstandings, editing out the wrong or spreading unconfirmed information, make sacred values are deflated and deformed in the totality which is not a good thing to lead to the theological confusion, cultural misappropriation, or become gaps of spiritual depth.

So, ensuring the authenticity of digital religious content is a systematic, multifaceted affair. Religious institutions need to be around content creation, however they do not own the place of production and therefore new materialism must fit itself within religious traditional foundations and contextual interpretation. It is accomplished through authoritative translations, commentary provided by recognized experts, and respect for canon tradition in conjunction with presenting the material in ways that are relevant to those who live now [20]. The use of technology to prevent unauthorized modifications such as blockchain for content verification, the official AI fact checking, materials watermark is also an alternative. Third, digital paradigms need to maintain the contextual pedagogy historical, linguistic, and cultural teaching contextualized within the context of knowledge that opens up the depth and space needed to liberate understanding as a critique against superficial or erroneous interpretations.

For child-like teaching elements regarding religion, the use of interactivity in terms of gamification, multimedia storytelling, or immersive simulation should not override the soulfulness and energy for spiritual depth and reverence. The solemnity, symbology, and ceremonial aspects of sacred teachings crucial for the transformation these impart must be faithfully preserved in digital renditions [21]. A good online religious education program should resemble traditional learning environments by promoting a mentorship in modeling practices, discussion forums, and community-building.

A global interconnection also plays a crucial role in serving the purpose of maintaining authenticity. There is also the possibility of online dialogue and information exchange, but it must also be done with boundaries being clear to maintain theological integrity and avoid syncretism. However, the technology in and of itself is neutral; it is that which it transmits and initiates into the world that can become good or evil with great power comes greater responsibility, which makes it crucial to foster collaboration between technologists, religious leaders, and educators in hopes of preserving purity of sacred teachings but also counterbalancing their appeal with innovative forms of digital religious education. In the end, protecting authenticity and rooting the truth inside digital religious content will guarantee that technology serves as a bridge not a barrier between ancient wisdom and modern learners, allowing religious education to preserve both connection with tradition as well as responsively for an ever-evolving world [22].

5 Sacred Values with Digital Pedagogies for Sustainability: Cross-Cultural Exchange and Global Interfaith Dialogues

Combining sacred values and digital pedagogies around sustainable development is a very strong way of ensuring transcultural interchange; as well as global inter-religious dialogues. Online course offerings in the fields of religion, ethics, and environmental studies provide new opportunities for learners from around the world who represent wide-ranging cultural, linguistic, and religious traditions to enter into impactful discussions on spirituality, ethics, and sustainable life. In this way, whole communities can adopt moral vernaculars across geography and doctrinal beliefs by embedding sacred values like compassion, justice, stewardship of the Earth and respecting human dignity into online educational platforms [23]. This common ethical ground is particularly useful when dealing with issues of global sustainability that require collective responsibility and joint efforts. It is through these virtual classrooms, webinars, and interactive forums that communities of individuals can come together to get educated on how their heritage approaches the subject of environmental care, social equity, and peace-building; thereby providing a much more richer and inclusive solution in response to these challenges.

Digital pedagogy facilitates cross-cultural and interfaith dialogues that help in creating a mutual understanding as well as breaking down of misconceptions, stereotypes, or prejudices that act as barriers for possible collaboration. These discussions each show a shared moral foundation among different religious traditions and permit a quilt of collective consciousness on sustainable development. Such as hosting a series of global webinars over the span of a year, inviting pairs of religious leaders for example: Christian and Islamic, Hindu and Buddhist, Jewish and Sikh, and Indigenous leaders to discuss their environmental ethics. These dialogues also promote countries to adopt local sustainability initiatives, through collective sharing of lessons and experience from other communities [24].

The interactivity and multimedia capabilities of digital pedagogy, for example, virtual reality tours of sacred landscapes, multilingual e-learning modules, help performers experience diverse cultural frameworks in a very direct way. They nurture an awareness of the lived lives of others, expand horizons, and deepen sense of responsibility for preventing harm to people and the planet. Importantly, however, when situated within such contexts of learning sacred values, sustainability is reframed not as an abstract asset but as a lived ethical responsibility [25]. For alongside the eternal wisdom of sacred values, it needs to utilize new digital modes to hold cross-cultural and interfaith dialogues to mobilize global solidarity and sustainable hope, where an overarching ethos meets mutual respect with a shared destiny of the Earth.

6 Conclusion and Future Prospects

Religious education, if combined with digital platforms, provides a novel possibility to integrate sacred values and serve as a new transformative pathway toward sustainability, global understanding, and moral responsibility. Values as compassion, justice, stewardship, and respect for life are sacred and provide a timeless ethical compass that rings true to all peoples of our diversified planet. In turn, where do these values overlap when played out through digital pedagogies that conserve spiritual heritage all the while lending itself to how religious-based teachings might convert into actionable commitments with the United Nations Sustainable Development Goals (SDGs). Combining tradition and technology allows for religious education to cross over international bodies politic and build more inclusive dialogues and collaborations across cultures to solve the environmental, social, and ethical challenges facing humanity today. Crucially, digital tools give room for interfaith dialogue, allowing different communities to find common moral ground while still honoring doctrinal divisions.

For the future prospects, this integration has an open path. New technologies like AI and AR/VR or blockchain religions can make religious content more accessible, authentic, and engaging. Religious leaders, educators, and technology providers can work together to design new interactive multilingual arenas that promote sustainable ecological living as a spiritual imperative. In addition, global interfaith networks that are online can be points of dissemination for best practices and organizing grassroots solutions and increasing empathy across lines of difference. Ultimately, this long-term effort to adjudicate sacred values with digital innovation may lead to the emergence of ethically literate faces ready for the complex challenges posed by modernity. It is our hope that by maintaining the true spirit of religious education while also harnessing technological development, it can help guide humanity toward a future where everyone can live together in greater peace, equity, and sustainability.

References

1. Bebbington, J., & Unerman, J. (2021). Accounting for the sustainable development goals: Towards a new research agenda. *Accounting and Business Research, 51*(2), 99–122. https://doi.org/10.1080/00014788.2020.1802958
2. Gardner, G. (2021). Spiritual traditions and environmental sustainability: The intersection of spiritual beliefs and nature conservation. *International Journal of Multidisciplinary Research and Growth Evaluation, 6*(1), 658–662.
3. Jones, R. H., & Hafner, C. A. (2021). Discourses of sustainability in a global context: The role of language and communication. *Applied Linguistics, 42*(1), 190–196. https://doi.org/10.1093/applin/amaa049
4. Khiewtam, R. S., & Ramakrishnan, P. S. (2021). Sacred groves as a model for sustainable conservation. *Ecology and Society, 26*(1), 3. https://doi.org/10.5751/ES-11985-260103
5. Lorenz, K., & Lal, R. (2021). The role of sacred sites in carbon sequestration and climate change mitigation. *Journal of Environmental Management, 298*, 113398. https://doi.org/10.1016/j.jenvman.2021.113398
6. Luetz, J. M., & Nunn, P. D. (2021). Spirituality, sustainable development, and climate change in Pacific Island countries. *Sustainability, 13*(11), 6140. https://doi.org/10.3390/su13116140
7. Selwyn, N., & Facer, K. (2021). Technology and the future of sustainable education. *Journal of Computer Assisted Learning, 37*(1), 29–43. https://doi.org/10.1111/jcal.12489
8. Campbell, H. A. (2021). Digital religion: The new media and religious authority. *New Media & Society, 23*(4), 847–865. https://doi.org/10.1177/1461444820986794
9. Kilonzo, S. M., & Omwalo, B. O. (2021). The politics of pulpit religiosity in the era of COVID-19 in Kenya. *Frontiers in Communication, 6*, 616288.

https://doi.org/10.3389/fcomm.2021.616288
10. Rotaru, I.-G. (2021). Religious communication in the digital age: A study of online religious communities. *Journal of Media & Religion, 20*(2), 87–92. https://doi.org/10.1080/15348423.2021.1963212
11. Setyoningrum, S., & Widiyono, M. A. (2021). Digital learning and its impact on Islamic religious education. *International Journal of Education and Humanities, 4*(1), 1–10. https://doi.org/10.32454/ije.v4i1.1578
12. Student, S., Jannah, S., & Aisyah, R. (2021). The role of digital learning in improving students understanding of Islamic religious education materials. *Journal of Islamic Education and Learning, 2*(1), 1–12. https://doi.org/10.22236/jiel.v2i1.458
13. Bencze, J., & Alsop, S. (2021). Pedagogical and ethical challenges of using digital media in religious education. *International Journal of Computer and Mathematical Learning, 26*(1), 77–112. https://doi.org/10.1007/s10758-020-09477-8
14. Anadón, M. (2021). Mixed methods research in religious education: Bridging qualitative and quantitative approaches. *Qualitative Research, 38*(2), 105–123.
15. Ben-Cheikh, I., Rachédi, L., & Rousseau, C. (2021). Online mourning and religious rituals in a multicultural context. *Frontiers in Sociology, 6*, 654321. https://doi.org/10.3389/fsoc.2021.654321
16. Campbell, H. A. (2021). The changing relationship between religion and the digital continent in the context of a COVID-19 pandemic. *Religions, 12*(9), 736. https://doi.org/10.3390/rel12090736
17. Hajri, H. (2021). The importance of religious education in the digital era for character development. *International Journal of Islamic Education and Research, 1*(2), 14–25.
18. Hamid, A. (2021). The use of social media for the dissemination of Islamic values and community building. *Journal of Islamic Studies and Culture, 11*(1), 45–60.
19. Insani, H. M., Dewi, R., & Furnamasari, Y. I. (2021). The role of Islamic religious education in character development in the digital age. *Journal of Education and Humanities, 5*(2), 101–115.
20. Aulia, N., Cahyono, A., & Nuha, A. (2021). Digitalization of spiritual understanding in the context of religious education. *International Journal of Religious Studies, 10*(3), 54–68.
21. Douyère, D. (2021). The mobilization of digital communication by religions: New challenges and opportunities. *Social Sciences, 10*(11), 431. https://doi.org/10.3390/socsci10110431
22. Duteil-Ogata, F. (2021). New religious practices in the online world: From computer-tombs to online rituals. *Online-Heidelberg Journal of Religions on the Internet, 13*(1), 11–19.

23. Helland, C. (2021). Online religion as lived religion: Methodological issues in the study of religious participation on the Internet. *Journal for the Scientific Study of Religion, 60*(2), 345–360. https://doi.org/10.1111/jssr.12702
24. Lövheim, M., & Lynch, G. (2021). Religious communication in a digital world: The challenges of mediation. *Journal of Communication and Religion, 44*(1), 1–15.
25. Hjarvard, S. (2021). The internet as a sacred space: How digital technologies are changing religious experience. *Journal of Contemporary Religion, 36*(2), 205–220. https://doi.org/10.1080/13537903.2021.1906754

CHAPTER 16

Digital Education and Sustainability: Policies and Regulations

Arunima Shastri and Khar Thoe Ng

Abstract The COVID-19 pandemic accelerated digital education's shift from a supplemental tool to an indispensable pillar of learning, exposing both its transformative potential and systemic inequities. This paper examines the governance gaps, policy imperatives, and regulatory innovations shaping post-pandemic digital education. It proposes a "Triple Policy Imperative" of quality assurance, equity, and risk mitigation, supported by a five-pillar framework: infrastructure & access, data governance, content & assessment, teacher student empowerment, and Artificial Intelligence ethics. Drawing on case studies from Singapore, Rwanda, and the UK, the analysis illustrates diverse approaches from centralized national

A. Shastri (✉)
CHRIST University, Bangalore, India
e-mail: arunima.shastri@christuniversity.in

K. T. Ng
Faculty of Education and Liberal Arts (FELA), INTI International University, Nilai, Malaysia
e-mail: kharthoe.ng@newinti.edu.my

P. K. Dutta et al. (eds.), *Digital Education for a Sustainable Future*, Sustainable Development Goals Series,
https://doi.org/10.1007/978-3-032-15433-0_16

strategies to equity-first innovations and agile regulatory sandboxes. The paper argues that sustainable digital education requires principle-led governance, public-private partnerships, and integration with broader social and environmental goals, including the SDGs. It concludes with a call for globally coordinated yet context-specific policies to ensure that digital transformation in education fosters inclusion, safeguards rights, and delivers high-quality learning for all.

Keywords Digital education policy · EdTech governance · Equity in learning · AI ethics · Sustainable development goals

1 Digital Education: The Post-pandemic Imperative

The COVID-19 pandemic presented a global stress test of education systems on a scale not seen before. Overnight, millions of entities moved to digital spaces in places and other items as forecast soon thereafter by educators, students, and policymakers. The sudden pivot put the spotlight on technology as a means to maintain learning integrity, but it also exposed the underlying systemic gaps. According to UNESCO, more than 1.3 billion pupils spent months without connection during the closure of schools while rural communities and low-income countries remained the hardest hit. Digital learning was more like a malaise which took it as an opportunity but for many, it emerged as an exclusion [1].

The crisis has forced us all into video instruction, AI-based tutoring, and digital collaboration tools: these provide proof of concept that technology can scale education delivery. More information + Critical questions on quality, access, and sustainability. Some schools took advantage of rich high-bandwidth immersive learning environments, while others could not even get base connectivity. The unequal nature of these distributions has also provoked greater impetus for policies that focus less on equal access and more on the underlying inequities of digital transformation.

The pandemic has, in short, unleashed a paradox: it showed the potential of digital education but also what could happen without oversight. In a post-pandemic world, this digital experiment is expected to be more policy-driven in nature rather than piecemeal and ad-hoc.

The Governance Gap

At a time where technology in education is evolving rapidly, policy frameworks remain outdated and reactive. New pedagogical methods in education such as AI-driven adaptive learning systems, virtual reality classrooms, and blockchain-based credentialing platforms are already transforming the environment, but regulation is lagging behind [2].

Key governance gaps include:

(a) There are no universal data privacy standards in EdTech: Data such as learning analytics and behavioral profiles of students often continue to be unregulated due to the paucity of stringent oversight.
(b) Automated grading or AI-driven admissions or career guidance tools: Algo-based decision-making such as automatic grading with AI, admissions with AI can be obviously biased and non-transparent of nature.
(c) Private EdTech providers lack strong accountability mechanisms—most provide courses without adherence to traditional education norms, which may render them guilty of providing misinformation, exploitative pricing, and sub-optimal quality of learning outcomes.

Without proactive governance, technology can outpace questions of ethics; ultimately it will put students at risk and leave public education subject to the demands of the private sector.

A policy for the digital future, however, must go beyond existing access-focused one-time engagements and move to equity, ethics, and accountability. This will entail a move from technology-focused use to principle-led governance.

The chapter argues for:

(a) Increased data privacy to protect student information and higher standards of algorithm transparency, making AI systems auditable and bias-free.
(b) Investment of public money into resilient digital infrastructure (i.e. low bandwidth & inclusive solutions, for use in underserved regions)

(c) Global cooperation to avoid regulatory fragmentation and establish common norms related to data governance, credential recognition, and ethical AI.
(d) In this way, the vehicle of effective policy is not a drag on innovation but, as we have seen here and elsewhere, rather an essential navigational tool ensuring that technological advancement moves compass-like toward roomy exiting goals like quality of education (SDG 4) and social equity.

2 Policy Matters, Why the Environmental Landscape is Changing: From Niche to Necessity

A decade ago, digital education was for the most part thought of as a supplement. While MOOCs in the early 2010s could attract millions of learners, they were very much on the periphery of formal education systems. By now, you would expect digital learning today is as much a part of the education infrastructure as roofs and bricks and clicks in the 2000s, but it was not always so (we even debate about what to call it nowadays).

This change was further expedited by the onset of the COVID-19 pandemic that served as a springboard for greater digital adoption on a mass level. Hybrid, then online learning gained ground and policymakers along with educationalists realized technology is no more an "optional supplement," it is a sine qua non for continuity and inclusivity. The global EdTech market is set to surpass $400 billion by 2030, driven mainly by the surge of AI, gamified learning platforms, and personalized adaptive technologies [3].

At the same time, however, we recognize that technology by itself does not nor never will single handedly ensure high-quality education for all students. In the absence of governance, this landmark shift toward digital education runs a severe risk of leading to an incomplete promise fragmented and inequitable systems driven by market forces, rather than public interest. And this is when policy really matters it's not just a hindering factor but an enabler for sustainability.

The Triple Imperative for Regulation

A Ensuring Quality and Efficacy

The Challenge: The explosion of unvetted EdTech tools has resulted in an app and platform marketplace filled with technology promos promising transformative results without empirical validation. Rollouts being done directly to the classroom without thorough validation means we have inconsistent results and in some cases, pedagogical harm [5, 6].

Policy Recommendation: Demand-side to protect against deterioration in quality, introduce national accreditation systems for digital content and tools. Example: The government of Estonia, through its "Digital Testing" framework, sets stringent standards required for educational technologies to be evaluated and certified before they are applied across the country. This includes ensuring that digital learning solutions are compliant with curricular needs, bring academic integrity, and drive evidence-based practices.

At the same time, teacher training systems and policies should require that teachers who use technology be proficient in assessing EdTech tools so that research can better inform classroom practice. When quality assurance is integrated within the policy framework, systems can evolve from experimentation to guided, outcome-based digital learning.

B Advancing Equity (SDGs 4 and 10)

Challenge: While technology has advanced more than ever, the digital divide still represents one of the most significant obstacle to education inclusivity. The percentage of households with internet access varies dramatically across regions. This is compounded by further exclusions that continue to be defined based on gender, income with rural and marginalized communities bearing the brunt of these disabilities.

Policy Solution: Digital Education Policy with Equity an agenda for digital education would need to be two-pronged, marrying infrastructure investment with smart inclusion strategies. In India, where India's "Digital India" campaign has been expanding access through the provision of subsidy infrastructure like devices, Wi-Fi hotspots at panchayat and gram panchayat levels, capacity building initiatives all seek to reduce the urban-rural digital divide. Public-private partnerships can help solve this problem: similar schemes in places such as Kenya and Brazil show that they significantly increase coverage and lower prices for students who are at a disadvantage.

Furthermore, creating equity in digital learning also calls for policies that cover representation along with access so online study material and modules are kept culturally responsive and translated into local languages. Here it provides an opportunity to ensure that digital education can be aligned with the Sustainable Development Goals (in particular SDG 4: Quality Education and SDG 10: Reduced Inequalities) and transform technology from being a driver of exclusion into an extraordinary equalizer [4].

C Mitigating Foundational Risks

Governance of EdTech: With the mass collection of student data in educational platforms such as behavioral patterns, learning histories and biometric details, the absence of explicit consent standards and possibilities for exploitation presents significant privacy issues. In the wrong hands, these can be manipulated to do things like data exploitation, profiling, and even commercial misuse.

Policy Solution: GDPR has been a global catalyst for privacy, it is not alone: new education-specific privacy regimes are emerging. For example, SOPIPA (Student Online Personal Information Protection Act) in California both restricts the commercial use of student data and requires that educational platforms used in K12 settings implement a high level of security measures to protect such information.

To ensure accountability, policymakers must require that EduTech companies practice transparent data governance providing information about the collection and storage of student data. These are also important for fairness and non-bias, especially when it comes to independent audits of algorithmic decision-making in automated grading and predictive analytics [7].

D The Policy Imperative

Quality, Equity, and Risk Mitigation becomes the Triple Policy Imperative for the Digital Education. They're sorting it out now, but going forward, the EdTech sector will likely become a wild frontier, complete with inadequate security, piracy-related issues, & student privacy concerns. But with governance that anticipates long-term needs, technology can be a real enabler of teaching and learning as articulated in the UN Global Goal for Education.

This is not merely good stuff for policy wonks. That foundation is essential to support sustainable and ethical digital learning ecosystem, one which can scale the seeds of innovation while at the same time gatekeeping human rights and integrity in education.

3 Cornerstones of a New Age Digital Education Policy

In the world of learning ecosystems, it has firmly entered the realm where digital education helps to create a seamless learning experience. However, in the absence of defined policy frameworks, digital transformation risks exacerbating inequality and eroding data privacy—not to mention feeding into greater propensity for algorithmic bias. This is why a future-ready regulatory architecture rooted in 5 highly inter-dependent pillars, Infrastructure & Access, Data Governance & Privacy, Content and Assessment, Teacher and Student Empowerment, as well as AI Ethics [8].

A Infrastructure and Access
Almost always, infrastructure is the achilles heel of digital education. Operationalization of any policy, without connectivity, devices, and sustainable energy solutions, cannot deliver the desired regulatory outcomes.

B Green Tech Integration
While the digital revolution of education scales exponentially, it has a considerable environmental footprint as well. With data centers that require a huge amount of energy and the average digital device already doing the environment more harm in its production, we are outputting a yearly growing amount of CO_2 into the atmosphere. In recognition of this, for example, the European Union has set binding targets on energy efficiency measures in data centers as well as the use of renewable energy. Such requirements should be applied in academia as well, where the environmental impact of online learning platforms and institutional IT infrastructure remains largely unexamined.

Policies that, for example, would compel educational institutions and EdTech providers to move away from carbon-intensive hosting services in favor of green cloud computing options. Governments could also promote the sales of low-energy apparatuses and recycling old hardware, thus reducing e-waste and at the same time supporting environmentally sustainable living. This congruence of educational policies with climate goals is critically important to make sure that digital transformation does not take root as a broader sustainability agenda.

C Public-Private Partnerships (PPPs)

Public funding alone will not get the job done, especially in low and middle-income countries, which require massive infrastructure expansion. A key part of the solution is strategic collaboration with the private sector. The Digital Literacy Programme [DLP] in Kenya Typifies the Might of PPPs. Then it shipped more than a million tablets to schools and trained teachers how to use them, creating localized digital content with the backing of technology giants like Microsoft and Intel. It showed how a combination of private-sector skills and government stewardship can move the needle on digital inclusion in a meaningful way [9, 10].

Apart from the same last-mile connectivity initiatives should be supported by policies. Community Wi-Fi programs like the one implemented in India's rural regions through Digital India enable block-level affordable internet access to even the remotest parts of the country. Central to this vision is the idea of using a regulatory framework that not only incentivizes telecom providers to provide broadband at affordable price points but also mandates them to commit these projects in those regions where connectivity is lacking in sectored areas like education and library.

D Data Governance and Privacy

The shift to digital learning in higher education has made student data a vital and sensitive commodity. The frequency and severity of data breaches, the opacity of algorithms, and the increasingly aggressive commercialization of personal information make visible the urgent need for strong mechanisms to govern these processes.

E Student Data Bill of Rights

Although the European General Data Protection Regulation (GDPR) has established a solid baseline of privacy and data protection, it is not sector-specific to education or minors. One step that could fill this gap would be for states to establish an education-specific Student Data Bill of Rights creating a right that explicit control over their data is in the hands of students and parents [11].

Key provisions might include:

Transparency: Schools and EdTech providers must be transparent about what type of personal data can be collected from the students or parents, for which purposes they intend to process such data, and how long it will be stored.

Limited purpose: Student data must only be used in service of educational value, and specficially not for any commercial purposes.

Deletion of data: Students and parents should be able to request the deletion of personal data.

Oversight must be independent: Monitoring compliance is the purview of regulatory bodies and penalties are imposed for any breach.

This will not just strengthen legal protections, but will also lay the foundation for rebuilding trust in digital education systems given some EdTech companies were recently caught selling student data.

F Algorithmic Audits

AI-driven (AI) tools, whether used for grading without human intervention, predicting student outcomes, or optimizing adaptive learning pathways, are susceptible to bias and opacity. To help mitigate these pitfalls, governments can and should require that educational technologies are regularly audited for the fairest outcomes.

So the New York City AI Transparency Act, which mandates that companies disclose their training datasets and bias mitigation strategy, is a good example. A similar regulation, specific to education, could also require EdTech providers to submit their algorithms for an independent review of fairness and explainability. Policies should also require companies to disclose a paper trail that enables educators, students, and regulators to re-create the hows and whys of algorithmic determinations [12].

Algorithmic accountability is needed to avoid systemic bias such as punishing non-native speakers with automated essay grading or discrimination against certain groups such as racial minorities.

4 Content and Assessment

It is true that digital learning goes beyond mere delivery mechanisms, but extends to content taught and assessment of outcomes. Regulation has a role to ensure that content quality and assessment integrity are maintained.

A Open Educational Resources (OER) Mandates
While digital learning resources are increasingly of better quality, students and schools still have less access to high-quality content due to the cost-prohibitive nature of proprietary materials. For a real-world example, consider Plan Ceibal in Uruguay where the government gives every student free access to digital textbooks, educational software, and learning resources online. Governments can use the process of embedding open educational resources (OERs) within national education strategies to:

(a) Save on proprietary learning materials.
(b) Succeed in cross-language content adaptation.
(c) Encourage educators and their respective universities to introduce the concept of collaborative content creation.

An OER mandate could also be established to facilitate the ongoing updating of materials, guaranteeing that curricula evolves as required by the needs of today's digital economy.

B Regulation of Anti-cheating Technology
As examinations have switched to online, so too have the tools associated with them including some questionable remote-proctoring applications that use technologies like eye-tracking, facial recognition, and keystroke monitoring. Some intrusive practices have been categorically restricted in Germany, since a number of technologies violate student privacy in a disproportionately severe way.

Policy for education should set definite standards on digitally proctored assessment and must focus more on asynchronous modes of assessments like randomized question bank, TCA tools, AI-based plagiarism detection, and oral examinations with supervised human proctors. The steps it is taking accomplish the right balance of preserving the integrity of education and ensuring students have appropriate privacy rights.

5 Teacher and Student Empowerment

Technology in and of itself and this is the most important point to be made does not impact learning cognition; that incorporation lies closest to the human level for teachers, how they view their roles, for students, how do they experience essentially digital-native environments.

A Digital Pedagogy Licenses

One of the few countries in a position to set such an example is Finland, whose teachers are now required to take AI Literacy and Digital Pedagogy training as part of their certification process. They are no longer only users of technology but have become critically conscious consumers of new tech that is contextual to their teaching [13].

Policies that oblige professional development in digital education would lead to retraining programs funded by the public sector.

B Student Digital Rights Charters

Empowering students is equally critical. Student Digital Rights Charter developed with student participation as part of the "Digital Schools Initiative" in Portugal. This charter codifies:

(a) Accessible and inclusive digital learning tools.
(b) Transparency in algorithmic grading and career guidance.
(c) Security from invasive surveillance during exams conducted online.
(d) Embed the student voice, and you can build education systems that elevate learner agency while promoting digital citizenship.

6 Guidelines for Ethical Research in the Education AI

One of the things AI promises to revolutionize is education from intelligent tutoring systems, automated grading, and predictive analytics. But rather than be a force for good, these tools can amplify bias, erode trust, and dehumanize already marginalized people when unleavened by ethical guardrails.

A Bias Mitigation

Diverse Datasets: AI algorithms are meant to be trained and subsequently deployed across a global market where gender, cultural, and lingual divides could easily muddy the waters. EdTech companies should be subjected to bias testing and certification in order to deploy AI tools in educational settings through policy. So long as the tools respect broad fairness standards, independent regulators could even be empowered to audit them periodically.

If not addressed, bias could actually reinforce disparities already in place. A trained AI tool cannot rule out bias for example, if the data used to train it has a majority of urban, English-speaking students then rural or multilingual learners would be excluded.

B Human-in-the-Loop Rules

AI should complement not replace human educators. The South Korean regulation requiring a teacher review of AI-generated feedback offers a good illustration of that process. That rule of thumb is meant to keep ultimate authority around the most critical educational decisions centered on educators and not pre-empted by an automated system.

Those rules might also prevent schools or other official bodies from relying solely on an AI system to make high-stakes decisions (admissions, standardized grading) and instead demand some form of human review to ensure that fairness and accountability are upkept.

C Policy Ecosystem for the Future

It also means that each of the five pillars of infrastructure, data governance, content and assessment, teacher, student empowerment, and AI ethics, is not alone but rather mutually reinforcing in terms of impact. This includes strategically integrating them with a broader policy framework that can be thought of as part of a system for tackling immediate crises and future shocks [14].

Ensuring digital education reaches and serves every learner regardless of geography or socioeconomic realities is the guiding principle of equity. It is the guarantee of ethics that technology respects privacy and human rights, and also a form of fairness. The commitment to sustainability between educational digital transformation and climate-related policies. Innovation will build the regulatory infrastructure around which EdTech can flourish safely.

This next-generation digital education system can be achieved by adopting a multi-pillar approach that turns COVID-era digital response into decades of sustainable, inclusive high-quality learning.

7 Case Studies in Policy Implementation

Policy frameworks are merely words on paper, and their practical fidelity is the yardstick of their success. Analyzing how digital education policies have been implemented in various countries provides useful lessons for understanding where success has been achieved, the extents of some challenges and what type of regulatory strategies may still need to be tailored depending on differences within a regional context. The study of Singapore Smart Nation for Education Strategy, Rwanda EdTech Policy Equity focus, and UK EdTech Innovation Regulatory Sandbox are represented under this section.

8 Highlight of Singapore as a Smart Nation in Education

Coincidentally, Singapore is one of the countries with the most considerable comprehensive educational policy ecosystems for digital education. Since the creation of its Smart Nation initiative in 2014, it has forcefully aligned education to become a strategic asset within its national digital transformation agenda.

A Holistic Policy Integration

Singapore, meanwhile, takes its education policy one step further it wants to do more than build and improve infrastructure; it is preparing for the integration of AI, cybersecurity, teacher training, and digital literacy as part of a cohesive masterplan. This is part of the national Student Learning Space (SLS) portal, where all schools are required by the Ministry of Education (MOE) to be on a digital learning platform that will link up every student and teacher. Adaptive learning tools, AI-driven assessment systems, and data-driven insights for educators are all at the very heart of this centralized platform.

Singapore has incorporated cybersecurity education into its curriculum as well. The government more recently took stock of rising dangers amid further digital transformation and teamed up with the Cyber Security Agency of Singapore (CSA) to introduce selected campaigns for safe internet use and digital ethics, moulding a new generation that is equipped to make judgments on the new opportunities and risks in the virtual realm.

B Teacher Training and AI Adoption

One key to success has been their commitment to developing teacher digital capabilities in Singapore. Teachers are continuously developed in AI-powered pedagogy, blended learning techniques, and digital classroom management via the National Institute of Education. This ensured that technology integration not just top down but also bottom up by digitally skilled teaching force.

All this has led to 98% of the Singaporean schools currently using AI enabled, adaptive learning tools. For example, these systems are capable of adjusting content to each individual student, freeing teachers up to provide personalized instruction rather than standardized, one-size-fits-all delivery.

C Outcomes

There are a number of direct benefits that the strategy has provided to the Smart Nation such as:

(a) Higher educational outcomes: Practically applied AI tools have resulted in up to 15% improvement in student performance (pilot programs conducted on mathematics and language learning).
(b) This helps to ensure digital equity: All students at the secondary level will have individual learning devices delivered to their schools, reducing the digital divide in APS.
(c) Cyber resilience: Incorporating cyber hygiene into education has allowed Singapore to establish a benchmark in high-security EdTech ecosystems with no or fewer recorded data breaches within school networks.

Its centralized, government-led model illustrates the ability of a country to align infrastructure, training, and regulation with national digital transformation aspirations.

D Rwanda's Equity-Focused EdTech Policy

Rwanda, on the other hand, represents low-resource setting and provides example of equity-led policy that is pushing digital education in this context.

A The Challenge

This was only 30% of rural schools access to electricity, a far cry internet connection in 2020 available in Rwanda. This was a major impediment to running any digital education project. In addition, teacher digital literacy was low and there existed a critical shortage of localized digital learning content.

B The Solution: Solar-Powered Digital Classrooms
To overcome these issues, the Rwandan government concluded agreements with the One Laptop per Child (OLPC) program as well as private sector providers to build solar-powered digital classrooms.

Based around but not solely inclusive of teacher training as a central component of the policy. Through the Rwanda Education Board (REB), teachers were trained in how to use digital pedagogy mechanisms, and followed through with proper integration of e-learning resources into lesson plans.

In addition, Rwanda announced a nationwide e-learning drive to create educational content in Kinyarwanda that all students living in the farmlands could study without being constrained to English and French [15].

C Outcomes
While Rwanda had limited resources, its equity-first approach has proven to be extremely effective. Expansion of digital literacy: By 2023, over 60% of rural schools had been fitted with solar-powered digital classrooms. Well-trained teachers: Tens of thousands of teachers have completed digital training programs and are now more comfortable using technology in their classrooms. Localized learning: More than 1000 digital resources have been developed in Kinyarwanda to cater for culturally appropriate learning content.

This is a crucial lesson in digital education policy: effective models do not have to be extremely high-tech, they just need to understand the underlying principle of what it going on—and innovate under that content. Rwanda has laid a powerful, scalable foundation for digital learning in low-resource settings by tackling infrastructure and teacher development together.

9 The UK's EdTech Regulatory Sandbox

On one extreme you have cases such as the deployment of Singapore and Rwanda, which are characterized by large-scale policy implementation; on another extreme footing stands the UK's regulatory sandbox approach to digital education governance where small-scale experimentation is carried out in a controlled condition.

A The Approach

In keeping with such a focus, the UK government previously introduced its EdTech Regulatory Sandbox jointly with the Department for Education (DfE) and the Office for Standards in Education (Ofsted), acknowledging that regulation could hinder innovation. With temporary regulatory waivers granted by CUE to campus partners, ABC serves as a testing venue for startups and educational institutions to pilot new technologies in actual classroom settings.

The sandbox framework provides:

Apprenticed testing situations for EdTech Tools

(a) Allows for certain compliance requirements to be skipped to ease into the pilot phases (flexible regulation).
(b) Private mechanisms to evaluate the effect of these technologies on whether people learn (os not) and if they lose any privacy as a consequence.
(c) The UK ensures that technology developers can work, safely within parameters, to ensure the prevention of any damages by creating a safe space for innovation [16].

Accelerating VR in STEM Education

A lead example of the latter is virtual reality (VR) in STEM education which has been one of the UK sandbox's most prized successes. The VR tools designed by startups based in the UK were deployed on a pilot basis across several schools in sandbox conditions, with educators providing structured feedback and regulators watching over data privacy compliance.

The findings were encouraging: VR teaching modules had led to greater engagement and understanding by students, particularly in areas like biology and physics. After such a successful trial, the accreditation for several of the tools was made formal before they were deployed within a bigger catchment of schools.

Outcomes

The sandbox model in the UK has led to three main outcomes:

(a) Faster innovation: Startups can get products into classrooms faster than the cleared regulatory processes.

(b) Evidence-based policymaking: Pilot study goes a long way in customizing the policies and schemes, applied to individual groups.
(c) Minimal risk: Encouraging innovation leads to assessment of risk at the preliminary level and creates ethical boundaries.

This balance has been achieved by a blend of flexibility and accountability, leading the UK to emerge as an exemplar in agile regulation for digitally distributed higher education [17].

B Lessons from the Case Studies
As the three studies show, there is no standard formula for digital education policy. However, several key lessons emerge:

(a) Inclusivity and Integration: Benchmarking Singapore, creating efficient infrastructure and systematic training and workshops led for teachers, can create more inclusivity for technology.
(b) Rwanda depicts a different and quite innovative picture where solar panels run classrooms, depicting out-of-the-box thinking and energy conservation, equitable distribution of resources in the classroom, including internet connectivity.
(c) The UK's sandbox approach aims at balancing and regulating innovations, leading the way to preserve the student rights and make them accountable of their actions.

We would argue that these examples illustrate the key point articulated throughout this chapter: that not only is policy a leveraged pathway approaching compliance mechanism, but one which does so in a manner creating digitally sustainable, inclusive, and innovative models for education.

A. Singapore's "Smart Nation" Education Strategy: A Global Leader in Digital Learning

The initiative led to a series of "enablers" to facilitate digitization across these six areas: Promoting intelligent solutions through testing and research partnerships. Fostering a culture of trial and continuous innovation. Sharing data via the open data portal and Smart Nation Platform, Investing in Research and Development (R&D). Establishing "living laboratories" for the creation and testing of technological solutions. Developing an ecosystem for industry and start-ups. Ensuring cybersecurity and data privacy—Enhancing computational skills. Educational initiatives at different levels, which include young children, secondary school students, and working adults. Skills upgrading initiatives like Skills Future. A Smart Nation Fellowship Programme that engages seasoned data scientists and engineers to collaborate with the government on technological solutions [18].

Teachers: The Backbone of Tech Integration

Technology alone doesn't transform education teachers do. That's why Singapore invests heavily in continuous teacher training through the National Institute of Education. Educators don't just learn how to use tools; they master AI-powered teaching methods, blended learning, and digital classroom management. This ensures tech adoption isn't forced from the top down but grows from a skilled, confident teaching workforce.

The results speak for themselves: 98% of Singaporean schools now use AI-driven adaptive learning tools, which tailor lessons to each student's needs. Instead of a rigid, one-size-fits-all approach, teachers can focus on personalized instruction, making learning more effective and more human.

Tangible Success: Measurable Impact

The Smart Nation strategy isn't just ambitious it works. Here's how:

- Better Learning Outcomes: Pilot programs in math and language saw student performance improve by up to 15% with AI-assisted tools.
- Closing the Digital Divide: By providing personal learning devices to every secondary student, Singapore has nearly erased inequities in tech access.
- A Safer Digital Ecosystem: By embedding cybersecurity into education, schools have minimized data breaches, setting a global standard for secure EdTech.

Why Singapore's Model Matters
Singapore proves that a centralized, government-led approach one that aligns infrastructure, training, and policy can turn digital education from a buzzword into real, scalable success. Other nations looking to modernize learning would do well to take notes.

10 Rwanda's Equity-First EdTech Revolution: Learning Against the Odds

While Singapore's high-tech approach showcases what's possible with abundant resources, Rwanda tells a different story one of ingenuity, resilience, and a relentless focus on equity. In a country where only 30% of rural schools had electricity in 2020, digital education seemed like a distant dream. Yet, Rwanda didn't wait for perfect conditions it built solutions from the ground up.

The Challenge: No Power, No Connectivity, No Teachers Trained Now What?
Imagine trying to teach digital skills in a classroom with no electricity, no internet, and teachers who had rarely used a computer. That was Rwanda's reality. Add to that a critical shortage of learning materials in Kinyarwanda, the language most students spoke at home, and the barriers seemed insurmountable.

But Rwanda saw these challenges not as dead ends but as problems to solve.

The Solution: Solar Panels, Offline Tech, and Teachers First
Instead of waiting for nationwide infrastructure, Rwanda took a leapfrog approach:

- Solar-Powered Classrooms: Partnering with One Laptop per Child (OLPC) and private companies, the government rolled out self-contained digital hub classrooms powered by solar panels, stocked with offline servers and laptops. No grid? No problem.
- Teachers as Change-Makers: Through the Rwanda Education Board (REB), educators received hands-on training in digital teaching methods, turning skeptics into confident tech users.

- Learning in Kinyarwanda, Not Just English: A national push created 1000+ digital lessons in Kinyarwanda, ensuring kids in remote villages could learn in their mother tongue.

Outcomes: Proof that Equity Works
By 2023, Rwanda's stubborn optimism paid off:

- 60% of rural schools had solar-powered digital classrooms doubling access in just 3 years.
- Thousands of teachers went from tech-shy to tech-savvy, transforming how they taught.
- Kids who once had no books now had digital lessons they could understand in their own language.

The Big Lesson: Innovation isn't About the Fanciest Tech
Rwanda's story proves that scarcity breeds creativity. You don't need cutting-edge gadgets to make digital learning work you need smart policy, local solutions, and a commitment to reaching the last mile. While richer nations debate AI in schools, Rwanda shows how a solar panel, a laptop, and a teacher who believes in change can rewrite the future.

11 The UK's Regulatory Sandbox: Where Innovation Meets the Classroom

While Singapore builds nationwide digital systems and Rwanda powers rural schools with solar panels, the UK is taking a different path turning classrooms into living labs. Here, the question isn't just *how* to bring tech into schools, but *how to test it safely* in the real world.

The Problem: When Red Tape Stops Progress
Imagine you're a startup with a groundbreaking VR tool for science classes. Before students can even try it, you're buried under months of compliance checks while teachers and kids wait. The UK's answer? A regulatory sandbox, where innovation gets a *temporary pass* to bypass bureaucracy but under watchful eyes.

Launched by the Department for Education (DfE) and Ofsted (the UK's school watchdog), the sandbox gives startups and schools a real-world testing ground:

- Test-drive new tech in actual classrooms no hypotheticals.
- Skip some red tape during trials (but keep core safeguards).
- Get instant feedback from teachers *and* regulators.

Think of it as a "safety net for bold ideas": experiment freely, but with experts ensuring nothing harms students.

Case Study: VR Takes Flight in Science Class
One standout success? Virtual reality for STEM. Under the sandbox, startups partnered with schools to let students explode 3D cells in biology or tweak gravity in physics all from their desks.

While kids were mesmerized, regulators tracked two things:

1. Did learning improve? (Engagement and test scores jumped.)
2. Was student data safe? (Checked and secured.)

The result? Fast-tracked accreditation for VR tools that proved their worth and are now used nationwide.

Why It Works: Speed, Proof, and Safety.

In 3 years, the sandbox has shown how to balance innovation with responsibility:

- Faster pilots: Startups test ideas 50% quicker without cutting corners.
- Smarter rules: Real classroom data now shapes policy (no more guesswork).

12 Conclusion: Toward a Global Policy Compact for Digital Education

While the proposed analytical framework proposes a comprehensive list of policy levers for digital education, it is important to recognize that all policy levers do not apply equally to countries according to their level of digital development/maturity. The state of digital development of each education system also determines the sequencing and timing of such policies. Countries with high shares of students lacking basic access to quality Internet connection or digital equipment for learning should begin by supporting investment in the provision of access to digital education technologies. In contrast, countries that are further ahead in the digitalization of their education systems can put a stronger emphasis on steering innovation in digital education technologies, enhancing the monitoring and evaluation of digital education to ensure the sustainability of its outcomes, but also on investing in forecasting and scenario planning to ensure that their policies adjust to evolving digital technology trends. Irrespective of education systems' starting point and their current state of digital exposure, this analytical framework provides a general checklist of policies to consider for enabling a more effective rollout of digital education. An assessment of where countries stand in the digital transformation of their education systems and the challenges they face as digital technologies increasingly permeate learning processes can provide a first step in guiding the sequencing of policies necessary to enable successful digital education.

References

1. Gajderowicz, T., Jakubowski, M., Kennedy, A., Kjeldsen, C. C., Patrinos, H. A., & Strietholt, R. (2025). The learning crisis: Three years after COVID-19. *arXiv*. https://arxiv.org/abs/2501.01260?utm_source=chatgpt.com
2. Tech Monitor. (2023, March 16). *Government backs UK AI regulatory sandbox*. Tech Monitor. https://www.techmonitor.ai/digital-economy/ai-and-automation/government-backs-ai-regulatory-sandbox?utm_source=chatgpt.com
3. ICO. (2025). *Regulatory sandbox final report: Department for Education*. ICO.https://www.techmonitor.ai/digital-economy/ai-and-automation/government-backs-ai-regulatory-sandbox?utm_source=chatgpt.com
4. UNICEF Innocenti. (2025). *Regulatory sandboxes and innovation in education*. UNICEF Innocenti. https://www.unicef.org/innocenti/media/11091/file/UNICEF-Innocenti-Regulatory-Sandboxes-Case-Study-2025.pdf?utm_source=chatgpt.com
5. UNESCO. (2025). *Digital learning and transformation of education: What you need to know*. UNESCO. https://www.unesco.org/en/digital-education/need-know?utm_source=chatgpt.com
6. Lee, A. V. Y., Koh, E., & Looi, C. K. (2023). *AI in education and learning analytics in Singapore: An overview of key projects and initiatives*. ResearchGate. https://www.researchgate.net/publication/375137743_AI_in_Education_and_Learning_Analytics_in_Singapore_An_Overview_of_Key_Projects_and_Initiatives

7. Government Technology Agency Singapore (GovTech). (2025, January 21). *AI in education: Transforming Singapore's education system with student learning space*. GovTech. https://www.tech.gov.sg/technews/ai-in-education-transforming-singapore-education-system-with-student-learning-space/?utm_source=chatgpt.com
8. EducationEstonia.org. (2025, May 26). Estonia eschews phone bans in schools and takes leap into AI. *The Guardian*. https://www.theguardian.com/education/2025/may/26/estonia-phone-bans-in-schools-ai-artificial-intelligence?utm_source=chatgpt.com
9. Complex Discovery Staff. (2025). *Estonia's AI leap in education: A model for future learning*. ComplexDiscovery. https://complexdiscovery.com/estonias-ai-leap-in-education-a-model-for-future-learning/?utm_source=chatgpt.com
10. World Bank. (2025). *Digital pathways for education: Enabling greater impact for all*. World Bank Publications. https://www.worldbank.org/en/topic/edutech/publication/digital-pathways-education-enabling-learning-impact?utm_source=chatgpt.com
11. World Bank Blogs. (2025). *Three mindset shifts to build digital and AI empowered education*. World Bank. https://blogs.worldbank.org/en/education/three-mindset-shifts-to-build-digital-and-ai-empowered-education?utm_source=chatgpt.com
12. EducationEstonia.org. (2023). *Estonia shared its digitalisation experience at the World Bank seminar*. World Bank. https://www.educationestonia.org/estonia-shared-its-experience-at-the-world-bank-seminar/?utm_source=chatgpt.com
13. PVKnowHow. (2025, March). *Rwanda expands solar power to electrify close to 1,000 schools by 2025*. PVKnowHow. https://africa-energy-portal.org/news/rwanda-expands-solar-power-electrify-close-1000-schools-2025?utm_source=chatgpt.com
14. Ignite Power & Government of Rwanda. (2023–2025). *Solar-powered internet school initiative*. Ignite Power/Rwandan Ministries. https://developingtelecoms.com/telecom-technology/energy-sustainability/15945-rwanda-partners-ignite-for-solar-supported-education.html?utm_source=chatgpt.com
15. Tech Monitor. (2023). *Regulatory sandbox frameworks in the UK government*. Tech Monitor. https://www.techmonitor.ai/digital-economy/ai-and-automation/government-backs-ai-regulatory-sandbox?utm_source=chatgpt.com
16. Lim, V., Wee, L., Teo, J., & Ng, S. (2017). Massive open and online courses and open educational resources in Singapore. *arXiv*. https://arxiv.org/abs/1708.08743?utm_source=chatgpt.com

17. EducationGov.sg. (2021). *Building partnerships and capabilities for Smart Nation: AI Centre for Educational Technology*. Singapore Smart Nation PDF. https://www.smartnation.gov.sg/files/press-releases/2021/building-partnerships-and-capabilities-for-smart-nation.pdf?utm_source=chatgpt.com
18. EducationEstonia.org. (2020). *How did Estonia become a new role model in digital education?* EducationEstonia.org. https://www.educationestonia.org/how-did-estonia-become-a-new-role-model-in-digital-education/?utm_source=chatgpt.com

CHAPTER 17

Strengthening Research Foundations for Data-Driven Digital Education in Institutions

Saurabh Chandra, Amar Pandey, and Rashi Yadav

Abstract Data-driven digital education can advance and thus help to strengthen educational quality, innovation, and equity in the digital age. In light of the increasing technological transformation of teaching and learning environments, there is urgency for theoretical research frameworks that can be applied in a systematic manner to examine data and inform policy and practice. The institutions need their own internal capacity to engage in data-informed decision-making, which requires investment in research infrastructure, professional development for educators and administrators alike about the importance of data literacy, and the kinds of decisions this allows us to make responsibility and a larger cultural shift toward an ethos of evidence-based decision-making. This may be related with the twofold approach to qualitative and quantitative research featured in toward an understanding of digital education

S. Chandra (✉) · A. Pandey · R. Yadav
School of Law, Bennett University, Greater Noida, India
e-mail: saurabhchandranls@gmail.com

P. K. Dutta et al. (eds.), *Digital Education for a Sustainable Future*, Sustainable Development Goals Series,
https://doi.org/10.1007/978-3-032-15433-0_17

and is necessary to gain as comprehensive overview of both more established features and newer elements. Linking across departmental divides, interdisciplinary research, and links to external stakeholders can enhance both the outputs of research in terms of publications, but also relate these outputs to practical benefits. In order to ensure that research benefits all learners and ensures equitable outcomes, institutional leaders must prioritize data ethics, privacy, and inclusivity. So, integrating research at the strategic heart of digital education initiatives enhances academic attainment and learner satisfaction, and directly supports national and global education strategies.

Keywords Data-driven education · Institutional research capacity · Digital learning innovation · Evidence-based practice · Educational policy and strategy

1 Introduction

Digital education coming into being is thought of the most transformative shift in learning and teaching. It involves the use of technology in the classrooms/online platforms but its more than that, it is a complete rethinking and reimaging of how educational delivery, engagement, and assessment can be done. Within the wider picture of changing digital landscapes, research is key to identifying what works in online education and how best practices can be scaled effectively. In the absence of rigorous, context-specific, and evidence-based research, institutions may run the risk that their digital strategy is misaligned to learner needs or pedagogical principles and/or fails to deliver on institutional mission and aspirations [1]. Ultimately, then, developing a robust research base is critical to creating, testing, and iterating digital education systems in an ethically sustainable way.

Research on digital education is essential to investigate the entanglement of learners, educators, technologies, and learning environments. Digital education is unlike traditional classrooms as it offers different types of modalities: everything from self-paced asynchronous online courses, to virtual real-time classrooms, AI-driven personalized learning systems, and immersive simulations. Each modality offers specific pedagogical, psychological, and technological challenges. Institutional research helps institutions to study these variables scientifically and take informed decisions over curriculum design, technology adoption, instruction strategies, or student support services. It is the perspective that we need to test, adapt, and scale educational innovations.

This path of a research-based data will make the roadmap for digital education initiatives to support pedagogy it is not about just following some tech trends. Researchers can then analyze this data to identify patterns and predict learning points that students may struggle with, which will allow them to work on interventions for it. These are the kind of insights that can enable a more adaptive learning experience, in which smart systems personalize content based on individual attributes to improve learning [2]. This body of work has the potential to contribute to a more inclusive digital education by shining light on differences in access and engagement across demographic groups, thus preventing digital education from further complicating existing systems of educational inequality.

Institutional research supports development of policy, quality standards, and framing for digital education from macro to micro ends. It provides a tool for policymakers and institutional leaders to evaluate the impact of national or institutional digital education strategies, make effective resourcing decisions, and benchmark against international measures. This is an important alignment especially in places where eLearning as a phenomenon is still emerging and will require a lot of learning based on the context. Research findings thus serve as the evidentiary base on which educational reforms and forward-thinking strategies can be grounded.

Digital education is not fixed and continues to change at a rapid pace due to new technologies, societal changes, and global crises. All this calls for a fresh investigation on rapidly evolving, acidified waters. In this pandemic, for example, there is an acute requirement to understand digital readiness and the well-being of students learning online and if it actually matters in attracting high school graduates even while instructional design may be improved and quality of educational media acceptable methods to reach learners remotely. They provided the foundational logic for crisis intervention in education, as well as foresight into hybrid and flexible models, impacting future of learning. Then institutions need to understand that constant research is the key in staying Agile and Resilient, even at times of uncertain future.

Research can also inform the development of teachers' competencies in digital environments. Action research, reflective practices, and participatory studies will enable this new pedagogy to be applied experimentally in the classroom then these experiences regularly reviewed. They help create a learning culture in organizations, giving professional educators opportunities to work with data, think about their practice, and contribute ideas to what is collectively known. Lastly, when teachers are engaged in the research process it highlights a democratic way to knowledge production and leads toward providing buy-in for digital initiatives which is essential for successful implementations [3]. This allows for an interdisciplinary view on digital education, combining views from the fields of computer science, psychology, sociology, and design. This work is very important for enriching the spectrum of inquiry and yielding comprehensive solutions to the great complexity in digital learning. Whether it is gaining insights into cognitive load in multimedia learning, the evaluation of user experiences in educational apps, or examining the ethical quandaries raised by artificial intelligence integrated with classrooms interdisciplinary research offers comprehensive and specific answers that are crucial toward facilitating a well-informed digital transformation.

With a simple conclusion and reminder that research is the lifeblood of a purposeful and long-lived digital education ecosystem. It empowers schools to make the most of digital technology, keeping their pedagogical core strong and holding on to equity, inclusion, and learner-centering at its heart. Institutional research capacity and widespread investments in it make digital education about more than just quality and relevance from the perspective of academic leadership, but a front-line vehicle to position institutions as innovative, accountable change agents that deliver results for their many different stakeholders [4]. In this time where technology is rapidly enabling education, research is no more a choice rather a must have.

2 Data-Driven Education: Linking Digital Pedagogy with Evidence-Based Practice

The fundamental pillars of modern digital pedagogy is data-driven education, which aims to use empirical evidence for planning decisions, to strengthen performance results among learners, and to contribute to continuous improvement in educational environments. In digital education, every learning platform generates a lot of data and we are at a point in time where institutions can tie back their teaching practices with clear measurable outcomes [5]. This merger of e-pedagogy with outcome-driven practice empowers educators and administrators to create dynamic, individualized models of learning driven by data rather than intuition.

The essence of data-driven education is the systematic process of collecting and analyzing data related to student performance, engagement, and behavior, and then using them. When used properly, this methodology ensures teachers can adapt course delivery to the unique requirements of students as well as identify 'at-risk students' in time, and intervene with the necessary action. For instance, real-time dashboards can show how many students participated in an activity, what percentage completed a quiz successfully or failed miserably, and the time they spent on tasks so that instructors can tweak the pace of instruction, mix learning styles up, or reach out with support. By providing these evidence-based practices, pedagogy comes into alignment with learning outcomes which in turn makes education targeted and meaningful.

Digital pedagogy morphs from the move traditional to embrace adaptive learning pathways which is owered by data analytics. These programs adjust in real time in response to student input and performance, providing students with the content and activities that specifically match their proficiency levels and learning modalities [6]. Data collected from these platforms does more than just underpin student-centered learning efforts, it also feeds institutional knowledge about what is most effective, for whom, and under what circumstances. The cycle of data use and inquiry reinforces a culture of inquiry in which teaching is ongoing tested and refined and reinventing schools within systems.

Data-driven education also enables decision-making at the policy and administrative levels. This will in turn allow institutions to make evidence-based decisions on curriculum redesign, technology investments, professional development opportunities, and resource allocation. A separate funding stream is available for large-scale impact assessments of digital learning interventions, ensuring that edtech innovations are not just taken up but also tested. Similarly, connecting evidence-based practice with the power of digital pedagogy via data-driven education converts teaching from a static interchangeable pattern of learning into dynamic, responsive, and learner-oriented approach [7]. It brings the instructional aspirations and the learning practices together providing institutions sharp tools through which to navigate digital education complexities with precision and foresight. With a foundation on principled data usage and open modalities, data-driven education can be an unparalleled quality driver as well as a new force for equity in the digital era.

3 Current Challenges in Institutional Research Capacity

Despite the increasing awareness that data-driven decision-making is an indispensable part of digital education, education institutions still suffer from a number of challenges when it comes to the development and upkeep of robust research capacities. The main obstacles are deficit in infrastructure and investment. In many developing regions, especially, educational institutions do not have access to research tools and platforms and due to the old-fashioned systems they are using for years as well as limited technological resources. In the absence of this foundational support, institutions will have difficulty in developing sustainable insights or mainstreaming evidence-based practices [8].

The critical problem is the scarcity of experienced personnel capable of performing research very well. Research approaches, data, and digital tools that are seen to be key for more robust institutional studies might not be familiar to faculties and administrative staff. The lack of opportunities in continuous professional development only makes the knowledge gap more extensive, which makes it harder for institutions to analyze data or extract meaning from findings. A divide typically exists between researchers, educators, and policymakers such that the outputs of research normally are not coordinated with institutional objectives. The other obstacle is cultural resistance to data use. Public institutions that view such research skeptically, or are afraid the data may be used punitively rather than to help a campus improve. The resistance to this can stymie innovation, and a collaborative effort is prevented from growing into an established culture of inquiry and accountability. Finally, against a background of fragmented data systems and the absence of standard frameworks, it is difficult to bring together or use broadly scattered data about learners across various departments or programs for institutional insights at scale [9].

Infrastructure and Resource Limitations

Shortages of infrastructure and resources serve as major barriers to improving institutional research capacity for most universities. With outdated computer systems, limited access to reliable high-speed internet, and antiquated data analytics tools, providers struggle mightily to collect and analyze educational data in a meaningful way [10]. The research labs, online repositories, and cloud-based resources are often non-existent or underutilized, particularly in poorly resourced or rural areas. In the absence of these building blocks, organizations won't be able to consolidate all their sources of information for big data processing or real-time analytics. The limited resources prohibit wider financial investments in promising or successful pilot research projects that can support long-term reform based on evidence. Overcoming them takes more near-term strategic prioritization of investments in digital infrastructure and technology-support systems, at every level [11].

Skills and Competency Gaps

Institutional research in digital education will largely hinge upon whether or not qualified staff who can work effectively within a labyrinthine data world are available. It is common for most of these institutions to lack personnel with adequate expertise from research design to data analytics and statistical tools to digital literacy. Educators and administrators are not often well-exposed to interdisciplinary research methodologies, or more technical aptitude on how to work with educational technologies and data platforms. It weakens the credibility, validity, and utility of research results.

Fragmented Data Systems

Most institutions have fragmented and disconnected data systems, which makes it difficult to bring information together across departments, units, or even campuses. Admissions databases, learning management systems, and tools for performance tracking tend to work in silos creating duplication and inconsistencies in the data passing through them. This lack of standardized protocols and interoperable systems only adds to the complexity. Institutions can solve these issues by developing a consolidated data management approach, using seamless digital platforms, and creating governance mechanisms for ensuring standardized, secure, and mission-relevant availability of the data across all levels of operations [12].

Cultural Resistance to Data Use

This cultural resistance to becoming data driven continues to be a key issue in education. Data use is often met with concerns about surveillance, punishment, or performance review and not seen as a part of development. This distrust can often be traced back to a lack of transparency, ungraceful communication, or past negative experiences with data abuse. This can discourage people from not only participating in research efforts, but also providing valuable criticism. The hierarchical nature of institutions and deeply entrenched bureaucratic systems often hinders open discourse regarding research findings and data, thereby limiting opportunities for innovation and progressive development. Convincing this will require the public data leadership to be transparent, use ethical qualitative age, and include key stakeholders in the design research process as well as communicating results to build trust and create a data skeptic organization climate [13].

4 Building Blocks of a Robust Research Foundation

A solid research base is a necessity for educational institutions hoping to fully leverage data-driven digital education. Creating such a foundation involves many different layers of structural, technological, human, and cultural aspects. In the first place, institutions need to institute a research framework with well-defined goals and scopes for how data should be gathered and processed [14]. That includes everything from prioritizing research around those objectives to ensuring that they are linked with a university's educational mission and digital priorities. Having a clear research agenda ensures that time and research efforts are focused in ways that bring value to the pedagogical and strategic investments being made. This framework is the access and valuing of tech layer capabilities. Secure digital platforms that are not codependent on the ERP must be of priority to ensure real-time data collection, learning analytics, and visualization. By combining platforms, cloud-based systems, integrated learning management systems (LMS), and reliable data warehousing solutions, scientists can obtain high-performance research resources for storing, retrieving structured/unstructured big data. Second, creating strong data governance is necessary for data quality, confidentiality, ethical use, and regulation. Having clear policies regarding data ownership, access, and sharing is a way to promote trust and accountability within the institution.

Any research ecosystem is built upon a well-funded support structure of personnel educational researchers, data analysts, its specialists, and faculty. Training in quantitative and qualitative methods, digital literacies, and approaches for ethical research requires continuous professional development for all to flourish [15]. These interdisciplinary research teams must combine in partnership academic, administrative, and technical skills to encourage creativity and allow for the inclusion of various perspectives that determine how data is understood and put into use. Building a culture of curiosity, cooperation, and openness is fundamental. Institutions need to foster critical self-reflection, experimentation, and data-informed decision-making throughout the system. Action research, learning communities, and feedback loops embed the routine of inquiry in daily practice, requiring that not just data be collected, but that it be acted upon as an improvement cycle for teaching and learning. The collaborative efforts with partners such as governmental agencies, industry, research consortiums, and other external bodies can offer richer resources, knowledge, and credibility to strengthen the institutionalized form of research.

It underscores that it takes time for a strong foundation of research to be developed. It needs sustained investment, strategic planning, and a collective vision if we are to draw on and get the most out of the collaboration for evidence-based progress. Institutions are constructing an ecosystem that supports robust research by prioritizing infrastructure, technology, human capital, ethical practices, and collaborative culture to help steer digital education onto the most innovative, effective, and inclusive path [16].

5 Institutional Strategies for Capacity Enhancement

The creating and sustaining data-informed digital education requires institutional research capacity developments that are deliberative, systemic, and durable. Such a comprehensive, multi-faceted approach requiring structural reform and integration of leadership commitment, stakeholder engagement as well as targeted investment across the institution is needed. This strategy is central to doing research that doesn't just deliver knowledge, but also helps drive a broader digital transformation for the institution. In other words, it means embedding goals of research inside the strategic plans of institutions and making sure that data-informed practices are not somewhere out there in good weather but rather at an all-time high overtaking quality assurance, shaping decision-making, and fueling innovation.

Leadership has a lot to do with pushing the capacity building agenda. Institutional leadership needs to create a culture that honors scholarship, inquiry, and improvement. This entails naming focused research units or committees which coordinates the research efforts, gives methodological direction, and tracks success in various departments. These structures need to be underpinned by policies that provide appropriate recognition, reward, and career progression for the involvement in research activities [17]. Institutional governance also needs to promote an interdisciplinary approach breaking old academic silos so that comprehensive/detailed research could be performed to seek answers for complex challenges in digital education.

Capacity development another key element is professional growth. Support institutions will be expected to facilitate continued education and mentoring in refinement of skills such as research methodologies, data analysis tools, digital pedagogy, and ethical research foundations. More emphasis should be placed on preparing faculty and administrative staff to not only do research but also interpret and apply findings in relevant ways. Introduction of workshops, advocacy training programs, i.e., research fellowships and collaboration with other research agencies could improve competencies or a conducive working environment to conduct research work. Investing in technology infrastructure strategically is also critical. Access to advanced learning management systems, research software, data analytics platforms, and secure data storage solutions must be available from the institutions. These tools need to be easy to use, interoperable, and able to produce actionable insights. Reliable sources of funding for private or public, internal and research grants are important for the long-term and large-scale projects that in majority are a part of research.

Some of the institutions also need to focus on data governance and ethic standards. Clearly defined data collection, privacy, consent, and use protocols must be in place to support trust among stakeholders and compliance with legal and regulatory frameworks. Clear communication of the goals and potential payoffs of research also helps to broaden the study's reach, as resistance to data use is diminished [18]. Collaboration with other educational institutions, policy bodies, edtech firms, and international organizations allows for exposure to best practices, benchmarking data, and a diverse set of perspectives. They also serve as mechanisms opportune in disseminating findings from research to inform broader education policy and practice. This should make clear that the answer is a very long way from being yet, but that better institutional strategies to improve our capacity must be systemic and anticipatory. This can be done by investing in the people, realms, governance, and partnerships to deliver an optimal quality and evidence base in digital education.

6 Monitoring, Evaluation, and Impact Assessment

The monitoring, evaluation, and impact assessment are key to both the establishment and sustainability of institutional research capacity, not least in an era of digital education fueled by data. Together, we have a complete and holistic view of how institutions can effectively document progress, evaluate outcomes, and determine impact associated with research efforts as well as digital strategies over time. In the absence of monitoring, evaluation, and impact assessment frameworks, educational institutions may implement reforms without an understanding of their true efficacy or value proposition whether this refers to long-term benefits and areas for growth [19]. Monitoring, evaluation, and impact assessment practices have thus become institutionalized on campus so that our digital education strategies are evidence-led, outcome-focused, and live-developed from in-practice feedback and impact.

Monitoring is the continual and systematic collection of data with respect to the implementation of digital education initiatives and research activities. This allows for monitoring projects to see they are being executed according to the plan, on time, and within the scope and objectives in mind by institutions as an example of monitoring, with a new digital learning platform, it would track usage metrics for user engagement, accesses per unit time, course completion rates, and incident reports [20]. It also sends timely signals for bottlenecks and allows learning which are quite essential to adjust their strategy or resource allocation so that those efforts are as per the institution standpoint.

Assessment is more than just monitoring and considers the utility, effectiveness, and sustainability of digital education initiatives. It takes on the big questions: Are the digital tools making quality teaching better? Is student engagement improving? Are outcomes being achieved by varied learner populations? Evaluations can take the form of being conducted during implementation to provide feedback and help with improvement or be done at the end to review and account for overall success. It involves both quantitative measures, for example, performance analytics, attendance rates, and assessment scores and qualitative feedback, for example, surveys, interviews, and focus groups which provide a more nuanced sense of the program's strengths and areas for improvement. Perhaps most importantly, evaluations lay bare the facts to stakeholders those who teach and learn, funders, and policymakers regarding what digital educational investments have actually produced.

The work of impact assessment falls within digital education ecosystem component, signifies a 'higher' level of maturity—measuring broader and more sustained outcomes following an intervention in digital education on institutional performance, learner success, equity, and innovation capacity. It explores whether such research-informed digital strategies are directly responsible for changes in practice, policy, or culture. An impact assessment would then ask whether the use of adaptive learning platforms was associated with benchmarks such as academic scores among disadvantaged student groups over the course of a few semesters [21]. It takes into account unanticipated positive and negative side effects, such as the digital divide, increased workload for educators, or heightened institutional visibility and competitiveness. Impact assessments are demanding a stringent methodology that frequently necessitates long-term or longitudinal studies to establish causality and control groups, which often need to be verified using multiple methods [22].

The cornerstone of any potent monitoring, evaluation, and impact assessment framework is the definition of objectives, indicators, and benchmarks from the very beginning of any such initiative by an institution. Performance metrics should be tied to the strategic priorities of the institution and regularly reviewed as well as updated with changes in context. Furthermore, institutions need to develop their internal capacity by training staff in MEIA tools, techniques, and ethical standards. To help streamline this process, technology provides data dashboards and other real-time analytics and visualization tools for monitoring and reporting efficiently.

So, involving stakeholder is as important in monitoring, evaluation, and impact assessment processes. The future adoption of MEIA outcomes will be facilitated when faculty, students, administrators, and external partners are part of the process to design and interpret them for promoting a shared sense of ownership and trust. Transparent dissemination of results via reports, seminars, or policy briefs makes globally sourced knowledge actionable. The study of monitoring and evaluation and impact analysis are vital to understand the worth, efficiency, and sustainability of institutional study in digital education [23]. They turn information into insights that can be acted on by institutions to learn from experience, to scale up what works, and to recalibrate what does not. So, integration of monitoring, evaluation, and impact assessment deep within institutional practice means that educational organizations build their malleability and support sustained quality enhancement, offering a more substantial grip on the fact that digital education work drives equitable learning change.

7 Conclusion and Recommendations

The building of institutional research capacity has never been more crucial for long-term data-driven change. Built on a background of evidence-based research consortium and integrated into institutional frameworks, the partnership will see digital strategies entrenched in research, aligned to meet learners where they are, and positioned to respond to emerging challenges. But turning that vision into reality means more than simply adopting technology, it requires a transformative approach to infrastructure development, capacity building, interdisciplinary collaboration, and a culture of inquiry and transparency. Challenges institutions face include lack of resources, siloed data ecosystems, human capital deficiencies, and data resistance. Institutions can only maximize the benefits of research-led practice for digital education when guided by synchronized and targeted efforts.

There are several major recommendations that can be made in this regard as the first was that before researchers might access sustained support, institutions needed to hardwire research into strategic plans and reserve space for basic robust funding to sustain their systems. This includes investing in learning management systems, data analytics platforms, and research software that enable efficient and ethical data handling. Secondly, the need for continuing professional development because training programs should be made available to faculty and staff that increase our knowledge in research methodologies, digital literacy, and ethical data practices. So, fostering interdisciplinary and cross-sectorial collaboration helps to improve the relevance and impact of research outputs. Collaborating with edtech companies, government organizations, and other academic institutions expands the sources of expertise and resources.

The institutions need to have robust data governance processes in place to maximize information accuracy, privacy, and consistency. Values and rules of ethics should be present throughout all steps of data collection, analysis, and application. Integrate monitoring, evaluation, and impact assessment mechanisms into all digital initiatives to gauge performance, inform telecoms decision-making, and ensure accountability. Trust is critical, and presenting the information to a critical objective audience in a clear and transparent manner drives trust even more so leading to advancement. The capacity in institutional research is not merely an enabling function but a strategic necessity in digital education. Through investment in these enhancements, educational providers can deliver more responsive, inclusive, and effective learning environments which have the potential not just to keep up with the changing nature of technology but influence its future utilization within education.

References

1. Gonugunta, K. C., & Leo, K. (2024). Role of data-driven decision making in enhancing higher education performance: A comprehensive analysis of analytics in institutional management. *International Journal of Acta Informatica, 3*(1), 149–159.
2. Botha, J., Webber, K., Williams, J., et al. (2024). Building capacity in institutional research: Collaboration and complementarity? *Tertiary Education and Management, 30*, 129–145. https://doi.org/10.1007/s11233-024-09139-0
3. Echtenbruck, M. M., Fühles-Ubach, S., Naujoks, B., & Kaliva, E. (2025). A data literacy competence model for higher education and research. *ar Xiv*. doi:https://doi.org/10.48550/arXiv.2504.15690
4. Fitsilis, P., Damasiotis, V., Dervenis, C., Kyriatzis, V., & Tsoutsa, P. (2024). Effective data stewardship in higher education: Skills, competences, and the emerging role of open data stewards. *arXiv*. https://doi.org/10.48550/arXiv.2410.20361
5. Sajja, R., Sermet, Y., Cwiertny, D., & Demir, I. (2023). Integrating AI and learning analytics for data-driven pedagogical decisions and personalized interventions in education. *arXiv*. https://doi.org/10.48550/arXiv.2312.09548
6. Komljenovic, J., et al. (2024). Turning universities into data-driven organisations: Seven dimensions of change. *Higher Education*. https://doi.org/10.1007/s10734-024-01277-z

7. Henderson, L., Nuttall, J., Wood, M., & Martin, J. (2024). Educational leadership in early childhood edu cation: Participant vulnerability and a rule of care. *Journal of Early Childhood Research, 22*(2), 297–312. https://doi.org/10.1177/1476718X231210641
8. King, R., Weber, Y., & Rienties, B. (2024). Toward a data-informed framework for the assessment of digital readiness of higher education institutions. *International Journal of Educational Technology in Higher Education.* https://doi.org/10.1186/s41239-024-00491-0
9. Ferguson, R., et al. (2024). A competence framework for educators to boost open educational practices in higher education. *Open Learning: The Journal of Open, Distance and E-Learning, 39*(2), 1–20. https://doi.org/10.1080/02680513.2024.2310538
10. Scott, H., & Smith, M. (2024). Innovation from necessity: Digital technologies, teacher development and reciprocity with organisational innovation. *Open Learning, 39*(2), 1–18. https://doi.org/10.1080/02680513.2024.2307627
11. Rafique, R. (2024). Supporting teachers through online professional development: A qualitative study in Bangladesh. *Open Learning, 39*(2), 1–10. https://doi.org/10.1080/02680513.2024.2316629
12. Mittelmeier, J., Long, D., Cin, F. M., et al. (2024). Learning design in diverse institutional and cultural contexts: Lessons from Africa. *Open Learning, 39*(2), 250–266. https://doi.org/10.1080/02680513.2024.2307627
13. Nascimbeni, F., Burgos, D., Brunton, J., & Ehlers, U.-D. (2024). A competence framework for educators to foster open educational practices in HE. *Open Learning, 39*(2), 1–20. https://doi.org/10.1080/02680513.2024.2310538
14. Smith, M. D. (2023). *The abundant university: Remaking higher education for a digital world.* MIT Press.
15. Hossain, D. (2024). Adapting to the digital age: An evaluation of online learning strategies in public health and social care education. *Education Research International*, 5079882. https://doi.org/10.1155/2024/5079882
16. Linklater, H. (2024). Skills required of academics to use digital technologies in open distance learning institutions. *Innovative Higher Education, 50*, 843–866. https://doi.org/10.1007/s10755-024-09758-w
17. Kelder, JA., Crawford, J., Al Naabi, I. et al. Enhancing digital productivity and capability in higher education through authentic leader behaviors: A cross-cultural structural equation model. *Educ Inf Technol 30*, 17751–17767 (2025). https://doi.org/10.1007/s10639-025-13422-x

18. OECD. (2023). *Digital education outlook 2023: Multi-stakeholder collaboration and co-creation: Responsible application of AI in education*. OECD Publishing.
19. Cui, Z., & Hamid, A. H. A. (2025). The impact of digital leadership in enhancing teaching capacity through datadriven strategies among faculty in education programs in China. *Eurasian Journal of Educational Research (EJER), 115*, 17–37.
20. Jin, R., Peng, Y., Wang, Z., Wang, J., Tang, J., & Zhang, M. (2025). Data-driven educational decision-making: How to enhance educational quality and management efficiency. *Journal of Higher Education Research, 5*(6), 550.
21. Yongli, G., Qi, D., & Zhipeng, C. (2024). Leveraging the synergy of ipv6, generative AI, and web engineering to create a big data-driven education platform. *Journal of Web Engineering, 23*(2), 197–226.
22. Li, G., & Liu, J. (2024). Improving physical education through innovative multimedia learning platform and data-driven instruction. *Soft Computing, 28*(2), 1567–1584.
23. Baidya, R., Lal, R., & Rena, R. (2024). Digital competency assessment and data-driven performance management for start-ups. In A. Khang, R. Gujrati, H. Uygun, R. K. Tailor, & S. Gaur (Eds.), *Data-driven modelling and predictive analytics in business and finance* (pp. 203–234). Auerbach Publications. https://doi.org/10.1201/9781003504327-10

CHAPTER 18

Utilizing Public Platforms to Support Marginalized Learners in Digital Education Arena for Sustainable and Secured Future

Kozma Dorottya Edina, Akshay Bhargava, and Rakhi Singh Chouhan

Abstract Leveraging public spaces to benefit underprivileged learners in changing digital education landscape is part of a key way to improve equity, resilience, and trust within learning ecosystems. Open educational resources (OERs), government-supported e-learning portals, and

K. D. Edina
University of Pannonia, Veszprém, Hungary
e-mail: kozma.dorottya.edina@gtk.uni-pannon.hu

A. Bhargava (✉) · R. S. Chouhan
Department of Law, Prestige Institute of Management and Research, Gwalior, India
e-mail: akshaybhargava1992@gmail.com

R. S. Chouhan
e-mail: rakhisingh.chouhan@prestigegwl.org

P. K. Dutta et al. (eds.), *Digital Education for a Sustainable Future*, Sustainable Development Goals Series,
https://doi.org/10.1007/978-3-032-15433-0_18

community-based digital hubs are public platforms, which facilitate egalitarian availability of quality education for learners from diverse backgrounds such as around socio-economic status. Strengthening cybersecurity through the development of cyber-resilient practices encourages secure engagement and protects individual data, facilitating confidence in digital services. Sustainable models focus on developing capacity, bundling digital literacy training, and creating local content in such a way that the learners are not just consumer of knowledge but become partners in the knowledge economy. Using public platforms strengthens educational equity, gives communities power, and reinforces global sustainable development goals like SDG 4 (Quality Education) and SDG 10 (Reduced Inequalities). A collaborative multi-stakeholder effort including governments, NGOs, technology providers, and local communities around this vision can transform public platforms into tools that build social resilience and increase economic opportunities, providing a bridge to a world in which all learners no matter who or where they are able to learn, adapt, and succeed safely and sustainably in the digital age.

Keywords Public platforms · Marginalized learners · Digital education · Sustainability · Educational equity

1 Introduction

Incorporating public platforms within digital education systems represents a unique opportunity to mitigate the educational divide of underprivileged learners and lead an inclusive, resilient, and safe learning environment. Public platforms, over open-access digital libraries; community-driven e-learning portals, government-run (Massive Open Online Courses or MOOCs); and non-profit educational repositories democratize access to high-quality educational resources which was otherwise your run-of-the-mill elite institution privilege. The marginalized learners are deprived of livelihood in the digital education space due to systemic barriers like inadequate infrastructural support, minimal digital literacy, and absence of local content. Public platforms deliver a reset by providing free or low-cost materials, multi-lingual content, and flexible delivery options for diverse interests, with assistive technologies as needed to accommodate disabilities. What makes the offers of this type more sustainable is that they are massifiable and incorporate feasible educational models for continuous, scalable, and reduced environmental impact which need fewer physical artifacts to provide education, reduce costs, and blur constraints in distance.

This also includes the need for safe and secure digital space is crucial, through which vulnerable learners can be well-protected with regard to cybersecurity, disinformation, or breaches of privacy [1]. This is where Governments, NGOs, and tech companies must combine to make sure that cyber-security requirements are strong enough to avoid incursion of willy-nilly viewpoints and at the same time platforms will have ETHICAL AI-driven moderator tools as well as verified repositories for academics. The public platforms should connect with Learning Management Systems (LMS) and Student Information Systems (SIS) as well in order to track learner progress, build personalized pathways, and make targeted interventions for underperforming learners. It should be available offline, optimized for low-bandwidth connection, and include AI-based translation and speech-to-text tools to cater to linguistic and literacy impairments.

For the marginalized learners, public platforms are also gateways to skill development, vocational training, and career readiness programs that impact positively to targeted SDGs, e.g., 4 (Quality Education) and 10 (Reduced Inequalities). Multi-stakeholder partnerships between policymakers, educators, technologists, and community representatives to co-create polices in favor of inclusivity, equity, and learner safety should be engaged on how these platforms are governed if we are to ensure the future is secured. Community engagement is also represented in the success of such initiatives building local champions who can support learners through using digital tools, providing peer learning, and integrating culturally relevant content.

Significance of Digital Inclusion for Marginalized Learners

The strategies such as data-driven analytics embedded in public platforms that tell policymakers about trends of learners, their engagement levels, and efficacy of content—to enable them to take reforms based on evidence. Sustainable funding models may involve public-private partnerships, crowd funding, and government subsidies to keep access to these vital resources affordable regardless of socio-economic background. While we continue to wrestle with the many significant issues facing America, from disparities in educational attainment and civic understanding to generational poverty and disenfranchisement, public platforms if architected properly at inception can be just the impetus that is needed: channels for lifelong learning thus helping marginalized learners succeed in the digital economy, fully participate in civil society, and finally break entrenched cycles of poverty and exclusion. Through open-access, secure, and inclusive technologies, societies can achieve a reimagined educational environment in which every learner regardless of socioeconomic background, geographic location, or physical ability will have access to the tools with which they can learn and the knowledge and self-assurance to prosper in an innovative and compliant future [2].

2 Marginalization in Education: Causes of Educational Exclusion in the Digital Era

Marginalization in education is a condition where certain groups of learners are systematically denied access to appropriate and meaningful learning opportunities, resources, and outcomes by any or all of the economic, social, cultural, geographical, and political. This phenomenon is particularly relevant for economic disadvantage, ethnic and linguistic minorities, rural and remote areas, refugees, persons with disabilities as well as the gendered impact which also interact with any one of the causes listed. Similarly, the learners who most need to reach are often up against multiple and intersecting barriers: poor infrastructure, no broadband connectivity, untrained teachers, inaccessible digital content, or lack of relevant policy that addresses their unique context.

Marginalization incapacitates children from accessing education now but also threatens to bequeath unfavorable financial circumstances, with high rates of unemployment and social inequality meaning that national and global developmental goals including the Sustainable Development Goals (SDGs), especially SDG 4 on quality education [3]. In the digital age, this divide has widened to technology where access to digital devices, affordable internet, and skills in digital literacy is a pre-requisite for engagement with contemporary education systems. In the absence of interventions targeted at these groups, both the digital divide and social exclusion are put at risk of becoming more entrenched. Providing marginalization homely environment, multi-dimensional strategies from pedagogies to be inclusive, fair resource allotment, and society participation engage in culturally relevant pedagogy. It is also calling for collective action between governments, civil society, technology providers, and international organizations to ensure that digital transformation in education leads to the inclusion of all learners a call against leaving anyone behind. The urgent call also challenges stakeholders to elevate marginalized communities and contributes to broader resilience, equity, and innovation in society.

The educational exclusion in the digital age is a multi-dimensional issue comprised of technological, socio-economic, and systemic factors. Certainly, the digital divide is one: Inequities that take place when some students lack access to technology and internet services prevent them from entering digital learning spaces [4]. Learners from rural, remote, and underserved communities do not have the same internet options as learners in urban and affluent regions, which lead to widespread disparities in online education access. Adding to this is economic inequality, where marginalized families may deploy resources for their hardline welfare as opposed to adopting technology in education. It also lacks sufficient digital literacy since it is not used optimally by both students as well as educators, reducing the benefits of available technologies.

The language barriers can also disenfranchise those who do not have mastery of a region's dominant language of instruction as in the case of learners in linguistically rich areas. But the unique requirements of marginalized groups, like learners with disabilities, refugees, or indigenous populations, are all too often eluded by systemic biases and policy vacuums in educational planning. There is similar gender inequality, such that cultural norms and societal expectations may continue to limit girls from access to the digital space. These factors place the most marginalized learners in some of the poorest countries at a significant disadvantage compared to their more affluent counterparts globally, inadvertently exacerbating the global equity gap in education which has been amplified by the digital era [5].

3 Public Platforms as Catalysts for Digital Inclusion

Public platforms as enabler: Public platforms set the stage for digital inclusion, acting as a metronome of change in promoting inclusivity by bridging the chasm among communities at margins and their right to learn, access resources and opportunities for progress entailment in the digital age [6]. Through their widespread availability and ease of access, they widen the possibilities to those who are otherwise bound by socio-economic, geographical, or infrastructural restrictions. Public digital platforms like a national e-learning portal, an open government data repository, or a digital library can provide educational content, skilling services, and portrait essential public services to citizens. They are democratizing forces, reducing digital divide between the privileged and lesser sections of society. For instance, initiatives like the DIKSHA platform in India or the eCitizen service in Kenya have done more to deploy learning resources and government services at scale than any boot camp ever could. These platforms typically include multi-lingual content, and have various learning tools within them assistive technologies for particular target user groups such as persons with disabilities. In addition, public channels can help to train in digital literacy through templates and interactive tools that allow users to improve their skills for a more efficient activity within the digital economy [7].

The interactive features include community building and knowledge sharing, so users can go from consumers of digital content to participants in a collaborative environment. Above all, this kind of platforms can help the government to implement and monitor policies using valid feedback mechanism which in turn brings transparency, accountability, and responsiveness in governance. Nevertheless, the sustainability of these public platforms is inseparably linked to a strong underpinning infrastructure and inclusive policy landscapes along with partnerships with civil society, academia, and private sector stakeholders. Equally important is the need to keep them free from over-monetization and misuse of data, so as to foster trust and preserve users' privacy [8]. So, while all that technology is pretty amazing to well-constructed open public platforms are not just technologies they are change agents, serving to broaden digital inclusion, reduce the digital divide, enhance social equity, and enfranchise everyone to be a full member of the information society. They help us build communities that are more durable, informed, and digitally literate; people who ban thrive in the twenty-first-century knowledge economy by emphasize accessibility, cultural relevance, and user empowerment.

Public Digital Education Platforms in Brief

Public digital education platforms are online systems established by government and community projects with the purpose of offering access to diverse educational resources across all sectors of society, most especially target populations. They provide a diverse array of educational resources, courses, and interactive tools over the internet which is generally integrated with mobile applications. They emphasize enabling free/low-cost access, open educational resources (OER), multilingual content, and inclusive pedagogy. Tech-based democratizers like Medixa have been playing a crucial role here to bridge the gap in education through mass-scale learning with technology and ensuring transparency, scalability, content, and delivery [9].

Accessibility and Access to Services

Affordability mitigates cost barriers by offering free core learning materials, zero-rated internet data plans, and low-data modes. Availability ensures educational content stays current, culturally adapted to local curricula, and available 24/7. These components combine to size the platforms and, in effect, give marginalized learners a new path to education long after educational costs have grown while also helping foster sustainable, inclusive learning ecosystems.

4 Technological Tools and Frameworks for Marginalized Learning Support

With the help of technological tools and frameworks, we can bridge this gap in education, by bringing scalable, adaptive, and inclusive learning solutions to marginalized learners. This is done through Learning Management Systems (LMSs) that offer a unique learning experience remotely, like Moodle and Google Classroom or platforms such as Canvas that facilitate better access to content organization, real-time collaboration, including abilities for teachers to track progress [10]. Much of this is immensely helped by AI-powered systems that are becoming increasingly embedded with and recommending the right learning paths, resources, and predicting at-risk learners for targeted interventions using analytics. Free, multilingual, and adaptable frameworks for Open Educational Resources (OER) directly address inclusivity, reduce financial barriers, and are supportive of culturally responsive pedagogy. M-learning platforms use smartphones to deliver chunked-down, micro-learning modules, video lectures, and gamified assessments suited for low-resource setting or rural settings.

At the policy and governance level, digial public infrastructure frameworks, such as India's DIKSHA Portal and UNSECO Global Skills

Academy, leverage centralized libraries, teacher-training modules, and analytics dashboards to align national education policies with global sustainable development goals under SDG 4 (Quality Education). In addition, cloud computing solutions support secure storage, sharing, and real-time collaboration across geographies which enables global educators to contribute to localized content repositories. If credentialing frameworks are based on a blockchain as employability, certification, and lifelong learning recognition becomes more inclusive surrounding for those that were left behind.

AI-driven tutoring bots and Immersive VR classrooms are some of the modern EdTech innovations redefining the way engagement is created by enabling simulations of problems in real-world environments abstracted out. Frameworks such as Universal Design for Learning (UDL) support the design of flexible curricula to meet diverse learning needs through digital pedagogy. This not only protects marginalized learners from potential exploitation or discrimination, but also integrates data protection frameworks (GDPR) and ethical AI governance [11]. It is not only about in fashion content dispensing but a triggering factor which demarcates and builds ecosystems exhibiting inclusivity on one hand and adeptness as well as cultural relevance on the other. By virtue of aligning fresh design and design metaphors with principles of affordability, accessibility, and sustainability there is a good chance that for the first time ever these digital infrastructures can actually be designed to support some marginalized learners to participate effectively in the rapidly evolving global knowledge economy.

Mobile Learning Applications

In the digital age when access to traditional educational resources is still nowhere near equal, mobile learning applications have risen as tools that could potentially transform the way marginalized learners are able to bridge their own educational gaps. These apps provide learning resources in interactive, multimedia-rich formats available anytime and anywhere by using the exclusive nature of smartphones and affordable data plan availability. Mobile app services are catering to a vast range of learners from metro literate to other low level learners with different local cultural, linguistic, and socio-economic barriers through localized content with multiple language options and adaptive learning features [12].

These apps are especially important in low-connectivity regions as their offline functionality facilitates uninterrupted learning without reliance on continuous internet service. Likewise, gamified learning modules and micro-learning approaches drive better engagement and retention and built-in assessment tools empower educators and policymakers to track progress through real-time data on where young people struggle in their learning. A more recent development is a collaboration between the government, NGOs, and private technology companies to integrate such apps into national educational strategies for sustainable development. Mobile learning apps are not merely technological tools of cognitive knowledge in marginalized communities, but elastic entry points to learning-threaded vocational skills, digital literacy, and social empowerment for the fact that they further remove barriers to bridge the digital divide as well as drive inclusive, lifelong learning pathways [13].

AI-Enabled Assistive Technologies

These are just some of the diverse learning needs that can only be competently addressed by AI through assistive tech tools that the world over have started using to aid marginalized learners who may have a disability, struggle with language barriers, or simply lack any significant prior educational exposure. Using artificial intelligence, these technologies enable adaptive learning experiences that adjust to the way each learner progresses, their learning style, and challenges. They include artificial intelligence that drives text-to-speech and speech-to-text converters, real-time translation software, and intelligent tutoring systems which can make it possible for learners to access quality education without traditional walls that prevent them from participating fully [14].

AI-powered screen readers, captioning tools, and predictive text support provide students with visual, auditory, or cognitive challenges with equitable access to educational content. In addition, the use of AI algorithms allows models to evaluate learner behavior and performance data in order to generate targeted suggestions. These suggestions can help educators design more personalized interventions and conduct more effective evaluations. Given that cloud-based integration means these tools can be accessible across any device, they make it practical even in low-resource environments. AI-enabled assistive technologies when integrated onto the very axles of digital learning ecosystems, therefore, not only drive marginalized learners toward academic success but help them gain confidence, autonomy, and social acceptance as well [15]. When supported with policy frameworks and teacher training, these innovations can contribute to creating a sustainable, safe, and inclusive educational environment that is in line with the global equity and quality education goals.

5 Ensuring Sustainability in Digital Education

Sustainable digital education is an approach that is need to be focused by ensuring development of systems, policies, and practices that are consistent over time in order to give a stable foundation or resilient support for playing their day-to-day routine roles, making them relevant and accessible to all learners especially the marginalized group. Sustainability does not pertain specifically to the keeping of digital tools but also implies continued environmental stewardship that establishes an environment [16]. Sustainable digital education must first combine eco-friendly technologies. This includes using cloud computing, energy-efficient servers, and recycling e-waste to minimize environmental footprints and linking education with a larger sustainability mission, like the UN Sustainable Development Goals (SDGs). Second, financial sustainability is essential. Digital education is often introduced through pilot projects that wither when initial funding runs out; therefore, longer-term financing models, including public-private partnerships (PPPs), service subscriptions offered at subsidized rates to schools and disadvantaged learners, or community-based financial mechanisms are important to avoid breaking the flow of access [17].

With enabling communities to actively engage within the digital learning ecosystem ensuring that local educators are trained, the curricula is adapted to the local context and that it is delivered in a language and an environment that includes cultural elements will help avoid digital alienation. Sustainable technology requires infrastructure to be updated regularly, compatibility with other systems and scalability of the platforms. Policy-level sustainability is equally critical. This needs robust regulations from governments and educational bodies on data protection, open educational resources (OER), unrestricted access to online platforms. Besides this, substantial faculty development in education on digital literacy, adaptive pedagogy, and tech assimilation ensures that teachers are well-prepared to handle the ever-changing academic environment as it unfolds. Sustainability in digital education depends on a holistic view that combines economic sustainability with the adaptability of technology, environmental sustainability, and social inclusion. Digital education can still be a positive force for lifelong and equitable learning throughout the twenty-first century by supporting resilient systems and strong communities [18].

6 Digital Literacy for Safe Online Learning

It includes not just the skills to use technology, but a range of abilities that allow learners to navigate their digital world with confidence and critical thought and a strong dose of ethical responsibility. Digital literacy for safe online learning is, at heart, the ability to evaluate digital content. College-bound students must be prepared to sort reliable from unreliable sources, a vital component in their college research, and as an immune system against the dissemination of falsehoods. This includes recognizing the subtleties of media bias, what certain websites are attempting to do with a piece of information and checking facts against other sources. The protection of personal information would be a second and equally important digital literacy component. However, given the proliferation of online platforms for learning, students also need to excel in securing their privacy settings, setting robust passwords in place, and recognizing the dangers associated with sharing sensitive information. They should be informed about phishing scams and dangerous software, so that they can watch out for potentially harmful links and attachments in emails. In addition to security, digital literacy for online learning includes the awareness of good digital citizenship and ethical behavior.

This means following good netiquette, being respectful in online conversations and knowing the hurtful impact of cyber-bullying. It pertains to understanding issues related to copyright and respect for intellectual property, being mindful of the law in order not to plagiarize when consuming information from digital sources. The embedding of digital literacy in the curriculum is to limit students from being mere receivers of information and sending them on as empowered, efficient, and responsible members of a global digital society so they can study, interact, and develop online but yet not fretting about dangers related to internet usage. It is critical that the promotion of these skills to be in place so that the potential of online education is harnessed productively and securely for every learner [19].

7 Global Collaboration and Policy Alignment: Knowledge Sharing and Cross-Border Learning with Sustainable Development Goals (SDGs) Alignment

For those at the margins to be included in an equitable and sustainable digital education ecosystem, international cooperation and policy harmonization are essential. In a field as dynamic and rapidly changing as education, knowledge exchange is crucial for sharing best practices, latest technologies, and teaching strategies that fit various contextual needs of different regions. This is no longer an aspirational goal, but one that is closely linked to the Sustainable Development Goals; especially SDG 4 (Quality Education) which empowers inclusive and equitable education for all [20].

Open educational resources (OERs), multilingual digital libraries, globally recognized competency frameworks, and public platforms (with international cooperation) are purpose-driven tools that can effectively take care of such disparities. Policy harmonization can help governments as well as institutions, on the academic side make sure platforms are interoperable, digital credentials standardized, and that skills recognition happens across jurisdictions, all key for students in central Africa.

Cross-border learning efforts motivate resource pooling that stretches from open-source technological tools to shared curriculum frameworks, thus allowing a stronger focus on end goals without duplication of effort and decreased costs of implementation. There is also the need for collaboration with international agencies, non-governmental organizations (NGOs), and technology providers to develop focused interventions including AI-driven adaptive learning systems, inclusive user interfaces to make sure learners with disabilities, rural learners, and linguistic minorities have equitable access.

The policy alignment helps establish consistent governance mechanisms that unify cybersecurity and data privacy regulations and ethical principles of AI, which is important for maintaining trust in digital education systems. It can build an alliance spirit to bring in and work on global digital divide narrowing action (SDGs Goal 17 partnerships for the goals). This cooperation also builds education system resilience to online educational disruption by crises like pandemics, natural disasters, or violence, and for the rapid adoption of successful practices that are proven elsewhere [21]. With embedding the principles of sustainability, cultural inclusivity, and fairness into its design by aligning policies with SDGs, digital education goes beyond attending to immediate access issues.

This is a social learning model leading to a worldwide tutoring network where knowledge can be sought and gained irrespective of your place; learners are breaking the barriers of geography and education ultimately becomes an instrument for social upliftment. By harnessing a coordinated global partnership approach and enabling policy coherence, the vision of sustainable, secure, and universally available digital education can become more than an ambition it can be a reality with no one left behind.

8 Monitoring and Evaluation Framework in Digital Education

The well-designed monitoring and evaluation (M&E) at every level are critical to high-quality, inclusive, and sustainable learning interventions in digital education, especially for the marginalized learner. The M&E frameworks offer systematic facilitation of the volume of progress, measurement of impact, and improvement areas which clubs in data-driven decision-making [22]. These frameworks combine factors both quantitative and qualitative, e.g., metrics of learner engagement, accessibility, technology adoption, and academic achievement results within the context of digital educational resources. GHAs also provide special consideration by assessing certain indicators that measure inclusivity, equity of access, and narrowing the digital divide for marginalized groups. Real-time monitoring through such advanced analytics and connected learning management systems (LMS) will enable educators, policymakers, and all stakeholders to quickly see any connectivity issues, or device availability problems, content relevance, or learner motivation before it escalates. The evaluation process is iterative and incorporates feedbacks from learners, educators, and communities to keep the solution grounded in culture and context.

This will involve M&E frameworks aligned with international best practices as well as the SDGs, particularly SDG 4 (Quality Education) and SDG 10 (Reduced Inequalities), hence ensuring outcomes contribute to global education equity objectives. With AI-powered dashboards, mobile survey platforms are few examples of these kinds of tools that can improve transparency and accountability for verifiable evidence of progress toward attaining a goal. In addition, the M&E process must be iterative—integrating planning, implementation review, and adaptive practice to ensure that solutions keep pace with technology developments and learner needs. In the end, a robust M&E mechanism is able to change digital education from a one-way content delivery to adaptive service for making sure that marginalized learners not only get access but also an outcome in terms of learning which is both meaningful and sustainable [23].

9 Conclusion

Digital education is a horizon that grants new prospects to democratize learning but will maintain exclusive divides in access, ability, and inclusion unless strategic actions are taken. Efforts like public platforms, technology innovations, and policy frameworks have the potential to convert education into a universally accessible resource but it needs to remain data-driven with continuous monitoring, evaluation, and adaptation. A sustainable and secure future in digital education will only be achieved through the coordinated efforts of governments and businesses, universities, schools, and teachers to address infrastructure gaps, promote digital literacy and affordability. By anchoring in sustainability principles and the SDGs, stakeholders can begin to weave together more renewable and forward-looking learning ecologies. A digital transformation of education should not simply address existing gaps, however, the future needs us to consider how technology will shape and be shaped by significant new forms of inequality so that no learner regardless of where they live or their socio-economic status or ability is left behind in the new global knowledge economy.

References

1. Siddiqi, M. M. (2024). Future of digital education: Inclusive, immersive, equitable. *MediaSpace: DME Media Journal of Communication*, *5*(01), 8–24.
2. Iyanda, J., & Raja, D. (2025). The role of online learning platforms in transforming African higher education. *Quality in African Higher Education: Development Perspectives from Selected Regions*, *20*, 249.
3. Bailey, L. E., & Nyabola, N. (2021, June). Digital equity as an enabling platform for equality and inclusion. *Pathfinders for Peaceful, Just, and Inclusive Societies/NYU Center on International Cooperation*. https://cic.nyu.edu/resources/digital-equityas-an-enabling-platform-for-equality-and-inclusion
4. Ojo, O. A., & Olugbade, D. (2025). Promoting inclusive education in developing countries: Innovations and technological frontiers. In B. I.

Edwards, B. L. Tanko, M. Klufallah, H. Abuhassna, & C. C. Chinedu (Eds.), *Reimagining transformative educational spaces: Technological synergy for future education* (pp. 317–331). Springer Nature Singapore. https://doi.org/10.1007/978-981-97-8752-4_17

5. D'Agustino, S. (2024). Social reproduction and equity challenges in learning management systems (LMS) within online education. In J. Keengwe & G. Onchwari (Eds.), *Digital literacy at the intersection of equity, inclusion, and technology* (pp. 20–48). IGI Global. https://doi.org/10.4018/979-8-3693-0619-0.ch002
6. Almén, L., & Bagga-Gupta, S. (2023). Digital tools and social-ecological sustainability: Going beyond mainstream ways of understanding the roles of tools in contemporary eduscapes. *Frontiers in Education, 8*, Article 1147402. Frontiers Media SA. https://doi.org/10.3389/feduc.2023.1147402
7. Taylor, C., Dewsbury, B., & Brame, C. J. (2022). Technology, equity, and inclusion in the virtual education space. In D. A. Thompson, A. M. O'Sullivan, & J. E. Lewis (Eds.), *Technologies in biomedical and life sciences education: Approaches and evidence of efficacy for learning* (pp. 35–60). Springer International Publishing. https://doi.org/10.1007/978-3-030-79036-8_3
8. Herrera, L. J. P., & Young, C. (2025). From shelter to server: Conceptualizing the intersection of housing insecurity, digital accessibility, and language teaching and learning. *Colombian Applied Linguistics Journal, 27*(1), 126–140.
9. Sidana, N., Singh, M., Bidhuri, Y., & Febriana, P. (2025). Education 4.0: E-learning as an economics catalyst in the digital age. In P. K. Paul, A. Bhuimali, & M. Dey (Eds.), *Immersive technology for the gig economy: Transformative business practices* (pp. 101–126). IGI Global Scientific Publishing. https://doi.org/10.4018/979-8-3693-1234-7.ch005
10. Ramkissoon, L. (2024). AI: Powering sustainable innovation in higher ed. In C. Fitzgerald & M. Cunningham (Eds.), *The evolution of artificial intelligence in higher education* (pp. 203–229). Emerald Publishing Limited. https://doi.org/10.1108/978-1-83753-640-220241012
11. Bhatia, K. V., Arora, P., & Gupta, S. (2024). *Edtech platforms from below: A family ethnography of marginalized communities and their digital learning post-pandemic* (pp. 1–15). Learning, Media and Technology.
12. Dobson, S., Svoen, B., Agrusti, G., & Hardy, P. (2024). *Learning inclusion in a digital age: Belonging and finding a voice with the disadvantaged* (p. 184). Springer Nature.
13. Huszka, B., Stark, A., & Aini, I. (2024). Linguistic sustainability: Challenges and strategies of preserving minority and indigenous languages—The case of Indonesia. Preservation, 7(6), 112–129. MDPI. https://doi.org/10.3390/preservation7060012

14. Aochamub, A., & Jacques, P. H. (2025). Building trust and attracting investment: A teaching case on digital diplomacy in Namibia's green industrialization strategy. *Journal of Behavioral and Applied Management, 25*(2), 62–74.
15. Lee, H., Kang, D. Y., Kim, M. J., & Martin, S. N. (2023). Navigating into the future of science museum education: Focus on educators' adaptation during COVID-19. *Cultural Studies of Science Education, 18*(3), 647–667.
16. Pérez-Escolar, M., & Canet, F. (2023). Research on vulnerable people and digital inclusion: Toward a consolidated taxonomical framework. *Universal Access in the Information Society, 22*(3), 1059–1072.
17. Swanepoel, J. A. (2024). Cohesive online education model using emergent technologies to improve accessibility and impact. *Education Sciences, 14*(5), 522.
18. Hamdan, M., & Anshari, M. (2024). *Green education to promote green technological skills Asfand Yar Universiti Brunei Darussalam, Brunei* (p. 72). Harnessing Green and Circular Skills for Digital Transformation.
19. Masih, M., Suleman, S., Khan, M. H., Sahito, Z., & Shahid, S. (2025). The future classroom: Integrating AI and social media for adaptive learning. *Inverge Journal of Social Sciences, 4*(3), 98–111.
20. Huszka, B., Stark, A., & Aini, I. (2024). Linguistic sustainability: Challenges and strategies of preserving minority and indigenous languages—*The case of Indonesia. Preservation, 7*(6), 112–129. MDPI. https://doi.org/10.3390/preservation7060012
21. Njau, G. W., Ndiga, B., & Kitonga, D. M. (2025). Exploring how students' online activism contributes to leaders' accountability by promoting transparency in resource management in selected public Universities in Nairobi, Kenya. *Journal of African Interdisciplinary Studies, 9*(7), 176–205.
22. Sharma, R. S., Mokhtar, I. A., Ghista, D. N., Nazir, A., & Khan, S. Z. (2023). Digital literacies as policy catalysts of social innovation and socioeconomic transformation: Interpretive analysis from Singapore and the UAE. *Sustainable Social Development, 1*(1), 45–63. Open Access Publishing House. https://doi.org/10.54517/ssd.v1i1.1861
23. Zubeyr, E., Kunasegaran, M., & Kunjiapu, S. (2024). Embracing youth volunteerism through digital literacy for a sustainable future. *International Journal of Academic Research in Business and Social Sciences, 4*, 1394–1403.

CHAPTER 19

Climate-Resilient Education Infrastructure: Adapting Education Infrastructure to Climate Risk and Disruption

Masanori Fukui, Ashok Kumar Sharma, and Amit Kumar

Abstract Climate-resilient education infrastructure is needed to ensure continuity of learning in the face of growing climate risks and disruptions, including floods, heatwaves, storms, and other extreme weather events. The school also has Disaster Risk Reduction, Sustainable Design, and Adaptive Planning as part of its living classroom. Green building

M. Fukui
Faculty of Software and Information Science, Iwate Prefectural University, Takizawa, Japan
e-mail: fukui_m@iwate-pu.ac.jp

A. K. Sharma (✉)
Faculty of Law, Meerut College, Meerut, India
e-mail: aksharmallm@gmail.com

A. Kumar
Dewan Law College, Meerut, India

P. K. Dutta et al. (eds.), *Digital Education for a Sustainable Future*, Sustainable Development Goals Series,
https://doi.org/10.1007/978-3-032-15433-0_19

materials, renewable energy systems, and water management solutions can help in reducing environmental losses by schools and improve their resilience in the long run. By onboarding early-warning systems, flexible learning spaces, and digital infrastructure, we guarantee that education continues to be available if emergencies are looming. A key element to strengthening resilience within an education system is that cooperation and support for action at the community level are not only reflected in policies but also safeguarded and participation of all included. Connecting it all to the SDGs (especially with objective 4 on quality education, having regard to objective 11 on sustainable cities and communities and empowered a connected society according to 13) ensures that this comprehensive environmental and educational approach is well-founded. Investment in climate-resilient education infrastructure protects the lives of students and staff but also secures long-term societal resilience, ensuring that education systems are robust enough to withstand, recover from, and adapt to the impacts of a changing climate.

Keywords Climate resilience · Education infrastructure · Disaster risk reduction · Sustainable development goals · Adaptive learning spaces

1 Introduction

The physical and institutional framework that facilitates the delivery of learning opportunities to communities is referred as the education infrastructure. This infrastructure depends on numerous systems that are more vulnerable to shocks now than at any point in history, as the climate influences everything from rapidly accelerating extreme-weather events to slow ingresses of atmospheric and oceanic degradation. Climate-resilient education infrastructure refers to the planning, design, construction, and maintenance of facilities which are strong by being robust or adaptive along with uninterrupted learning processes. Schools, colleges, and training centers are at a growing risk of damage from floods, cyclones, extreme heat-waves and droughts, and wildfires affecting the built environment for schools life routines, displacing facilities outages, or closing them down altogether; together with deepening existing educational inequalities. It will require a proactive, holistic strategy for protecting learning environments against the ravages of climate change and obviate an approach in which climate adaptation is relegated to the dustbin as an afterthought while policymaking expands around teachers, students, and their schools.

In the past, educational facilities had been largely designed with economic accessibility and population sizes in mind at the expense of resilience to environmental conditions. Even in many low- and middle-income countries, schools are frequently built with little regard for the changing climatic threats, instead relying on outdated architectural standards that do not take increased exposure to rising sea levels, wind loads, or heat stress into account. The additional vulnerability is fixed by poor maintenance, minimal emergency preparedness, and low investment in disaster-resilient construction. As the children in the cyclone-impacted coastal areas on certain parts of Indian coast are frequently forced to vacate their schools due to the loss of learning spaces caused by weak building materials and poor structural design as a result of extreme weather, they face prolonged educational disruption. In areas prone to water shortages, or where the risk of heatwaves is high but no passive cooling system, efficient facility-wide water tank storage and shaded teaching venues are available; the harsh climates generate student/teacher intolerable conditions leading to reduced attendance and underperformance. Its design fails to incorporate structural features that mainstream climate resilience into the educational infrastructure agenda.

Scope and Significance

The exposure to climate change is not the only domain in which the relevance of climate-resilient education infrastructure is prevalent. In crises of natural or enforced political origin, schools can serve as alternative emergency shelters for the community, sources of information, and emergency aid supply channels. Therefore, aside from preserving the loss of infrastructure investment, resilient climate infrastructure can also be accessed regularly to ensure flexibility and durability of the infrastructure. With the introduction of climate-resilient infrastructure into the educational mainstream; thus, investments in infrastructure could not only ensure sustainability but also preserve considerable investments in development. In the context of sustainable development goals SDG 4: Quality Education, SDG 9: Industry, Innovation, and Infrastructure, SDG 11: Sustainable Cities and Communities, and SDG 13: Climate Action, putting sustainability in improving infrastructural design becomes an urgent priority. The importance of studying the impact of climate-resilient education infrastructure is salient in the address of the equity gap prevalent in education. Children from marginalized communities usually survive in the areas where infrastructural support lacks, thus interrupting their education.

Schools that are integrated with resilience measures, for example, that have flood-resistant buildings, use a renewable source of energy like solar, are well ventilated, and allow for flexible learning space, help is ensuring inclusivity. This means that all children, regardless of the environment they are exposed to, are protected and ensured of their right to access education. They also offer co-benefits, primary being an enormous reduction in operational costs, better learning opportunities, and healthy living for the students in question. This perspective offers resilience a new meaning as it serves as a beneficiary and a change enabler to adapt to the climate situation. It also aligns with the climate resilience and adaptation method in society. Since the likelihood of sharp climatic changes occurring, awareness, research, and efforts to combat this potentially dangerous threat turn into a new domain requiring urgent action. The awareness and research of the existing vulnerabilities, partly due to climate-induced conditions and research on cross-sector collaboration between educationalists, architects, engineers, policymakers, and climate experts is essential to guarantee the learning environment in the change of climate issues. The literature seeks intensive contribution in the field, including the integration of these measures guaranteed in the identified necessary policies and the existing streams for implementation. Therefore, the literature offers practical enlightens for implementation by policymakers, and actors in the field [1].

2 Climate Resilience in Education: Intersection of Education Infrastructure and Climate Risks

The point of intersection between infrastructure in education and climate risks represents one of the most important landmarks for sustainable development because learning environments need to be not only resistant but adaptable to changes in more severe environmental circumstances. Education infrastructure is a crucial element of the basic educational system, including school buildings and furniture, utilities, e.g., electricity, water, transportation, digital connectivity, and central to knowledge delivery/development. The continuity, accessibility, and safety of educational systems are threatened by climate change-induced risks worldwide including: increased flood impact, cyclones, heatwaves, wildfires as well as the rise of sea levels. Service disruptions in some regions due to damaged facilities, closed roads, and schools not reopening for an extended period of time after a catastrophic event can thwart educational advancement and deepen disparities.

The communities most at risk from the climate crisis are often similarly disadvantaged by under-resourced schools, where design decisions and ongoing maintenance and contingency planning miss the mark for climate resilience. Examples of this integration include designing adaptive building designs, employing locally available construction materials with reduced carbon footprints, implementing renewable energy systems, and establishing comprehensive DRR strategies in construction to promote climate resilience education infrastructure. Physical adaptations are dimension of resilience, and the other is digital infrastructure that allows remote learning during times when it would be otherwise interrupted. In doing so, they will not only be protecting continuity in learning but also promoting awareness, preparedness, and adaptability of generations to come, keeping education aligned with the principles of climate-resilient systems making it a pillar for stability in this era marked by environmental instability.

Global and Regional Trends in Climate Impacts on Education

Climate change and its effects on education are increasingly being recognized as a more widespread problem, although these impacts are heavily dependent upon the difference in geographies, socio-economic status, and infrastructural divide between countries. Despite this, the impact of rising sea levels and more intense storms that strike low-lying coastal and island nations often damage schools, displace communities, or disrupt academic calendars. Traditional agricultural practices in many rural communities struggle with recurrent floods and droughts, which depress attendance rates and force families to pull girls out of school often due to the need for domestic or economic labour.

As extreme heat events have become more frequent, schools in places like the Middle East, North Africa, and parts of Australia are closing early or sometimes for days on end to protect students from unsafe conditions. Conversely, growing wildfire and hurricane threats in the high-income zones of Europe and North America demand climate-resilient schools and increased emergency response. While this digital transformation has been an improvement for some, it often deepens gaps and disparities due to the uneven availability of remote learning technologies. Regional patterns also indicate that although climate effects on education are global in nature, the potential vulnerability and capability to respond have a broad range attributable to governance norm strength, resource availability and educational infrastructural quality. So, knowledge of these global and regional trends is critical to identify where interventions can be targeted aimed at both immediate climate risks, and long-term resilience within education systems globally.

3 Climate Risks and Disruptions Affecting Education Infrastructure

An entire component of education infrastructure, school buildings, transport networks, energy systems, water supply, and digital connectivity is more exposed to the multiplying impacts of a changing climate. Classrooms, libraries, labs, and sports facilities are often directly hit by the cyclones, hurricanes, floods, and wildfires that school infrastructure damaged from the impacts of extreme weather events which frequently renders them not just unsafe for use in a matter of weeks or months around yet but can further reinforce this problem for years to come.

When this happens in regions that suffer from flooding, vertically penetrating water weakens building foundations, damages educational materials, and stimulates mold growth all of which represent health risks for students and staff. Water also becomes scarce in drought-affected areas, sanitary facilities are not as proper thus closing schools due to unhygienic conditions, and increased disease susceptibilities [2]. In addition to causing students and teachers to overheat, extreme heat is also a maintenance nightmare for summer cooling systems, especially in older buildings operating without the benefit of energy-efficient gear. School construction is also expensive, and the issue of design exacerbates this challenge; rural and remote schools often struggle with both poor initial climate-resilient design as well as a lack of financial resources to rebuild, rendering them highly vulnerable to repeated damage. Even if they could be bused in from elsewhere, transportation disruptions by landslides, damaged roads, or inundated routes mean getting to school might be impossible for kids living in geographically remote areas.

Climate risks extend to digital infrastructure power outages and connectivity breakdowns undermine the continuity of remote and blended learning, a critical adaptation mechanism during climate emergencies [3]. The compounding effect of repeated climate-induced disruptions erodes community trust in the reliability of education systems, increasing dropout rates and hindering long-term educational attainment. The post-disaster reconstruction often prioritizes rapid reopening rather than integrating climate-resilient design principles, leading to a cycle of damage and repair that is financially and socially unsustainable. Building robust, climate-resilient educational infrastructure requires proactive planning, incorporating green building materials, flood- and wind-resistant designs, renewable energy integration, and reliable digital systems. Such an approach not only safeguards physical assets but also ensures uninterrupted learning, thereby strengthening the capacity of education systems to adapt to and withstand the growing threats posed by climate change [4].

4 Principles and Frameworks for Climate-Resilient Education Infrastructure

Climate-resilient education infrastructure builds on principles and frameworks that holistically consider sustainability, disaster risk reduction, and adaptive capacity within the planning, design, construction, and maintenance of learning spaces. The principles should protect the safety, functionality, and accessibility of schools during and after climate-related hazards in order to maintain the right to education. The first principle is risk-informed planning, where projects are backed by climate risk assessment, hazard mapping, and vulnerability analysis to identify natural hazards such as flooding, extreme heat, or storms specific to a location. Adaptive nature of the design encourages this kind of approach making the structure supple to accommodate changing climate patterns and future uncertainties. The materials and construction should find natural investment in sustainable ways of building, where low-carbon, energy-efficient, and resource-conserving principles work to reduce the ecological footprint while ensuring maximum longevity through good quality [5].

The frameworks that influence climate-resilient education infrastructure are often dependent upon global policy instruments the Sendai Framework for Disaster Risk Reduction (2015–2030) and international agreements including the Paris Agreement and the UN Sustainable Development Goals, particularly SDG 4 on quality education, SDG 9 on resilient infrastructure, and SDG 13 on climate action. These frameworks focus on integrated strategies that connect educational planning to national adaptation and mitigation climate-related actions. The Comprehensive School Safety Framework (CSSF), for example, is a favored model by the global community as it centers on safe learning facilities, school disaster management, and educational aspects of risk reduction. Recommendations of the UNESCO–UNICEF Global Partnership for Education also suggest mainstreaming resilience into education sector plans, with climate-proof infrastructure and renewable energy, water harvesting, and digital connectivity suitable for learning continuity.

Equity and inclusivity is another key principle to make climate-resilient schools not only available to all, but also, with attention to not deepening inequalities for those who are located in hazard-prone areas or marginalized communities. The participatory planning is required to involve a wider range of actors from local citizens and educators to students, engineers, and policymakers in co-design processes that blend traditional with technical expertise. Climate-sensitive grant programs and long-term maintenance and monitoring frameworks are also key to ensuring the resilience of UHI projects. When integrated into strong governance systems, climate-resilient education infrastructure goes beyond structural adaptation; it also serves as an enabler of community resilience, educational continuity, and socio-economic stability over the decade in which we can expect regular climatic interruptions [6].

International Guidelines and Best Practices in Digital Education with Sustainable Development Goals

Digital education is one of the aspects that international guidelines and good practices start to harmonize with Sustainable Development Goals (SDGs) recommended by United Nations, including but not limited to SDG 4 (Quality Education) and SDG 13 (Climate Action). UNESCO, UNICEF, and the World Bank all endorse digital learning tools that can help to bridge gaps in access to technology based on global needs of equity, inclusivity, and environmental sustainability. These are frameworks that focus in part on building inclusive ICT infrastructure, clean energy-supported digital tools and climate-resilient systems prepared for environmental shocks. Best practices include utilizing green technologies, delivering low-carbon footprints in educational technology deployment, and incorporating climate literacy into curricula [7].

The Regional Initiative on Digital Learning and Skills for Africa advocates for mobile learning and the use of small-sized, environment-friendly digital kits; the UNESCO Greening Education Partnership calls on countries to integrate environmental sustainability in their digital education planning; while the Global Partnership for Education is backing financial instruments that promote climate-resilient digital solutions. Education for Sustainable Development (ESD) concept also emphasizes the application of technology to improve the capacity to take decisions related with climate change. The guidelines also emphasized the role of teacher education in digital competencies, toward building resilient learning environments for urban as well as rural scenarios. Incorporating sustainability imperatives in digital education strategies can not only serve to improve the quality of education but may also be part a tool used to reduce insulation and advance nations toward global climate action commitments.

5 Design and Technological Solutions: Climate-Responsive Architecture and Green School Building Materials

Sustainable development, education, climate-responsive architecture, and the use of green school building materials all meet in a nebulous apex of environmentally friendly construction. It combines traditional architectural design concepts with the latest technologies in smart buildings to develop learning spaces that are energy efficient, resilient against climate change and can sustain research-based pedagogical practices [8]. Climate-responsive architecture is based on the premise that we have to design buildings that adjust naturally to local climatic conditions as positioning for ventilation, daylight, and passive cooling or heat systems in order to minimize the need for energy-demanding technical solutions. The use of technologies such as Building Information Modeling (BIM) and digital simulations allows architects, planners, etc. to evaluate environmental performance during the design stage so even before breaking ground maximizing energy potential and minimizing negative impact on the environment.

A secondary advantage of green school building materials is the positive impact on sustainability. Materials like recycled steel, bamboo, low-VOC paints, rammed earth, reclaimed wood, and solar-reflective roofing are chosen for their longevity in application, sustainability, and health benefits to occupants. They frequently have more reliable indoor air quality, lower greenhouse gas emissions, and better thermal comfort. This has turned schools into living, breathing proponents of environmental consciousness integrating measures like PV façades, rainwater harvesting systems, and smart energy control solutions into the very structure of education [9].

The designs are directly supportive of SDG 4 (Quality Education) and SDG 13 (Climate Action), creating resilient and inclusive learning environments to ensure students are holistically prepared for careers in climate-conscious industries. Schools in cyclone-prone areas, for instance, might use reinforced green materials and built on columns schools that are elevated; and those in arid zones could build with high thermal mass materials to lower indoor heat. Green roofs, vertical gardens, and biodiversity-friendly landscaping enable environmental learning first hand, while reducing impacts of urban heat islands.

In addition to providing optimal thermal comfort, these low-energy and water use climate-responsive school design features have the potential to reduce operations costs and as well allow more funding resources that go toward educational programs. Based on this research there are widespread calls by governments and international bodies such as UNESCO, UNEP that not only these principles shall be adopted in the policy but also technical guidelines should developed, funding incentives shall be provided, and capacity building initiatives may be undertaken before implementing it [10]. If educational environments can internalize sustainable material choices and improve their existing structures, they serve as models of ecologically sound practice for students, staff, and community members. Thus, both climate-responsive architecture and green building materials are not only as physical solutions but also other face of the coin for culture, through movement for education toward the resilient of a global warming problem and ethical values with using environment-friendly beliefs.

Smart and Digital Infrastructure for Continuity of Learning

The effectiveness of disaster-related interruptions in education is spearheaded by smart and digital infrastructure. Schools should incorporate technology-driven solutions to accommodate their maximum learning scenario, one where physical attendance is no longer a viable option due to flooding or storms or heat-waves or whatever other pathways climate hazards take [11]. Teachers and students can connect remotely through digital learning platforms, virtual classrooms, and cloud-based educational resources which help in curtailing the academic losses. Interactive tools, AI-powered personalized adaptive learning solutions, and downloadable educational content cater to the inclusivity of areas with poor or no connectivity.

Climate-resilient ICT infrastructure also helps in sustainable digital operations by solar-powered computer labs and energy-efficient servers, and also climate-proof data centers reduce carbon footprints. Broadcasting ensures all students are informed immediately, allowing schools to be better prepared and react more swiftly to budding weather situations in real-time communication systems along with early warning applications. The deployment of smart technologies such as IoT-enabled monitoring systems also facilitates being-building safety energy optimization and resource management. Smart infrastructure supports SDG 4 on quality education and SDG 13 on climate action by helping build future-ready, inclusive, and resilient education systems. In the end, it is about creating designs that enable people to safeguard learning against climate shocks and build a system that will continue advancing sustainability and innovation [12].

6 Climate-Resilient Education Policies and Legal Frameworks

To ensure that both learning systems are not affected by the impacts of climate change, as well as to develop adaptive capacity in students and educators alongside institutions these must incorporate quality education. This means that climate adaptation and mitigation strategies are mainstreamed into educational planning, curriculum design, and infrastructure development in these areas. With climate literacy integrated from K to 12, the framework is ensuring that students develop the competences, understanding, and values essential for coping with contemporary environmental issues. Schools may be mandated by law to adopt green building standards, use renewable energy with the reinforcement of disaster-resilient infrastructure that can help reduce their vulnerability to extreme weather events.

A strong policy and legal framework also facilitates the integration of disaster risk reduction (DRR) measures in education sector planning, which encompasses school preparedness, rapid response capacity, and recovery [13]. The frameworks often coincide with international agreements like the Paris agreement, Sendai Framework for Disaster Risk Reduction, and UNESCO's Education for Sustainable Development Goals that help nations to synchronize their climate action in education sector. Most significantly, they will need to grapple with the issue of equity by directing financial, material, and other resources as well an access to climate-resilient educational facilities to support disenfranchised and socially just vulnerable communities.

Legal provisions can go far toward requirements for building codes incorporating green standards in schools as well, incentives to promote lower carbon technologies and integration of early warning systems into education sector planning. Policies enabling the collaboration of governments, private sectors, and civil society to finance and develop cutting-edge climate-resilient educational interventions [14]. Administratively, that includes making certain that digital and remote education options are woven into the regular patterns of governance and backed with policy language—so that when physical access goes out the window, educational continuity does not follow.

Dynamic and evidence-based climate-resilient education frameworks will be most effective in light of new scientific understanding as well as evolving climate risks. They must be monitored, evaluated for impact, and kept relevant by engaging stakeholders constantly [15]. And because these policies and legal frameworks serve not just to protect our educational systems from climate disruption, but also as a springboard for creating climate smart societies educating generations to come on the importance of being sustainable agents, while ensuring access to uninterrupted, quality education even with environmental uncertainties.

7 Community Engagement and Capacity Building: Role of Teachers, Students, and Parents

Community engagement and capacity building play a critical role in delivering climate-resilient education infrastructure by making adaptation measures inclusive, participatory, and sustainable. It is our teachers, students, and parents who are the very pulse of education systems; their roles not only include delivering classroom learning but also in shaping a culture that are climate aware, prepared, and resilient. As the most important catalyst of learning process, teachers have a role in strengthening climate change knowledge becomes inseminated into regions, especially instilling environmentally sound behavior and organizing disaster drills preparedness [16]. Teachers can gain the necessary knowledge, aptitude, and innovative digital tools to identify climate-related risks, implement protective measures for, e.g., safety protocols in schools and remote or hybrid teaching strategies during climate-induced displacements of students through continuous professional growth and targeted training programs.

Students are the future safeguarders of a just and sustainable development. Through being involved in environmental clubs or school greening projects, and participating in climate actions, it helps to form a sense of responsibility for the environment as well. Incorporating real-life knowledge about water conservation, use of renewable energy and means to reduce waste can enable students by providing them with life skills that will help them cope with the challenges posed by climate change [17]. They can be equally catalytic at spreading climate literacy among their families and communities to connect carbon-neutralization within school-based interventions all the way through to impactful societal shifts [18].

Meanwhile, parents help by reinforcing at home what children have already learned in school and keeping their kids safe during extreme weather events or school closures. Through their participation in school decision-making processes (e.g., parent-teacher associations, community consultations, infrastructure planning committees), they ensure the new need of their students to be considered within climate adaptation strategies [19]. These stakeholders help to create a climate-literate learning ecosystem with an alignment of knowledge, infrastructure, and community support. Community ownership: getting communities involved keeps a sense of responsibility alive, allows resources to respond to disasters as they arise, and makes the interventions culturally appropriate and context-bound which is very important when preparing for coping with climate change. An informed and united school community has what it takes to ensure learning continuity during climate risks, while most importantly looking after the physical, emotional, and intellectual well-being of their students. This collaboration turns schools into centers of resilience supporting societal climate change adaptation beyond the immediate crisis.

8 Future Scope

Climate-resilient education infrastructure is the long-term answer about emerging innovative, adaptive, and inclusive systems having resilience that can survive and get back to their functions as quickly as possible after any climate-related disruption. The adoption of renewable energy sources, real-time AI-triggered early warning system, and digital platforms that are climate responsive to ensure learning never stops. Multi-disciplinary research nexus of architecture, environmental science, and EdTech pragmatic solutions while being scalable and contextualized to most vulnerable geographies. Developing global and regional partnerships will create the space for best practices sharing, resource pooling, and technical know-how. Climate literacy integrated with traditional curricula can help drive future generations to start becoming a force in these climate-resilient efforts. Green building certifications, sustainable materials, and adaptive planning are some of the ways that policy will make a difference. It is about building education systems in which infrastructure, teaching and learning, and governance combine to protect this right from the potentially catastrophic impacts of climate change and do so sustainably [20].

9 Conclusion

In a world of increasing climate catastrophes, building climate-resilient education systems are not optional anymore; it is imperative to protect the universal right to learning. The rebuilding of schools and learning spaces should be carefully contemplated to make use of sustainable design, green building materials, and adaptive technologies for adequate safety, functioning, and energy efficiency. The integration of smart infrastructure, renewable energy solutions, and disaster-preparedness mechanisms to lessen vulnerability can increase resilience, which in turn can ensure the continuance of education in times of crises. The equal significance are climate-resilient policies, legal frameworks, and community participatory action such as resilience plans for educational institutions that involve teachers and students and parents in preparedness. They help build a culture of preparedness and adaptation through environmental awareness, capacity building, and ownership at the local level. It needs to be a joint effort requiring proper levels of funding and international cooperation to develop infrastructure for advancing powerful infectious disease surveillance. A climate-resilient education ecosystem is more than just saving time and learning; it's about instilling sustainability and resilience in future leaders to come back with their creations that make our communities great.

References

1. Basu, A., Chatterjee, A., Ghosh, R., Dasgupta, S., Roychowdhury, T., Dutta, P. K., Bhattacharya, P., & Tanwar, S. (2024). Analysis and performance of text summarization tools applied on Indian languages. In Y. Singh, P. K. Singh, P. J. S. Gonçalves, & A. K. Kar (Eds.), *Proceedings of International Conference on Recent Innovations in Computing* (ICRIC 2023) (Lecture Notes in Electrical Engineering, Vol. 1194). Springer, Singapore. https://doi.org/10.1007/978-981-97-2839-8_28
2. Pal, A., Tsusaka, T. W., Nguyen, T. P. L., & Ahmad, M. M. (2023). Assessment of vulnerability and resilience of school education to climate-induced hazards: A review. *Development Studies Research, 10*(1), 2202826.
3. Argyroudis, S. A., Mitoulis, S. A., Chatzi, E., Baker, J. W., Brilakis, I., Gkoumas, K., Vousdoukas, M., Hynes, W., Carluccio, S., Keou, O., Frangopol, D. M., & Linkov, I. (2022). Digital technologies can enhance climate resilience of critical infrastructure. *Climate Risk Management, 35*, 100387.
4. Nalla, V., Johnson, C., Ranjit, N., Sen, G., Peddibhotla, A., Anand, M. C., Bhatia, N., & Bazaz, A. B. (2023). Considering curriculum, content, and delivery for adaptive pathways: Higher education and disaster resilient infrastructure in the Indian urban context. *Sustainable and Resilient Infrastructure, 8*(Suppl. 1), 143–156.
5. Schipper, E. L. F., Eriksen, S. E., Fernandez Carril, L. R., Glavovic, B. C., & Shawoo, Z. (2021). Turbulent transformation: Abrupt societal disruption and climate resilient development. *Climate and Development, 13*(6), 467–474.
6. Pelling, M., Chow, W. T., Chu, E., Dawson, R., Dodman, D., Fraser, A., ... & Ziervogel, G. (2022). A climate resilience research renewal agenda:

Learning lessons from the COVID-19 pandemic for urban climate resilience. *Climate and Development, 14*(7), 617–624.
7. Shammin, M.R., Haque, A.K.E., Faisal, I.M. (2022). A Framework for Climate Resilient Community-Based Adaptation. In: Haque, A.K.E., Mukhopadhyay, P., Nepal, M., Shammin, M.R. (eds) *Climate Change and Community Resilience*. Springer, Singapore. https://doi.org/10.1007/978-981-16-0680-9_2
8. Rees, N. (2021). *The climate crisis is a child rights crisis: Introducing the children's climate risk index*. UNICEF.
9. Rane, N., Choudhary, S., & Rane, J. (2024). Artificial intelligence for enhancing resilience. *Journal of Applied Artificial Intelligence, 5*(2), 1–33.
10. Mason, J. G., Eurich, J. G., Lau, J. D., Battista, W., Free, C. M., Mills, K. E., ... & Kleisner, K. M. (2022). Attributes of climate resilience in fisheries: From theory to practice. *Fish and Fisheries, 23*(3), 522–544.
11. Dodman, D., B. Hayward, M. Pelling, V. Castan Broto, W. Chow, E. Chu, R. Dawson, L. Khirfan, T. McPhearson, A. Prakash, Y. Zheng, and G. Ziervogel, 2022: Cities, Settlements and Key Infrastructure. In: Climate Change 2022: Impacts, Adaptation and Vulnerability. *Contribution of Working Group II to the Sixth Assessment Report of the Intergovernmental Panel on Climate Change* [H.-O. Pörtner, D.C. Roberts, M. Tignor, E.S. Poloczanska, K. Mintenbeck, A. Alegría, M. Craig, S. Langsdorf, S. Löschke, V. Möller, A. Okem, B. Rama (eds.)]. Cambridge University Press, Cambridge, UK and New York, NY, USA, pp. 907–1040, https://doi.org/10.1017/9781009325844.008
12. Xu, L., Feng, K., Lin, N., Perera, A. T. D., Poor, H. V., Xie, L., Ji, C., Sun, X. A., Guo, Q., & O'Malley, M. (2024). Resilience of renewable power systems under climate risks. *Nature Reviews Electrical Engineering, 1*(1), 53–66.
13. Ackerl, T., Weldemariam, L. F., Nyasimi, M., & Ayanlade, A. (2023). Climate change risk, resilience, and adaptation among rural farmers in East Africa: A literature review. *Regional Sustainability, 4*(2), 185–193.
14. de Abreu, V. H. S., Santos, A. S., & Monteiro, T. G. M. (2022). Climate change impacts on the road transport infrastructure: A systematic review on adaptation measures. *Sustainability, 14*(14), 8864.
15. Raghunathan S, Darshan Singh A and Sharma B (2022) Study of Resilience in Learning Environments During the Covid-19 Pandemic. *Front. Educ.* 6:677625. https://doi.org/10.3389/feduc.2021.677625
16. Apollo, A., & Mbah, M. F. (2021). Challenges and opportunities for climate change education (CCE) in East Africa: A critical review. *Climate, 9*(6), 93.
17. Olufemi-Phillips, A. Q., Ofodile, O. C., Toromade, A. S., Igwe, A. N., & Adewale, T. T. (2024). Strategies for adapting food supply chains to climate change using simulation models. *Strategies, 20*(11), 1021–1040.

18. Mottahedi, A., Sereshki, F., Ataei, M., Nouri Qarahasanlou, A., & Barabadi, A. (2021). The resilience of critical infrastructure systems: A systematic literature review. *Energies, 14*(6), 1571.
19. Betts, R A, Haward A.B., Pearson, K.V. (eds)]. Climate Change London.
20. Malik, I. H., & Ford, J. D. (2025). Monitoring climate change vulnerability in the Himalayas. *Ambio, 54*(1), 1–19.

CHAPTER 20

Enhancing Institutional Research Capacity for Evidence-Based Digital Education with Emerging Technologies

Kittisak Wongmahesak, Bhrigu Raj Mourya, and Arun Prakash Singh

Abstract This chapter provides a study of how educational institutions can improve their own research capacity to facilitate the formulation of a data-informed digital education strategy. Schools implementing AI, machine learning, or learning analytics will now have to go beyond the

K. Wongmahesak
Faculty of Political Science, North Bangkok University, Bangkok, Thailand

Publication Research Institute and Community Service, Universitas Muhammadiyah Sidenreng Rappang, South Sulawesi, Indonesia

Faculty of Business and Management, Universiti Sultan Zainal Abidin, Terengganu, Malaysia

Shinawatra University, Pathum Thani, Thailand

B. R. Mourya (✉)
MATS University, Raipur, Chhattisgarh, India
e-mail: brmourya.mourya321@gmail.com

P. K. Dutta et al. (eds.), *Digital Education for a Sustainable Future*, Sustainable Development Goals Series,
https://doi.org/10.1007/978-3-032-15433-0_20

mere adoption of these tools to a real evaluation and impact on learning outcomes. That means moving from answering the question of tech implementation reactively, in near real-time, to doing it proactively and evidence based. The abstract discusses the challenges of defining an institutional research infrastructure, suggests a new model for developing it that leverages emerging technologies to foster a culture of inquiry, and provides it with essential human and technical architecture. The hope is for its K-12 platform to enable educators and administrators to not only use high-quality digital tools, but also produce data that can guide pedagogical innovation while guaranteeing fair and equal access for all students. This way he feels will enable institutions to maneuver the complex digital world fruitfully which would then lead to major educational reforms that are not only impactful but capable of sustenance as well.

Keywords Institutional research · Digital education · Emerging technologies · Evidence-based practice · Learning analytics

1 Introduction

Digital transformation, a key enabler, is fast turning into the lynchpin in the dynamic world of education for improving pedagogy, student success, and administrative processes. Institutes across the globe are embracing digital education to enhance accessibility, engagement, and learning results. But for digital education to be effectively implemented and improved, an institution must have the reliable research capacity needed to provide its academics with evidence-based information. Strengthening this capability is essential for schools to inform decisions, develop effective services, and stay ahead of the curve. The integration of artificial intelligence, big data analytics, cloud computing, virtual reality, and other emerging technologies provides unprecedented opportunities to enhance institutional research capabilities and drive evidenced-based practices in digital education [1].

A. P. Singh
Bakey Bhihari College of Law, Budaun Sadar, India

Institutional research capacity refers to the capacity of an educational institution to gather data, analyze data, interpret and re-use them for policy, curriculum design, pedagogy, or resource allocation. It is fundamental to instill this capacity if we are going to enable a culture of continuous improvement and accountability. In the sleep of things that holds true, institutional research has newly gotten into digital education beyond conventional metrics to gather details about technology use, learner engagement tech abilities, and pedagogical practices. Through new technologies, the information will be improved and the data collection methods will not only be sophisticated but also generate insightful outcomes that help shape decision-making based on evidence.

However, while the need may be clear, and the opportunity real, many falling short when it comes to creating sustainable digital education research capacity in institutions. Challenges include limited tech infrastructure, insufficiency in researcher and faculty skills, data management and privacy concerns, and efforts at research being fragmented. To meet these challenges requires a strategic, systemic response which involves technology investment, human capital development, methodological innovation, and collaboration.

The challenges can be not only difficult but also life threatening; this is where emerging technologies come to provide a saving hand. Through machine learning and artificial intelligence algorithms, it helps inform predictions and research on personalized learning. They use big data analytics to make sense of the huge educational data, and discover patterns for purpose of adjusting curricula and providing other support for learners. Cloud computing gives volume, flexibility, research space, and virtual and augmented reality tests the interaction and pedagogical imaginations. Implemented well, these technologies (when integrated) have a transformative ability to enable institutions to expand and support their research efforts with enduring impact in the exigent digital-educational-future space.

Importance and Relevance of Institutional Research Capacity

Institutional research capability is essential for higher education institutions to generate and collect data effectively to inform decision-making in support of the scale and effectiveness of digital learning. This also can facilitate the regular collection, analysis, and interpretation of information regarding teaching/learning practice and the deployment of technology that should lead to ongoing enhancements. Strong research capacity underpins an evidence-based policy, funding, and curriculum development, ensuring that digital education initiatives meet learner needs, as well as institutional goals. It also facilitates accountability, transparency, and responsiveness in education systems that enable institutions to react to rapid technological change and shifts in learner requirements. An essential element of innovation, reducing equity gaps, and maintaining educational quality in the digital era is the improvement of institutional research capabilities.

Purpose and Objective of the Chapter

This chapter seeks to identify ways in which institutional research capacity might be improved to support evidence-based digital education using new technologies. It describes current research capacities, technology and human resource requirements, and best practices for data management and analysis. The remit covers examining how technologies such as AI, big data, and cloud computing can be used to enhance the research process. The study highlights capacity building issues and advances frameworks for research-use in policymaking. In conclusion, this paper aims to offer practical advice to institutions on how they can create research ecosystems that help sustain a research program for quality and innovation in digital education [2].

2 Evidence-Based Digital Education: Principles and Practices

The strength of this method comes in the fact that decisions about educational technologies, pedagogical strategies, and policy interventions are based on evidence-based analysis without relying on un-evidenced intuitions or tradition. The guiding principle of evidence-based digital education is to increase learning and equity by using what works, continuously testing it in practice. The core principles of an evidence-based approach to digital education is that one needs access to good-quality, relevant data which captures a broad spectrum of roles in the learning process. That may be numeric data as learner engagement metrics, assessment results, technology usage logs, or qualitative insights from learner feedback, teacher observations, and wider case studies. Aggregating and harmonizing these diverse data types facilitate a more holistic view of what works, for whom, and under what conditions.

The critical step is the application of rigorous research methods, including randomized control trials and longitudinal and mixed-method studies, to ascertain the effectiveness of digital education tools and interventions. Such methods can be used to disentangle the impact of individual technologies or teaching practices, provide insights into what are effective ways to teach, and help identify some of the barriers that may prevent learning from happening. This careful evaluation is necessary to scale successful innovations and to reallocate resources away from less effective programs. Evidence-based digital education also needs continuous monitoring and iterative improvement [3]. Formative assessments and real-time data analytics are embraced by institutions which in turn monitor students' progresses, analyze their engagement levels, and offer timely interventions immediately to cater the needs of each student. By providing the educators with teaching aids such as learning analytics platforms and dashboards: easily digestible information that enables them to better understand how best to proceed, while personalizing learning pathways, student motivation skyrockets, in conjunction with academic achievement.

In order to foster, teach, and learn better, evidence-based digital education drives accountability and transparency among stakeholders. Policymakers, administrators, teachers, and learners all benefit from transparent evidence-based information to answer questions about the impact of programs, use of resources, and equity outputs. It creates a transparency process that builds trust and encourages all parties involved to decide collectively, ensuring that the educational objectives align with the needs of society and the workforce. The implementation of new technologies like artificial intelligence and big data analytics are revolutionizing evidence-based practices as they increasingly allow for more comprehensive data support and even predictive modeling. These tools are able to unearth underlying patterns, forecast where learners might struggle, and suggest custom strategies, thereby making digital education more effective and equitable. It practices design research utilizing innovative methods and new technologies to improve educational outcomes, avoid reinforcing discrimination, and create environmentally friendly digital learning ecosystems. In doing so, colleges and universities can anchor their digital education initiatives in enduring concepts and best practices that align with the emerging needs of learners and society [4].

Role of Emerging Technologies in Educational Research

Emerging technologies are transforming the field of educational research, opening possibilities for new methodologies and access to granular data. Today, learning analytics and artificial intelligence are driving many studies that rely on large-scale collections—the infinite troves of data made possible by digital platforms allow researchers to automatically collect and analyze millions or billions of signals about student behavior, engagement, and performance. This shift away from more traditional surveys and tests allows for a hopefully livelier, ongoing recognition of the ways in which learning occurs. The tools powered by AI can also run predictive modeling to recognize at-risk students or analyze student work at scale using automatic content analysis. And that, at the same time, immersive technologies virtual reality (VR) and augmented reality (AR) in fact turn out to be really awesome research environments. For instance, it is very difficult in a traditional classroom to create certain kinds of controlled simulations that are necessary for the study of complex cognitive phenomena, for example, cognitive load, situated learning. With the help of these tools, more sophisticated and data-based insights can be produced that are based on evidence, enabling data-driven interventions informed also by the creation of better and individualized learning strategies in digital age [5].

3 Current Landscape of Institutional Research in Digital Education

The current landscape of institutional research in digital education includes major breakthroughs alongside enduring dilemmas. Higher education is realizing there are now ways to extract data and research to help write the rules of digital learning and policy. Educational research units and even centers in higher education institutions, or school systems, which undertake study on learners via data by using digital tools depending on their contexts and needs to look for learning or instructional design improvement [6]. This movement is characterized by an increased focus on the use of evidence to guide decisions, and this emphasis on data-driven practices has never been more important than in today's technology-rich educational settings.

The advent of technologies like learning analytics platforms, AI-based data processing, and cloud-based collaborative tools elevated the institutions to pool a lot of educational data thereby enabling them for deep analysis. These solutions offer understanding of student behavior in attendance, learning path, and tech performance to give the faculty real-time feedback and personalized learning interventions based on individual needs. The inclusion of digital surveys, video analytics, and online assessments has increased the wide-ranging data points available for institutional research [7]. Despite these improvements there are significant disparities in research capability remain across institutions. These include limited technology infrastructure; a lack of expertise in data science and educational research; and fragmented, uncoordinated purpose or partnerships.

Research activities can also be difficult for researchers as data privacy and ethical concerns sometimes prevent access to some learner data. Variability in these tools across regions and institutional resources, coupled with inequality to access technology threaten equity within research and education. Although progress is underway, collaboration between academic researchers, policymakers, and technology developers remains limited. These complex challenges are often solved by models with cross-institutional partnerships that include industry experts. Also, broader scale structures that intertwine research activities with institutional strategies and policy frameworks are much needed. The field of digital education institutional research is growing and changing, thanks to technological innovation and in recognition of the increased demand for evidence-based practice [8]. But institutions need to tackle infrastructure, capacity, and ethical issues as well to truly reap its benefits and grow research ecosystems that foster digital education improvements over the long term.

4 Key Emerging Technologies Supporting Research Capacity

Digital education is sweeping into higher educational space and innovations in emerging technologies are taking an active role in building the research capacity of institutions. These tools help in better data collection, new level of analytics, and richer insights to support decision-making. Some of the most influential include artificial intelligence, big data analytics, cloud computing, and virtual/augmented reality, to name a few each in their own way helps enable new and enhance existing technology stacks that in turn, equip researchers with powerful tools to extend the frontiers of knowledge. Using artificial intelligence and machine learning to analyze data has changed what we expect from our systems, automating a large number of complex tasks: particularly those such as pattern recognition, predictive modeling, or natural language processing. In education research, AI algorithms can analyze gigantic datasets to look at patterns in student performance, engagement, and learning behaviors. With this capability, institutions can build predictive models which will help predict learners need timely intervention to improve their outcome. AI helps you in your research by assisting with data collection through surveys or interviews while increasing reach and efficiency.

Big data analytics are providing larger tools and techniques for dealing with entirely large amounts of data that are created out of digital learning environments. Learning management systems, online assessments, and education apps result in humungous amounts of structured and unstructured data. Big data platforms are allowing researchers to pull these datasets together so that they can better understand how curriculum effectiveness, resources used, and learners' diversity. Advanced visualization tools help transform sophisticated findings into formats suitable for both policymakers and fellows, transferring knowledge for better decision-making in policy and educational measures.

Institutional research of today would not be possible without the scalable and flexible infrastructure provided by cloud computing [9]. Through cloud-based data storage and computational resources, institutions can break down silos of on-premises systems and facilitate seamless collaboration across departments or even across different institutions. Cloud platforms offer advantages in real-time data sharing, versioning management, and huge analytical capabilities without an extensive upfront capital expenditure. This democratizes research ability, very important for institutions lacking a large brick-and-mortar apparatus.

Augmented reality (AR) technologies also open new avenues of research, as a result of their ability to create fully immersive learning environments. These simulations reflect real-world challenges and help researchers explore learner engagement, motivation, cognitive processes, etc. Furthermore, these technologies empower experimental approaches which are complicated to execute otherwise and produce qualitative as well as quantitative data. VR and AR also allow educators to be trained in a more interactive experience and researchers for capacity building.

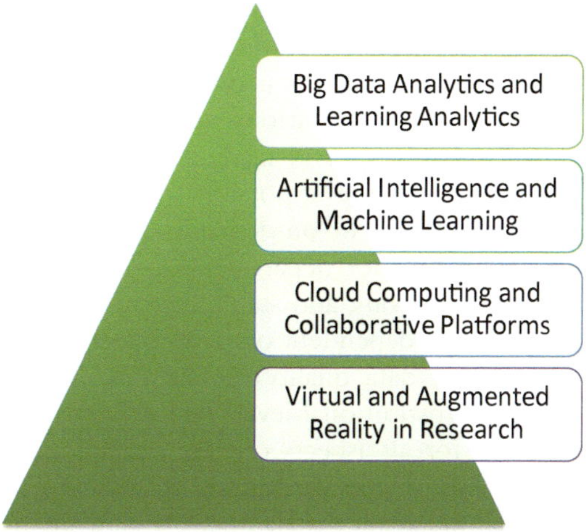

Fig. 1 Shows the points on key emerging technologies supporting research capacity (self-created by Author)

Individually and together these are often very powerful new technologies providing the seamless infrastructure to support much more capable future-oriented institutional research [10]. Their use helps to provide a richer characterization of processes and outcomes in digital education with the aim of informing the design of effective, equitable, inclusive, and innovative learning experiences. It is clear that long-term investment and support will be required to sustain this level of research excellence in digital education as technology continues to develop as discussed in Fig. 1.

5 Building Infrastructure for Institutional Research

The establishment of a disciplinary infrastructure is key to this as institutions need to build the capacity for institutional research embedded within an institution in a rapidly moving field such as digital education. Infrastructure that works includes all the stuff, the physical hardware and software systems, along with how that stuff is wrapped with good frameworks for data management, security, and interoperability. It provides a central platform for collecting, storing, curating, analyzing, and disseminating research data which helps the institution in creating both timely evidence and right kind of data thus help in decision-making [11].

Building infrastructure is setting up reliable technical resources such as high-performance servers, secure data centers, and cloud computing services. These systems need to be scalable to sense the socioeconomic education data from various sources namely learning management system, digital assessment, and learner engagement tools. Instead, cloud-based infrastructure makes it possible to store and access data at will with lower costs by the use of on-demand storage and computational power thus making it easy for departments to work together as well with external partners. A strong and stable internet connection is important since the whole app is dependent on data transfer and real-time analytics.

A robust data quality requires an efficient data management infrastructure. Institutional-level data governance policies should establish a standard for all aspects of data collection, storage, sharing, and use of data to ensure consistency and reliability. This work also includes efforts to make metadata management of data at the appropriate granular level, standardized data formats for better interoperability that enhance the integration of the combined datasets from different educational technologies. The more robust data catalog systems can increase the efficiency of researcher access to and discovery of needed datasets.

The infrastructure does not develop overnight and like other aspects of the technology landscape requires regular updates and innovation simply to keep up with new technologies and data complexities. By using strategic planning and sustainable funding models, infrastructure can grow in response to the research requirements [12]. A robust infrastructure consisting of technical capabilities, data management, and security, and support services collectively establishes the base for institutional research capacity. This infrastructure allows institutions to access all the benefits of digital education data, fueling real-time improvements and innovation.

6 Human Resource Development and Capacity Building

Human resource development (HRD) and capacity building are phenomenon that have become the foundation of organizational growth and sustainability, but they operate at a different yet interconnected level. It mostly concerns the employee as an individual, including all the actions that aimed at improving their knowledge, abilities, and skills. This can be more formal training programs, as well as mentorship, career pathing, and performance management that are designed to educate an individual about how better to do their current job and how they compare in the spectrum for potential future roles [13]. The goal of HRD is to develop a competent, active, and committed workforce which is resolved by providing an environment for learning and development. More recently, this includes providing up-skilling and reskilling to enable employees to adapt with the rise of technology, such as artificial intelligence while also accommodating for changes in industry demand. A focus upon investing in people through their times of challenge equips an organization to better serve itself and to keep talent that is pleased; it optimizes the organization.

Capacity building provides a more comprehensive and systematic approach to strengthening an enterprise from top-down enabling it to better pursue its purpose. While HRD is an essential element of this, capacity development extends to wider systemic and structural issues. This includes revitalizing the internal processes of an organization, improving governance and leadership practices, enhancing technology infrastructure, and promoting external partnerships. This wants to form an efficient organization that is also robust, flexible, and sustainable. A capacity-building program could target better financial management systems, adopt new data analytics tools, or enhance communication channels to improve interdepartmental coordination. Successful capacity-building strategy ultimately integrates individual HRD practices with inherent organizational objectives, realizing UN synergy where skilled workforce operates on efficient and solid functioning organization. The two-pronged approach means the firm can handle everything that comes its way today and plan ahead for whatever may lie ahead tomorrow [14].

7 Methodologies and Frameworks for Evidence-Based Digital Education Research

Evidence-based digital education research is built upon methodologies and frameworks that provide systematic means to collect, analyze, and interpret educational data. Using the right research methods that can provide valid, reliable, and actionable findings improves in informed decision-making on teaching, learning, and policymaking in digital settings. Researchers also regularly employ quantitative methods, building on experimental designs and surveys to track the utility of digital tools as well as learner outcomes and engagement patterns [15]. Controlled experiments and randomized trials can be used to isolate the impact of particular interventions or technologies by design this way, giving policymakers much more rigorous evidence of cause-and-effect. Through large-scale surveys and learning analytics it is possible to get numbers on such patterns across thousands of learners and thus support generalizable conclusions.

They complement quantitative approaches, which are based on measuring the scale of phenomena to instead provide a picture of students their contexts, experiences, and motivations in digital education. Work such as interviews, focus groups, and case studies provides in depth qualitative data providing behind statistical trends. The results of mixed-method research can be used which combines the quantitative and qualitative methods to provide a more complete view. This methodological approach advances rigor by using multiple sources of data and measuring both quantitative results and qualitative experiences. By conducting student interviews as well, learning analytics could indicate not only what patterns of learning exist but also why they are present, therefore highlighting areas where more effective interventions may be needed.

Theories such as the Technology Acceptance Model (TAM), Community of Inquiry (CoI), and SAMR (Substitution, Augmentation, Modification, and Redefinition) are used to inform the design and evaluation of online educational interventions. Specifically these frameworks help situate findings among theoretical constructs offering tools for a systematic analysis of technology adoption, engagement, and pedagogical transformation [16].

Research frameworks also must consider ethical aspects, including data privacy, consent, and equity. Researchers must follow guidelines that protect the rights of participants, as well as encourage a level of transparency and being held accountable. A range of methodologies and well-established frameworks provide researchers a means to produce strong evidence in digital education. In doing so we will better be able to fill the current gap around understanding challenges and improvements in these critical learning environments, as well as promote increasing quality of technology-enhanced leanring, equity considerations, and innovation as shared in Fig. 2.

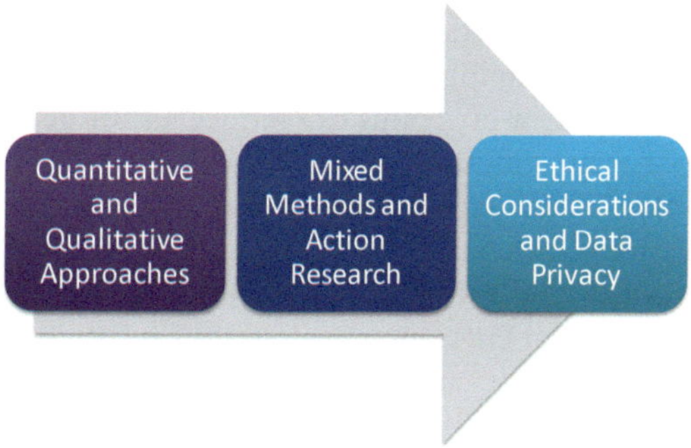

Fig. 2 Methodologies and frameworks (self-created by Author)

8 Utilizing Research Findings for Policy and Practice

Appropriate and evidence-informed use of findings is essential to close the data-to-policy-practice gap in digital education. Institutional research produces important evidence about the efficacy of technologies, pedagogical strategies, and learner success; yet such work has only as much impact as the degree to which this understanding is put into implemented policies or changes in teaching practice that actually improves educational quality and equity. This process of research generating products that meet the need for dissemination in a variety of formats accessible to multiple constituencies, such as policymakers, educators, administrators, and learners themselves, represents one organization's milestone. An executive summary, policy briefs, and an online interactive dashboard can make complex data much more digestible, laying out clear recommendations for how to act in response. Within established communication and stakeholder engagement pathways, both trusts are built up along with a collaborative dialogue that ascertains the research evidence is understood, realized, and applied appropriately.

It is a challenging and time-consuming process because policymakers require specific type of information which sometimes not aligns with the goals of research institutions. It informs resource allocation, curriculum development, and infrastructure investments, making sure that digital education projects are not only efficient but also robust. For instance, research identifying digital divides or areas of skill deficiency can be used to help shape equity concerns and capacity building in funding programs or professional development efforts [17]. This translation of research into the innovation of classroom involves supporting educators with training, tools, and continued feedback loops. The professional development programs can induce a shift in teacher methodology leading to better adoption of evidence-based instructional strategies and technology use which translates into enhanced learner engagement and learning outcomes. With formative assessments and learning analytics it is possible to monitor and adapt in an ongoing fashion leading to nimble pedagogical environment.

Monitoring and evaluation systems, integrated within institutional frameworks can oversee that policies and practices remain responsive to changing requirements. Feedback loops allow incremental changes over time, keeping institutions up-to-date with the latest in evidence and technology. The assimilation of research evidence in policies and practices helps develop a dynamic ecosystem with greater scope for growth, and drives a culture of ongoing improvement in digital education. Institutions can facilitate broader conversations, create buy-in, build capacity, and employ iterative evaluation to make the most out of research and ensure that digital innovations lead to meaningful learning experiences for everyone [18].

9 Fostering Collaboration and Partnerships: Industry-Academia Partnerships, International and Cross-Institutional Collaboration

Inter-collaboration and partnership are all the more important for increasing our capacities in institutional research and promoting innovation across evidence-based digital education. Successful digital education projects are built in partnership, where different expertise, resources, and perspectives come together to enhance the quality of research and provide relevance and scalability. With connecting academic research with technological innovation and workforce demands, industry-academia partnerships unlock powerful synergies. Tech companies and educational institutions work together to develop digital tools, exchange data, and test new learning platforms. These partnerships can allow for much faster translation of new and/or cutting edge applications such as AI, virtual reality, and big data analytics into the educational space. This also ensures that curricula is industry-relevant and prepares students for jobs of the twenty-first century. These collaborations typically open the door for funding as well as technical expertise and infrastructure that may expand an institution's research capacity beyond its in-house limits.

However, international collaboration broadens research perspectives and encourages cross-cultural cooperation, comparative work, and sharing of expertise across a variety of educational settings. By working in global partnerships, digital education practices can be benchmarked and the successes and challenges of institutions across the world can benefit each other. Consortia and networks work to standardize research methodologies, collecting data in parallel across multiple studies—increasing the comparability and validity of findings. The partnerships also provide capacity building by offering joint training, workshops, and conferences to help train scientists in new skill sets and approaches.

Resource sharing among different entities both within and across national boundaries in international networks drives reduction of duplication and improvement of joint research impact. Collaborations among many institutions in research projects allow for a larger and more heterogeneous collection of data and higher statistical power. These platforms and cloud-based tools encourage real-time data sharing and joint analyses available to researchers in any discipline or sector, supporting multiple perspectives on digital education challenges. Therefore, collaboration and partnerships are indispensable to form robust, responsive, and inventive institutional research ecosystems [19]. Educational institutions can accelerate research, improve the relevance and quality of digital education while also meaningfully contribute to the global shift in education by effectively tapping into industry, academia as well as international and institutional networks.

10 Sustainability in Digital Education and Future Directions

In the digital education space, sustainability is about building learning systems that are evidence-based and equitable but also remain robust and malleable over time. Sustainability demands the continued investment in technology infrastructure, human capacities, and political systems that promote dynamic change and widespread access. Affordable internet access and device availability are among the most fundamental pieces required for ensuring fairer learning experiences for all students, which is why these digital divides must be addressed with cost-effective security solutions. So, combining green technologies and energy-efficient habits can make digital schooling less harmful to the environment in tune with wider sustainability strategies.

Sustainability for digital education requires a holistic approach that aligns progress in technology with ethical, social, and environmental concerns. Educational institutions can secure the enduring accessibility, relevance, and impact of digital learning for all, by reinforcing resilient infrastructures, inclusive policies, and forward looking innovations. The next moves in digital education look exciting: personalized learning through machine intelligence, immersive experiences facilitated by VR and AR, to name a few, with better data analytics for real-time feedback at scale. With emerging technologies continually updating the way education is implemented and evaluated, curricula must be agile and educators as well as students professionally developed to tackle more difficult tasks. In conclusion cross-sector collaboration and global partnerships will be critical to foster the sharing of best practices, resources, and research results at scale [20].

11 Conclusion

Rigorous research provides evidence for policymakers, funders, and stakeholders regarding the efficacy and equity of digital education interventions. It promotes transparency, accountability, and commonality of educational objectives with workforce and societal needs. Innovation often remains at the grassroots level and the capacity of institutions to carry on modern research further gets hampered, as long as digital education continues to boom world-over it is imperative that more research should support new ideas into open educational resources. The chapter draws on the complexities of increasing institutional research capacity for digital education underpinned by evidence-based practices and emerging technologies. It starts with a look at current capabilities and gaps, key technology enablers, human resource and infrastructure needs, and best practices on how to take research into policy practice. Aims to provide an overarching model that will allow institutions to develop a coherent narrative about how they create robust, adaptive, and beneficial research ecosystems which enable them to deliver digital excellence in education today and into the future.

References

1. Timotheou, S., Miliou, O., Dimitriadis, Y., Sobrino, S. V., Giannoutsou, N., Cachia, R., Monés, A. M., & Ioannou, A. (2023). Impacts of digital technologies on education and factors influencing schools' digital capacity and transformation: A literature review. *Education and Information Technologies, 28*(6), 6695–6726.
2. Whitelock, D., Goshtasbpour, F., Pitt, B., Ferguson, R., & Cross, S. (2024). Capacity building for digital education. *Open Learning: The Journal of Open, Distance and e-Learning, 39*(2), 105–111.
3. Gaebel, M., Zhang, T., Stoeber, H., & Morrisroe, A. (2021). *Digitally enhanced learning and teaching in European higher education institutions.* European University Association absl.
4. Alenezi, M. (2023). Digital learning and digital institution in higher education. *Education Sciences, 13*(1), 88.
5. Okoye, K., Hussein, H., Arrona-Palacios, A., Quintero, H. N., Ortega, L. O. P., Sanchez, A. L., Ortiz, E. A., Escamilla, J., & Hosseini, S. (2023). Impact of digital technologies upon teaching and learning in higher education in Latin America: An outlook on the reach, barriers, and bottlenecks. *Education and Information Technologies, 28*(2), 2291–2360.
6. Burhan Ismael, N., Jabbar Othman, B., Gardi, B., Abdalla Hamza, P., Sorguli, S., Mahmood Aziz, H., Ali Ahmed, S., Sabir, B. Y., Ali, B. J., & Anwar, G. (2021). The role of training and development on organizational effectiveness. *Ismael, NB, Othman, BJ, Gardi, B., Hamza, PA, Sorguli, S., Aziz, HM, Ahmed, SA, Sabir, BY, Ali, BJ, Anwar, G. (2021). The Role of Training and Development on Organizational effectiveness. International Journal of Engineering, Business and Management, 5*(3), 15–24.
7. Zickar, M. J., & Keith, M. G. (2023). Innovations in sampling: Improving the appropriateness and quality of samples in organizational research. *Annual Review of Organizational Psychology and Organizational Behavior, 10*(1), 315–337.
8. Garlinska, M., Osial, M., Proniewska, K., & Pregowska, A. (2023). The influence of emerging technologies on distance education. *Electronics, 12*(7), 1550.
9. Giannakos, M. N., Mikalef, P., & Pappas, I. O. (2022). Systematic literature review of e-learning capabilities to enhance organizational learning. *Information Systems Frontiers, 24*(2), 619–635.
10. Afzal, A., Khan, S., Daud, S., Ahmad, Z., & Butt, A. (2023). Addressing the digital divide: Access and use of technology in education. *Journal of Social Sciences Review, 3*(2), 883–895.
11. Tariq, E., Muhammad, A., Iman, A., & Sulieman, A. H. (2021). The effect of digital marketing capabilities on organizational ambidexterity of the

information technology sector. *International Journal of Data and Network Science, 6*(2), 401–408.
12. Bhuiyan, M. R. I., Faraji, M. R., Rashid, M., Bhuyan, M. K., Hossain, R., & Ghose, P. (2024). Digital transformation in SMEs emerging technological tools and technologies for enhancing the SME's strategies and outcomes. *Journal of Ecohumanism, 3*(4), 211–224.
13. Alenezi, M., Wardat, S., & Akour, M. (2023). The need of integrating digital education in higher education: Challenges and opportunities. *Sustainability, 15*(6), 4782.
14. Jacobsen, C. B., Andersen, L. B., Bøllingtoft, A., & Eriksen, T. L. M. (2022). Can leadership training improve organizational effectiveness? Evidence from a randomized field experiment on transformational and transactional leadership. *Public Administration Review, 82*(1), 117–131.
15. Ng, D. T. K., Leung, J. K. L., Su, J., Ng, R. C. W., & Chu, S. K. W. (2023). Teachers' AI digital competencies and twenty-first century skills in the post-pandemic world. *Educational Technology Research and Development, 71*(1), 137–161.
16. Adam, I., & Fazekas, M. (2021). Are emerging technologies helping win the fight against corruption? A review of the state of evidence. *Information Economics and Policy, 57*, 100950.
17. Bristol-Alagbariya, B., Ayanponle, O. L., & Ogedengbe, D. E. (2022). Developing and implementing advanced performance management systems for enhanced organizational productivity. *World Journal of Advanced Science and Technology, 2*(1), 39–46.
18. Wang, C., Chen, X., Yu, T., Liu, Y., & Jing, Y. (2024). Education reform and change driven by digital technology: A bibliometric study from a global perspective. *Humanities and Social Sciences Communications, 11*(1), 1–17.
19. Zhang, J., Long, J., & Von Schaewen, A. M. E. (2021). How does digital transformation improve organizational resilience?—findings from PLS-SEM and fsQCA. *Sustainability, 13*(20), 11487.
20. Mhlongo, S., Mbatha, K., Ramatsetse, B., & Dlamini, R. (2023). Challenges, opportunities, and prospects of adopting and using smart digital technologies in learning environments: An iterative review. *Heliyon, 9*(6), e16348.

CHAPTER 21

Global Cooperation in Digital Education Partnership Models to Advance Digital Education Access

Hammouch Hind, Ambuj Sharma, and Pushan Kumar Dutta

Abstract Global efforts in the harmonization of digital education partnership models play a fundamental role in promoting equitable access to quality education across the globe. Partnerships encourage governments to collaborate with education institutions, technology providers, or international organizations, and are addressing the many layers of

H. Hind
University Sidi Mohamed Ben Abdellah, Fez, Morocco
e-mail: elmalali.hind@gmail.com

A. Sharma (✉)
Kamkus College of Law, Ghaziabad, India

P. K. Dutta
Department of Electronics and Communication Engineering, Amity School of Engineering and Technology, Amity University, Kolkata, India
e-mail: pkdutta@kol.amity.edu

P. K. Dutta et al. (eds.), *Digital Education for a Sustainable Future*, Sustainable Development Goals Series,
https://doi.org/10.1007/978-3-032-15433-0_21

the challenge as digital divide; resource discrepancies; and pedagogical innovation. When it comes to partners, they bring complimentary skills and resources to create scalable digital education models for various types of learners in varying geographies. International cooperation enables information sharing, standardization, and capability building which helps ensure that digital education responses are relevant and sustainable. Collaborative frameworks help propagate inclusive policies that remove socio-economic and geographical restraints making digital learning possible for the excluded populations. With the acceleration of digital transformation, an even stronger emphasis must be made on international partnerships to spur innovation, increase equity, and achieve sustainable development goals. This chapter addresses different models of global cooperation in digital education, opportunities, and challenges that they face as well as future perspective to enable truly inclusive digital learning ecosystem for all.

Keywords Global cooperation · Digital education · Partnership models · Digital access · Educational equity

1 Introduction

As an essential tool to drive the democratization of quality education worldwide for people in all regions and circumstances, digital education partnership models are coming into age as a means of global cooperation. The current era of fast-paced technological progress and digitalization brings both complex challenges and opportunities for education systems around the world, which require holistic solutions. Among them is the digital divide, which amounts to inequalities in technology access, connectivity, and digital skill levels; a significant obstacle that remains for inclusive education, especially in low-resource settings with vulnerable populations. But bridging this divide will require more than isolated national efforts, it demands global strategies and partnerships that build on the mutual strengths of governments, educational institutions, technology companies, international organizations, and civil societies. These partnerships are also an avenue for pooling resources, knowledge, and innovations, which can all be harnessed to increase delivery of digital education through sustainable pathways.

Digital education partnership models are diverse, including government-to-government partnerships, public-private partnerships (PPPs), academic and research networks, and multilateral organization-led initiatives. Although each model has its own strengths and challenges, they all share the common aim of facilitating the development of inclusive and scalable digital learning environments. Through these partnerships, the necessary mix of technology infrastructure, financing mechanisms, policy frameworks, and pedagogical capabilities can be assembled to provide solutions customized according to local requirements yet leveraging global knowledge base and standards. Beyond driving the pace of innovation, this cross-border pollination also helps align educational goals, quality assurance, and digital literacy standards across the globe.

There is an increasing recognition of the central role education plays in shaping the overall social and economic prosperity which underscores the need for a global cooperation. Digital learning has the potential to change traditional modes of learning by making it adaptable, learner-centric, and transcending geographical and socio-economic barriers. Yet the promise of these innovations will be realized only to the extent that education systems are able to effectively and equitably adopt new digital complements to core components of their work. Despite demand and demonstrated impact, emerging technology solutions often do not achieve the scale most needed. Coordination across sectors is difficult to establish at sufficient levels due partially to fragmented efforts, limited resources in individual settings, and lack of coordinated policy frameworks. Global partnerships can uniquely help facilitate this integration by promoting alignment, scaling up successful approaches through expanded technical support networks, and leveraging additional investment from donors.

Global collaborations help in developing digital literacy, teacher training and reforms, and research capacity that lead to the improved quality and relevance of digital education. Partnerships bring together a multitude of stakeholders, which ensures that digital education initiatives are tailored to the local context and local development priorities. Additionally, they ensure sustainability by setting up control mechanisms and financial structures that enable running the platform in the long run.

This chapter sets out to map a spectrum of international cooperation in digital education partnerships, in terms of their forms, but also strategies; achievements; and challenges. This will issue and evaluate how these models support access to digital education, equity, and innovation.

By focusing on case studies and promising practices, the study aims to provide concrete lessons that can help enrich the work of policymakers, educators, and partners who are leveraging global learning networks as a strategy for catalyzing educational improvement. Ultimately it is to show that through collective effort and shared vision, digital education can be useful for inclusive development and lifelong learning globally [1].

Importance of Global Cooperation in Digital Education

Digital education, dealing with widespread problems of access, equity, and quality in learning for everyone and everywhere, cannot be managed without global cooperation. Although access to digital technologies is enabled in education, the disparities in infrastructure and connectivity as well as the weaknesses of digital skills continue, especially in low-income and marginalized communities so that they do not get equal educational opportunities. Global challenges are cross-cutting, and no country or institution can go it alone in dealing with them as such cooperation allows sharing of resources, know-how, and best practices across borders.

Collaborative partnerships are key for coordinated responses to the digital divide, working together on solutions that can scale and are user-centered for a wide range of learner populations. In addition, international cooperation also helps to promote a consistency for educational standards, data privacy protocols, and policy frameworks across countries in order to have well-coordinated and effective digital education ecosystems. Global cooperation fosters innovation and capacity building by linking governments, the private sector, academia, and international organizations to enable education systems in keeping up with a dynamic technology area. In the end, this type of collaboration is key to unlocking the change potential that digital education represents for open, equitable, and lifelong learning.

2 Digital Education Partnerships and Models of Global Cooperation

In twenty-first century, skills are indispensable for a seamless integrated world, so to draw some personal and professional details about the myriad opportunities opened up by digital education. But it can only reach full strength if we work together across national borders and silos of sector.

Partnerships are fundamental to the success of digital education, particularly international cooperation that can play a crucial role in scaling access, making quality improvements, and sustaining new forms of digital learning everywhere. These partnerships unite governments, public and private educational institutions, technology companies, multilateral organizations and NGOs, and community groups as all of them possess particular resources, competence, and viewpoints. The different partnership models define processes of global cooperation in digital education, structures, functions, advantages, and disadvantages of aforementioned partnership models build up a full picture of how collaboration leads to educational transformation.

Government-to-Government (G2G) partnerships are of global cooperation in digital education, and they typically pave the way for cross-border educational efforts. The collaboration usually involves two or more parties entering into bilateral or multilateral agreements to pool resources, align policies, and co-invest in digital infrastructure and capacity building. For example, regional blocs, such as the European Union (EU), have devised a framework that allows countries to work on digital education across borders with common standards, funding, and mobility of learners and educators. G2G partnerships have the potential to unleash significant political will and financial resources for scale, such as national digital learning platforms, cross-border virtual classrooms, and joint research endeavors. Nevertheless, the collaborations must be carefully negotiated to marry differing national priorities and regulatory regimes, educational outlooks.

Allied to G2G efforts, public-private partnerships (PPPs) have emerged as successful models for leveraging private sector innovation and resources. PPPs are collaborations of governments or educational institutions with technology companies, content providers, and/or service organizations. These often include infrastructure, supply of software and hardware, and training for teachers. Technology companies have recent experience and SaaS solutions, and public entities complete regulatory requirements. They include global tech giants collaborating with ministries of education to roll out digital classrooms in underserved regions, complemented by programs that train teachers to use them effectively. PPPs provide efficiencies and innovations, but can increase existing inequalities and make education overly commercialized unless governance challenges are overcome to ensure full accountability and equitable sharing of benefits.

A critical model is shown connected to the academic and research institution networks which enable universities and educational resources across the globe to work closely. These consortia facilitate curriculum co-creation, digital pedagogy research, and transfer mechanisms for leveraging teaching/learning holistically. These relationships help spread scientific strategies, as well as mobilize resources through information sharing and collaborative projects. Such an approach is exemplified by networks like regional alliances in Africa, Asia, and Latin America that promote cross-institutional learning and advocacy around digital education policies. Academic partners regularly focus on pedagogical innovation and inclusivity that drives culturally sensitive digital education solutions tailored for diverse learners [2].

Global cooperation models are also influenced by international organizations and multilateral agencies. UNESCO, UNICEF, the World Bank, and the International Telecommunication Union (ITU), for example, enact multi-stakeholder partnerships that incorporate policy advocacy; funding; technical assistance; and capacity building. These organizations will give advice to coordinate action across countries, set worldwide education targets, and advocate for standards on quality and equality in digital learning. Many multilateral initiatives attempt to reach the poorest of the poor, have approaches that integrate gender equity, disability inclusion, and rural access from inception.

Without effective governance, it is difficult to balance interest of multiple stakeholders and assign clear roles and responsibilities between them which will automatically prompt collaboration using trust. A number of successful partnerships develop collaborative governance mechanisms such as joint steering committees, working groups, or advisory panels made up representatives from each of their participating sectors. Such constructs make way for a continuous discourse, conflict resolution, and synchronization of goals. Equally important, flexible partnership models that can be adapted to unique local contexts and changing needs are not only more sustainable but also more effective.

3 Global Challenges in Digital Education Access

Even with all the available opportunities, international cooperation in digital education encounters a number of difficulties. This is a view seconded by many experts, who see policy fragmentation as the biggest challenge of all and with national regulations on data privacy and intellectual property such as the EU's GDPR or recent accreditation examples in Switzerland, to name but a few, the road ahead for cross-border initiatives can become even more complicated. Reconciling these policies without abrogating sovereignty will demand diplomacy and international protocols that value regional autonomy while encouraging collaboration. Even in less high-profile use cases, resource differences between developed and developing countries can serve as a barrier to entry since low-income regions might not have the infrastructure or expertise do more than participate passively. In order to correct these disparities, partnerships should be structured around joint production agreements that are sealed through destination-specific funding mechanisms designed for technology transfer and capacity building [3].

These cultural differences and linguistic hurdles, in turn, pose added challenges to collaboration that can impact our ability to develop curricula that remain relevant are interesting enough to engage learners as well as the communication among partners. Good partnerships value culturally relevance, and the participation of local communities and educators in processes of decision-making, customization of content and multilingualizing. Partnership dynamics are increasingly influenced by innovation. Across the university, faculty are incorporating new technologies artificial intelligence; blockchain; immersive learning environments; and more into partnerships that aim to expand individualized education, verify competencies for future employers; and improve engagement. Incorporating these advancements will coupled with data analytics provide deep, interesting insights to help enable adaptable policies and practices which makes partnerships better equipped to answer the call.

The future of technology in education will likely be shaped by digital education partnerships and models of global cooperation that promote equitable, quality digital learning worldwide. They combine forces and ideas across sectors and borders, focusing on problems that no one of them is powerful enough to solve alone. The forms of these adaptation partnerships are diverse ranging from government collaborations to public-private initiatives and academic networks but they share principles of inclusivity, shared governance, and adaptability [4]. As digital education solutions evolve, the challenge for all stakeholders remains to build on these initiatives and strengthen global cooperation in order to create inclusive, resilient, and future-proof education systems that enable learners everywhere.

Digital Divide and Inequities

The digital divide is a core block to universal access to digital education thereby also reflecting disparities in technology availability, internet connectivity, and skills among different groups of people. Urban and rural areas, high-income and low-income communities, developed and developing countries are among those with the widest divides. Lacking in resources, cultural biases and endemic deprivation of opportunity mean that girls with disabilities and minority ethnicities often confront a double burden. These inequities limit students' access to remote or hybrid learning and impact their future trajectory. Overcoming this gap will need interventions focused on things like affordable internet access, devices and digital content that is culturally appropriate [5]. Digital education for the sake of it, without addressing the digital divide potentially reifies and entrenches current social inequalities rather than ameliorating them, frustrating global attempts to foster inclusive quality education for all.

Infrastructure and Resource Gaps

Basic infrastructure services benefits like electricity, broadband internet, and access to right tools such as computer or tablets are often absent or not reliable in the underserved areas. Schools and colleges may not have the technical capability or resources to properly maintain digital systems or perform software updates; making this functionality limited. The absence of localized and contextual educational content makes the learning process irrelevant and this lack of reliability creates disinterest among socially marginalized learners. These missing or deficient physical and human resources represent systemic barriers to scaling digital education; particularly in low- and middle-income countries. Piecing together these missing services requires collaborative investment in both physical infrastructure and technologies that are truly sustainable. International aid, public-private partnerships, and other new financing mechanisms must be set to bridge these gaps so that digital learning environments are available everywhere [6].

Policy and Regulatory Barriers

The primary barriers to the internationalization of digital education are policy and regulatory challenges. There are variances in state laws regarding data privacy, intellectual property rights (IPR), online education accreditation, and digital content governance which lead to challenges for cross-border collaborations and technology adoption. Weak or missing policies also may discourage investments in digital infrastructure or impede the adoption of new educational technologies. The regulatory uncertainty may slow innovation and can prevent scale of successful digital education models. Without solid digital education strategies many countries scramble to connect individual projects which costs significant resources [7]. This requires the articulation of coherent, inclusive policies that safeguard user rights and quality standards and foster public-private collaboration to set up enabling environments. Adopting and harmonizing standards between regions, forms of international association agreements, and the means by which content can be licensed are examples of standardization that would contribute to ease in creating partnerships and increasing reach, thus further working toward a worldwide digital education experience.

4 Types of Partnership Models in Digital Education

In trying to address similar issues of equity, quality, and sustainability within digital education, the approach has been increasingly based on a variety of forms of partnership. Models, bringing together multiple stakeholders: governments, private sector companies, academic institutions, CSOs, and international bodies to contribute resources, expertise, and innovative efforts on digital learning initiatives [8]. A widely accepted framework to classify partnership models in digital education helps in illustrating how partnerships can address the challenges involved in digital transformation due to their multifaceted nature.

The most high-profile has been government-to-government (G2G) partnerships official agreements between countries or regions to work together on digital education programs. Such collaborations tend to concentrate on exchanging experiences, aligning policies, and co-financing infrastructure and capacity building. G2G partnerships on the other hand can make it possible for things like cross-border online learning platforms to be built at scale, mutual recognition of digital credentials, and coordinated national or regional teacher training efforts [9]. Governments could expedite the transition to digital education by consolidating political will and resources, particularly in areas where collective action can lead to economies of scale; they rely on a robust diplomacy and congruence of an educational target.

The second most popular model used is public-private partnerships (PPPs). These partnerships combine the technical capacity, innovative thinking, and resources of the private sector with the public mandate and access of government. This has included expanding broadband infrastructure, developing educational software and hardware through public-private partnerships (PPPs), and providing teacher professional development. Tech companies commonly offer digital tools or platforms in obvious discounted prices or as part of their Corporate Social Responsibility schemes, while governments would work toward the deployment and integration into education systems [10]. While the right PPPs can drive innovation and rapid scaling, they are extremely sensitive to design features such as governance arrangements, conflicts of interest, and primary motivations behind project initiation, and distribution of benefits to avoid over-commercialization.

Partnerships as well are being made with the academia and research institution networks in knowledge creation, curriculum development, and pedagogical innovation. Higher education: Institutions such as universities and colleges come together across borders to collaborate with one another over how best to share research findings, co-create open educational resources (OER), and implement joint digital learning projects. The networks will encourage EBP methods and support educator and researcher capacity development, to ensure that digital education initiatives are pedagogically sound and locally contextual. These partnerships could also advocate for policy reforms informed by research to augment the entire digital education landscape [11].

International organizations and multilateral agencies facilitate multi-stakeholder partnerships that gather governments, private sector, civil society as NGOs, and broader under coordinated frameworks. Such partnerships frequently address global or regional challenges, such as improving digital inclusion for disadvantaged communities or responding to educational disruptions exemplified by the COVID-19 pandemic. There are delivering mechanisms such as UNESCO, UNICEF, and the World Bank which provide technical assistant, funding and policy guidance, supporting connected-action across different sectors and regions. They are partnerships that focus on equity, sustainability, and capacity building in a way that supports local mechanisms to further international education goals. Programs are designed and run by local non-profits, parent groups, grassroots organizations—many of which work directly with learners and educators to cater programming to community interest [12]. Supports marginalized learners, advocates equitable policy implementation, and forms partnerships with employers that help close the technology literacy gap.

There are several partnership models in digital education which synergies the best strengths of all actors to explore and address access, quality, and equity issues. The future-ready digital learning ecosystem will be strengthened all over the world by partnerships that governments can collaborate with and work together in public-private, academia networks, cross-border coalitions, community and interface agencies to build resilient diverse equitable educational systems. These global partnerships will continue to require improved governance, mutual accountability, and context-sensitive approaches in order to be most effective and sustainable.

5 Role of Technology Providers and Industry Partners

As digital education continues to evolve, so must the fragmented ecosystem of technology providers and implementation partners that are instrumental to its growth. They play a critical role, not just providing the tools and infrastructure needed but also bringing innovation, expertise, or resources that might be hard to access for many educational institutions or governments yourself especially in low resource settings. This symbiotic relationship between the education segment and industry partners strongly influences the way digital learning environments mature, how outreach gets faster and outcomes they generate keep getting better [13].

The technology providers create and deliver the necessary digital infrastructure for education in the digital world. This refers to computers, tablets, and smartphones; located learning management systems (LMS), virtual classrooms, online content platforms, etc. consumerization of learning: Industry partners also design and deliver scalable, cloud-based platforms that facilitate remote learning and real-time assessment through interactive multimedia content; these solutions aim to convert traditional classrooms into modern, learner-centered experiences. The cloud computing and AI enterprises, with their adaptive learning capabilities, deliver personalized instructions to individual learners resulting in higher levels of engagement and better performance. The digital education promise to serve different learning styles and paces would be a hard one to keep without such innovation.

The technology providers lead infrastructure development and connectivity programs that help extend digital education access. The tech companies have teamed up with governments and NGOs to enhance broadband access in underserved communities, one of the primary downsides of digital inclusion [14]. These efforts range from delivering inexpensive satellite internet services, creating cheap hardware and software solutions or synchronous educational solutions for areas with limited connectivity. Industry partners innovate in energy-efficient and durable hardware designs, which are useful for tough environments where power may be less reliable such into schools.

The most essential functions that external partners perform are in capacity building and professional development. As the saying goes, technology is only beneficial if it works for you. In this sense, companies collaborate with schools and other educational institutions to carry out programs that train teachers and school administrators, teaching the pedagogical use of digital tools and effective management of virtual classrooms. These often also involve workshops, online tutorials, and certification courses that improve digital literacy and instructional design capability. Technology providers should empower educators in that middle to ethically use the tools available in a meaningful way and thus progress from merely offering technology into enriching technology.

Industry partners also help fund digital education through corporate social responsibility (CSR) programs. Some companies direct resources to charitable efforts that chip away at these inequalities, from device giveaways to connectivity initiatives and open educational resource funding. Whether private sector CSR can ever be as effective is debatable, but in many countries where public budgets are tight, social enterprises have the potential to lead transformational change while still being cheaper and more efficient than nonprofits. Companies are frequently vocal supporters of policies that encourage digital education and share their experience in constructing inclusive and innovative regulatory settings [15].

It also collaborates with industry partners that drive research and innovation in the space of digital education as well. Partnerships with universities and research institutions support the creation of innovative education technology that marries pedagogical theory and evidence. Partnerships around ethics in AI to guide its use in education ensure that technological solutions are designed responsibly, for example, by keeping learners' data private, and by ensuring fairness. Industry players iterate digital tools through pilot projects and user testing, tailoring them to the diverse needs and contexts of learners in a cycle of continuous improvement.

But the technology providers and industry partners that are now involved are causing new problems. This concerns surrounding commercialization and data privacy. This includes concerns with respect to consent, security of learner data, and ethical use of it. Transparent responsible systems embodying appropriate privacy principles need effective governance and oversight frameworks that span across the different stakeholders. ESG is proud to act as a catalyst; yet there is also that danger of focusing on technology solutions that emphasize return and thereby perpetuate an unequal distribution of resources if it does not reach all populations. Therefore, developing responsible partnerships with common values and accountability mechanisms is very important.

Digital transformation of education is a giant global task, and technology providers are definitely the partners needed to make an impact as well. The roles include supplying innovative tools and infrastructure, increasing access, developing capacity, and enabling research and advocacy. Working ethically and together, these partners provide the foundation to a global digital education ecosystem that is inclusive, scalable, and sustainable supporting learners across the world. It is essential that their efforts are in line with educational aims and equity principles to enhance their positive effect to meet the myriad issues of digital education access along with quality [16].

6 Conclusion and Suggestions

The advent of digital learning represents a major opportunity to change our experience of learning, to improve its access and build these necessary skills for the evolving Digital Age. But unlocking this potential will not be easy there are major infrastructure, equity, capacity, and policy hurdles to clear. These challenges can only be overcome with global cooperation and a variety of collaboration models that include governments, technology providers, academia, and civil society. Effective collaboration allows us to pool resources and knowledge, as well as scale innovative solutions in a way that is specific to the different contexts. Technology providers and industry partners can be part of the solution, providing infrastructure, innovation, and capacity building, but we must ensure it is done in a way that respects individual privacy rights and promotes an inclusive approach to benefit sharing.

A number of recommendations emerge about how to build a sustainable and equitable digital education agenda. The first, investing in infrastructure and specifically linking-up the unconnected regions are essential to narrowing the digital gap. This will include expanding access to affordable broadband, offering devices, and supporting continued power supply. All educators need to have ample digital literacy, and training from professional development is a must to get the most out of the pedagogical process through technology. The policies and regulations that are inclusive need to be established for international harmonization in order to promote cross-border cooperation without compromising data privacy or fairness. Supporting open educational resources and relevant local content can create a more engaging and meaningful learning experience. Digital schools will be supported by ongoing monitoring and evaluation allowing iteration on performance to meet changes in needs and scaling based on evidence. The global education community can use these strategies to leverage digital transformation for the benefit of all learners by building more resilient, inclusive, and quality learning environments.

References

1. Gupta, T., & Khan, S. (2023). Education and international collaboration in the digital age. *Globus: Journal of Progressive Education, 13*(1), pp. 79–87.
2. Alenezi, M., Wardat, S., & Akour, M. (2023). The need of integrating digital education in higher education: Challenges and opportunities. *Sustainability, 15*(6), 4782.
3. Abduvakhidov, A. M., Mannapova, E. T., & Akhmetshin, E. M. (2021). Digital development of education and universities: Global challenges of the digital economy. *International Journal of Instruction, 14*(1), 743–760.
4. Singh, A., Sharma, S., & Paliwal, M. (2021). Adoption intention and effectiveness of digital collaboration platforms for online learning: The Indian students' perspective. *Interactive Technology and Smart Education, 18*(4), 493–514.
5. Alenezi, M. (2023). Digital learning and digital institution in higher education. *Education Sciences, 13*(1), 88.
6. Karabacak, M., Ozkara, B. B., Margetis, K., Wintermark, M., & Bisdas, S. (2023). The advent of generative language models in medical education. *JMIR Medical Education, 9*, e48163.

7. Afzal, A., Khan, S., Daud, S., Ahmad, Z., & Butt, A. (2023). Addressing the digital divide: Access and use of technology in education. *Journal of Social Sciences Review, 3*(2), 883–895.
8. World Health Organization. (2023). *Digitalized health workforce education: An elicitation of research gaps and selection of case studies*. World Health Organization.
9. Ng, D. T. K., Leung, J. K. L., Su, J., Ng, R. C. W., & Chu, S. K. W. (2023). Teachers' AI digital competencies and twenty-first century skills in the post-pandemic world. *Educational Technology Research and Development, 71*(1), 137–161.
10. Wang, C., Chen, X., Yu, T., Liu, Y., & Jing, Y. (2024). Education reform and change driven by digital technology: A bibliometric study from a global perspective. *Humanities and Social Sciences Communications, 11*(1), 1–17.
11. Alenezi, M. (2021). Deep dive into digital transformation in higher education institutions. *Education Sciences, 11*(12), 770.
12. Archambault, L., Leary, H., & Rice, K. (2022). Pillars of online pedagogy: A framework for teaching in online learning environments. *Educational Psychologist, 57*(3), 178–191.
13. Mhlongo, S., Mbatha, K., Ramatsetse, B., & Dlamini, R. (2023). Challenges, opportunities, and prospects of adopting and using smart digital technologies in learning environments: An iterative review. *Heliyon, 9*(6), e16348.
14. Singh, J., Evans, E., Reed, A., Karch, L., Qualey, K., Singh, L., & Wiersma, H. (2022). Online, hybrid, and face-to-face learning through the eyes of faculty, students, administrators, and instructional designers: Lessons learned and directions for the post-vaccine and post-pandemic/COVID-19 world. *Journal of Educational Technology Systems, 50*(3), 301–326.
15. Sato, S. N., Condes Moreno, E., Rubio-Zarapuz, A., Dalamitros, A. A., Yañez-Sepulveda, R., Tornero-Aguilera, J. F., & Clemente-Suárez, V. J. (2023). Navigating the new normal: Adapting online and distance learning in the post-pandemic era. *Education Sciences, 14*(1), 19.
16. Kaputa, V., Loučanová, E., & Tejerina-Gaite, F. A. (2022). Digital transformation in higher education institutions as a driver of social oriented innovations. *Social Innovation in Higher Education, 61*, 81–85.

Index

P. K. Dutta et al. (eds.), *Digital Education for a Sustainable Future*, Sustainable Development Goals Series,
https://doi.org/10.1007/978-3-032-15433-0

GPSR Compliance

The European Union's (EU) General Product Safety Regulation (GPSR) is a set of rules that requires consumer products to be safe and our obligations to ensure this.

If you have any concerns about our products, you can contact us on ProductSafety@springernature.com

In case Publisher is established outside the EU, the EU authorized representative is:

Springer Nature Customer Service Center GmbH
Europaplatz 3
69115 Heidelberg, Germany

Batch number: 10523116

Printed by Printforce, the Netherlands